The
Flowering
of
Art
Nouveau

The Flowering of Art Nouveau

by Maurice Rheims

HARRY N. ABRAMS, INC.
Publishers, NEW YORK

Translated from the French by Patrick Evans.
Library of Congress Catalog Card Number: 66-10988.
Copyright in France by Arts et Métiers Graphiques, Paris.
Illustrations printed in France.
Text printed in the Netherlands.
Bound in the Netherlands.

Contents

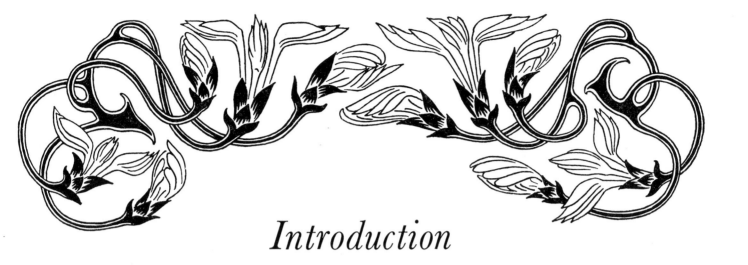

Introduction

To André Breton

Aʀᴛ Nouveau was a great artistic movement, one which, however, has been constantly misrepresented. It has been identified, wrongly, as an aspect of the *Belle Époque*, and the many names given to the style have merely camouflaged this blunder: for example, 1900, Nouille ("noodle") Style, Stile Liberty, Stile Floreale, Morris Style, Métro Style, Whiplash, Sezession, Yachting Style, Glasgow Style, Jugendstil, Lilienstil, and Wellenstil (respectively "youth style," "lily style," and "wave style").

It is therefore essential, as a preface to this study, to analyze briefly the political, social, and psychological forces amid which Art Nouveau was born, and then to show the repercussions of these forces in the aesthetic field.

Toward the end of the nineteenth century the evolution of the modern world (which had begun in the middle of the sixteenth century) was showing signs of stabilization. The European countries, so often divided and redivided by war, settled down; the frontiers had been redrawn; the map looked permanent. But European expansion was marking time and the prestige of the Old World was diminishing. Skills developed by Anglo-Saxons and Latins had been exported from Europe to the United States and were now rebounding across the Atlantic; vigorous American competition was already a force to be reckoned with. Only yesterday the New World countries had been scorned by Europe; now they were hurrying to catch up and even had the audacity to dream of overtaking her. The Americans actually dignified their giant factories and office blocks with a homemade aesthetic label, the Saracenic Style.

The European powers no longer had to defend themselves against military aggression; but internally a number of social and political problems were threatening the security of the middle classes, all sections of which (except in Russia) had been deeply shaken by the consequences of the Revolution of 1848, the reverberations of the Paris Commune in 1871, and the economic crises of 1875. The big cities of Western Europe housed a poverty-stricken proletariat which was aware that its numbers implied strength and which was struggling desperately to organize itself. Industrial advances which the middle classes themselves had brought about, together with Socialist propaganda and the upsurge of democracy, had created new and bewildering situations.

Faced by the proletarian threat, the bourgeoisie did everything it could to strengthen its position. Politically, it used nationalistic aspirations as a disguise for its natural greed; and on the social plane it successfully confused the issue by the exercise of a moralizing authoritarianism. Trade unions were permitted but strikes were suppressed. Universal suffrage was declared but the issue of voters' cards was held up. Free education was granted as a concession to popular demand, but designed in such a way as to preserve social conformity and class divisions.

Poverty, the struggle for better wages and conditions, and the conflict between paternalistic employers and Communistic workers, all made their presence felt in the painting and caricatures of the time, like watermarks in paper. The titles and subjects of the pictures exhibited in the Salons between 1896 and 1900 reveal the cares lurking behind the façade of a period which people liked to think was happy and prosperous. *Firedamp Explosion*: a handsomely bearded industrialist, with a watchchain looped across his ample paunch, is pinning long-service medals on the victims' corpses; a young lady in her nightdress, sporting a pair of wings and carrying a laurel wreath in her hand, is the dominating figure in the composition. *Christ the Carpenter*: in a wretched workshop a doddering old man gazes with wonder at Christ. The Saviour has a plane in his hand and is putting the finishing touches to the old man's coffin.

Until the Congress of Amsterdam in 1904, the mood of the Socialists and Communists remained conciliatory; after the strikes in London, Brussels, and Paris the employers made certain definite concessions to the workers and calm was restored. Unity between capital and labor still appeared possible. Cheap industrial production provided the customers of the big stores—lower-middle- and working-class people—with goods which, if not exactly works of art, were at any rate pleasant to own; and a few half-hearted attempts to solve the housing problem put a brake on demands which nowadays would seem extremely modest.

With the abolition of child labor, and the fourteen-hour work day; with voters' cards, Sunday suits, and a day trip to the seaside once a year; with "artistic tile" decoration in cafés, and the hope of one day possessing a bicycle, the proletariat gained some sort of respectability and were able to identify themselves to some extent with the middle classes. This hopeful atmosphere supplied the setting for the endeavors—tinged more or less with the earlier socialism of Saint-Simon or François Fourier—of William Morris, Henry van de Velde, and the School of Nancy. All these artists came of middle-class origins.

It is clear that the dawn of democracy had shed a disturbing, confusing light. The propertied classes conceded a growing importance to those below, gave them a limited degree of political scope, and abandoned some of the old taboos; the result was a profound psychological shock which made itself felt at all levels of society.

This upheaval stands out even more glaringly in the religious field. For the better part of four centuries religion had been drying into rigidity, changing from a spiritual attitude into a moral code. Authorities and flock alike had become negative, sinking deeper and deeper into habits of faultfinding and life denial. Formalism reigned. In his encyclical, *Quanta Cura* (1864), Pope Pius IX sweepingly rejected modern society and the spirit of 1789 (the French Revolution), setting up a complete opposition between the Catholic ideal and the liberal spirit. He was adamant against secular education and the freedom of the conscience and the press. Leo XIII was more accommodating, and in 1891 enunciated a social doctrine for the Church, but the resulting democratic movement was condemned soon after by Pius X with his attacks on the errors of modernism. Religious adherence had become a matter of social position; religious practice, merely the result of early training. In some localities the presence of working-class people at Mass was strictly supervised, and in all parishes the "servants' Mass" was held early on Sunday mornings.

All that the established churches had to offer to eager hearts was a monotonous and, as time went on, thoroughly superficial rule of conduct. It was, therefore, only to be expected that some people should search for God elsewhere, reviving old beliefs or creating new ones, and indulging in spiritual activities condemned by authority as dangerous or sinful. Magic and spiritualism had never had so many supporters, and when Hyacinthe Chantelouve pursued terror and exaltation along strange paths, including diabolism, she was perhaps struggling to assuage desires she no longer dared to confess to a priest.

Atheism had opened a void which worried a number of churchmen, university teachers, writers, and artists. Cardinal La Vigerie, who was especially active against *boulangisme*, a reactionary movement led by General Boulanger, opened the way to those who thought it possible to be both republican and Catholic. J. K. Huysmans and Aubrey Beardsley were converted to

Catholicism. Ferdinand Brunetière, in 1895, protested against the bankruptcy of science and speculated on the means of rescuing a soul for God. Confusion meanwhile was total: the French secularists were even accused by the Christians of being reduced to worshiping a mysterious individual named Léon in place of the banished Christ: "Léon is watching us"; "There is only one Léon," run the captions on a caricature depicting a classroom in a secularist school. It was in this climate that the *Affaire Dreyfus* burst on public attention.

A glance at history and society during the so-called *Belle Époque* discloses a state of utter confusion—moral, social, religious, intellectual. The world was no longer in tune with Europe; Socialism was no longer the expression of generous impulses; love and marriage were incompatible; and art was aimed at the senses, not the soul. The churches were empty of God. In these circumstances Art Nouveau was simply the aesthetic manifestation of a deep hunger for something different, something new.

Along with these moral and material perplexities arose another problem, as important as it was unforeseen: that of woman, or rather, women. The real-life originals of the women in the novels of Stendhal, Balzac, and Flaubert were middle-class female objects, passive and subservient—at least economically, and usually in other ways as well. They might choose a confessor or a lover to suit themselves, but that was the limit of their freedom. "Adultery," proclaimed Willy (Colette's husband, and a well-known author), "is the foundation of society: by making marriage bearable it ensures the survival of the family."

Certainly in literature, from Balzac to Henri Becque, marriage is depicted as a social and commercial institution almost entirely unconnected with love. A girl is taught from her childhood how to please the opposite sex; her upbringing is based not on absolute moral standards but on recipes for seductiveness. Feminine behavior degenerated into a handful of conventional, artificial attitudes set in motion by conditioned reflexes.

The whole life of women, and hence morals, literature, and the art of love, was controlled by fashion, and any feminine gesture might supply the subject matter for a supposed work of art. To take off a glove with deliberate slowness was calculated, by the standards of the period, to throw a man automatically into a frenzy of desire (*Woman with Pink Gloves*, by Jacques-Émile Blanche). *In the Garden*, by Georges de Feure, helps us to understand the taste of the time for certain evocative aspects of nature, for rare flowers, and for lace petticoats embroidered with hearts and vines. Never had there been such a flurry of legs in the air, of conspiratorial fingers, of skirts hitched up (Seurat's *The Cancan*). On gusty Sundays, young men leaving church after Mass are thrilled by the fleeting revelation of a girl's ankle (*Joli mois de Marie*, by Paul Chabas). And in the evening, with their top hats rammed down tight on their skulls, the same young men are spectators at the crude unveiling of sexual mysteries in the form of professional dancing which is merely a rhythmical exhibition of garters and bloomers (*Le Cabaret de la Souris*, by Bottini).

Cartoons in the daily press show us other facets of the situation: for example, a handsome girl, half covered by her rumpled bedclothes, teases her departing elderly lover, as he gloomily puts on his jacket, with its buttonhole displaying the rosette of the Legion of Honor: "Poor old pussycat, I wonder how you'll manage to honor the mother of your children tonight!"

The lives of working-class girls had run into an intolerable dilemma. The urban proletariat had increased enormously; so had prostitution. In the closing years of the century it was as if the influx of population to the towns had been followed by a similar movement of the *jus primae noctis*; in the London, Vienna, and Paris of 1895, anyone with enough money in his pocket enjoyed the same freedom as a feudal lord. Laborers' wages were low; girls, whose labor was mostly piecework, earned even less, and their only hope lay in finding a rich "protector." In one of Forain's cartoons a thirteen-year-old girl is selling long loaves of bread; a financier whispers into her ear, "No need to go on toting those great things about; I can tell you where to find smaller ones."

Various writers, especially Zola, made society aware of its responsibilities. Feminism, which in France at any rate was a resolutely Socialistic and at times revolutionary movement, attracted women of all classes. Society, fondly imagining that the lot of Woman had been unalterably decreed for all eternity, suddenly found itself confronted with the problems of real, live women.

Here we must interrupt this historical survey for a moment to define two words. The first is "historicism." By this we mean that excessive fondness for past styles which was the great weakness of the nineteenth century; preferring pastiche, however mediocre, to anything new, historicism stifles all attempts at original creation. The second word is "Mannerism." Today it is generally used in reference to the highly refined, subjective exaggeration of artistic canons, subject matter, or composition that developed at the end of the High Renaissance; but in discussing nineteenth-century art we shall use the word in an unfavorable sense: Mannerism is the spirit which is set on achieving something precious and rare at all costs; it falls readily into preciosity, tends toward decadence and the bizarre.

A new intellectual elite had arisen. Its leaders and standard-bearers were such artists as Gustav Klimt, Beardsley, and Thomas Theodor Heine, who had given graphic expression to the psychopathology laid bare by Freud and the Nancy school of psychologists, and writers such as Huysmans and Lorrain, who had rejected ordinary morals to seek the savor of life in various kinds of irregularity—"forbidden loves," drugs, and alcohol. Two distinct viewpoints, sensuousness and sexuality, became the poles round which two opposite artistic principles took shape: the apostles of the first principle were the Symbolists and the artists of the Sezession; the second was exploited in the salacious pictures and illustrations turned out by the prize-winning painters of the Salons.

The arts enable us to decipher the whole attitude of a society or a country. In the present context, the relevant question is the degree to which the modern world was rejected or accepted. The monuments, paintings, furniture, and objects of the time all reflect one of two trends. On the one hand there was bourgeois Mannerism, the final expression of an aesthetic already on its deathbed; on the other, a bold, prophetic, revolutionary impulse which prepared the ground for the art of today.

This duality manifests itself even in the humblest artistic productions. The posters, political pamphlets, and educational journals published during that period make it clear that the entire left-wing camp in France—Syndicalists, Socialists, Anarchists, and the campaigners for the secular control of education—had been stimulated by both Symbolism and Art Nouveau. In one of these publications there is an illustration of a schoolmaster inspired by a Marianne with naked bosom, who points to the rising sun. The title page of a journal on higher primary education is decorated with Japanese flowers which might have been drawn by Félix Bracquemond. Propaganda posters, such as "Soldier! When are you going on strike?" or a capitalist's offer to a starving proletarian: "Send your children to the monks to be educated, marry the Church, and then we'll give you a job," are treated in the popular style dear to Théophile-Alexandre Steinlen.

Correspondingly, Royalist, Christian, and anti-Dreyfus propaganda remained faithful to a more or less classical style. The fashionable, cold-hearted humor of Jean-Louis Forain, and the titillations of Adolphe Willette, gave the moneyed classes what they wanted.

In the visual arts, the unrest underlying bourgeois Mannerist society reared its head in the form of a misguided and excessive use of symbolism. Comparable symptoms appeared in literature; lyricism became heavily tainted with decadence. This superpreciosity, this exaggerated straining after novelty and refinement, infected not only minor figures like Fénéon and René Ghil, but also poets of such significance as Jules Laforgue and Jean Moréas. Some of the word-coinings and metaphors of that period make hilarious reading today. No doubt our grandchildren will be equally amused by many of the laudatory articles and prefaces now being published about contemporary artists.

The political, social, and moral upheavals in the latter part of the nineteenth century were paralleled by the passionate warfare constantly raging in the artistic world. Art Nouveau was particularly distinguished by its determination to break with academicism and to create an aesthetic in harmony with the needs of the age. This drive and, indeed, vocation, which was a common factor of the movement in Brussels, Chicago, Glasgow, London, Munich, Nancy, and Vienna, was often emasculated by a certain predilection toward folk art and the like; the success of the English architects emulating the Tudor style, or Louis Sullivan when his work is too "Oriental," is not entirely convincing. But in spite of the charges leveled against it, including that of going astray in Mannerist blind alleys, Art Nouveau has the honor, particularly in the architectural realm, of having been the first movement to recognize the demands of the modern world. Moreover, it was also the first to participate in Freud's clarification of human issues and, by purging the symbols of art of their outmoded elements, to strip the mask from the human face to reveal its naked anxiety. Sincerity was restored.

One of the weapons Art Nouveau forged for itself was the understanding of ornament, which it developed to a state of perfection; all the representatives of the movement, whether they are Symbolists like Leonardo Bistolfi, Henri Cros, or Hector Guimard, or modernists like Van de Velde and Josef Hoffmann, are as determined as any primitive artist to achieve harmony between the object and its decoration. This is equally true whether it concerns a sculptural mass, a vase, or the façade of a building. But the greatest triumph of Art Nouveau was that achieved by the painters, who boldly threw off their technical shackles and created new color effects which remain unequaled even now. No one until then, neither among the Impressionists nor even the Pointillists, had dared to conceive such unexpected chromatic delights: emerald, ruby, and violet, and astonishing opalescent tones abruptly juxtaposed with an inimitable turquoise hue.

Whenever it walked in Pre-Raphaelite footsteps and made obeisance to the obsolete dogmas of John Ruskin or William Morris—turning its back on industrialization and preaching a universal return to crafts and guilds—Art Nouveau had no claim to novelty; but it was genuinely new whenever it sought unusual, original effects, and was colorful, consistent, harmonious, and functional, prefiguring the shape of things to come—the Bauhaus, Surrealism, and abstract art.

So protean is Art Nouveau in its manifestations that it demands to be studied country by country. But we should first dispose of a possible misconception: it is common to think of France as a center and of Paris as the capital of Art Nouveau, as its French name implies. On the contrary, however, in France the new possibilities opened up by the movement were neither welcomed nor understood. If we describe Art Nouveau as the creation of an appropriate setting for modern life, more particularly in architecture and the applied arts, we have to admit that it did not originate in Paris and, what is worse, that the French remained blind to it. It may be objected that in the work of Émile Gallé, France can be credited with having given birth to an original and charming style, but that style soon died out because it made no attempt to satisfy the demands of its epoch.

By 1910 almost the only traces of Art Nouveau in France were Jules Aimé Lavirotte's Céramic Hôtel in Paris, De Feure's faded flowers, and Sarah Bernhardt in her seventies; the country had exhausted its imagination and had simply turned over and gone to sleep again. Lethargic complacency lay over all—a spell so deep that only the First World War could break it; but that blow was too heavy: instead of awakening, France was shattered. By 1925, she was beginning to rediscover, with amazement, things which had been conceived a quarter of a century earlier in Austria, Germany, and the United States.

Surrealism—the most passionate voice that has ever been raised against banality and staleness in life and art—left the majority of the French indifferent. Following the example of the Goncourt brothers in an earlier generation, they preferred to linger among the desiccated charms of a bygone age. What a paradox that, in 1964, Paris, proud of its heritage, should have held its Antique Dealers' Fair (an interesting exhibition but essentially a conservative gesture) in a building which was one of the "high places" of modernism: a palace in the 1900 Style!

Architecture

Until the beginning of the nineteenth century no one felt the urge to beautify a commercial building; it did not occur to anyone that such a mundane object should or could be beautiful. After 1815 the rise in the material and social status of tradesmen brought about certain changes for the better, and the interest in historic styles, with their evocation of past glories, caught the favor of the newly rich. In 1839, in the then heart of New York, Richard Upjohn built Trinity Church in the Gothic style; meanwhile in Paris, where a multitude of façades with floral or pseudo-cathedral decoration were making their appearance, Théodore Ballu built his inimitable Sainte-Clotilde.

Others preferred classicism to this medieval revival. Karl Schinkel in Berlin, Kornhausel in Vienna, Raffaello Stern in Rome, Monferran in Saint Petersburg, Alexander Thomson in Glasgow, A. J. Davis in New York, Visconti and Lefuel in Paris, Espérandieu in Marseilles—with such architects as the leading spirits, "Parthenons" and "Forums," duly edited in the spirit of Ledoux or Sir John Soane, proliferated on every side.

Along with these two tendencies there can be detected, from about 1830, the development of modernist trends. Industrial progress and the first large-scale constructions in iron (both due to the initiative of the most affluent section of the middle classes) had opened up substantial new possibilities; an interval of forty years separates the Palais du Commerce et de l'Industrie in Paris by Grisart (1838) and the Provident and Trust Company Building by Frank Furness (1879) in Philadelphia. Ten years later, in St. Louis, Sullivan was constructing his first buildings, and in 1899, Horta's Maison du Peuple (plates 60 and 84) was opened in Brussels.

The means of expression of Art Nouveau were extremely varied and even, at times, mutually exclusive, with the result that we cannot apply simple classifications like "Louis XV" or "Louis XVI" or "Empire." The ambiguities and hybrid forms which are so common in the realm of the decorative arts have equally striking parallels in architecture. Two such different creations as Charles Rennie Mackintosh's Glasgow School of Art (plate 32) and August Endell's Elvira Photographic Studio (plate 39) both date from around 1897, and both are examples of Art Nouveau.

Thus, there is not a single Art Nouveau style, but a number of movements with a great variety, even conflict, of stylistic traits (the symbolism of some making a violent contrast to the modernism of others) which nevertheless were ultimately and amicably joined in a single cause, that of trampling on the established order and clearing the way for all the revolutionary manifestations of the twentieth century.

In this chapter we shall have to deal with the sinuous arboreal structures of Guimard (plate 13), Sullivan's Carson Pirie Scott & Co. Department Store (plate 79), and Sommaruga's buildings (plates 21 and 22)—a medley which represents the contradictions of the period more eloquently than any words.

It may indeed be objected that Hendrik Petrus Berlage's Amsterdam Stock Exchange and certain Scandinavian buildings in the "Viking" style should have been passed over. But they possess characteristics which make it seem logical to classify them as Art Nouveau—the use of dreamlike symbolism, for example, or a highly conscious manipulation of space. Like the medieval revival in the middle of the nineteenth century, the 1900 Style varied from place to place; it was wildly exuberant on the banks of the Rhine, but it was serious and restrained in Northern Italy.

Art Nouveau was a great moment in the evolution of artistic styles; the works of Horta (plate 63), Guimard (plate 5), and Gaudí (plate 27) showed that the art of the past could be carried to an ultimate stage, while those of Josef Hoffmann (plate 36), Sullivan (plate 56), and Tony Garnier were among the first to point to the promise of the future.

The architecture of Art Nouveau can be likened to the flight of a Fourth of July rocket. Some architects, such as Auguste Perret and Sullivan, chose the moment at which the trajectory is starting to curve and fall away; others, such as Guimard and Horta, subjected conventional materials to convolutions which recall the spirals that appear when the rocket bursts and floats down, opening like a fiery flower.

FRANCE

The beginning of the Second Empire saw a wave of expansion taking place in the environs of Paris; farms and parks gave way to heavy, gloomy, high-rent apartment buildings designed by uninspired hacks.

The decorations of the façades of these disastrous edifices—which were hopefully dubbed "eclectic," "hygienic," or "economical," and which are dotted about in an area bounded by the Gare de l'Est, the Colline Montmartre, and the Gare Saint-Lazare—show an alarming tendency to break out into excrescences (heads of Minerva in consternation, or muzzles of snarling lions) on the rectangular masses of their funereal balconies.

In the eyes of the promoters, already numerous in the time of the French President Thiers, the newly affluent classes were better accommodated by those conventional, massive dwellings than by the charming but over-modest little Parisian houses of the "keepsake" type (for example, 20 Boulevard des Italiens, 1 Rue Vineuse, and 9 Rue Victor-Massé).

While bourgeois classical architecture was expiring, a few "engineers," as these innovating architects were slightingly called, conceived the idea of using iron girders as the framework for industrial buildings. Iron and glass made their first appearance as early as 1833, in Rohault de Fleury's greenhouses for the Jardin des Plantes, Paris. Finally, in 1863, by inaugurating his lectures at the École des Beaux-Arts with his famous series of *Entretiens sur l'architecture* (*Discourses on Architecture*, 2 vols., Boston, 1875–81), Viollet-le-Duc was to sow dismay among the defenders of eclecticism. He was a convinced medievalist, but at the same time an equally convinced and even excessive rationalist; he made it his business to debunk the ideas of the Gothic revival, so dear to mid-century designers and decorators. In his view the thirteenth-century architects had been primarily technicians, engineers in fact; as for decoration, they had used it to soften and humanize the austerity of the pointed arch, so well adapted to sustaining the most daring thrusts of their architecture.

But where Viollet-le-Duc showed himself most prophetic and influential was in his suggestion that it might be possible to erect an armature—a lightweight metal skeleton—and cover it with masonry. Thirty years later, Sullivan, Horta, Frantz Jourdain, Perret, and Tony Garnier, replacing stone with iron, concrete, and glass, bore witness to his genius. Just how far he anticipated and shaped Art Nouveau can be seen from the tributes paid him by Camillo Boito, Berlage, and even Gaudí. Viollet-le-Duc was a rationalistic force; and although legend had tended to turn him into a disciple of Lenoir, a kind of Goncourt of the medieval movement, in reality he was like Otto Wagner and Mackintosh. His ultimate ambition, like theirs, was to conceive architecture as an integral whole which, "in order to be aesthetically pleasing, must be functional."

French Art Nouveau architecture belongs almost exclusively to what we shall call the Latin school, as distinct from the Scottish and Viennese schools. In France, Guimard created this architecture; but to Perret belongs the honor of having subjugated the excesses of the movement, preventing it from suffocating in its own preciosity, and saving it from premature decease.

Guimard showed courage and imagination in designing the Castel Béranger in Paris (1897); the extent of his courage and imagination can be seen by taking a walk along the Boulevard Haussmann, the Rue de Maubeuge, or the Rue de la Pompe. It was in this building that for the first time, at least in France, the principles of Art Nouveau had been embodied in a house built expressly for leasing to middle-class tenants. The Castel Béranger gave people a shock; at the time, it was described as "a building which seems to have sprung up out of nothing." Moreover, its perfectly integrated design was an unkind comment on the banality of the surrounding architecture. As in the work of Horta, symmetry and the straight line had been eliminated wherever possible, yet the building as a whole had a curiously unified air. Both inside and out, Guimard allowed lavish scope for sculpture and color; by using a two-toned variety of brick, and also a glazed brick with a graduated blue shade, he succeeded in creating a distinguished chromatic effect both on the façade and in the inner courtyards, similar to that achieved by Otto Wagner at 40 Linke Wienzeil in Vienna.

Like Horta, Guimard designed buildings in complete detail, even specifying the locks and bolts, fastenings for windows, the tradesmen's entrance, and the fireplaces (a remarkable example is found in the concierge's room in the Rue La Fontaine house of 1908). In a house on the Avenue de Versailles he made use of a bend in the stairs, between one floor and another, as the place for a couch, which becomes an integral part of the general décor. He surrounded doors with hypnotic arabesques, his fireplaces seem to blaze by themselves, and his perversely twisting lines have nothing to learn from the allurements of the Sezession Style.

Destiny, it seemed, intended this unusual art to be placed within everyone's reach: Guimard was commissioned to design station entrances for the Métro (plate 114). Up from the sidewalk there sprang a profusion of interlacing metal, bouquets of aquatic plants, luminous tulips, gorged with the rich disturbing sap of Paris, its cellars, and subsoil.

Imprisoned in his own aestheticism, Guimard began imitating himself—which he did very well in 1908, as seen in the enchanting private house at 60 Rue La Fontaine (plate 5). But by this time Peter Behrens, Van de Velde, and Frank Lloyd Wright had appeared on the scene, and Tony Garnier's prodigious plan for the city of Lyons had been in existence for seven years.

At the beginning of the century a certain number of French architects, stimulated by contact with German theorists, became passionately interested in exterior decoration. Their desire for active collaboration with artists in wrought iron and sculptors in wood or stone enabled them to achieve a striking unity in the finished building.

The mansion by Georges Pradelle, in the Rue d'Orléans at Neuilly (about 1904), was the result of excellent teamwork between this architect and the decorative sculptor, Armand Seguin. Seguin displayed an aptitude for composition which lent gaiety to a commonplace façade. The balconies, which are particularly successful, the charming sunken door leading to the cellar, and the front gate, which foreshadows characteristics visible in French painting of 1925, were designed and executed in iron by Émile Robert.

※

Xavier Schoellkopf, who graduated from the École des Beaux-Arts in 1895, deserves especially high praise; his buildings, particularly Yvette Guilbert's house (plate 6) in the Boulevard Berthier, Paris (now unfortunately destroyed), put him among the best ornamental architects of his time. It is true that his excitable, emotional style sometimes runs off into superfluities, but his well-modeled masses and his decorative motifs are felicitously blended together. The façade of 29 Boulevard de Courcelles, Paris, with sculptures by Rouvière, shows the architect's desire to attain a flexible form in the modeling of the stone. The surface is shaped into wavelets which rise gently from the stone and melt back into it; the effect is one of planes interpenetrating and fusing. But simplification of some of the decorative detail (overlapping foliage, flowers, and shells) would have been an improvement. Like Charles Plumet, Schoellkopf continually conceals his appetite for Art Nouveau under imitation eighteenth-century effects; both these architects appear to have felt slightly ashamed of their predilection for this odd new style.

※

Plumet, a "rationalistic Symbolist," was one of the first to humanize the appearance of commercial buildings by reconciling the medievalist leanings of his contemporaries with the financial demands of the real-estate developers. Like many architects of his time, Plumet wanted art to be everywhere: in the concierge's room, on bakers' shopfronts, in brasseries. Reactions were sharp: "Ever more insolently, art is slopping out into the streets, on the fronts of shops and houses.... What a disgraceful mess! If you want something outstanding you must look to men of outstanding talent; if not, be content to have something decent and ordinary" (Camille Mauclair).

The strictures of Mauclair are merely a symptom of the ambiguous state of affairs which arises whenever an important new creative development is in question. (A similar situation arose around 1948, when art directors in the film world were handing out Surrealism of the kind usually associated with hairdressing establishments.)

Plumet and his partner Tony Selmersheim enriched the Paris scene with a number of elegantly designed buildings which have since disappeared (the entrance of the Hôtel du Havre, the Kohler chocolate shop, the Maison Cadolle, the establishment of Roddy the shirtmaker, and the Restaurant Édouard in the Place Boïeldieu). Among buildings by this partnership which have escaped destruction, 39 Avenue Victor-Hugo claims our attention by a certain stylishness and a somewhat forbidding sobriety—although it might have been improved with a little warmth, a touch of madness somewhere. The decorative stonework, whose airy, supple carving is by Lucien Schnegg, is nicely in harmony with the façade.

The architect L. P. Marquet succeeded in marrying new forms with an apparently classical style. His bow windows are incorporated into the façade by ingenious floral decorations. In the front doors of the Rue Hermel and at 2 bis Avenue des Gobelins in Paris, Marquet felicitously combined wrought iron with the stone carvings of Émile Derré and Seguin.

※

Auguste Perret began his career in the Art Nouveau period, as is evident from his building, 119 Avenue de Wagram, Paris. Though the façade hardly forecasts the genius of his future work, several unusual details can be seen: the weight-supporting consoles beautifully integrated with the general mass of the building; the two trees climbing audaciously up the front; and the simplicity of the iron balconies, which foreshadow the staircase in the Rue Franklin.

The residence designed in 1903 by Perret at 25 *bis* Rue Franklin (plate 15) marked the end of Art Nouveau in Paris, and the erection of the first house in what can properly be called a contemporary style. It was also the first time any architect had used such a diversity of materials —glazed tile sheathing, faïence mosaics, glass bricks, asbestos cement, ferro-concrete and concrete—which Perret humorously described as "rich man's concrete on poor man's concrete."

Jules Lavirotte is undoubtedly one of the most attractive figures of Art Nouveau because, like Gaudí and some of the Italian architects, he was first and foremost a Symbolist. His building in the Avenue Rapp, Paris (plate 4), with its asymmetrical yet balanced façade, its consoles and their thistle decoration, its hues of greenish gray and faint blue, its roofs which evoke the Gothic past and the more dreamlike parts of German Romantic literature, is one of the strangest buildings in the world. His Céramic Hôtel in the Avenue de Wagram, with its pebble-dash decoration by Bigot, soon acquired an appearance of preciosity equal to that of the Chinese pavilion at Drottningholm, built two centuries earlier. Lavirotte was more decorator than architect; this is what distinguishes him from Horta and Guimard. He tended to get carried away and to exaggerate, and though the parts are often admirably unusual, they do not always add up to a happily integrated whole, a charge which can never be brought against Guimard.

The disappointing curve described by French architectural development can be gauged by looking at the Liceo Italiano at 12 Rue Sédillot (1899), then at 151 Rue de Grenelle, and finally at 23 Avenue de Messine (1908). Like Horta, and probably for the same reasons (middle-class clients' passion for imitation Louis XVI), Lavirotte retreated into prudent conformism.

Between 1900 and 1910 most architects borrowed from the new style, some because they really wanted to, others because it was the fashion; touches of Art Nouveau can even be found on exteriors dated 1930. Along some main Parisian arteries, such as the Avenue des Gobelins, Avenue Victor-Hugo, Avenue Henri-Martin, and Boulevard Raspail, dozens of buildings show similar traces.

The influence of Guimard and the School of Nancy was great in the provinces as well. The works of Mienville and Eugène Vallin, who designed the entrance gallery of the Decorative Arts Exhibition in Nancy, are characteristic of the style of that city. Their buildings, and especially those of Vallin (often named as the leader of the School of Lorraine), are well balanced and have great power; they are closer to Guimard than to Lavirotte, but often lack the grace of the first and the singularity of the second. Weissenburger, who designed the Magasins Réunis de Nancy, continued what Émile Gallé had begun; his style is characterized by the use of wide bays separated by robust pillars with clean, sober lines.

About 1903 or 1904, various building firms put up what were called "hygienic dwellings" for tenants of modest means, such as members of the liberal professions and the lower ranks of the civil service. Despite low costs and the unpromising soubriquet, architects like Henri Sauvage and C. Sarazin did manage in some cases to give these houses a pleasant, welcoming appearance. Instances can be found in the Rue Damrémont and at 7 Rue Trétaigne in Paris; the fronts of these houses have a pair of bow windows, each window being surrounded with tiles and surmounted by a rounded cornice. The brightly painted window frames, the stained-glass windows lighting the stairs, and the floral decoration of the banisters, all combined to give the visitor an artistic impression. Finally, an interesting new note was struck by bathrooms embellished with decorative tiles, the first attempt in France to make such installations beautiful as well as comfortable.

It is impossible to discuss Art Nouveau without saying something of the petit bourgeois houses which sprang up everywhere in outer Paris. Some day, if they are not mown down by time and real-estate developers, we shall start noticing that these innumerable tiny villas built of millstone grit, usually regarded as a standing joke, are not without charm. Fanciful, saucy, dainty, they well deserve a few moments' contemplation. Built on plans imported from England, they were in most instances adapted to French ways of life by the architect Bliault. The price had to be kept down; these little houses were economically built—no paneling, and a minimum of other interior woodwork; no moldings and often no wainscoting, so that sweeping and dusting were made easy. The usual price was 7,000 francs (about $3,000 at that time); furniture, designed by the architect, came to about 1,500 francs; and another 500 francs went toward painting and decorating.

To sum up this section, we can say that between 1895 and 1910, French architecture remained decorative rather than functional; in eluding the clutches of historicism (the recent rediscovery of the eighteenth century by the Goncourt brothers was still very much in the air), it frequently fell into the pitfalls of Symbolism, from which only Perret and Tony Garnier were capable of extricating it.

ITALY

Apart from a few new achievements such as the Café Pedrocchi, built in Padua by Giuseppe Jappelli in 1816, and famous for a façade which succeeds in being both academic and functional, Italy in the nineteenth century remained faithful to the traditional glories of her architectural past: Palladio, Vignola, and Sangallo. After the Risorgimento, the appearance of Italian cities began to change, a process to which speculative builders had, inevitably, contributed. By constructing new main avenues, the Italian emulators of Haussmann modified the archaic character of Rome and Milan; they gave these cities a bourgeois "New Look."

The middle of the nineteenth century was the heyday of bourgeois historicism throughout Europe. The monument to King Victor Emmanuel erected in front of the Forum in Rome, and the Galleria dei Mercanti which was put up in Milan to connect the Piazza del Duomo with La Scala, were dubbed "Stile Umbertino."

Out of an entire generation of conventionally oriented colleagues, the Roman architect Camillo Boito, about 1860, was one of the first Europeans to argue the priority of function over decoration. (Berlage was to do the same thing some twenty years later in Amsterdam.) In 1871, Boito built the hospital at Gallarate. He achieved the feat of putting the service rooms all on the same level, and he kept his decoration simple; the building is functional, but the monotonous severity of the bare brick walls is broken here and there by a frieze with a trefoil motif, and by the ornamental metalwork of windows and gutters. The Ricovero dei Musicisti (Milan, 1899) confirms the fact that Boito remained a servant of historicism and never became a real adherent of Art Nouveau.

The birth of the Stile Floreale, the name given in Italy to Symbolistic Art Nouveau, is elusive. No date can be assigned to it. From 1885 onward, in Turin and more particularly in Milan (in and near the Via Mozart), buildings with unfamiliar outlines began to appear. This may have been an effect of the historical ties between Northern Italy and Austria, or it may have been due to the influence of Symbolism. But many of these Floreale houses exhibit a Mannerist character, a feeling accentuated by curious statues which seem to explode from the stone.

Two men deserve a special place in the architectural history of this period: Raimondo d'Aronco, whose buildings reflect his admiration for the Sezession and for orientalism; and Giuseppe Sommaruga, in whom the Floreale tendency was impregnated at once with historicism and modernity.

Raimondo d'Aronco stands out as the most important Italian architect of his generation. In his early works he was still dominated by Romantic historicism; such are the Porta Tenaglia (Milan, 1882), the façade of the architectural exhibition in Turin (1890), and the Ponte Maria Teresa (Turin, 1893). The latter reminds one of another bridge, at that time still unbuilt, the Pont Alexandre III in Paris.

It was not long before the artist in him threw off the restraints of orthodoxy and allowed his imagination to range at will. In 1899, after a violent earthquake devastated much of Constantinople, D'Aronco was invited to Turkey by Sultan Abdul Hamid. Like Gaudí in Barcelona, Josef Maria Olbrich in Darmstadt, and Sullivan in Chicago, but in his own fashion, D'Aronco sought to fuse traditional Moslem art and the spirit of Art Nouveau. In Constantinople, in 1900, he designed a slender, tall, gaily impudent house for Edem Bey which, with its sloping roof, makes one think of a young woman, her hat perched on the side of her head and coming down over one eye.

D'Aronco was represented at the Exhibition of Decorative Arts in Turin (1902). Nothing now survives of that remarkable display; only from photographs (*see* plate 23) can we conjure up a mental picture of its extravagance, its exaggerations, its Mannerism. The exhibition sounded the death knell of the Stile Liberty. With the passing of the years, D'Aronco's imagination progressively dried up; his Palazzo Communale at Udine (1909) shows a partial return to the clichés of orthodoxy.

The architectural style of Sommaruga has the peculiar interest of providing a bridge between eclecticism and rationalism. A passionate proponent of Boito's theories, he built, in 1901, the Casa Castiglioni in Milan (plates 21 and 22). This rebellious masterpiece, with its striking decoration and its base of bare, rusticated blocks of labradorite, seems at first glance to be in the Baroque tradition, a late Baroque which has nothing in common with Horta's "Whiplash" manner or with the abstract, increasingly stylized forms pursued in Glasgow, Vienna, and Darmstadt. It was by his handling of contrasting planes that Sommaruga showed his modernity in this building; his guiding principle seems to have been a feeling for space. The staircase, one of the functional themes which appears to have had an especially intoxicating effect on this architect, acquires maximum importance, becoming as it were the respiratory system of the building as a whole.

Sommaruga built a number of villas, of which the most remarkable is the Villa Faccanoni at Sarnico. This most unusual dwelling, rising from a base of untrimmed masonry, abounds in interesting details: twin vaulting which intersects at a forty-five-degree angle over the main door, elliptical bow windows, and little Gaudíesque tufts of stone crowning the roof.

In 1908, on a hill overlooking Varese, Sommaruga embarked on the construction of a hotel; the result, with its two main blocks connected by a high, vaulted passageway, is something titanic, bizarre, and almost frightening.

To sum up, Art Nouveau architecture in Italy was the work of isolated individualists. Delightful buildings in this key are to be found here and there, at Pesaro (plate 25), Florence, or in Sicily; no one can remember who designed them.

SPAIN

In the course of a journey in Catalonia toward the middle of the nineteenth century, Queen Isabella II conferred her approval on the plan for extending Barcelona. The Ensanche, the wide, gently sloping plain which surrounds the old town, became the training ground for young men from Barcelona's new school of architecture, founded in 1880. Census figures tell what was achieved: in 1860, Barcelona had 17,000 houses and 200,000 inhabitants; by 1905, the figures became 40,000 and 600,000 respectively. In addition, due to the contributions of Gaudí, Barcelona had once more regained her stature as an artistic and liberal center temporarily free of Spanish (Catalonians consider themselves Catalonians, *not* Spaniards) domination.

Antoni Gaudí was born at Reus, Catalonia, in 1852. He showed an inclination for drawing and architecture from early youth. In 1869, he entered the old School of Architecture in Barcelona, but had to earn the money for his fees and so did not take his diploma until eight years later. Between 1870 and 1880 he worked as assistant under Juan Martorell and José Fontseré on a large number of commissions, one of which was the monumental waterfall in the Parque Ciudadela in Barcelona. Interested in technique rather than aesthetics, young Gaudí was at this stage still deeply under the influence of medieval architecture. In 1880, he completed the Casa Vicens (plate 26), which gives a foretaste of all his work to come, but the full character of his style did not emerge until 1885, when he set about designing the Palau Güell.

A passionately devout Catholic who walked several miles to church every day, and a patriotic Catalan who declared himself unable to speak Spanish properly, Gaudí with his originality and eccentricities is one of the most fascinating characters in the whole history of art. Even his death was strange. At six o'clock on the evening of June 7, 1926, he was knocked down by a trolley bus and dragged along for several yards. No one recognized the victim; he was just an old man raggedly dressed, and the taxi drivers declined to pick him up. He died on June 10, in the public ward of the Santa Cruz Hospital, without regaining consciousness. When his death was announced, all Spain went into mourning, and his funeral two days later was followed by a procession two-and-a-half miles long. Many Catalonians regarded him as a saint.

Gaudí's work is based on a profound, abnormal, almost monstrous knowledge of all the styles of the past, which he transmuted with astonishing ease into something all his own. The intense power of his imagination confronts us irresistibly in the double parabolic design of the doorways of the Palau Güell, mysteriously veiled by the serpentine reticulation of the iron gates behind which they stand. A boundary wall of dressed stone, as sinuous as the brick walls built by John Palmer a century earlier at Bath, encloses the sumptuous park. It carries overtones of medieval castles and modern machine-gun nests; its mosaic decoration, composed of ceramic fragments, bears a resemblance to some of the surfaces contrived by Klimt.

About 1900, he gave free rein to his imagination. The chapel of the Colonia Güell (1898–1914) is a most extraordinary attack on conventional architecture and decoration. Everything which normally appears solid and stable (walls, columns, towers, roofs) has been transposed into a new, wild key; architecture and its mathematical laws are translated into the stuff of dreams.

In the Casa Milá (1905–10), Gaudí declared war on everything rectangular. It is as if he had succeeded in making a cast of the ocean surface on a stormy day; decoration based on plant life hangs from the edge of parapets and balconies, as if left stranded by a receding tide. The windows have soft, melting outlines and are placed according to the vagaries of the form, with the result that they reflect the light from a number of angles. The unclassifiably shaped chimneys, formed rather like totem poles, appear to be ready to take wing at the command of a disquieting, mysterious messenger.

It would be altogether too simple to catalogue Gaudí's creations under the general heading of Art Nouveau. They make one think of the fantastic flights of certain medieval architects or, again, of what would happen if the torrential verbal visions of Victor Hugo could be cast in concrete.

Four architects, none of them rivaling the genius of Gaudí, also made their contributions to the beauty of Barcelona. The works of Lluis Domenéch y Montaner belong to Art Nouveau in much the same way as do those of Lavirotte in Paris. Like the latter, and like Sommaruga in Milan, Domenéch y Montaner showed his originality in his irregular windows, the floral designs of his decorative details, and sculptural figures which seem to come surging out from the walls (Paséo de Gracia). He embellished his brick walls with white enamel, blue figures, and coats of arms in curling relief, so that his buildings strike a note of wealth, gaiety, and extravagance.

Don Henrique Sagnier used medieval, Rococo, and Art Nouveau effects side by side, not without a certain success and elegance. He had an unusual way with balconies, making them look a little larger than life. The five-windowed mirador projecting from the first story of one of his apartment houses is like the woodwork of an Austrian or Baroque organ.

With Don José Puig y Cadafalch and Artiges, traditional Spanish architecture resumed its sway and Catalonian architecture fell into a long, deep sleep.

SCOTLAND

Charles Rennie Mackintosh stands out as a leading figure in the history of Art Nouveau. His architectural abilities, no less than his genius and versatility as a designer of decoration, caused the style he created to be named after him.

Born in Glasgow, where his father was a police superintendent, Mackintosh found his vocation at an early age; at sixteen he was already working under the architect John Hutchinson and going to evening classes at the Glasgow School of Art. During the next eight years his name was always in the lists of prizewinners at the school. In the National Competition of 1888, he won a bronze medal for a design for a mountain chapel; in 1890, he won the Thomson Prize with a design for a town hall in the classical style. Armed with a scholarship, he set out on a tour of Italy.

While still a student he became friendly with Herbert MacNair. He and MacNair later married the Macdonald sisters (Mackintosh married Margaret in 1900), both of whom had some influence on the development of the Glasgow Style. Known as The Four, this coalition of complementary talents quickly won a reputation extending far beyond Glasgow and Scotland, and in 1902 The Four took part in the Turin Exhibition.

Mackintosh turned his hand with equal readiness to the design of houses, posters, fabrics, and furniture, and his versatility rapidly caught the attention of artistic circles in Munich, Darmstadt, and Vienna. In 1920 Mackintosh, who had left the group, retired to Port-Vendres, France.

Viewed as a whole, the work of Mackintosh reveals a sharp contradiction. His architecture proves he was a modernist. His style, always extremely severe, was subordinated to functional demands, and though it gives off an occasional whiff of musty Celticism, it reflects the rigid standards of his native society, austere and habitually devoted to industrial work. But he was also an aesthete whose hypersensitive sense of line flaunted its charms in Miss Cranston's Buchanan Street Tearooms in Glasgow.

Mackintosh's first big architectural job was the Martyr Public School at Glasgow (1895). The door, despite a bulky portico, is a success; otherwise this massive building, with its tall rectangular windows, is thoroughly commonplace. But with the new Glasgow School of Art, in 1897 (Library Wing in 1907–09), he showed his mettle (plate 32); difficulties brought out the best in him, as they did in Gaudí. He took advantage of the sloping site to make the front of the building rise up sheer for eighty feet, giving the impression of a Highland stronghold. Like Edward William Godwin in the White House, Mackintosh mellowed a large blank wall by piercing it with small windows placed asymmetrically, and the drainpipe from the gutter was exploited to emphasize the midline of the pattern. The northern part of the building, with its enormous bays and irregular arrangement of windows (four in the west wall, three in the east), strikes a different note from the rest. The entrance would appear overbearing were it not for the curving ironwork support at the foot of the stairs, which restores the visual balance. The impression of height from the south and west aspects is increased by the vertical rectangular block jutting out from the façade, dominating the main entrance. The appearance of the building as a whole is that of an impregnable fortress.

In 1901, Mackintosh built Windy Hill, at Kilmacolm. At first glance, the outside of this small country house offers nothing surprising to a Continental eye, but certain details (the chimneys, the boundary wall through which the front gate passes, and the shifting planes of the walls of the house itself) are clearly from the same hand as the School of Art. Hill House (1902–03) shows Mackintosh's imagination in a quieter mood (plate 31); this country house, complete with dovecot, is less functional than the rest of his work.

The fundamental differences between the architectural thinking of Mackintosh and that of Guimard or Sommaruga remind us yet again that Art Nouveau was a movement rather than a style.

AUSTRIA

By ordering the demolition of the ancient fortifications of Vienna and building the Ringstrasse, a great external boulevard, the Emperor Franz Joseph opened the capital to new sources of inspiration. For half a century the city had been subjugated to that overpowering, solemn, bourgeois architecture which has been so well named the "Bureaucratic Style."

In 1897, the architects Otto Wagner, Joseph Maria Olbrich, Josef Hoffmann, Koloman Moser, and Adolf Loos, united by their resolve to shatter the conservative spirit of Viennese society, formed a group and made their breakaway—the Sezession, as their movement came to be called and, with it, the whole of Austrian Art Nouveau. It was, incidentally, just at this period that Freud's early studies first became available to the public in book form.

Whereas in England, Scotland, France, Belgium, and Italy, Art Nouveau grew out of the old familiar styles, such as medieval or Rococo, in Vienna no connection can be drawn between Austrian traditional styles and the Sezession. Indeed, the creations of Hoffmann and Loos are visible evidence of the disdain of that generation of artists toward the Mannerist Baroque which had been held in highest esteem in their country for nearly three centuries. Another striking fact, paralleled only by the difference between Barcelona and the rest of Spain, is that no Austrian city other than Vienna was excited by Sezessionism.

Otto Wagner occupies a preponderant position in the history of Austrian architecture, but because he was of the Symbolist generation his relation to Art Nouveau is ambiguous, rather like that of Gustave Moreau in painting. Wagner's titanic achievement, with its variety and apparent contradictions, is often hard to define.

As early as 1863, he put forward a revolutionary project for the Kursalon in Vienna's municipal park. In 1880, after building a number of apartment houses, he designed the Artibus building and the offices of the Giro und Kassenverein, in which he epitomized all the fundamentals of European architecture, in so far as the latter can be regarded as a definable entity.

In 1891, he produced a project for the Berlin Cathedral in which, despite an accumulation of superfluous accessory features, the underlying vigor of the structure makes itself felt. In 1894, he built the Kaufhaus Neumann; the pure, austere lines of its rectangular façade, ornamented with floral designs, prefigured his future work. The same elimination of inessentials appeared in the Ankerhaus (1894), a work which reminds us of Sullivan's Wainwright Building in St. Louis and the Guaranty Building in Buffalo.

In his inaugural lecture at the Vienna Academy in the same year, Wagner declared: "Only what is practical is beautiful," and again: "The essence of the structure of a building, and the material employed, must be left visible."

Wagner's project for the Hofburg, in 1898, showed how Van de Velde's "*déblaiement d'art*," the clearing of the ground in the arts, had been put into practice. Decorative encumbrances were banished and the architectural mass thus purified had an undeniable majesty of its own. The curious project for the Stadtmuseum (1901), with its happy distribution of the principal masses and its sober lines—marred, however, by an exaggeratedly statuesque quality—at the same time looks back to the Symbolist period and forward to the world of tomorrow.

Between 1903 and 1907, Wagner built the church of Sankt Leopold and the Postal Savings Bank (plate 35). The Villa Wagner (1912) proclaimed that he had left the Sezession behind and was henceforward a European.

The most substantial figure among Austrian architects and decorators of the early twentieth century was Josef Hoffmann. Born at Pirnitz (Moravia), he campaigned for the reform of Austrian aestheticism from the beginning of his student days, when he entered the Austrian Academy of Fine Arts. He represented the geometrical element in the Sezession group, the tendency later known as the "Quadratel Hoffmann."

In 1898, he collaborated with Olbrich to build the offices of *Ver Sacrum*, a magazine which played a leading part in spreading the influence of the Sezession. In 1899, with Koloman Moser, he designed the Apollo store, whose decoration, based on the classical volute, shows that Hoffmann had not yet discovered his true path. In 1901, he built a number of small houses on the Hohe Warte in Vienna; the strangest of them is a villa for Koloman Moser, conceived in terms of large planes broken up in various ways—an unexpected balcony here, a bow window there. The Punkersdorf Sanatorium (1903) was his first resolutely modern work on a large scale. The rigor of the planes and the limpid structure make it Europe's first attempt at a rational architecture.

In 1904, disgusted by the poor quality of Austrian peasant crafts, Hoffmann founded the *Wiener Werkstätte*, a group of studios and workshops in which, with the help of professional colleagues, particularly Koloman Moser, he designed furnishings and interior decoration of every kind—furniture, carpets, and all the appurtenances of everyday life. Like Van de Velde, Guimard, and Mackintosh, Hoffmann obliterated the distinctions between fine and applied art.

He was just thirty-five when he produced the work which above all others bears the characteristic stamp of his genius, the prodigious Palais Stoclet, a private house in Brussels (plate 36). In later years the Hoffmann style, ruthlessly stripped of inessentials, tended toward monotony; his rounded masses, unrelieved by slenderness anywhere, became ponderous. The last traces of the Sezession spirit had disappeared.

Adolf Loos stands somewhat apart from the other architects and designers of the Sezession. He disliked symbols and rejected excrescences. Whether he was concerned with business premises (such as the shop for men's clothes, designed by him in Vienna in 1898) or a café (the Café

Museum), the emphasis throughout was on structure. The Villa Karma (Geneva, 1904) testifies to his concentration on the ever more perfect distribution of volumes. To him, architecture existed as a function of new needs: "Every epoch must create its own style."

As time went on, Loos exhibited an increasing urge toward synthesis: witness the smooth, massive front presented to the world by the Looshaus (Michaelerplatz, Vienna, 1910). In the Steiner house (Vienna, 1910) he used big convex surfaces, cubes in step-formation, and plain compact blocks. The façade and interior of the Rufer house (1912) were completely up to date, based on the latest architectural advances. In 1926, he built a house in Paris for Tristan Tzara and, the following year, a shop for Knize, a firm of shirtmakers, on the Avenue des Champs-Élysées.

The artistic personality of Loos is such that one cannot neatly pigeonhole him as a member of the Sezession; like Sullivan, Auguste Perret, and Frank Lloyd Wright, he transcends the limits of Art Nouveau.

It was not long before the Sezession acquired the stature of a school. The charms of the new movement gained adherents among the younger Hungarian architects, who broke with the Bureaucratic Style and affirmed the existence of a national style in Budapest. Some, like Odon Lechner (plate 38), showed great originality; others, like Karoly Kos and Béla Zrumeczky, who built the Zoo, and Aladar Arkay, the architect of the Zebegeny church, subscribed to an architecture bearing folk-art overtones, rather like that developed by the Finns.

The tendency most closely related to the Hoffmann Quadratel was represented by Béla Lajta, whose remarkable Rossavolgyi house is most Viennese in feeling, very much a child of the Sezession. Later, Béla Malnai (who designed the Credit Bank), Moritz Pogány, and Istvan Medgyaszay (the first Hungarian architect to design a building in reinforced concrete) pioneered in the modernization of urban aesthetics.

GERMANY

The monument to Frederick the Great, designed in 1797 by Friedrich Gilly, exhibits the nostalgia for Roman antiquity which was prevalent at that time in Germany. The same attraction was one of the ingredients of German Romanticism throughout the nineteenth century; examples of it are the Trinkhalle designed by Heinrich Hübsch at Baden-Baden in 1840, the Johanneum built in 1836-39 by C. L. Wimmel and G. J. Forsmann in Hamburg, and the museums in Munich by Leo von Klenze, a pupil of Gilly.

Soon, however, the clash of Wagnerian cymbals heralded a new arrival, the Rundbogenstil (Romanesque style), a militant architectural movement addicted to a mixture of ancient and musty recipes—a passion for the Middle Ages and a nostalgia for romantic fifteenth-century Italy. Germany broke out into a rash of granite and brick, the medium employed by Gottfried Semper at Dresden for the Opera House, the Museum, and the Synagogue, and at Vienna for the Burgtheater.

Alfred Messel revolted against historical eclecticism and the charmingly preposterous castles of Ludwig II of Bavaria. Inspired by the use of iron and glass in France and the United States, he applied the same methods in designing the Wertheim Department Store (plate 83) in Berlin (1896-1900). At about that time, intellectual circles—Symbolists and Liberals—in Hamburg, Berlin, and Munich, with support from individuals here and there in the ranks of the bourgeoisie, became enamoured of Art Nouveau. Julius Meier-Graefe with his magazine, *Pan*, Bernard Pankok, Bruno Paul, and Richard Riemerschmid with the *Münchener Vereinigte Werk-*

stätte (United Workshops of Munich) played influential parts in Teutonizing the various doctrines from abroad.

But though Jugendstil (youth style) showed real originality in typography, posters, furniture, and the decorative arts, its success in the architectural field is by no means so clear. With the exception of August Endell, the Germans were receptive rather than creative.

It was in 1897 that Endell was called in to design the studio of the photographer Elvira (plate 39). The façade was all straight lines—it brings to mind Perret's Théâtre des Champs-Élysées (1913). Within this frame the windows and doors were placed asymmetrically; their upper corners were cut off and rounded, and the leading of the window panes described whimsical arabesques.

Many Germans found this variety of Mannerism too Latin for their taste; they preferred the simplicity of the Sezession or the Edinburgh School, which had appeared on their horizon in 1898, in Mackintosh's contributions to the Munich Exhibition.

Between 1898 and 1910, three men devoted themselves to ensuring the triumph of the Jugendstil: Olbrich, Peter Behrens, and Van de Velde.

By his design for the Sezession building at the Vienna Exhibition in 1898, an astonishing structure which prefigures the work of Hoffmann, Olbrich (plate 34) asserted his independence not only of the Austrian classical school, but also of his early mentor, Otto Wagner. It was this building which, in the following year, earned him the task of planning a miniature city of the arts on the Mathildenhöhe, in the suburbs of Darmstadt. The Grand Duke Ernst Ludwig of Hessen-Darmstadt, an ardent admirer of the new creative architecture in Britain, financed the undertaking.

Olbrich achieved a remarkable synthesis of British and Viennese theories, and in so doing abolished all traces of Symbolism and historical lyricism. The whole complex of buildings on the Mathildenhöhe (plates 41–44), in whose design Behrens was also involved, took over ten years to complete. The finished work is less than homogeneous, so that it hardly seems possible to speak of a "Darmstadt style," and certain features—the shapes of some of the roof-ridges, the colors of mosaics, the bottom of the reflection pool (plate 42), the porch of the Ernst Ludwig Haus (plate 41), and the fountainlike roof of the Hochzeitsturm (plate 44)—show a decided infusion of orientalism.

Peter Behrens, after making his contribution to the Mathildenhöhe, took part in the Turin Exhibition of 1902, and the Düsseldorf Exhibition of 1904. A disciple of Mackintosh, Voysey, Sullivan, and Hoffmann, as time went on he modernized what he had learned from them and adapted it to suit German taste. In 1910, he produced designs for the turbine factory of the AEG (Allgemeine Elektrizitäts Gesellschaft) in Berlin, which stamp him definitively as a man of the twentieth century.

German architecture over the last fifty years has received an equally strong imprint from Van de Velde who, after spending some time at Krefeld, designed several buildings (examples are the Folkwang Museum at Hagen and, in 1914, the Werkbund Theater in Cologne).

To sum up, we may say of the Jugendstil and the Darmstadt School, those remarkable offshoots of the Sezession, that both of them, especially the latter, if not always successful in living up to Otto Wagner's dictum, "Only what is practical is beautiful," did succeed in clearing the air. They counteracted the intoxicating influence of Symbolistic idealism on a Germany still throbbing sympathetically to the memory of Wagnerian cyclones, and thus prepared the way for Walter Gropius and the Bauhaus.

ENGLAND

For the average Londoner, unversed in architectural problems, it would be difficult to describe the progress made between 1830 and 1900. New ground was won discreetly, not by sweeping revolutionary advances; we must look for it in matters of detail.

Nineteenth-century London had two faces. One was classical, elegant, and contained—the character imposed by Soane and Thomson on public buildings and investment buildings; the other was "period"—medieval, Queen Anne, and the Gothic Revival, which eventually grew into High Victorian Gothic. The men who, between 1860 and 1910, were to transform traditional architecture were recruited mainly from the medievalists. Unlike the Europeans and the Americans, the English were not much interested in the problems of designing big buildings or big groups of buildings; they devoted themselves to improving the structure and decoration of private houses. The heavy English cottage, half buried in the damp soil, and burdened with its clusters of chimneys, was to become lighter, rise to the surface, and open out to the light.

In 1859, with the Red House (built in Bexley Heath, Kent, for William Morris), Philip Webb, a friend and collaborator of Morris, blazed several unobtrusive little trails which in time became the path leading to English Art Nouveau. The brick walls of the Red House are a composition of successive vertical planes which are broken here and there by a gutter or by a room jutting out on a slender console (this reminds one of the slim supporting column used forty years later by Lavirotte in Paris in a corner of the Square Rapp), the purpose of which was to counterbalance the chimney stack. It was at this period that Webb, Ford Madox Brown, Edward Burne-Jones, and Dante Gabriel Rossetti, the leaders of the Arts and Crafts movement, set up the firm of Morris and Company with a capital of £100; their aim was to revitalize the dwelling house and everything in it.

Even before the Glasgow School started, there were a few architects who had had enough of medievalist flummeries and were turning in the direction of the purely functional. The contrasts of light and dark in the White House (plate 45), built in London in 1879 by William Godwin for his friend, James McNeill Whistler, its asymmetry, and the unfinished look of the façade (a lapse from good taste by conventional standards), prefigure some of Le Corbusier's works.

Unobtrusively, Richard Norman Shaw showed similar preoccupations. Though less severe than the White House, his Old Swan House, London (1876), is remarkable for the irregular arrangement of the seven windows on the third floor, an asymmetry which is cleverly masked by the projection of three of them outward from the façade. The decorative tracery and stylized foliage on the masonry band dividing the ground floor from the first floor are particularly happy touches. The light-colored horizontals, standing out against their background of dark brick, impart a decided vigor to the building. Holy Trinity Church, Latimer Road, London (1887), also by Shaw, proved that gaiety could replace the gloom so frequently associated with religious buildings; in this case the effect was achieved by the airy, graceful lines of the leading in the stained-glass windows. Shaw's inspiration was diverse; he passed from the perfectly orthodox Dutch style of his Albert Hall Mansions, London (1879), to tiresome exercises in the manner of Ledoux, while the Piccadilly Hotel, London (1905), is different from both of these. He is an example of how difficult it is to apply to the English architects of the end of the century a single, simple definition or descriptive phrase.

The work of Charles Harrison Townsend is closer to European ideas than any of his contemporaries. The front of the Whitechapel Art Gallery (plate 47), one of the most startling buildings in London, is like a fortress designed by a Moslem for a Spanish king; the doorway, with its Gaudiesque arch, strikes an exotic note in English architecture. In the Church of St. Mary the Virgin at Great Warley, in Essex (1904), Townsend, with the assistance of Sir William Reynolds-Stevens, created something which was entirely Art Nouveau; certain details of the interior are reminiscent of Josef Hoffmann's decoration, and the pillars are clenched to their bases in a way which recalls a device that had already been used by Horta in the Maison du Peuple in Brussels.

Arthur Heygate Mackmurdo, one of the most dexterous figures of the whole Arts and Crafts movement, was responsible for the celebrated Cadogan Gardens, London (1899); the private mansion there, with the purity of its unornamented façade featuring strong parallel lines with vertical emphasis, and its oblong windows nearly two stories high, reminds one of German and Austrian buildings of the same period.

The works of W. R. Lethaby (for instance, Avon Tyrrel, Hampshire, 1891), with their careful arrangement of masses and the geometrical simplicity of the forms employed, with calculated contrasts between lines, are related to both the Viennese school and to that of Mackintosh.

Charles Francis Annesley Voysey, at the outset of his career, took a much livelier interest in decoration than in architecture. His earliest buildings had a stocky, very Queen Anne appearance, but soon, in his houses in Bedford Park (1891) and Hans Road (plate 50), he displayed an urge toward a more sophisticated refinement. Given a small site and having to build high in consequence, he avoided the narrow-gutted look which afflicts so many London houses by proportioning the windows in such a way as to give breadth and lightness to the façade. But it was by radically transforming the style of English country houses (plate 48), yet at the same time preserving traditional appearances, that Voysey really made his mark. His ideas seemed so new and original that he became even better known than the young Frank Lloyd Wright.

In the Julian Sturgis house (1899) and "The Orchard," Chorley Wood (1900), Voysey handled rectangular windows in groups of four in such a way as to give the gabled fronts of these houses a simplicity which borders on perfection. An equally startling flair is to be found inside—the unusual staircase and banisters, for example, and the way the brickwork of the hearth makes a frame for the fire. Like Wright, Voysey leveled off the chimneys with the top of the roof, thus lightening and simplifying the form of these small houses. As is the case with Sullivan, Behrens, and Perret, Voysey's insistence on simplicity of line makes him a man of the twentieth century rather than a practitioner of Art Nouveau.

In 1904, in London, the designer and architect Charles Robert Ashbee built 38 Cheyne Walk, Chelsea (plate 51), one of the most harmoniously conceived houses of the earliest part of the century. Like the sixteenth-century Italians, he juggled with visual effects, framing the front door with an arch, and sketching an imaginary porch with a thin half circle of wrought iron. And though the necessity of ensuring that his rooms were adequately lighted forced him to use excessively high windows, he restored the balance with an asymmetrical pediment which soars like an arrow.

So varied was English architectural talent at this period that it hardly seems possible to speak of English Art Nouveau. The main conclusion seems to be that, between 1850 and 1910, the best English architects strove to break the chains of historicism, but they were not invariably successful in doing so. In general, Latin and Symbolist influences did not take hold in Great Britain. Harrison Townsend's few essays in this direction, and the highly Parisian Michelin Garage in London (plate 75) were, so to speak, medicinal doses of a Continental Art Nouveau of which the islanders had no great opinion.

HOLLAND

Holland remained deeply loyal to her own architectural traditions. Her charming small houses, many of them dating from the "golden age," proved perfectly adaptable to the needs of local life under modern conditions and, as ever, were admirably integrated with the landscape.

To satisfy urban needs, P. J. H. Cuypers and subsequently Berlage were commissioned to design large-scale complexes, such as railway stations. Cuypers, classically trained and unimaginative, built the Rijksmuseum and the Amsterdam Central Station in the medieval style. To Berlage fell the task of rejuvenating large-scale architecture without running counter to Dutch style and national character. But first came his trip to Chicago. He also fortified himself by studying the techniques of Boito, Sullivan, and Frank Lloyd Wright. Only after this preparation did he undertake the Amsterdam Stock Exchange. Although he used ornament sparingly, avoided gratuitous effects, and restored large flat surfaces to their proper value, Berlage, like Godwin, Shaw, and Richardson, could not refrain from little, over-picturesque details here and there.

The town-planning ideas he achieved in Amsterdam and The Hague (*see* plate 52) made Berlage the indisputable leader of the younger generation in Holland. To contemplate the works of this sturdy Dutchman takes us into an entirely different world from the exotic Symbolist blooms of Horta, Guimard, or Sommaruga.

UNITED STATES

Until the middle of the nineteenth century, American architects were followers of François Mansart, Claude-Nicolas Ledoux, and Sir John Soane, and despite a marked bias in favor of pediments and colonnades they created many highly elegant, graceful buildings: witness Thomas Walter's State Capitol building, Columbus, Ohio (1839–61); James Bucklin's Washington Buildings, Providence, Rhode Island (1843); William Strickland's Philadelphia Merchant's Exchange (1832–34); and Russell Warren's buildings at Newport. Consequently, when James Bogardus designed the Laing Stores in New York, in 1849, one of the first functional buildings, he was not so much reacting against the vices of an American historicism as responding to the needs of a nation of businessmen and industrialists.

American contractors subscribed to the revolution in building techniques sooner than did their European counterparts. New materials (iron, concrete, Bessemer steel) were used by William LeBaron Jenney in Chicago, and Elisha Graves Otis presented the first elevator at the New York International Fair in 1853. Innovations like these made deep inroads on the traditional methods. Soon the new spirit assumed visible shape in buildings of monumental character but relatively small dimensions, such as in the Provident Life and Trust Company by Frank Furness, Philadelphia (1879). Bogardus and Jenney were technicians of architecture; those who came after them were decorative architects. Henry Hobson Richardson, who was born in New Orleans and studied under Henri Labrouste in Paris, succeeded in his Trinity Church (Boston, 1873–77) and Crane Library (Quincy, Massachusetts, 1880–83) in assimilating and Americanizing European medievalism to a certain extent. But if we compare Richardson's Marshall Field Wholesale Store (Chicago, 1885–87) with Adler and Sullivan's Wainwright Building (St. Louis, 1890–91), we see that Richardson already belonged to a past epoch.

Curiously, it was on the especially difficult marshy soil of Chicago that the young Louis Sullivan elected to build his first skyscrapers. Sullivan was born in Boston in 1856. In 1872, he entered the office of Frank Furness as a student, but the current economic depression caused him to return to Chicago a year later and take a job under William LeBaron Jenney. In 1874, he decided to go to Paris and become a pupil of Émile Vaudremer (designer of the Église Saint-Pierre in Montrouge), from whom he acquired the orientalist leanings which became one of the characteristics of his work.

In 1881, Sullivan (in partnership with Dankmar Adler) built the Rothschild Store in Chicago which, with its four stories of large glass windows, was an early embodiment of spatial exploration with the accent on light. The Ryerson Building (Chicago, 1884) shows us a Sullivan still under the influence of Richardson, but it has an unusual façade composed of rectangular elements stamped, as it were, on contrasting vertical planes.

The Troescher Building (1884), the Knisely Building (1884), and the Wirt Dexter Building (1887), all in Chicago, illustrate Sullivan's preoccupation with mass: he distributes masses by tapering his buildings upward. The influence of the new English architecture can be seen in his smaller buildings, such as the West Chicago Club (1886). In the same year, work was begun on the Auditorium Building—a colossal creation, with foundations of monumental dimensions carrying a tower weighing 15,000 tons. In the Walker Warehouse (Chicago, 1888–89) the theme of the entrance with its sets of huge double arches is a prelude to the twin volute of the interior stairs.

Sullivan varied the size and form of his buildings to suit the local climate. Thus in the Opera House Block (1890) in Pueblo, Colorado, an amusing pastiche reminiscent of Florentine palazzos, the windows are sunk into the façade as if they had gone into hiding, whereas in the very Hanseatic style of the St. Nicholas Hotel in St. Louis (1892–93) they show up, in a series of three-sided outward-jutting bays, in the English manner. The Chicago Cold Storage Exchange Warehouse (1891) is a blind, purely functional, double rectangular mass.

Sullivan's work became more and more rigorous as his career proceeded, as seen in the Stock Exchange Building, Chicago (1893), and the Guaranty Building in Buffalo (1895) (plates 56 and 93). And though the façade of the Carson Pirie Scott & Co. Department Store, Chicago (1899–1904), is robed in exuberant decoration (plate 79), the body of the building is perfectly functional, presaging the architecture of our own day.

BELGIUM

About 1890, tendencies which had first seen the light in England nearly half a century earlier began to appear on the other side of the Channel, but with their scope and impact enlarged. The theories of Morris, Mackmurdo, and Mackintosh, and Liberty's bold ventures, now started fusing with Continental developments.

Between 1880 and 1890, Brussels became a crucible seething and bubbling with new trends. The process was initiated by Octave Maus, founder of the Cercle des Vingt and the Libre Esthétique movement. Glancing through his book, significantly titled *Trente années de lutte pour l'art* ("Thirty Years of Struggle for Art"), one is dazzled by the richness, boldness, and versatility of his thinking. He organized an exhibition of the sculpture of Rodin in 1884, and of Georges Minne in 1886. The prestige of the Symbolist movement, and also its ambiguities, ensured that everyone whose thoughts were tending in new directions felt himself immediately involved. Van de Velde joined the Libre Esthétique in 1889, and Jan Toorop followed him the year after. Soon the Nabis were to follow suit, and Symbolism triumphant was to assure the victory of a certain Mannerist tendency which was already beginning to appear in Nancy.

The greatest of all nineteenth-century Belgian architects was Victor Horta. His style was to fertilize the majority of European buildings for a number of years. Under his teacher, Alphonse Balat, an orthodox architect of first-rate quality, Horta studied the various creative ways in which Viollet-le-Duc had used iron, and was moved to announce: "The realization of any and every undertaking involves the empirical execution of a program which is technically appropriate to the purpose in hand."

As Van de Velde was also to do a little later, Horta eliminated the endless corridors, then in common use, by placing vestibules at different levels so that the other rooms became independent entities. He conferred nobility on the humblest materials—stone blocks, steel girders, and rivets. His houses showed their muscles and viscera, as if an anatomist had presented a skeleton not dead but alive; he left exposed everything which Haussmann's architects had been at pains to conceal.

In Brussels people were scandalized by Horta's work, and the aged Balat, the rebel's former master, was said to have burst into tears on seeing the Tassel residence (1892–93). Within a year, architects and designers from all over Europe were flocking to see Horta's buildings.

The Solvay residence (plate 63), which looks more spiky and rococo than the Tassel residence but is in fact more fluent and "musical," expresses the perfect maturity sometimes achieved by Art Nouveau at the crossroads of Latin and Anglo-Saxon impulses. Everywhere, on the exterior and interior, runs the famous Horta line—insidious, sibylline, voluptuous, light as air. In a more vigorous form but airy as ever, it was to reappear in the Van Eetvelde residence; it is the magic knot, the common factor connecting all his works. Among the uninspired buildings which surround them, Horta's discreet and harmonious façades make an immediate impression of good taste; the traditional decorative vocabulary of garlands, foliage, masks, caryatids, and lions' muzzles is nowhere to be seen.

Won over by Horta's modernism, the Belgian Socialist Party decided that this revolutionary architect was the right man to design their headquarters. The Maison du Peuple (plates 60 and 84) was opened on April 2, 1899, "to symbolize," as the official inscription declares, "the energetic and persevering endeavors of the Brussels working class."

For some reason—critical opposition or perhaps lack of continued bourgeois support—Horta's inspiration expired about 1900. It fell to the French, and especially Hector Guimard, to continue and perfect his work.

To find a suitable label for Henry van de Velde is indeed a bafflingly intricate task. Perhaps men of his scope and stature existed in the early thirteenth century, under the wing of Christianity. This Belgian, who worked mainly in Germany but remained essentially Flemish, could design a house and its decoration, and coordinate everything in it and about it; he was also a goldsmith, ship designer, bookbinder, engineer, and typographer. He built residential blocks, museums, and even a hairdresser's salon (Habig's, in Berlin). Ardent but clear-headed, Van de Velde was born to lead the modernist movement. "The destiny of art," he declared in 1894, "will attain its consummation in the Far East."

He started as a painter and exhibited in Brussels at the Salon des Vingt, but soon switched over to architecture. In his early work it is difficult to tell how much is due to English and Scottish influences. His first house, Bloemenwerf, in Uccle (plate 59), was built in 1896, and is simply conceived, closely akin to Voysey's manner. After the completion of this house he wrote: "The truth is that just now we are experiencing the dark night of reason. We have come to regard the maddest things as reasonable and the most reasonable ones as madness.... A stroke of luck has enabled me to build a house, and every time a funeral goes past it, this house makes cheerfulness suddenly and irrepressibly break through the ranks of pallbearers. And yet it differs from the nearby houses only in its modesty and by the fact that it is built in a completely logical way and is devoid of ornament." The house does indeed exhibit an exact congruence between design and purpose; the function of every part is clear and unequivocal.

In 1897, Julius Meier-Graefe and the Parisian art dealer Samuel Bing commissioned Van de Velde to design four rooms for the Dresden Exhibition, and in 1902, by which time Horta had abandoned Art Nouveau, Van de Velde was summoned to Weimar.

"The character of all decorative and ornamental work springs from one aim and one only: the application of reason." The opportunity had now come for him to apply his theories by embodying them is his own designs. It was during his Weimar period that Van de Velde finally abandoned the symbolic style of ornament so dear to the French (Guimard, Lavirotte); this element appeared henceforward only in a subtly schematized form, the Van de Velde line which, like a reptilian body, continually changes direction as its activities may require but always remains graceful.

He was fascinated by the potentialities of rectangular relationships and conceived the notion of "the cube as such," as his biographer Karl Ernst Osthaus puts it, "whose corners can be rounded and modeled at will." Not a cube, therefore, with the sharp edges favored by Hoffmann, but a mass firmly anchored to the ground by means of occasional sculptural additions. Hohenhof, the house built by Van de Velde for Osthaus near Hagen in 1907, is the earliest expression of these ideas; they were to remain characteristic of his art until 1914.

From 1910 to 1940 Van de Velde kept on designing with unabated ardor—railway cars, yachts, the Kröller-Müller Museum in Otterlo, Holland.... He was over ninety when he died.

He invented the Belgian style which Goncourt defined in a phrase which caught on prodigiously, the "Yachting Style." Nevertheless, Van de Velde wrote: "I assert that I have discovered nothing; unless you call someone a discoverer for merely having realized that to be a man of sense is enough to distinguish him from humanity at large." By combining beauty with comfort and serviceability, Van de Velde successfully created a new aesthetic; today we call it "functional."

Horta and Van de Velde were the masters of Belgian architectural Art Nouveau. They quite overshadow their contemporaries. It would nevertheless be unjust to overlook such men as Paul Hankar, Adolphe Crespin, and A. Waesbergue.

Hankar, who designed houses in the Rue Defacqz (plate 61) and the Rue Ruysbroeck, as well as the astonishing grill-room of the Grand Hôtel de Bruxelles, followed Horta's example in preaching the virtues of a style adapted to utilitarian needs. People used to say of his house in the Rue Defacqz, with a disapproving shake of the head: "Just the sort of house an artist would have!"

Brussels also fell under the influence of the English and Scottish architects. Between 1895 and 1910 a number of charming houses were built on the same general lines as Voysey's; hence the tall, narrow windows, which conflict with the medieval traditions so lovingly cherished in the Belgian capital.

DENMARK

Danish architecture, which had been sensitive for many years to the ancient Teutonic and Viking sagas, yielded to the attractions of Art Nouveau from about 1895.

It would seem as if Martin Nyrop felt obliged to transplant the new doctrines under conservative wrappings. For the façade of his imposing Copenhagen Raadhus, or town hall (plate

65), he used traditional red brick, heightened with granite and white stone, but he left the interior to the imagination of his decorators (plate 64). The capitals of the burgomasters' staircase are carved with animal details reminiscent of those in the Nancy-School glassware designed by Walter. The floral ornamentation of both the staircase and the loggia of the great hall, the sculptures by Niels Hansen which represent craftsmen building the Raadhus, the extremely stylized botanical decoration of the doors, containing various characters in medieval dress, and the tiles by Hermann Koehler transform this public building into an Art Nouveau complex.

The world's opportunity to discover Danish Art Nouveau came with the Universal Exhibition of 1900 in Paris. In such details as the very modern entrance by Bindesboell, and the agriculture and food pavilions by K. Arm Petersen, the influences of Hoffmann and the Sezession are to be seen. The progress achieved can be gauged by comparing these with the Danish pavilion, in which the architect Koch failed to free himself from the chains of folk art and the Viking tradition.

FINLAND

As soon as the Finnish pavilion, by Herman Gesellius, Armas Lindgren, and Eliel Saarinen, was erected in Paris at the Universal Exhibition of 1900 (plate 66), a chorus of exclamations arose from the visitors, and astonishment soon turned into admiration. What they saw was an enthralling, dreamlike building—contrasting gables, vaulted doorways, roofs bearing small spires, and a swelling campanile; this building might have illustrated a dream of Albert Robida, the highly imaginative French painter and poster designer, had he been a Finn or a Slav.

Such a gesture from Finland—a country which had been subjected for a good half-century to the Imperial Teutonic style first imported about 1830 by the German, Engel—was in line with the desire for national independence.

Two men were to contribute to the awakening of patriotic feelings; the painter Akseli Gallén-Kallela, who illustrated the old epic legends of the *Kalevala*, and the writer and designer Louis Sparre who, after travel and research in Karelia, was able to prove the existence of an ancient, national, Karelian style. Anyone who looks at those massive, archaic churches and castles and their heavy pillars—roughly trimmed tree trunks or granite columns, ornamented with mysterious geometrical signs—will at once be aware of the sources drawn upon by the Finnish architects who built the Northern Bank (plate 67) and the Pohjola building (plate 68). These monumental buildings, at once Cyclopean and functional, which contain sumptuous offices and whose interior decoration frequently bears traces of the Sezession, are the beginnings of the remarkable, lively, and youthful Finnish art of our own time.

1 ⬚ A. Singery and P. Jouannin. 61–63 Rue Réaumur. 1895. Paris.
This hybrid building is typical of the disorientation rampant in architectural design between 1840 and 1900. Byzantinism and medievalism are jumbled together here with dire results.

2 ⬚ Édouard Arnaud and François Hennebique. 1 Rue Danton. 1899. Paris.
The first building constructed entirely in concrete, it was built by Hennebique after the designs of Arnaud. The total cost, including elevator, heating, and partitions, was 235,000 francs, a high price for the period.

3 ⬚ Charles Klein. 2 Rue Eugène-Manuel. 1903. Paris.
The intention here is preponderantly decorative, as in the Céramic Hôtel (1904) in the Avenue Wagram. The Céramic Hôtel is more graceful than this building, but less powerful. Certain features—the arches over doors and windows, the elaborate ironwork, the remarkable use of "thistle" decoration, and the exterior covered throughout with ceramic tiles—make this building a part of French Art Nouveau.

4 ⬚ Jules Lavirotte. Private House. 1901. 29 Avenue Rapp, Paris.
Designed by Lavirotte who, like Guimard, was a native of Lyons, this is one of the most surprising houses in the world. It is also the first Western example of such a lavish use of ceramic facing in an ordinary building (glazed tiles are imbedded in the stone or in the reinforced brick and cover much of the façade). The design for the doorframe, by the sculptor Jean-Baptiste Larrivé, was carried out in glazed terra cotta, thus avoiding the expense of molding and casting. The ceramic decoration was the work of Alexandre Bigot. The sculptors Sporrer, Firmin-Marcelin Michelet, and Alfred-Jean Halou also took part in the building of this house which would have enchanted Jules Verne.

5 ⬚ Hector Guimard. Private House. 1908. 60 Rue La Fontaine, Paris.
It was in buildings of this kind that Guimard displayed the full scope of his genius. This small private residence is a good illustration of the architect's astonishing mastery; note, for example, the small door of the tradesmen's entrance, surmounted by the sloping triangular roof edged with floral ornament. Here, Guimard juggles his materials, mingling glazed with unglazed brick, and rusticated with dressed stone.

6 ⬚ Xavier Schoellkopf. Yvette Guilbert House. 1900. Boulevard Berthier, Paris.
A delightful piece of work (unfortunately destroyed), this house designed for the chanteuse Yvette Guilbert is a reminder of the style, at once French and Gaudíesque, whose spirit is also to be found at 140 *bis* Rue de Rennes, Paris. Schoellkopf disliked sharp edges: "The eyes and mouth, which are to a face as windows

to a façade, are not abrupt, crude openings; they are softened by their rounded and inclined forms."

7 ⬚ Unknown Architects. Two Houses. 1896–1901. 14–16 Rue d'Abbeville, Paris.
This pair of joined houses illustrates the architectural situation at the beginning of the Third Republic, just at the end of the century. On the house at far left (the oldest of the two), a pair of naiads do their best to invigorate a hybrid façade. With its Louis XVI consoles, balconies, and windows, and its masks from the time of Napoleon III, this pastiche is something the Germans have called "Rundbogenstil." The façade of No. 14 (nearest the viewer), whose bow windows are as effective as those by Lavirotte in the Avenue Rapp, bears the stamp of Art Nouveau.

8 ⬚ Cavelli. 7 Avenue Pictet-de-Rochemon. 1902. Geneva.
The wrought iron on this building is by Alex Vailly. If one could imagine a rest-home for tired octopuses this would be it! Here we find ourselves between Guimard and Gaudí. The picture-book folklore style of the roof, the plump juicy arabesques which form consoles for the balconies, and the embellishments round the windows, are slightly reminiscent of the buildings erected in the Rue de Rennes and Rue Réaumur in Paris for the Société Félix Potin. Art Nouveau architectural attempts in Switzerland remained sporadic; the architect E. Fatio was almost alone in attempting to start a Sezession Style in his country.

9 ⬚ A. Bocage. 6 Rue de Hanovre. 1904–05. Paris.
The general lines of this building seem to be borrowed from Perret; what makes it remarkable is the decorative treatment of the surface, done by the ceramist Alexandre Bigot. The façade in golden-brown stoneware, with seaweed and shells, and the opalescent ceramic tiles of the entrance, are an echo of the grotesques of earlier centuries.

10 ⬚ Unknown Architect. "Les Arums." C. 1900. 33 Rue du Champ-de-Mars, Paris.
This building, with its groups of bow windows, is noteworthy for both the general harmony of the design and the felicity with which the sculpture, even freer than that of Schoellkopf, is applied.

11 ⬚ Pierre Roche. Theater for Loïe Fuller. C. 1900 (now destroyed). Paris.
Pierre Roche is one of the most original artists of the entire Art Nouveau period. As a sculptor, he left the exquisite monument, *Avril*, which graces the façade of the Palais Galliera, Paris. In his architectural capacity he designed this small theater for the dancer Loïe Fuller. The walls are like the veils which the American star loved to drape and whirl around herself. Some of the works of Pierre Roche, his reliefs in plaster for instance, are so "evanescent" as to verge on abstraction.

12 ☒ G. P. Chédame. French Embassy. 1901–09. Schwartzenbergplatz, Vienna.
This elegant building is thoroughly Parisian; it recalls some of the houses in the Avenue Victor-Hugo, but it also has touches of the Sezession Style—the deep-set window niches at either end, for example. The garden railings and some of the fixtures inside, such as door-handles, window-catches, and lighting installations, are particularly typical of French Art Nouveau.

13 ☒ Hector Guimard. Castel Henriette. 1903. Sèvres.
The Castel Henriette was referred to by a journalist of the time as "the dwelling of Mélisande." The unusual combination of materials—brick, coarse aggregate, and rusticated rock of a type similar to meteoric stone—gives the house even more character than it would otherwise have had. The balconies and especially the railings of the flat part of the roof (top right in the illustration) look as if they had been inspired by Mackintosh. A strange, attractive house, which is now threatened with demolition.

14 ☒ Unknown Architect, possibly Édouard Autant. 29 Rue Émile-Meunier. 1905. Paris.
An unusual small house, hard to relate to anything in the French architectural tradition. The asymmetrical façade composed of large stone blocks is open to the light and makes one think of the German, Austrian, and English architects: Loos, Behrens, and, still more, Townsend.

15 ☒ Auguste Perret. 25 *bis* Rue Franklin. 1903. Paris.
The frontier between Art Nouveau and our own contemporary art runs through this apartment house. Here Perret is still making slight concessions to Art Nouveau: the design of the ceramics on the façade is carried out in a graceful composition of leafy boughs, and there is decoration around the doors. But Perret's verticals are totally opposed to Guimard's arabesques. The different angles at which the lines of the windows face the light should be noted; so also should the rigor of the balconies and staircases and the use of bottle-glass decorating the vertical stretches of the façade (the latter is also found in a house by Guimard in the Avenue de Versailles).

16 ☒ Émile André. Maison Huot. 1902–03. Quai Claude-Lorrain, Nancy.
Superficially this house might appear to be copied from Guimard, but it actually belongs to the folk-art-cum-medieval species so much favored by the School of Nancy. The front door, the window to the right of it, and the stone balcony above the tradesmen's entrance are particularly successful.

17 ☒ Unknown Architect. Pavilion. C. 1900. 36 Rue Sergent-Blandeau, Nancy.
This little pavilion adjoining the Musée de l'École de Nancy is hardly typical of the style of the School of Lorraine. Its arches, and its base of rough masonry, make it not unlike certain Italian works by Sommaruga.

18 ☒ Michelazzi. 99 Via Scipione-Ammirato. 1901. Florence.
This is a far cry from the dreamlike, Mannerist style which had developed in Italy. What is the dominant influence? Guimard, perhaps, or the Sezession, or Shekhtel's Ryabushinsky house (plate 69) in Moscow? A difficult question; but in any case this Florentine house is a masterpiece.

19 ☒ Unknown Architect. Façade of the Trianon Theater. 1902. Milan.
To save it from destruction, this façade was cleverly superimposed on a new building a few years ago. The striking décor, with the sculptures seeming to surge outward and detach themselves from the façade, is typical of Italian Art Nouveau.

20 ☒ Unknown Architect. Apartment House. C. 1900. Milan.
This building in the style of Sommaruga is reminiscent of the Old Palace at Tsarskoe Selo (Leningrad). Certain features—the rusticated stone at the base, the ironwork, the floral ornamentation on the interior—combine to make it one of the most successful buildings in Milan.

21 ☒ Giuseppe Sommaruga. Casa Castiglioni. *Detail of door.* 1901. 47 Corso Venezia, Milan.

22 ☒ Giuseppe Sommaruga. Casa Castiglioni. 1901. 47 Corso Venezia, Milan.
Sommaruga designed a number of buildings in Milan, Sarnico, Stresa, and Varese in a neo-Baroque spirit quite different from that of Parterna Baldizzi, Ernesto Basile, and the tendencies of D'Aronco—partly Sezession and partly orientalist. Everything about this building is remarkable, from the rusticated masonry supports at the base, which stand up like monoliths, to the elaborate workmanship of the wrought iron by Giovanni Magnoni.

23 ☒ Raimondo d'Aronco. Central Rotunda. 1902. Turin Exhibition.
For the Turin Exhibition of 1902, D'Aronco designed a series of buildings in which an Oriental touch mingles with Darmstadt and Sezession styles. A contemporary critic described them as "trapezoidal structures suggesting some kind of neo-archaism derived from Mycenae or Carthage."

24 ☒ Raimondo d'Aronco. Pavilion of Decorative Arts. 1902. Turin Exhibition.
The functionalism and rigor of the lines of force, qualities inspired by Otto Wagner and Olbrich, have here been smothered under a Mannerist décor—too

many statues (though some of those by Rubino are noteworthy—see plate 261) too much mimicry of vegetable matter, and too many consoles. The Turin Exhibition marked at once the culmination of Art Nouveau and the beginning of its decline.

25 ☒ UNKNOWN ARCHITECT. House. C. 1900. Pesaro.
At Pesaro, by the sea, and keeping company quite happily with the skyscraper beside it, stands one of the strangest, most exquisite of all Stile Floreale houses. The architect's inspired creativeness would have delighted certain eighteenth-century princes. There are surprises everywhere: sculptured plant forms, submarine motifs winding their way right across the façade, consoles under the eaves in the form of lobsters, and fountain basins representing other crustacea. This fascinating house is slightly reminiscent of the Restaurant de la Belle Meunière built by Tronchet for the Paris International Exhibition of 1900.

26 ☒ ANTONI GAUDÍ. Casa Vicens. 1878–80. Barcelona.
This building may look like an example of Moorish revival, but it is in fact thoroughly imbued with modernism; note, for example, the window openings and the width of the balconies. The diversity of the decorative materials and the elegant twists and turns of the ironwork announce Gaudí's golden age.

27 ☒ ANTONI GAUDÍ. Casa Batlló. 1905–07. Barcelona.
Roofs and balconies, seemingly modeled by some wayward breeze rather than by the human hand, are a striking example of the strange Art Nouveau of Catalonia.

28 ☒ LLUIS DOMENÉCH y MONTANER . Palau de la Música Catalana. 1906–08. Barcelona.
A rival of Gaudí, Domenéch y Montaner's career paralleled the former's in many ways, but he was more traditional than Gaudí and carried out a large number of institutional commissions, such as hospitals and hotels. In this façade, Domenéch seems to be taking joyful liberties with functional necessities (for example, the semicircular balconies with the slender balusters). Attention should also be drawn to the mock-solemn note sounded by the busts of famous composers (Beethoven and Bach are seen in this view).

29 ☒ ANTONI GAUDÍ. Casa Batlló. *Detail of the façade.* 1905–07. Barcelona.
Note the gaiety and ease with which the architect instills a sense of movement into a functional structure.

30 ☒ CHARLES RENNIE MACKINTOSH. Library Wing. 1907–09. The Glasgow School of Art, Glasgow.
The Glasgow School of Art is Mackintosh's most important work, the definitive monument to his genius. The windows of the long line of immense bays on the first floor (plate 32) give maximum light to the studios. The east and west parts of the building, in contrasting styles, both display reminiscences of ancient Scottish fortresses. The Library Wing, which is ten years later in date, has been called "a masterpiece of the utilization of architectural space." The bold, dramatic character of the whole is emphasized by the three tall projecting windows lighting the various levels of the library.

31 ☒ CHARLES RENNIE MACKINTOSH. Hill House. 1902–03. Helenburgh, Scotland.
This country house outside Glasgow is reminiscent of the fortified houses built in Scotland in the sixteenth century, although windows have replaced loopholes. No concessions are made to decorative display.

32 ☒ CHARLES RENNIE MACKINTOSH. The Glasgow School of Art. 1897–99. Glasgow.
In giving a new impetus to the art of the ironworker, Mackintosh yielded briefly to the prevailing appetite for ornament, for which purpose he designed unusual, highly stylized plant forms, as seen in the wrought iron on this façade.

33 ☒ OTTO WAGNER. Imperial Underground Station. 1894–97. Vienna.
Both the design and the decorations of the Imperial Underground Station in Vienna were by Otto Wagner. The entrance for the Emperor's carriage or motorcar was in the little building at the side. A large drawing room was at the sovereign's disposal as a waiting room, with a separate room for his suite. Everything, including furniture, wallpapers, and curtains, was in the style of the Sezession.

34 ☒ JOSEPH MARIA OLBRICH. Exhibition Hall of the Sezession. 1898. Vienna.
The Sezession building is one of the key monuments of Art Nouveau. The façade, with its simple decoration of stylized foliage, is guarded by three gorgons; the gilded cupola is in the shape of a trimmed laurel bush.

35 ☒ OTTO WAGNER. The Postal Savings Bank. 1904–06. Vienna.
The simplicity of this building is emphasized by the balustrade at the top, and the two monumental statues flanking it.

36 ☒ JOSEF HOFFMANN. Palais Stoclet. 1905. Brussels.
In 1903, while traveling in Austria, the rich Belgian industrialist Adolphe Stoclet was so impressed by the talent of Josef Hoffmann that he commissioned the thirty-five-year-old architect to design him a contemporary house. Reticular or cube-shaped architecture, formerly practiced in Europe exclusively by a few adepts, now emerged into life. To avoid an overwhelmingly massive effect, Hoffmann sheathed the walls with big sheets of white marble from Turili (Norway), and to soften the sharp corners of the building, he graced them with lines of chiseled, gilded bronze. Four marble athletes, by the sculptor Metzner, crown the tower.

I ◪ OTTO WAGNER. The Majolika Haus. 1910. Vienna.
The Majolika Haus is the archetype of functional buildings in which the architect aims at providing
the tenants with a well-lit, aesthetically pleasing environment which can be leased at moderate rents.
The polychrome ceramic decoration, the graceful ironwork, and the airily projecting balconies at
either side make the surrounding buildings look cruelly mediocre and commonplace. Note that the
flanking balconies at each end replace bow windows as a formal element.

37 ◪ JOZSEF and LASZLÓ VAGÓ. Woodland Theater.
1913. Budapest.
This most graceful building is typical of the transition
between the Sezession and Art Décoratif styles.

38 ◪ ODON LECHNER. Postal Savings Bank. 1899–
1902. Budapest.
One of the most remarkable architects produced by the
Sezession in Hungary, Lechner designed the church of
St. Ladislas, which is in a neo-medieval style, the
Museum of the Decorative Arts, and this, the Postal

Savings Bank. Its façade, free of the slight residue of
historicism still apparent in his Museum of the Decorative Arts, displays rigor tempered with fantasy: note
the serpentine line above the third-floor windows, and
the way the roofs are hidden behind a Gaudíesque
drape of stone.

39 ◪ AUGUST ENDELL. Elvira Photographic Studio.
1897–98 (now destroyed). Munich.
August Endell was largely self-taught. He began by
studying philosophy, but became a passionate devotee

of architecture and decorative arts. This building, one of the strangest, most fantastic creations of the Jugendstil, was torn down on the personal orders of Adolf Hitler as a prime example of the most decadent type of architecture.

40 ▨ UNKNOWN ARCHITECT. 75 Schlieperstrasse. 1904. Berlin.
Before the Second World War, there was no lack of Jugendstil buildings in Berlin. Those which have survived are of no great quality. The architect of this building could not escape his eclectic tendencies; the façade is Renaissance, the doorways medieval, and the incidental decoration seems to have been inspired by Endell.

41 ▨ JOSEPH MARIA OLBRICH. Ernst Ludwig Haus. 1901. Mathildenhöhe, Darmstadt.
In 1894, Olbrich joined Otto Wagner's office. In 1897, with Klimt, he founded the Wiener Sezession, for which he designed his first building, the Sezession Exhibition Hall (plate 34). In 1899, he was summoned to Darmstadt to collaborate in the building of the artists' colony on the Mathildenhöhe. He was a resolute enemy of empiricism and pointless decorative additions; here, in the façade of the Ernst Ludwig Haus, he succeeded in uniting functionalism and poetry.

42 ▨ JOSEPH MARIA OLBRICH and PETER BEHRENS. Reflection Pool. 1901. Mathildenhöhe, Darmstadt.
The shimmering pattern on the bottom of this pool is deliberately designed to mingle with the play of light on the surface of the water. The pool is one of the most successful features of the entire Darmstadt complex. The robust but elegant pillars are nicely congruent with the general rhythm of the buildings, and the little Russian church in the background strikes a lively note.

43 ▨ PETER BEHRENS. The Architect's House. 1900–01. Mathildenhöhe, Darmstadt.
In the setting of the artists' colony at Darmstadt, built under the patronage and with the support of the Grand Duke Ernst Ludwig of Hessen-Darmstadt, Behrens designed his own house in a style completely independent of local tradition. It is as bare of ornament as any of the Edinburgh School houses, and by using a pointed arch, the architect has succeeded in giving the front, with its vertically separated planes, a quasi-Slavonic grace.

44 ▨ JOSEPH MARIA OLBRICH. Hochzeitsturm (Wedding Tower). 1907. Mathildenhöhe, Darmstadt.
The Hochzeitsturm at Darmstadt, overlooking the Exhibition Hall, terminates in a roof shaped like a hand, symbolizing the marriage of Grand Duke Ernst Ludwig and Eleonore von Solms-Lich. The construction and decoration of the entire Mathildenhöhe complex, inspired by the example of Baillie Scott and Ashbee, was designed by Olbrich, Behrens, Christian-

sen, and Huber. The average age of this group was thirty-two; the youngest was only twenty.

45 ▨ EDWARD WILLIAM GODWIN. The White House. 1879. Tite Street, London.
The White House was designed by Godwin for James McNeill Whistler. The architect and his client were among the few Westerners of that period capable of appreciating the singular and rarefied beauty of the Japanese aesthetic. In designing this house, Godwin defied orthodox canons. The windows are positioned asymmetrically, almost haphazardly, like the rocks in the gardens of the Ryoanji in Japan. The rain gutters play an aesthetic as well as a utilitarian role—they connect the surfaces of the façade horizontally and vertically. We are reminded of Loos and also of Le Corbusier. (Unfortunately, the building has been greatly altered, and the architect's original design somewhat bastardized.)

46 ▨ EDWARD WILLIAM GODWIN. The Tower House. 1885. 46 Tite Street, London.
Enormous bays let in the light, and bow windows with beautiful proportions stemming from their design banish monotony from the left wing.

47 ▨ CHARLES HARRISON TOWNSEND. The Whitechapel Art Gallery. 1897–99. London.
The Whitechapel Art Gallery and the Horniman Museum, both in London and both by Townsend, are examples of the adaptation of English medievalism to Art Nouveau—plain surfaces, round towers, wide openings flooding the ground floors with light. Similar objectives had been obtained earlier by Sir John Soane in England and Frank Furness in Philadelphia.

48 ▨ CHARLES FRANCIS ANNESLEY VOYSEY. House for Canon L. Grane. 1897. Shackleford, Surry.
Voysey's work was not revolutionary; he was nevertheless the virtual leader of the new school in Britain. Like Boito in Italy and Berlage in Holland, he was an innovator who at the same time respected all that was best in his own national tradition. Where he excelled was in the handling of details: arches, moldings, the pitch of roofs. His art is related to that of Frank Lloyd Wright, who published the designs of his first prairie houses about this time.

49 ▨ HALSEY RICCARDO. 8 Addison Road. 1906–07. London.
The general appearance of this house places it in the historicist style, but by reading between the lines of the Renaissance design we can see a desire for modernity —tall bays, and the vivid note sounded by the flanking panels bearing the house number, and, inside, the orientalist wall tiles by William de Morgan.

50 ▨ CHARLES FRANCIS ANNESLEY VOYSEY. Hans House. 1891. London.
In addition to his architectural work, Voysey was pas-

sionately interested in the decorative arts; he designed wallpapers, fabrics, and furniture. The façade of Hans House, with its generous openings, its bay windows, the simplicity of its decoration—arabesques in the front porch, but nowhere else—is functional. Baillie Scott said: "Voysey eschews the tiresome method employed by the Renaissance architects, which consisted of coating the body of the structure with extraneous forms; thus he avoided the deplorable effects of that imitative architecture." For his roofs, Voysey commonly used greenish slate; doors and windows he surrounded with carved Bath stone. For exteriors in the country he recommended a rendered finish, to protect the brickwork against heat and dampness.

51 ☒ CHARLES ROBERT ASHBEE. 38 Cheyne Walk. 1903. London.
Charles Robert Ashbee, architect and writer, founded The Guild and School of Handicrafts in 1888. This building designed by Ashbee is typical of the new British architectural tendencies. Ashbee was one of the first European supporters of Frank Lloyd Wright.

52 ☒ HENDRIK PETRUS BERLAGE. Insurance Company Building. 1893. The Hague.
A building that illustrates the preoccupations of this great Dutch architect. He respected his compatriots' love of tradition; at first glance the building resembles those of the Dutch golden age. At the same time he observed complete functionalism, using wide, well-lighted bays and avoiding monotony by means of asymmetry and polychromed sculptural motifs.

53 ☒ JEAN FRANÇOIS RAFFAELLI. *Mr. Fletcher's New York Residence.* Oil on canvas. C. 1893. The Metropolitan Museum of Art, New York.
This house still stands on the southeast corner of Fifth Avenue and 79th Street. It is a Renaissance affair very similar to those adorning the Parc Monceau in Paris during the same period, and exemplifies the taste of a typical wealthy American at the end of the nineteenth century.

54 ☒ DANIEL HUDSON BURNHAM and JOHN WELLBORN ROOT. The Monadnock Building. 1891. Chicago.
This is the first skyscraper: with bearing walls of brick, it was built without a steel frame. With its vigorous lines—there are no concessions anywhere to historicism or decorative redundancy—its well-proportioned façade, and the gentle outward curve of its base and cornice, this building prefigures the most successful examples of present-day architecture. Godwin in Great Britain, and Richardson and Burnham in the United States, pointed the way which Tony Garnier and Frank Lloyd Wright were to follow.

55 ☒ DANIEL HUDSON BURNHAM and JOHN WELLBORN ROOT. The Monadnock Building. *Detail of the façade at ground level.* 1891. Chicago.
Because it was built without a steel framework, the

walls had to be thicker at the bottom to support their weight. This was brilliantly realized by the pleasing proportions of the slight curve of the enceinte, which is echoed in the coved cornice at the building's top.

56 ☒ LOUIS SULLIVAN. Guaranty Building. 1894–95. Buffalo.
This is one of Sullivan's masterpieces. Combining rigor of line with graceful orientalist and medieval decoration, it has now become a historic monument. (In the United States there are now collectors of buildings; thus, the Monadnock Building, for instance, is now the property of a member of the Board of Trustees of the Art Institute of Chicago. "We don't buy Renoirs any more," say the sons of old Chicago families, "we inherit them from grandmama.") The Guaranty Building is halfway between the nineteenth-century commercial buildings, such as H. H. Richardson's Schiller Building and the Marshall Field Wholesale Store, and major twentieth-century buildings. The tall vertical travises—of which the first user in Europe was Paul Sédille (*see* plate 76)—give the building an appearance of lightness.

57 ☒ LOUIS SULLIVAN. Albert W. Sullivan House. 1892. Chicago.
The façade, half austere and half ornate, of this small house which the architect built for his brother, was occupied by the architect himself from 1892 to 1896. The house is modern in character despite its date. One's attention is caught by the simplicity of the lower window which looks out on the street. One can also detect Sullivan's preference for orientalist decoration, the Saracenic Style dear to Tiffany. The house cost $12,000 to build.

58 ☒ LOUIS SULLIVAN. The Bayard Building. 1897–98. 65–69 Bleecker Street, New York.
This is the only building by Sullivan in New York City. Its lean, elegant lines and its perfectly integrated orientalist and medievalist decoration, make it one of the finest monuments of American Art Nouveau. The average cost of buildings of comparable size at this period was about $400,000. The ground floor was faced in white stone a few years ago, thereby destroying much of Sullivan's decoration, and ruining the architectural unity of the building. A sad attempt at modernizing a masterpiece.

59 ☒ HENRY VAN DE VELDE. Bloemenwerf. 1895–96. Uccle, Belgium.
At the age of thirty-three, untutored in architecture and working by the light of nature, Van de Velde built his own house at Uccle, near Brussels. To present-day eyes it is an innocuous country home, but contemporaries thought it revolutionary to the point of irritation. When Toulouse-Lautrec saw it, he observed, "Dreadful! Never saw anything like *that* before! Really, the only decent parts are the ones painted in white enamel —the bathroom, dressing rooms, and the nursery."

60 ⌀ Victor Horta. Maison du Peuple. 1897–99. Brussels.

It was on a confined, steeply sloping site that Horta, with iron and glass as his materials, created this delightful and functional monster, whose irregular façade curves fluently to accommodate a window space, or house a flight of stairs. The consoles of the iron balconies harmonize happily with stone supports modeled on plant-forms. The fundamental structure and rhythm of the building unfold like a melody. In fact, Horta did think seriously of a musical career for some time, and in its own day the Maison du Peuple was as striking and unusual as a work by Debussy. Slim, exaggeratedly tall columns, and subtle networks of lines, abstract in some cases, plantlike in others, amalgamate technical fulfillment with ornamental beauty (*also see* plate 84).

61 ⌀ Paul Hankar. 48 Rue Defacqz. 1897. Brussels.
Apart from Horta, the greatest of the Belgian Symbolist architects was Paul Hankar. This private house shows his strong predilection for the Far East, especially Japan. The door at the bottom left has been subjected to alteration at a later date.

62 ⌀ Paul Cauchie. 5 Rue des Francs. 1905. Brussels.
This little house was designed by the painter, Paul Cauchie. It is at once rigorous and graceful, with its tall verticals and its decoration which is a mixture of Belgian and Sezession styles.

63 ⌀ Victor Horta. Solvay Residence (now the Wittamer de Camps Residence). 1895–1900. Brussels.
The Solvay residence (fortunately preserved intact by the present owners, M. and Mme. Wittamer de Camps) is one of Horta's most remarkable creations. No borrowing here; this is a completely original work of Art Nouveau. In the façade, the great Belgian architect combines harmony of proportion with the unexpected—a fact readily confirmed by a glance at the flanking buildings.

64 ⌀ Martin Nyrop. Interior of the Raadhus. 1893–1902. Copenhagen.
Here, function takes precedence over decoration. The interior of the building was designed by Nyrop, Wenck, and Vischer (who built the Hotel Bristol, Copenhagen), and is less equivocal than the façades.

65 ⌀ Martin Nyrop. The Raadhus. 1893–1902. Copenhagen.
One's instantaneous reaction might well be to exclaim, "pastiche!" But in reality the architect has contrived to camouflage a monumental functional building, whose lines are soberly elegant, by dressing it in historicist costume. With its façade, which is a simple elongated rectangle interrupted by two bow windows, its bell tower, which is some 320 feet high—higher than any hill in Denmark—and its pleasant color scheme of gray and white stone with warm brick, this building deftly eludes criticism.

66 ⌀ Herman Gesellius, Armas Lindgren, and Eliel Saarinen. The Finnish Pavilion at the Universal Exhibition of 1900. Paris.
This Pavilion expresses the poetic and artistic aspirations of the Finnish nation. It was, however, Louis Sparre, born of a Swedish father and an Italian mother, who restored the folk-art traditions of Finland to life.

67 ⌀ Herman Gesellius, Armas Lindgren, and Eliel Saarinen. Pohjoismaiden Osakepank (The Northern Bank). 1907 (now destroyed). Helsinki.
The façade of this building combines inspiration drawn from ancient local legends with the daring theories of the younger generation of Finnish architects.

68 ⌀ Herman Gesellius, Armas Lindgren, and Eliel Saarinen. The Pohjola. 1901. Helsinki.
The Pohjola, one of the most characteristic Art Nouveau buildings in existence, rises from a massive stone base like those used by Sommaruga in Milan. The pleasantly startling decoration (less well integrated, however, than that of Gaudí or the Italians) is based on a symbolism comprehensible only to readers of the *Kalevala*: Pohjola, the name of the land and the people of the north (Lapland) and Kullervo, the spirit of evil. The names can be seen carved over the entrance. Also shown are animals inhabiting the forests of Finland: lynx, wolf, and squirrel. The building houses the offices of an insurance company.

69 ⌀ F. O. Shekhtel. Ryabushinsky House. 1905. Moscow.
F. O. Shekhtel, who also built the Yaroslavl Station in Moscow, imported the art of the Sezession almost unmodified into Russia. The stocky, powerful lines of the porch are the only concession to Muscovite architecture.

70 ⌀ Sergei Malyutin. House. C. 1890. Talashkino. Smolensk, Russia.
Princess Tenisheva set up a craft center at her estate at Talashkino around 1890. There, professional artists and the peasants were invited to give free rein to their talents in woodworking, the illumination of manuscripts, choral singing, and architecture—all based on traditional styles. The façade of this little house includes a bow window; touches of Sezession influence are added to traditional Slav decoration.

2

3

4

5

6

7

8

10

9

11

12

14

15

16

17

18

19

20

21

22

23

24

26

27

28

29

33

34

35

36

37

38

39

40

41

42

43

44

45

46

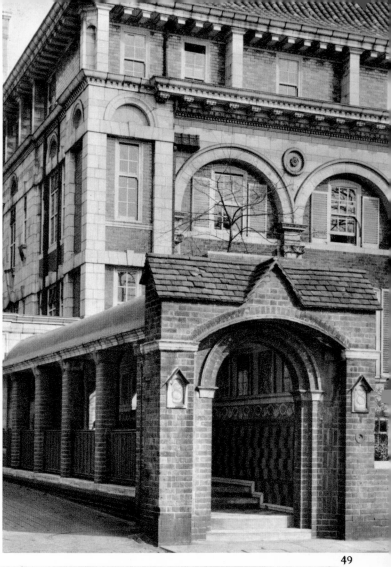

50

51

53

54

55

56

58

57

59

60

61

63

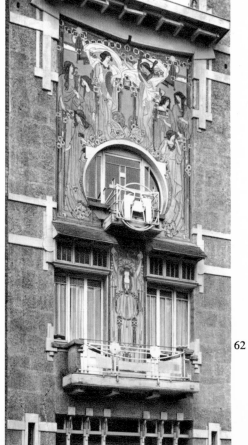

62

64

65

67

68

69

70

Commercial Architecture

THE birth of Art Nouveau is closely related to both an economic revolution and a shift in mores. The street and its countenance—shops, cafés, and restaurants—faithfully reflect this development and give us not only an accurate picture of the most transitory fashions, but also a thousand-and-one illustrations of the life of the people for whom these fashions were conceived.

Large department stores made their appearance in cities well before the end of the century. Zola, in *Le Bonheur des Dames*, traces the history of one of these giant establishments which, like a many-tentacled monster, reaches out to devour the surrounding shops. As early as the third quarter of the nineteenth century, small businesses were threatened with extinction, but it was to be a prolonged death; staving off the throes of dissolution and trying to adapt to modern conditions, small business was sporadically reanimated, and Art Nouveau played a large part in this. When the initial panic caused by the opening of the big stores had died down, those small ones which had not yet been brought to ruin by competition understood that they still had a chance for survival, provided they made a new start on a new basis.

Standing up to these threatening giants forced the smaller businessmen to make their establishments attractive, to give them a cachet and a personality which would make them stand out against the standardization and anonymity of the big stores. There was no future for those modest little shops whose very humility and reticence were a guarantee of genuine goods and service. Small business had to slough off its Victorian modesty; to win customers and influence sales it had to catch the eye: it had to charm women, tease them into affection, reassure them. This meant having recourse to everything that modern decoration could offer. It left posters and billboards to big business and used its own window displays as a publicity medium, abandoning quiet colors and adopting the wavy lines and the new materials (notably ceramics) as a setting for its goods. Better to take the risk of being a bit shocking than to blush unseen.

It would be a mistake, however, to regard this transformation only as an economic rescue operation on behalf of small shopkeepers; the artists who conducted it were impartial and served large and small alike.

At their disposal was a gamut of new materials and forms which they could use very much as they liked. A big shop was simply a framework or skeleton whose flesh and blood were supplied more by the wares it displayed than by the materials of which it was built. The early twentieth-century architects treated such a shop as a cage of iron and glass, freely permeated by the light of day. Superfluous decoration was out of the question; there was no longer room for sculpture, and the building materials, especially iron, had to evince their intrinsic ornamental value. In smaller establishments, wooden window frames with plump, seductive curves, were an important part of the façade just because they supported the glass. Glass had become a prime factor; the light was reflected from its decorative panes, which might be either enameled or engraved, and color was added by ceramics and metals (shapes cut from sheet copper were a special favorite). Shop fronts took on a lightweight brilliance, and their varied, graceful novelty broke up the monotony of the streets.

Cafés and restaurants, which mean so much in the lives of city dwellers, were a fertile environment for rich, fantastic growths. The café was the meeting place of artists and writers, and if it were famous, it had its own regular customers and its own specialty. There were Symbolist cafés, Anarchist cafés, painters' cafés, literary cafés, not to mention the humbler ones whose names were legion and which, with their faïence-tiled decoration, were places of refuge and escape for the miserably housed working class.

It was important for the cafés and restaurants to preserve the character of intimacy which the larger shops were losing. The cafés often retained a modest exterior, but the interior was sumptuous. They took advantage of every technical advance: the effect was based on the use of rare and exotic woods, with inlays or incrustations, surrounding mirrors or ceramic panels; the supple branches of these frames reached up to the ceiling which was frequently of stained glass. The handles and push-plates on doors were often of metal, designed to set off the choice woodwork. These trappings of luxury were not only the sign of a legendary and indeed somewhat mythical *Belle Époque*, but rather one of the many indices of a certain need: the craving for harmony—a warm, intimate, and exquisite unity—which is the major constant of Art Nouveau in all its aspects. Mackintosh's series of Miss Cranston's Tea Rooms or the Établissements de Vichy, the humblest provincial café or the notorious Maxim's—the same hunger for comfort and a unified décor is manifest everywhere and shows up as a common factor in the most disparate contexts.

The big hotels likewise went through an Art Nouveau phase, and this was a progressive step in the development of their furnishing and atmosphere. Some hotelkeepers had the vision to employ decorators of high repute to refurnish their rooms and public salons.

Preoccupation with hygiene and cleanliness was another noteworthy feature. Firms of decorators and furnishers strove to provide pleasant hotel bedrooms, well lit, comfortable, and easy to look after. They chose simple furniture, upholstered with washable fabrics; "practical" and "comfortable" became their watchwords. The guest was no longer shoved into a bedroom which he might or might not like, but had, in any case, to accept; the aim now was to make the room fit his needs so that, even in the neutral territory of a hotel, his surroundings were intimate and friendly.

Theater fronts were modernized, and inside, the traditional red plush and gilt stucco gave way to a simpler décor. Without these changes the theater would have been doing itself less than justice. Theater-going was playing an increasingly large part in the lives of ordinary people. Never had playwrights enjoyed so large an audience, not only in the upper classes of society, but also in the middle and lower classes. The theater became a "cultural activity"; at one time it was important to have been seen at the play; what mattered now was to have seen the play. Production and stage-sets took a new lease on theatrical life, and acting swung away from melodramatic pomposity to become more spontaneous and natural.

There was also theater outside the theaters. There was a tremendous vogue for the *café concert*, the *cabaret chantant*, the admirable *ombres chinoises* of Henri Rivière at the Chat Noir, and so on. Cinema and the dance must also be mentioned. The former developed rapidly and became the leading form of popular entertainment. The technique of the second was profoundly revolutionized by the innovations of Loïe Fuller, Isadora Duncan, and Ida Rubinstein.

The new aesthetic became familiar to everyone; it was visible in the new appearance of streets and subway stations, in lighting and shops and auditoriums.

II ▨ Jules Trezel. Decorative panel in the Restaurant Julien (*also see* plate 86). C.
1900. Paris.
During this period the figure of woman, slightly orientalized, was one of the favored motifs
in decoration. Here she appears as a pensive temptress on one of a series of large panels
executed in enamel and "American" glass. Enveloped in a concealing robe (and her own
mysterious atmosphere), this visitor from the dream world belongs as much to the vegetable
kingdom as to the human. She is a sister of one of Mucha's figures (*see* plate 223).

71 ⊠ Unknown Architect. Barbershop. 1904. Pesaro. As everyone knows, the *barbiere* is a key figure in everyday Italian life. The styling of his shop reflects, because it has to, the taste of the times. Here the lines of the architrave have been interrupted, the symmetry broken up, and curves and eddies have been introduced everywhere. The result is distantly related to the Baroque.

72 ⊠ Alphonse Mucha and Auguste Seysse. Jewelry shop of G. Fouquet. C. 1901. 6 Rue Royale, Paris.
In his choice of decorators, the jeweler Fouquet displayed as much talent as the jewelry designers whose work he displayed: René Lalique, Philippe Wolfers, and Emmanuel Jules Joé-Descomps. His shop was styled both inside and out by Mucha, with the collaboration of the sculptor, Seysse. No sign could have been as effective as the shop front and window displays in suggesting the beauty, rarity, and opulence of the articles for sale.

73 ⊠ A. Moulins. The Café Americain. C. 1900. Paris.
This café has lost none of its 1900 charm. The curves of the woodwork are demure and well behaved; the space above the lintel is adorned with flowers in relief; other very typical details include the way the flowery designs on the plate glass interrupt its transparency, and the supple, open forms of the lettering, which is executed in enameled glass.

74 ⊠ Charles Rennie Mackintosh. Willow Tea Room. 1904. Sauchiehall Street, Glasgow.
Mackintosh designed this façade in a completely modernist spirit. Sober design, beautiful proportions, and the straight line are in command here.

75 ⊠ Unknown French Architect. The Michelin Garage. n.d. London.
This building belongs to Art Nouveau because of its decoration rather than because of the design of its façade. The tall central arch, surmounted by an architrave and flanked by pilasters, is a very free translation of the large stables of an earlier day.

76 ⊠ Paul Sédille. Magasins du Printemps. 1881–89. Paris.
In the construction of this store, Sédille was an innovator insofar as he made liberal use of metal and plate glass. Traditional features, however, were to survive for twenty years or more—the masonry pilasters, the swags and garlands, and the sculptured female figures, Classically draped, with their backs against the façade.

77 and **78** ⊠ Frantz Jourdain. Magasins de la Samaritaine. 1905. Paris.
In 1905, the task of extending the Magasins de la Samaritaine was entrusted to Frantz Jourdain. Real innovations made their appearance here, as the illustrations show. The metal frame of the building has been left clearly visible. The vertical and horizontal

beams form a crystal-clear network, the angles of which have been softened (especially on the higher floors) with decorative ironwork. Oblong panels of vitreous enamel adorn the horizontals; these panels, glowing in various tints of orange, carry floral decorations alternating with the names of the goods on sale, and provide a vivid contrast to the blue of the ironwork. The large panel at the top, carrying the store's name, was designed by Eugène Grasset. The building is crowned by a dome whose surface is of glass bricks, and whose armature is clearly visible. Air and light are let in everywhere. The architect has used the concavities of the vertical girders as a housing for his ventilation and heating systems. Much simpler than the Grand Bazar in the Rue de Rennes by H. B. Gutton, the Samaritaine enjoys, as it were, birthright membership in the world of modern architecture. Several factors make it one of the great successes of early twentieth-century commercial architecture: its decoration, derived from the material itself; its polychromatism; the ornamental use of lettering; and finally, the sheer boldness of line.

79 ⊠ Louis Sullivan. Carson Pirie Scott & Co. Department Store. 1899–1904. Chicago.
Sullivan's thoroughly individual sense of ornament is well demonstrated on this façade. By coincidence rather than influence, this is very similar to the curvilinear style in vogue in Europe at that time.

80 ⊠ Émile Robert. Arcade. 1903. Salon de l'Auto, Paris.
Iron and glass in architecture and decoration were a sign of modernism. They were, consequently, particularly appropriate for housing a display of automobiles. For the Salon de l'Auto of 1903, the firm of A. Clément called in Émile Robert, the most famous specialist in ironwork in Paris at the time, to design this triple arcade with a broad horizontal band across the front. This ephemeral, glowing, openwork type of architecture, so light and fragile in appearance, is very much of the *Belle Époque*.

81 ⊠ Auguste Perret. Garage. 1905. Rue de Ponthieu, Paris.
This celebrated garage was built in the same year as the Magasins de la Samaritaine, but the two buildings have nothing in common except their date. Here, Perret moves away from Art Nouveau in search of "a modern classicism." He gives to concrete that lightweight, luminous quality which a metal framework renders possible; this façade already contains all the essential elements of his aesthetic.

82 ⊠ Lars Sonck and Walter Jung. Privatbanken. 1904. Helsinki.
These monolithic columns with their cubic capitals are a feature of this bank, whose decoration was by Walter Jung. The whole construction reflects clearly the tendencies of Finnish Art Nouveau: a return to

national traditions, a predilection for clear, slightly barbaric forms, and primitive type decoration, partly geometric, partly figurative.

83 ✎ ALFRED MESSEL. The Wertheim Store. 1896 and 1900–04. Berlin.
The Wertheim Store was built by Messel in two phases. In the first part, much use was made of iron and glass, and the tall windows between the pillars ran the total height of the building. This was certainly much closer to Art Nouveau than the second part (closest to the viewer in this photograph), which is quite clearly of latter-day Gothic inspiration.

84 ✎ VICTOR HORTA. Maison du Peuple. *Auditorium.* 1897–99. Brussels.
In the Maison du Peuple (*also see* plate 60), Horta allowed the structural framework to remain visible. The most successful part of the building is the auditorium, entirely composed of iron and glass. He elicited a highly decorative effect from essentially structural components, namely the girders and the openwork formed by their ties. Along the galleries at the side, the metal balustrades, with their graceful curves, echo the form of the framework.

85 ✎ H. A. A. DEGLANE, L. A. LOUVET, and A. F. T. THOMAS. The Grand Palais. *Interior.* 1898–99. Paris.
Structural iron had been used by British and French architects since the eighteenth century, but for a long time it was allowed to remain visible only in the interior of buildings. This was the case with the Grand Palais, whose interior was designed quite independently of the exterior. The staircase is a real masterpiece. The

stringboard is supported by light, graceful consoles, and porphyry columns enclosed in vertical ribs of iron form the trunks of these luxuriantly branching metal trees.

86 ✎ JULES TREZEL. Restaurant Julien. *Interior.* C. 1900. Paris.
All the favorite themes of the period are concentrated in the interior decoration of this restaurant. Colorplate II, page 77, shows a detail which is clearly visible at the far right of this photograph.

87 ✎ UNKNOWN DECORATOR. Gare de Lyon. *Dining Room.* 1900. Paris.
This restaurant interior was executed in 1900. Nevertheless, with its heavy arches and their embellishments in deep relief, its ceiling cartouches supported by large figures, its massive chandeliers, and the opulence of the decoration, it remains loyal to the bourgeois tradition.

88 and **89** ✎ LOUIS MARNEZ and LÉON SONNIER. Restaurant Maxim's. 1899. Rue Royale, Paris.
This famous restaurant was completely renovated in a few months during 1899 under the direction of the architect Louis Marnez, with the collaboration of the painter Léon Sonnier. The ample curves of the mirrors are surrounded by mahogany frames, brightened by satinwood inlays or decorative copper. Similar frames enhance the discreet murals, in which nude girls bathing can be seen in soft morning light. Here, as at the Brasserie Cadéac and the Café Voisin, we find the main constants of French Art Nouveau: straight lines are never allowed to become curt, and the décor is based on flowers and plant forms.

71

72

73

74

75

76

77

78

79

82

83

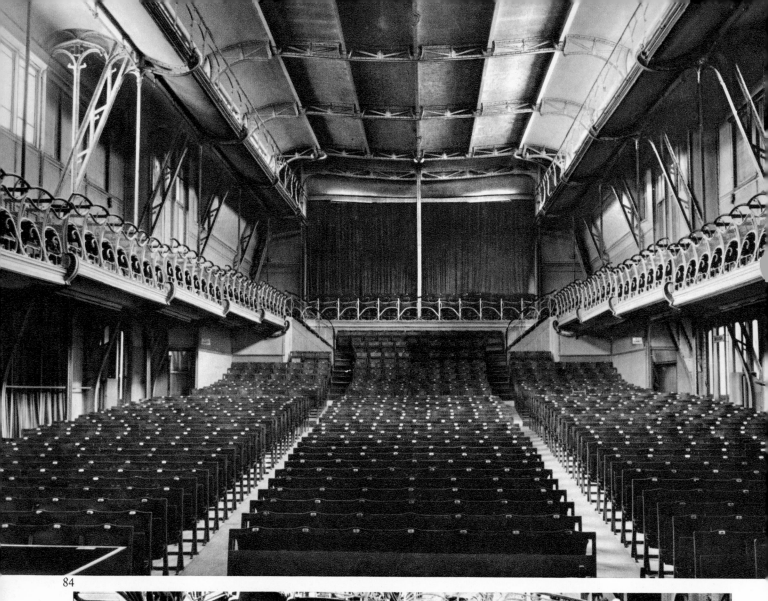

84

85

88

89

Decoration in Stone and Wrought Iron

ONCE the first flurries of creative exploration were over, the new appearance assumed by Paris in the Art Nouveau period was plain to see. Not just an isolated house here and there, but whole streets and even neighborhoods were in the new style. But alas, very few of the many buildings embodying the new aesthetic were as original, or as extravagant, as the Castel Béranger, or 29 Avenue Rapp. They were simply middle-class houses whose architects had obediently made concessions to the fashion of the time. However, perhaps we gain a truer idea of the new décor of the streets from this diluted form of the style than we would from a few exceptional creations.

What strikes one immediately is the abundance of sculptured vegetation: flowers, fruit, and foliage are everywhere. Not one species per building, but several on a single façade, the combination varying from story to story. Surprisingly, the resulting impression is one of unity. In some places, the leaves melt into the wall, losing themselves in the stone; in others, the wall itself seems to be swelling with sap and bursting into vigorous growth.

It did not take long for this wave of vitality to reach other European countries, passing from Catalonia to Italy, and from there to Germany. And although every country had its own preferences in the matter of ornament, Art Nouveau buildings of all nationalities display common characteristics: an abundant use of sculpture projecting from the wall surface—Italy may well have been the pace-setter in this—and an evident fondness for bay or bow windows, whether with undulating outlines as with Gaudí, or rectilinear (as in Scotland, Austria, and France), in the work of Perret.

This decorative stonework is partnered by the wrought-iron doors and balconies, which blossom with an even greater freedom. In France and Italy, the dominant style was floral, with results often very similar to eighteenth-century ironwork. The curving lines of Belgian Art Nouveau were admirably served by iron. Belgian ironwork, from which Guimard in France drew much inspiration, made such play with the interstices between the iron and with the suppleness of its lines that it created, both outside and inside buildings, a new kind of space—mobile, almost fluid, and very characteristic of the 1900 aesthetic. A curious feature to be noted is that the designers of the Glasgow and the Sezession styles, despite their preference for straight lines and emphatic angles, allowed wrought iron to remain as sinuous as possible. Finally, a place apart must be made for Gaudí, whose work belongs to Art Nouveau but rises above and beyond its limits. Until he embarked on his cubical phase, Gaudí decorated his structures with strange metallic efflorescences, disturbing forms, like dragons or monsters from some imaginary "other side," things from a dream world rather than items from any established repertory of ornament.

But it was not only ironwork and sculpture that composed the new décor of city life. In many capitals it was under the surface, invisibly, that the streets harbored the great novelty of the century—the subway. Stations and station entrances, both of which were made into true works of art by Guimard in Paris and Otto Wagner in Vienna, set up a new pulsation in the arteries of the city. Glass and cast iron were combined in hitherto undiscovered visual forms, suitably underlining the presence of this revolutionary means of transport.

90 ▨ LOUIS COMFORT TIFFANY (?). Glass and metal canopy. C. 1899–1902. 2 East 91st Street, New York. This glass and metal canopy is attributed to Tiffany. Its fragile opulence overhangs the door like a protective parasol, contrasting with the heavy balcony and consoles. The influence of Eastern art—Near, Middle, and Far—is strongly noticeable in Tiffany's early work. He is best known for his vases in *Favrile* glass, but his initial explorations were in the realm of stained glass. Windows in opalescent glass by Tiffany date back as far as 1876. This mansion, formerly the residence of Andrew Carnegie, now houses the Columbia University School of Social Work.

91 ▨ ÉMILE DERRÉ. 276 Boulevard Raspail. C. 1900 (?). Paris.
Derré was always the sculptor of love. From the *Chapiteau des Baisers* to the *Fontaine des Amours*, with a long series of Parisian house façades between, the tender passion is manifested in all its forms. In the example shown here, the *Three Ages of Love* are portrayed on the consoles supporting the long balcony. They stand out from among clumps of foliage which spill out copiously over the walls and window arches. With the name of Derré, we should also recall those of Schnegg, Baptiste Seguin, Rispal, and above all, Lefèvre and Paul-Jean Baptiste Gasq, whose signatures appear on the beautiful building at 103 Avenue des Champs-Élysées.

92 ▨ RUPRICH-ROBERT. Door. 1900. 50 Avenue de Ségur, Paris.
This building takes only incidental borrowings from Art Nouveau. The façade is plain and flat-chested, merely decorated here and there with gigantic flowering branches. The same hesitation between tradition and the new fashion is found in the door. The imaginative arabesques which surround and emphasize the arch are held severely in check by the molding which partially surrounds them. In the two panels of the door itself, the artist has used curved lines, but has arranged them regularly, in a symmetrical pattern. The little daisies look out demurely at the world; they have the form and grace of the original plant, but not its vitality.

93 ▨ LOUIS SULLIVAN. Guaranty Building. 1894–95. Buffalo.
In the Guaranty Building, Sullivan achieved the ideal large-scale office building, constructed in a new spirit and with new techniques. However, this did not force him to dispense with ornamentation; the iron framework is overlaid with terra cotta molded in low relief, a decoration in Sullivan's own style which has been identified sometimes as Art Nouveau and sometimes as

Proto-Art Nouveau. Consisting of a delicate tracery which combines geometrical with botanical elements, this ornamentation owes much to the Byzantine, the Celtic, and the Late Gothic art, as well as to that of William Morris. At the same time, it is perfectly original.

94 ▨ LOUIS SULLIVAN. The Bayard Building. *Main Doorway*. 1897–98. 65–69 Bleecker Street, New York.
When the building's ground floor was refaced a few years ago (*see* plate 58), this magnificent doorway was luckily left untouched. The same spirit seen in the decoration and ornamentation of the Guaranty Building is evident here, where the dense, carved foliage and the thousand-and-one combinations of the volute celebrate a joint triumph of exuberant design.

95 ▨ RENÉ LALIQUE. The Artist's House. *Doorway*. 1902. 40 Cours la Reine, Paris.
For the decoration of the house which he designed for himself, Lalique chose the pine tree as a motif. A trunk rises on either side of the front door; some branches have been lopped off, others spread out against the wall and melt into it in a softly modeled gradation. Without being interrupted by the door, the foliage is continued into the expanse of glass. While we undoubtedly see here the keen and realistic observation of nature of which this artist was so fond, we also notice the decorative instinct and sense of proportion which safeguarded him against excesses.

96 ▨ EDGARD WILLIAM BRANDT. Door. 1909. Rue de Prony, Paris.
By 1909, decoration had become more refined. The sap was becoming thinner; the plant had begun to wilt. In this door, the pine needles and pine cones have dwindled into a mere frame, and the greater part of the surface is occupied by rigidly straight bars. A far cry from the luxuriant vegetation designed by Émile Robert, for example.

97 ▨ AUGUSTE PERRET. 25 *bis* Rue Franklin. *Doorway*. 1903. Paris.
Within the context of a sober frame composed entirely of straight lines, this doorway is characterized by its extreme simplicity (*see* plate 15). Glass plays a large part in the design and construction of this doorway (and, indeed, the entire building); the lower third of each door panel is composed of interlaced iron strips which create a firm, rectangular pattern. The only feature reminding one of the period is the slender laurel branch connecting and continuing the brass door handles. But this detail is so delicate, so subtle, as to pass unnoticed under the impact of the ensemble.

III ▨ UNKNOWN DESIGNER. Rue d'Abbeville. *Service Door*. C. 1898 (?). Paris.
The tradesmen's entrance was not overlooked: indeed, it was often seized upon as an opportunity for typical Art Nouveau decoration. In this example, the lines are suitably sober, but the word "Service" stands out gaily in green on a metal plaque. The fanciful lettering dances along; the edges of the plaque, all curves and cusps, are decorated here and there with little flowers. No pains have been spared to make this door as attractive as possible.

98 ▨ UNKNOWN ARCHITECT. Pharmacie G. Lesage. 1904. Douvres la Déliverande, Calvados.
Art Nouveau in France was not confined exclusively to Paris. The movement also spread to the provinces: witness this building in Normandy with its flat façade, the ground floor and first floor of which have been adorned with curves wherever possible. The beautiful flowering lines of the ironwork should be noted, as well as the anachronistic Renaissance dormers of the top floor.

99 ▨ WAGON. Door. 1906. 24 Place Félix-Faure, Paris.
Fat, juicy stems, full of movement, springing from well-defined roots, frame the door of this building. The same dancing curves are echoed in the ironwork of the door itself, but in a more delicate and airy way. The artist has retained the emphatic vertical bars over and around which the tall irises go wreathing their way; stems, blossoms, and buds shoot out freely all over the surface, underlining the asymmetry of the whole.

100 ▨ GIUSEPPE SOMMARUGA. Casa Castiglioni. *Iron Gate*. 1901. Milan.
This curious iron gate is symptomatic of the passion for renewal which swept through Europe at the beginning of the twentieth century. Here, the designer has tried to conceal the very purpose of the object, twisting the rigorous vertical components waywardly this way and that like ribbons, and mingling them with volutes, flowers, and short horizontals. He has deliberately denied the symmetry and regular rhythm which dominate the work of previous centuries, preferring to foster an illusion of anarchic fantasy in which a nice balance is maintained between botanical and purely linear elements.

101 ▨ VICTOR HORTA. Solvay Residence (now the Wittamer de Camps Residence). *Balustrade*. 1895–1900. Brussels.
The Solvay residence was the most inclusive commission ever undertaken by Horta. He designed everything, from the building itself to the door handles. An outstanding feature is this staircase and its balustrade, an admirable piece of ironwork. Its design, derived from vegetable forms, is as abstract as some of Gaudí's. The only aspect of the plant which Horta has kept is the organic curve, the dynamic twisting movement which he transforms into a purely decorative interplay of airy stems, between which the light percolates abundantly. At the same time, he does not conceal the characteristics of his materials and the ways in which they are worked (hinges, for example, play their part in the visual composition). Iron is a major determinant in the work of Horta. He was one of the first to use it for decorative effect, notably in the drawing room of the house he built for Baron Eetvelde.

102 ▨ UNKNOWN DESIGNER. "The Dakota" Apartments. *Cast-Iron Railing*. C. 1881. 1 West 72nd Street, New York.

Until about 1890, America's attitude toward Europe was provincial and subordinate. She always adopted Europe's fashions with a time lag, adjusting them to meet her own needs, but initiating few herself. It is therefore not surprising to see on this New York City building (one of the first apartment houses built for the wealthy) this decorative cast-iron motif derived from the Renaissance, consisting of a semi-herm flanked by two dragons.

103 ▨ HERMAN GESELLIUS, ARMAS LINDGREN, and ELIEL SAARINEN. The Pohjola. *Staircase.* 1901. Helsinki.
This staircase designed for the Pohjola (*see* plate 63) antedates those designed by Van de Velde (*see* plate 106) and Perret (25 *bis* Rue Franklin, Paris). Its plan—all flowing lines without a single straight one—recalls the pioneering architectural thought of the period. At the same time it has a banister railing of astonishing simplicity and sobriety: no flowers or undulations, just a straightforward rectangular iron network. The style of the lamp standards on the landings is a long way from that of Horta.

104 ▨ OTTO WAGNER. The Majolika Haus. *Elevator Gates.* 1910. Vienna.
On this pair of gates the architect has repeated the motif already used on the stair railings. The stalks of the stylized flowers are arranged to form the necessary grill. But tradition, defied in the lower half, reappears in the upper, in the form of the vertical bars across which the ornamentation has been applied. In spite of their novelty and attempted originality, these gates go back to the still highly tenacious tradition of the eighteenth century. Perhaps only men like Gaudí, Guimard, Mackintosh, and Perret succeeded in throwing it off.

105 ▨ UNKNOWN DESIGNER. Elevator Cage. C. 1900(?). Leningrad.
Elevators were in common use in Europe from the beginning of the nineteenth century. Originally hydraulic, they were, by 1900, more often electro-hydraulic. Their gates, whether merged into the line of the stairway or treated as a separate feature, gave designers a new theme on which to exercise their imaginations. In this Leningrad building the designer chose a plant-form motif and developed it symmetrically about the vertical median line. Here, the metal plays no structural role: it is simply a decorative frame, allowing the artist to use large blank surfaces and play freely with the curves.

106 ▨ HENRY VAN DE VELDE. Folkwang Museum. *Banister.* 1902. Hagen, Germany.
This astounding creation is made of wood and wrought iron painted white. It uses a three-dimensional motif which in itself is fairly simple, but as one goes up the stairs it offers many different combinations of shapes, continually changing and undulating, and the eye searches in vain for the single underlying form.

107 ▨ UNKNOWN DESIGNER. Stair landing and elevator enclosure in a lobby. C. 1902. Milan.
The flora which invades this lobby in a Milan house gives us some notion of the unified, harmonious effect pursued by certain artists around 1900. Rather stylized thistle blooms rise from tall, vertical stems. The elevator gates are decorated with the same theme in a broader treatment. Plaster, paint, and wrought iron are combined here in a décor whose opulence and abundance are decidedly Italian. Other examples, conceived along the same general lines but executed with greater subtlety, possess inexhaustible charm.

108 ▨ JOSEPH MARIA OLBRICH. Door. Inlaid wood. C. 1900. Collection Dr. Wichmann, Starnberg.
This is not merely a decorated door, but one which has been conceived exclusively as a decorative panel. The purely abstract ornamentation, formed by the different varieties of inlaid wood which compose its surface, is just as important as the little picture at its center. This bold, unusual conception can be regarded as epitomizing the whole art of the Sezession—simple forms, rich materials, and dematerialized, ethereal line drawing.

109 ▨ LOUIS SULLIVAN. Metal Grill. C. 1898.
This delicate linear design, often found in Sullivan's terra-cotta ornamentation, is here transcribed as a metal grill. It was too frail to withstand the ravages of time; a few curves have been bent out of shape and a wire has been broken off here and there. But its highly individual character survives, especially in the T-shaped central ornament in which we can recognize the little detached leaf and the thread-like tracery of lines which also appear on the same designer's door handle and plate (*see* plate 129).

110 ▨ ERIC EHRSTRÖM. Bronze Door. 1907.
This cast-bronze door exhibits the sober, restrained line characteristic of Finnish art in general. Here, each rectangular panel represents a different species of undersea life, carefully and accurately delineated. Although the subjects are taken from nature, just as in much of Art Nouveau, the result is not Art Nouveau. The subject has been used in a different way: it no longer plays a formal and essential role in the ensemble, but merely fills the frame. The simplification and clarity of this decoration point toward more contemporary art.

111 ▨ CHARLES RENNIE MACKINTOSH. Glasgow School of Art. *Weathercock.* Wrought iron. C. 1898. Glasgow.
Apart from Mackintosh in Glasgow and Harrach in Munich, few artists concerned themselves with weather vanes or weathercocks. This one is at once modern and thoroughly Glasgow School, with its lines forming a somewhat rigid abstract composition.

112 ▨ CHARLES RENNIE MACKINTOSH. Mirror for the "Room de luxe," Willow Tea Room, Glasgow. 1904. Collection University of Glasgow.

Mackintosh showed a marked predilection for decorative ironwork. He used it abundantly both in the Glasgow School of Art and in his tea rooms. In this mirror we find his characteristically sober line which repeatedly moves forward, only to turn back on itself, finally launching forth decisively. This abstract motif, in which intersecting rectangles are combined with ovals, is typical of the Scottish designer's style.

113 ▨ OTTO WAGNER. Project for the Wiener Stadtbahn. India ink and watercolor. 1898. Historisches Museum der Stadt Wien, Vienna.
Although Otto Wagner used iron and glass in this railway station in Vienna, and was thereby modern, he showed himself much less revolutionary than Guimard. His station building corresponds exactly to the preference of his epoch for a lightweight, transparent architecture, with lacy metalwork and slender armatures. This drawing indicates that Wagner, then about to break away for good from an aesthetic which was by then dated, was for the time being still very *fin de siècle*.

114 ▨ HECTOR GUIMARD. Métropolitain Entrance Gate. Painted cast iron and colored glass. C. 1900. The Museum of Modern Art, New York.

These compositions in metal were greeted with dismay followed by ridicule. They were about to be destroyed when a great collector thought of re-erecting one of them on his estate, and the Museum of Modern Art in New York made haste to acquire one of the finest examples. In its setting in the Museum's garden, it recovers all the strangeness it must have had for Parisians at the beginning of the century. Then it framed the entrance to a subterranean abyss; now it stands out against the disturbing nudity of a plain brick wall which accentuates its elegant lines. The material is just right for the curves adored by Guimard; the ample, fluent modeling suits the viscous quality of cast iron, which discourages sharp edges and curt, tight-lipped forms.

115 ▨ ANTONI GAUDÍ. Finca Güell. *Dragon Gate.* C. 1887. Barcelona.
Wrought iron played such an important part in the decorative side of Gaudí's buildings that he chose to make most of its with his own hands. This gate, typical of Catalan art at that time, attains new heights of technical perfection, and its circumvolutions, powerful curves, and decorative value make it a harbinger of Art Nouveau.

91

92

28

PRUDENTIAL

93

65

94

95

96

99

98

100

101

104

105

107

108

109

110

111

112

113

114

Heating

FIREPLACES, which for a century and a half had become progressively smaller and less imposing, now returned to favor and offered both neo-medievalists and Art Nouveau designers a field in which to exercise their virtuosity. English and German architects strove to outdo one another in showing imagination in designing fireplaces.

In France, that trusty servant the *salamandre* (a cast-iron slow-combustion stove) was almost universal. From the first, it had been intended to stand in front of the fireplace. Fireplace and stove combined as a unit now became a stimulus to designers. Many artists gave their attention to the stove itself, seeking to improve its shape or decoration; Paul Follot and Tony Selmersheim were among those who designed *salamandres*. Others created a complete setting, including ceramic tiles, mirrors, cupboards, and copper edgings (cornices in the carpenter's, not the architect's, sense of the word). At present, these stoves are out of fashion; perhaps the day will come when they are as much sought after as the faïence stoves of Lorraine.

116 ▨ JOSEPH MARIA OLBRICH. Interior. 1900. Universal Exhibition, Paris.
At the Universal Exhibition of 1900, the Darmstadt group was represented by this interior, whose corner heating arrangement was designed by Olbrich. A stove stands in the hearth; what would normally be the mantelpiece is a panel of brass and vivid faïence. Since the stove allows no flames to be seen, the artist has compensated by using the theme and colors of his decorations to suggest fire, and has also laid out an amusing smoke motif on the adjacent walls. Discreet elegance is heightened by both wit and gaiety—in the decoration and by attention to comfort. All in all, a novel combination.

117 ▨ UNKNOWN DESIGNER. Maison des Gueules Cassées. *Fireplace.* 1902. Rue d'Aguesseau, Paris.
More than any other interior feature, the fireplace lent itself to a reincarnation of medieval and Renaissance styles; examples in châteaux and museums are legion. One of these would appear to have been faithfully copied here. The designer has provided an enormous wooden structure rising to the ceiling; the outer sides contain niches above and columns below. A touching family scene balances the tall, wide opening of the fireplace. The whole seems monumental, medieval, bourgeois—and unoriginal.

118 ▨ HALSEY RICCARDO. Fireplace at 8 Addison Road. 1906–07. London (*also see* plate 49).
It was a long time before anyone in Europe was willing to rely on anything except an open fire. Central heating was still in the experimental stage and not yet widely adopted. The open hearth set designers searching for new forms and decoration and, like any other accessory feature, it went through a number of styles and fashions. Toward the end of the century it was frequently executed in marble, like this English essay in would-be Classicism. A column on either side supports an "entablature" (the mantelpiece). The panel of the overmantel, long regarded as an essential counterpart to the opening below, is embellished with three shallow, arched niches.

119 ▨ EUGÈNE VALLIN. Fireplace. 1903–06. Musée de l'École de Nancy.
With this fireplace in the famous dining room designed for M. Masson by Eugène Vallin, of the Nancy School, we find ourselves fairly launched into Art Nouveau. Although its general lines recall the graceful curves of the Louis XV style, it is not a pastiche but an original piece of work, rigorously constructed and perfectly in harmony with the entire room. The dynamism of its lines is modeled on that of vegetation characteristic of the Art Nouveau of the Nancy School. The assembly is

not an inert mass standing on the ground and abutting on the wall; the wood shoots upward into curves, and branches rise and fall, as if still full of sap and life. This translation of vegetable growth into a style fairly close to that of the eighteenth century is one of the typical qualities of the Art Nouveau of the Nancy School.

120 ◪ ANTONI GAUDÍ. Fireplace. 1889 (?). Barcelona.
Gaudí added electric light fixtures to this Gothic design of his (pleasant, harmonious Gothic, be it said); he was never afraid to undertake a difficult problem.

121 ◪ LUDWIG GUIGNES. Fireplace. 1902. Private Collection, Clamart.
The fireplace enjoyed, among others, a Symbolist phase. Was it not, after all, the ideal setting for expressing the poetry of the seasons? Here the designer has revitalized the decoration, if not the form. The hearth is flanked by a pair of columns supporting a straightforward mantelpiece, but the capitals are carved with expressive faces denoting joy and sadness, in a style very similar to that found on the façades of buildings: soft, gentle modeling, with floating tresses flowing up over the abacus, makes the stone come alive. The nude figures on the lintel are more or less Classical in inspiration, but the dreaming mask in the center is completely in the taste of the time. A Japanese ceramic jar stands at either end of the mantelpiece of this thoroughly architectural structure, with a ceramic bust of the artist in the middle.

122 ◪ VARIOUS DESIGNERS. Room Setting. C. 1899. (No longer extant.)
Northern Symbolism was very different from that of southern Europe; in the present example it refers to ancient legends in which fire is represented as the source of life and love. The meaningful decoration is carried not by the fireplace itself but by the tapestry above it, designed by Gerhard Munthe in a deliberately archaic, folk-art style. This ensemble, exhibited in Berlin in 1899, is the work of several artists: the copper fireplace is by Robbins, the carpet by Frank Brangwyn, and the tables, stand, and lamps are by Louis Majorelle, Wilhelm, Charles Plumet, and Tony Selmersheim. Despite this mixture of nationalities the result is fairly representative of the northern idea of an interior: simple, rustic, and full of folk traditions.

123 ◪ GEORGE WALTON. Interior. C. 1900. (No longer extant.)
This interior is designed as a complete unit with the fireplace as its focal point. It exhibits the spindly straight lines dear to the Scottish and English designers. Sobriety dominates, but is quite different in quality from the somewhat massive simplicity favored by northern Europeans. Walton sought an airy, elegant refinement, which he obtained at the expense of comfort. The arrangement is pleasing to the eye, and the room has plenty of light, but would visitors sitting on the benches get much warmth?

124 ◪ UNKNOWN FINNISH DESIGNER. Fireplace. 1900. (No longer extant.)
There is no decoration, either symbolic or floral, around this ceramic-tiled fireplace, shown at the Paris Universal Exhibition of 1900. It was new just because it was so simple. It borrows from no style, it is heir to a primeval tradition, and it is simply—and solely—a source of warmth and comfort. These stripped-down forms and the sober decoration were peculiar to the Scandinavian countries at the beginning of the century. What makes them part of the vast and varied movement of Art Nouveau is the intention to which they testify: the search for an art at once functional, original, and national.

125 ◪ RAPIN and BLONDEL. Sketch for Fireplace. C. 1902. (Whereabouts unknown.)
This team of decorators made the stove the central motif in this comfortable library for a private house. Ceramic tiles, with a central medallion, and curved wings of woodwork flank the fireside, creating a niche for the fireplace. Each wing embodies a seat describing a quarter of a circle, with bookshelves above so that the reader can take full advantage of the heat provided. This secluded corner is rendered still cozier by two wooden baldachins over each seat-and-shelf unit.

126 ◪ GEORGE WALTON. Fireplace. C. 1900. (Whereabouts unknown.)
Another fireplace by Walton, this time in a billiard room. The opening of the hearth is framed in polished iron. This is surrounded with leaded panes of opaque glass alternating with faïence tiles. The marker for recording the players' scores runs across just under the mantelpiece and its lines of white numbers on a dark background make it a very original decorative motif. In their different styles, this billiard room by Walton, the dining room by Vallin, and the drawing room by Olbrich, all express the same purpose: the builder is no longer left free to install any fireplace he chooses, regardless of the furniture and decoration; on the contrary, the fireplace is considered not only as a piece of furniture in its own right but also as a center of life, and must therefore be given a form and arrangement which suit the room as a whole, and the function fulfilled by the fire in that particular setting. That is just what makes the present example so interesting: the link between the hearth and the billiard table is created by the marker and has nothing arbitrary about it. What more natural, from the players' point of view, than these repeated journeys between table and fire? This regard for logic, suitability, and comfort was new at the time; we can even say that it is, in itself, Art Nouveau. It reveals a new conception of interior arrangement. Drawing rooms, billiard rooms, and so forth, are no longer simply reception rooms in which the host hopes to dazzle his guests with his wealth and acquired luxuries; instead they have become spaces to be lived in. Simple as this sounds, it was in fact a great novelty.

116

117

119

118

20

121

c'est·ainsi
que·l'amour·s'alume·dans·le·coeur

122

123

124

125

126

Locks and Fastenings

T HE art of the locksmith had dwindled sadly; Art Nouveau restored it to the status it had enjoyed three centuries earlier. Guimard, Lavirotte, Sullivan, and Gaudí captured various strange creatures, some real, others imaginary, and laid spells on them, transforming them into door handles, gongs, or keys.

127 ◨ UNKNOWN DESIGNER. Mouthpiece of speaking tube at the front door of a house. 1902. Milan.
"Walls have ears." An Italian designer, taking the familiar saying literally, has replaced the usual doorbell with an immense ear. This decorative motif in bronze provides communication between visitor and porter. An ingenious combination of humor and symbolism.

128 and **130** ◨ VICTOR HORTA. Solvay Residence (now the Wittamer de Camps Residence). *Door Handles.* 1895–1900. Brussels.
Just as every French designer eventually worked out his own floral repertory, so every Belgian designer had his own linear style. Van de Velde's line is abstract, mobile, and nervous; by contrast, Horta's is more static, closer to its vegetable origins. It is applied here to door handles whose formal and decorative qualities the architect sought to re-create and revitalize. In these two examples the handle is adapted to the grasping action of the hand, and is backed no longer by a smooth blank plate, but by a subtle weave of interlacing contours. By means of these and other fixtures, Horta emphasized a plant-like linear quality in the room and its furnishings; even hinges were converted unobtrusively into essential decorative factors.

129 ◨ LOUIS SULLIVAN. Door Handle. C. 1900. Private Collection, Chicago.
See caption to plate 109.

131 ◨ HALSEY RICCARDO. Door Handle. 1906–07. 8 Addison Road, London (*also see* plate 49).
The little English leaf shows no very startling developments, but it grows everywhere. Here it is used as a border on an extensive escutcheon which is otherwise unadorned except for a few butterflies. The practical

English attitude is at work. Decoration is relegated to places where it will neither get dirty nor get worn away, but this inevitably means banishing it from the main body of the object. The French, German, and Belgian approach was different.

132 ◨ HECTOR GUIMARD. Door Pulls. Gilt bronze. 1911–12. The Museum of Modern Art, New York.
The irregular shapes and gentle lines of these handles are inviting to the hand, but the modeling is softer and less firmly accented than Horta's. These two great designers were not the only ones who strove to make their decoration consistent down to the last detail. At the beginning of the century, the locksmith's art was flourishing all over Europe. Alexandre Charpentier, with his outstanding sculptural talent, turned his attention to it; Ville Vallgren depicted a sad story within the confines of a door knocker; and many other artists with an interest in the applied arts designed handles and escutcheons.

133 ◨ HALSEY RICCARDO. Plates for light switches. Hammered metal. 1906–07. 8 Addison Road, London. These plates exhibit some of the favorite motifs of English Art Nouveau. Small, trilobed leaves form a triangular arrangement, harmonize with the geometrical interplay of the stems, and fit neatly into the area of the plate.

134 ◨ HENRI GUÉRARD. Cast Metal Keyhole Plates. C. 1900. Museum für Kunst und Gewerbe, Hamburg. To Henri Guérard, a keyhole was an open mouth around which to invent a face. He devised amusing and original variations on this theme, rather like some decorative details from the Middle Ages and the sixteenth century.

Bathroom Design

No amount of sociological scrutiny will tell us as much about private life in respectable society fifty years ago as the pages of the Countess de X., in her prolix *Bréviaire de la femme* ("The Woman's Breviary"):

"There are some women who take particular care of their beauty; one can reproach them only as regards the publicity which surrounds such matters in these days. There are others, alas—and their name is legion—who have no aesthetic sense whatever and even—cruel though it be to record—no standards of elementary cleanliness. So narrow is their mental horizon that they regard virtue and dirt as natural partners, and equate innocence with the absence of soap and water.

"Certain details of personal cleanliness are completely unknown to them, and if the mere glimmer of such an idea succeeds in penetrating their minds it is dismissed at once, with indignation, as a piece of shameful immodesty.

"So powerful is their sense of chastity that it prevents their bathing in pure water those parts of the body which a morality, as austere as it is stupid, forbids them to include in the same category as the parts which they submit to a more or less complete toilette every day.

"A sad state of affairs for any husband who loves beauty and the ideal woman."

The design of bathrooms was slow to evolve. The interior of a bathroom could be laid out in any number of different ways, yet very few bathrooms were frankly and openly sanitary. Not only was a room "reserved for hydrotherapy" regarded as a luxury, it was often disguised to look like something else. Usually it resembled a drawing room in which sanitary equipment had been discreetly accommodated. As the Countess puts it: "The buckets and foot baths, and the article which one straddles, are shrouded in invisibility; the last-named [the bidet] may be permitted to appear in the elegant guise of a Louis XVI chair." This is not the only form of expensive fancy dress which the bathroom may be compelled to wear. "The bath is either ordinary or luxurious; in the latter event it may be a sunken pool of pink marble at floor level, with steps leading down into it, or of Bohemian glass with a gold border." In neglecting the practical side, the decorators sometimes omitted certain elementary precautions; wallpapers with painted patterns and a poor resistance to heat and damp were frequently used in bathrooms.

What we are witnessing here are the infant footsteps of an art which, in the nature of things, could not grow faster than the social changes which produced it. It is well known that in designing working-class houses in the early part of the century, architects often provided for a rainwater supply on the first floor (bedrooms and sanitary arrangements), and that sanitation was meager in most apartments and villas. "Their *cabinet de toilette*," as the Countess relates in her description of society ladies, "is so sketchy that if they have one at all they can take it away with them whenever they go travelling." Servants' bedrooms never had running water; "the latter is reserved for their masters," and as for the bathtub:

"The famous tub has come to us direct from the kingdom of Britain; imported on the wings of snobbery, it is by no means useless to those who have acquired the smart habit of 'taking a tub' [*tuber* is the word she uses], and of making their friends and acquaintances aware that they are addicted to these exercises in cleanliness. By using the tub one plays to the gallery; it is one of the forms of snobbery which have infiltrated into our way of life.

"Little children take their tub, mama and papa do likewise; chambermaid and valet are summoned to perform as tub attendants in the bedroom. So it may be said that they know the ultimate secrets of those whom they serve; before their omnipotence, the last veil has fallen."

In Europe, hygiene was one of the great discoveries of the twentieth century—Europe after 1918, that is. Most of our grandparents, on the other hand, must have regarded it as a craze, and a perilous one at that.

135 ✐ WILLIAM BURGES. Washstand. 1880. The Victoria and Albert Museum, London.
This washstand is above all a piece of furniture, and a handsome one at that, seeming almost too good to be banished to the bathroom. Imagine for a moment the basin and soap dishes having been taken away; with its miniature columns and its somewhat medieval decoration it is more like a piece of ecclesiastical furniture. In the mid-nineteenth century the design and decoration of bathrooms did not yet exist in their own right, and this was one of the fields in which Art Nouveau had a challenge to meet.

136 ✐ UNKNOWN DESIGNER. Toilet Bowl. Vitreous ceramic. Private Collection, France.
The most private places and unexpected objects were not immune to invasion by ornament. This toilet bowl has been dignified by decoration—Renaissance foliage and urns—both inside and out. Though this does not affect the shape, it does represent an attempt to disguise the function, and to promote this humble but necessary item to the rank of an *objet d'art*. (Note the name of this model: "Le Desidératum.")

137 ✐ HENRI SAUVAGE and SARAZIN. Sketch for Bathroom. C. 1902. (Whereabouts unknown.)
This bathroom is decorated throughout with ceramic tiles by Bigot. Here we see only part of the room; the bathtub is set back in a niche and takes up very little room. The few bathrooms of which illustrations can be found in magazines of the period are immense. Indeed, one of them, installed by Simas at about the same time as the one illustrated, is equipped with a miniature swimming pool, no less, in enameled mosaic tiles. The present example is more ordinary, with tiled walls. Near the base of the wall, large slabs in relief form a plinth. The bath is made of the same tiling as that covering the walls; its inside is smooth, its outside covered with decorative relief. The color scheme is yellowish and gray, heightened by such details as runnels and ledges for the soap in green and blue.

138 ✐ LOSSOW and WICHWEGER. Bathroom. C. 1900. (Whereabouts unknown.)
In 1900 a bath was still a luxury. There may have been straightforward bathrooms at a modest price but, if so,

few signs of their existence can now be found. Documentary evidence from the period shows us only artistically decorated bathrooms. An example such as this, executed in faïence by the Dresden firm of Villeroy und Boch, is typical of this pursuit of luxury for luxury's sake. The bath is at floor level, set back in a niche or alcove. Decoration proliferates both around and above it. On the back wall two naiads and clusters of monsters are bathing, and the niche is framed with shells and seaweed. The whole is intended to create the illusion of a natural grotto. Was this not, in a sense, a way of evading the whole problem? The decoration is certainly aquatic, but it is rather like a stage-set disguising the essentially hygienic function of the bath. Bathroom design is groping for the way ahead but has not yet found it.

139 and **140** ✐ BRUNO SCHMITZ and ERNST BARLACH. Wall Fountains. C. 1900. Museum für Kunst und Gewerbe, Hamburg.
Wall fountains enjoyed a vogue in Germany around 1900. They were made of metal or stoneware, with decoration in relief. In one of these examples, Bruno Schmitz of Cologne has used a graceful design of water lilies and fish, while in the other Ernst Barlach has employed grimacing masks. Barlach's, like his commemorative plaque in honor of Justus Brinckmann (*see* plate 557), was realized by the ceramist Hermann Mutz.

141 ✐ GEORGES HOENTSCHEL. Bathtub. C. 1900. (Whereabouts unknown.)
Georges Hoentschel worked with Jean Carries for a number of years. He concentrated mainly on earthenware, in which he obtained a warm, soft patina. It was with this material that he executed the interior of the bathroom whose bath is shown in the illustration. Far from being conceived as an isolated receptacle, the bath is integrated into a decorative ensemble circumscribed by an arch. Plants hang down over its edges, and the designer has given it flowing, melting contours everywhere. Aquatic plants invade and almost hide it. It is not the bath which carries the decoration but, as if by some happy whim of nature, the decoration which permits the presence of the bath.

131

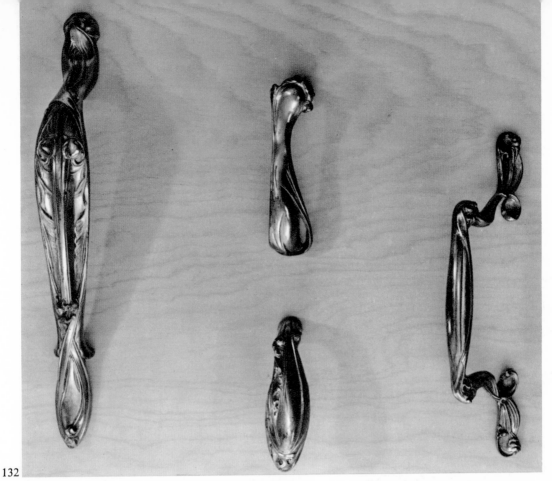

132

133

134

135

137

136 138

139

140

141

Painting

I N the year 2020, it will doubtless seem possible to sum up the many tendencies of present-day painting by using some simple, general phrase such as "the 1960 Style." In just the same way, the appellation "1900 Style" does not even begin to cover the various artistic manifestations flourishing at the beginning of the present century: Post-Impressionism, bourgeois Realism, Populism, Symbolism, Pointillism, the Nabis, Expressionism, and the beginnings of Abstract art.

To most people, "painting in 1900" probably means no more than the depiction of a certain kind of long-extinct elegance, with an infusion of sprightly gaiety in some cases and of pornographic humor in others: Slav-cum-Italian princesses by Boldini, pastry cooks by Chocarne-Moreau, and Parisian dressmakers' errand-girls by Béraud. Yet it is quite obvious, and has been increasingly so since the exhibition held in Paris in 1960–61, entitled *Sources du XXe siècle* ("Sources of the Twentieth Century"), that we have no clue to that deeply disturbed epoch unless we also look at both Symbolism, with its new interpretation of love, and the then nascent science of dream interpretation. These reflect more truly the impact of the political, social, and moral problems then current, and the effects of both scientific progress and psychoanalytical self-examination.

THE SOURCES OF ART NOUVEAU

Art Nouveau arose out of Symbolism, and its sources are as diverse and bewildering as those of the parent stream. It is customary to point to Piranesi and Blake, two precursors who whipped up the pack of satanic creatures and twilit forms so carefully excluded from the pastoral world of the Trianon. But are not the possessed women portrayed by Stuck and Klimt related as closely to Dürer's *Melencolia*, a Flora of Niccolo dell'Abbate, the Titans of Göltzius, or the disturbing androgynes of the elder Luigi Sabatelli? And have not Gustave Doré, Grandville, Bracquemond, and Manet—with his surprising poster *Les Chats* (1869)—just as good a claim to the paternity of the movement as the Christian Mannerist Philipp Otto Runge, for whom color itself had a symbolic value, or as the "Nazarenes," who played a part in turning religious Romanticism toward a Symbolistic mysticism which is found again in the work of the Pre-Raphaelites?

THE PRE-RAPHAELITES AND GUSTAVE MOREAU

The Pre-Raphaelites, because of their minute treatment of nature (one of them declared it had taken him three months to paint a tree) and the facility with which they combined the reasonable and the irrational, had an important influence on the development of Symbolism.

First cousins to the women depicted by Ingres, Chassériau, and Moreau (and also distantly related to Emma Bovary), the Anglo-Italian ladies of Burne-Jones and Rossetti are all the fairer and more desirable for being perpetually lost in mystical reveries. In fact, Pre-Raphaelite paintings and illustrations, apparently devoted to piety and mystical revelation, are really far more concerned with sensuality, which Romanticism had banished from both picture and word for nearly half a century.

Gustave Moreau, last of the Romantics and first of the Symbolists, opened wide the doors of the underworld and gave a face to faceless creatures—chimeras and lost souls—but did not cancel out their strangeness in so doing. His originality, however, is to be found essentially in his relation to religious myths; he is so clever at exciting disturbing, ambiguous feelings that no one can say to which element his work owes more, the liturgical, or the erotic. His surprising blend of cruelty, sadism, and brilliant barbarity, a mixture which had already delighted the German engravers of the sixteenth century, explains why André Breton and the Surrealists admire him so much. Moreau was a Christian in quite as ambivalent a way as J. K. Huysmans showed himself to be around 1895. His painting made him the iconographer of Satanism and the other strange cults then current (1888 saw the revival of the Rosicrucian Order by Sàr Mérodock Péladan), and his influence turned an entire generation—from Max Klinger to Carlos Schwabe, and from Jan Toorop to Aubrey Beardsley—toward the murky world of dreams, the paranormal, and the cultivation of sensuality: Heinrich Heine's *Lorelei*, Gérard de Nerval's *Balkis* (a lily surrounded by jonquils), and Stéphane Mallarmé's *Phénomènes naturels*. "Art does not live by will alone," said Gustave Moreau. "Everything depends on docile submission to the inrush of the unconscious."

Women or youths—men count for little or nothing in the inspiration of Symbolism—whether painted by Burne-Jones, Moreau, Beardsley, Lucien Levy-Dhurmer, or Franz von Stuck, always seem to be plunged in a dream or trance, and the frigid beauty of their faces never expresses anything but perverse, furious sensuality.

The difference between Symbolist Art Nouveau and the other pictures being produced around 1900 can be gauged from the women in them. There is nothing in common between Boldini's fake princesses on the point of taking off their clothes in a bachelor flat somewhere on the Plaine Monceau, and the haughty, drug-eyed ladies of Klimt (*see* plates 175 and 176). It is worth noting that out of the forty-one possessed, hallucinated characters in the paintings we have selected, twenty-five have closed eyes.

The works of Moreau, Beardsley, and Toorop are a constant reminder of the affinities between Symbolist poetry and the various other arts. Painting, sculpture, and the applied arts, fighting under the same flag at the time, were truly Symbolistic whenever they succeeded in giving form and substance to myths and chimerical visions, without regard for the poetic cast of the subject matter.

In the first section of the illustrations accompanying this chapter, the reader can judge for himself how various were the inspiration and genius of Eugène Carrière, Maurice Denis, Gauguin, Van Gogh, Klimt, Munch, Puvis de Chavannes, Giovanni Segantini, Toorop, and others. He will also observe the connective power of Symbolism, which makes a unified mosaic out of such a medley of personalities as Gustave Moreau and Odilon Redon, Max Klinger and Puvis de Chavannes, Jan Toorop and Eugène de Feure, Gustav Klimt and Edvard Munch, Joseph Maria Olbrich and Frank Kupka.

At the dawn of the twentieth century, Symbolism, in painting at any rate, sloughed off its old skin. Color was broken up into a mist of tiny particles, but whereas the Impressionists and Pointillists controlled this new fluidity by thinking about it in terms of physics, Symbolist painting and sculpture let it flow and made it volatile. Women and the stems of flowers are enormously elongated, and bronzes look molten. The arabesques of Toorop and Segantini herald abstract art; Klimt's bejeweled patchwork prefigures the ovoid masses of Miró; and the demonologist's world of Klee is already implicit in the disturbing evolutions of Kupka, F. Matusek, Riemerschmid, and Hans Schmithals.

Jean Cassou, in the remarkable preface he wrote for the catalogue of the exhibition *Sources du XXe siècle* (now published in the book, *Gateway to the Twentieth Century*, New York, 1961), points out the parallel between Symbolism and man's transient feelings, refining themselves ad infinitum. This, he says, "enables us to understand the resonance produced in German idealism, on contact with the linear and compositional simplifications of Gauguin, and his 'will to style,' [and to understand also] the effect of the outsize allegorical performances of Puvis de Chavannes and Hodler on a Germany still vibrating sympathetically to the memory of Wagnerian cyclones."

THE DECLINE OF SYMBOLISM

We come next to the pseudo-Symbolists. These were Mannerists who were lost in admiration for a decadent Hellenism or a witless historicism but who, by a more or less adroit idealization of their models, tried to show that they were adherents of Art Nouveau when in fact they were simply its contemporaries.

The results are equivocal and make uneasy viewing. If, as he may well be, the spectator feels baffled by Max Klinger's *Judgment of Paris* (*see* plate 151) because he cannot decide how much in it is genuinely poetic and how much mere paraphernalia, what is he to make of Mademoiselle Dufau's mythological hodgepodge (*see* plate 203)?

What we see in or about the year 1900 is Symbolism in decline; the virtue had gone out of it. A hopeless attempt was being made to combine Symbolism and Classicism and thus attain "supreme expression," a tendency which appears in literature with the last words of Henri de Régnier, Francis Jammes, Samain, Charles de Guérin, and Madame de Noailles.

Mannerisms topple (like the Biblical Gadarene swine) into an abyss of the worst vices of *petit bourgeois* grotesquery. In the mad race for gold medals, artists ground out an enormous number of choirboys, pastry cooks' apprentices, ecstatic communicants rolling their eyes as they imbibe the consecrated wine, and historical groups, such as the conspirators of Amboise. In Europe and the United States there was a swarm of pseudo-Symbolist artists who, in salons and academy exhibitions, sought to satisfy the customer with infernos peopled by corseted and hatted ladies surrounded by grinning demons. Some of the paintings are so silly that they come full circle and are comically charming, in the same vein as the following scene from the biography of Madame de Charmailles:

"The undulating, twisting torsos of flower-maidens emerged from enormous bluish lilies; tresses, whose incredible golden hue hovered between mahogany and egg yolk, surrounded their faces; bloodless faces like those of girls fresh from the operating table, with their pupils still enlarged by the anesthetics. Further on, in the tangles of coral and fleshy madrepores, where the seaweeds and submarine creatures swayed slowly to and fro like a pendulum, were the livid flesh tints of drowned women, whose terror-stricken faces crowned by grass-green manes of hair personified [Wagner's] three Rhinemaidens: Flosshilde, Woglinde, and Wellgunde."

Besides these *ersatz* Symbolists, there were a number of painters of varying talent—Jean Béraud, Jacques-Émile Blanche, Giovanni Boldini, Frederick Karl Frieseke, William Glackens, Paul Helleu (*see* plates 219, 221, and 227–229)—who have left us a pitiless record of the attitudes, customs, morals, and vices of the society of their time: an asocial society, conformist and paternalistic, sexual and satirical, rather than genuinely free and flippant in matters of the heart and senses—and cowardly on occasion. (A Parisian duchess, the day after the fire at the Bazar de la Charité, exclaimed: "At Montmartre they'd have saved the women!") On the whole, this society got the painters it deserved.

Guided by the same urge as the poets Tristan Klingsor, Paul Fort, Guillaume Apollinaire, and Francis Jammes, poets whose aim, in the words of Marcel Raymond, was to "reanimate the world of simple things and feelings," there were a few artists such as Carrière, Constantin-Émile

Meunier, Minne, Picasso, Steinlen, and Joaquin Sunyer who succeeded in blending Symbolism with the spirit of popular naturalism, despite having shed some of the artifices of the former; examples of their work have accordingly been included in this book (*see* plates 160, 236, 238, 242, 264, and 265).

FLOWERS, NATURE, LANDSCAPE

Flowers have such a peculiarly sensitizing effect on both Symbolism and Art Nouveau that they require special mention. Flower painters at the beginning of the nineteenth century, notably Redouté and his pupils, had achieved perfection in their art: the rose was never without its opaline pearl, so dear to Van Huysum. Flowers became the allotted province of well-bred girls, who were encouraged to pick them, limn them in watercolors, and preserve them pressed and dried in albums. After about 1850, when greenhouses had been improved and horticulture reached a new level of excellence, amateurs delighted in cultivating the dazzling blooms which Bracquemond and Owen Jones, followed by Grasset, De Feure, Ashbee, and Morris not long after, were to introduce into the environment of daily life, in the form of decorated books, fabrics, wallpapers, and other items.

Des Esseintes (in J. K. Huysmans' *À Rebours*, published in 1884) delights in flowers which have "textures like skin" and are "furrowed with imitation veins... eroded by syphilis and leprosy... damascened with eczema... studded with sores... pitted with ulcers and embossed with chancres."

The reason why Art Nouveau fell into such disrepute was probably that its notions of representation were so completely opposite to those of Impressionism. Impressionism was concerned with one problem only: the impact of light on objects, and the way the light is refracted and reflected at different times of day. It enjoyed increasing success for a couple of generations; it was a positive and physical doctrine, and was consequently reassuring. Painters like Renoir never arouse introspection or raise awkward social problems; objects are everything, the soul disappears behind a mask of flesh, and eroticism browses happily on caryatids *à la* Rubens and the heartless faces of the Misses Cahen of Antwerp.

An entirely different world emerges in the pictures of Thomas Theodor Heine, Xavier Mellery, and Carl Strathmann. These painters loved to lure the spectator to desolate shores overhanging treacherous, slimy lakes in which ghastly fishes swim, and into which the dreaming soul, despite shudders of revulsion, can hardly forbear to venture. *Gli Amanti del Lago* by Boccioni (*see* plate 184) is an example: the vegetable monster on the right-hand side of the composition has nothing in common with the happy, expansive landscape beloved of the Impressionists—dense wheat fields spangled with cornflowers and poppies, rivers on which leisurely barges move.

In conclusion, we must point out that this chapter—devoted to a medley of the unusual, the precious, and the poetic, with overemphatic lyricism sometimes spilling into absurdity—aims only at providing a broad panorama.

It was because no one had defined the necessary critical standards that writers of the time who dealt with Art Nouveau were so often at loggerheads. Between 1895 and 1905, manifestos and such periodicals as *Jugend, Pan, Art et Décoration, The Studio*, and *Mir Iskustva* reproduced works which seem to oppose our conception of the movement, and omitted others which today we would include.

It seems to us that in drawing up the ideal inventory of Art Nouveau, we can use great latitude: we can, and should, admit any work in which the Symbolist brew has been modified (even minutely) by the cult of the dream world, studied or otherwise unusual sensuality, Satanism, and humor.

"Symbolism," Marcel Raymond has said, "is one of those verbal fetishes which are all the more suggestive for being loaded with complex meanings, difficult to formulate." (*De Baudelaire au Surréalisme*, Paris, 1963.) Under no other designation could we have gathered such a disparate group of paintings, which set out to charm the spectator by appealing to the irrational side of his nature.

SYMBOLIST PAINTING
(Sources — the Dark Side, the Dream World, Slavic Folklore)

IV ◪ Sir John Everett Millais. *Ophelia*. Oil on canvas. 1852. The Tate Gallery, London.
   "Thus did Ophelia, sanctified and damned, float [on the surface of the stream] all night long."
                                                                     (Jules Laforgue, *Moralités légendaires*)
Psychoanalysis soon had plenty to say about the "reflections on the melancholy water," those deep, semi-stagnant waters in which the hallucinated dreamer is lost and drowned. The Symbolists were obsessed by Ophelia.

142 ◪ Philipp Otto Runge. *Der Morgen* (second version). Oil on canvas. 1808. Kunsthalle, Hamburg.
The German Romantic Runge painted striking "inhabited" portraits and pictures in which *putti* as chubby as the models of Mabuse wander like sleepwalkers, surrounded by strange, wan hieroglyphs in a primordial landscape setting. Albert Béguin writes of Runge: "The forms of the people, objects, and even landscapes are always duplicated by ornamental accessories around the edges of the picture and on the frame as well—interwoven flowers, angels, lines, and abstract figures. It seems that what the painter was trying to do was unobtrusively to dematerialize the real faces and objects in the middle of his canvas." (*L'Âme romantique et le Rêve*. Paris, 1963.)

143 ◪ Henry Fuseli. *Paradise Lost*. Oil on canvas. n.d. Neue Pinakothek, Munich.
Fuseli and Blake crossed the frontier of the unknown and entered the antechambers of Symbolism. Their characters, racked by frenzy, anguish, and depravity, howl in the night.

144 ◪ Eugène Delacroix. *The Death of Ophelia*. Oil on canvas. 1858. Neue Pinakothek, Munich.
Delacroix here joins the Ophelia cult, but is timid in his handling of its dark enchantment. Ophelia's eyes are still open, and she clutches desperately at the tree (and at life). Hair was a favorite theme of the *Emblématistes* (painters who made much use of traditional symbols, "emblems"), and is of course a perennial

sexual symbol; note that this Ophelia has short hair. It was the Romantics who made Symbolism possible by shattering the bolts and bars of Classicism. In tracing the origins of Art Nouveau, it is usual to cite Fuseli, Blake, and the Pre-Raphaelites as precursors. But surely Delacroix, a virtuoso of the vast Romantic keyboard, was one of the leading forerunners of those contradictory movements, Impressionism, Symbolism, and Expressionism.

145 🖾 GEORGE FREDERICK WATTS. *Hope.* Oil on canvas. 1885. The Tate Gallery, London.
The work of the Englishman Watts, a hermetic painter, borders on Symbolism: that is, on the style which was a natural reaction against naturalism and Impressionism and which found an esoteric pictorial language for suggesting emotions without making them explicit.

146 🖾 SIR NOEL PATON. *Quarrel of Oberon and Titania.* Oil on canvas. 1850. Royal Scottish Academy, Edinburgh.
This picture (which was very popular in Scotland) was exhibited in 1850 at the Royal Scottish Academy. It certainly shows Pre-Raphaelite influence (Paton was a friend of Millais'), but the painter's determination and fastidiousness in the choice of both his subject-matter and his means of expression enabled him to achieve a refinement which sets him apart from that celebrated English school. With its multitude of tiny figures, purity of line, and enchanted atmosphere, this canvas claims a place in the lineage of strange independent works which runs from Bruegel to Dali.

147 🖾 DANTE GABRIEL ROSSETTI. *The Beloved,* or *The Bride.* Oil on canvas. 1865. The Tate Gallery, London.
Blake, Fuseli, John Martin, Dante Gabriel Rossetti, and Burne-Jones were the first artists since the Florentine Mannerists of the sixteenth century to emphasize "spleen" in the female face. The elegant British version of disordered emotion (which some little touch in the expression of the eyes may be enough to show) is very different from the riot of movement which Géricault and Delacroix delight in. Here, there is no orgy of line but a minute study of detail.

148 🖾 FORD MADOX BROWN. *Foscari in Prison.* Oil on canvas. 1870. William Morris Gallery, Walthamstow.
The ways of perverse emotion are beyond anyone's power to fathom. In order to take advantage of them, Ford Madox Brown, one of the most perversely seductive of the enchanters who came after Pre-Raphaelitism, uses every available weapon: madness, religion, and fine sentiments.

149 🖾 GUSTAVE DORÉ. *The Death of Gérard de Nerval.* Lithograph. n.d.
It was fitting that Gustave Doré who, like Louis Boulanger and Grandville, had affiliations with the Romantic minority which ventured over the threshold of the

supernatural, should depict the death of Gérard de Nerval. Doré anticipated Victor Hugo in giving human semblance to buildings; his medieval castles grin sardonically, like *Landsknechte.* Long before Toorop and Segantini, he distorted his lines and elongated his figures to suggest a certain fantastic atmosphere. It is only a step from some of Doré's work, like his illustrations for the *Contes drolatiques* of Balzac, to the *Femme à 100 Têtes* of Max Ernst.

150 🖾 JAMES HAMILTON. *The Last Days of Pompeii.* Oil on canvas. 1864. The Brooklyn Museum, New York.
Ce moment que tout m'échappe, que d'immenses lézardes se font jour dans le palais du monde.

"This moment when everything slips out of my grasp and immense cracks appear in the palace of the world." (Louis Aragon)
Though the spirit of Symbolism did not find many followers in America, a few painters such as James Hamilton, Ralph Albert Blakelock, and Albert Pinkham Ryder (whose works are reminiscent of the charcoal drawings of Redon and Seurat) were attracted by unusual subject-matter and atmospheres.

151 🖾 MAX KLINGER. *The Judgment of Paris.* Triptych. Mixed media. 1885–87. Kunsthistorisches Museum, Vienna.
Un excès de réalisme ne se trouve plus en ce cas extrême d'autre support que l'intervention de la poésie la plus emblématique.

"In this extreme case, the only support left to excessive realism is to have recourse to poetic accessories of the emblematic type."
(André Breton, *L'Art magique*)
An enormous, complicated work combining painting and sculpture, Klinger's triptych has an odd, disconcerting lyricism, and is upsetting to those who like art to have a slight but definite Mannerist slant. Our generation, loving simplicity and in some case biased in favor of archaism, can scarcely believe that Max Klinger's contemporaries visualized Classical antiquity by the standards set forth in *The Judgment of Paris.*

152 🖾 WILLIAM DEGOUVE DE NUNCQUES. *The Angels of the Night.* Oil on canvas. 1891. Kröller-Müller Museum, Otterlo.
William Degouve de Nuncques was enamored with the tenderest, most refined aspects of experience. But this does not imply that he gave way to emotional flabbiness or facile technique. Even at the height of his Symbolist period, his pictures retained a firmness reminiscent of Seurat. This one closely prefigures the works of the Belgian Surrealists, but is sharply differentiated from them by its angelic atmosphere. Dream has been divested of its disturbing elements, leaving only its immaterial purity.

153 🖾 THOMAS THEODOR HEINE. *The Hammock.* Oil on canvas. 1892. Bayerische Staatsgemäldesammlungen, Munich.

V ⌀ Gustave Moreau. *The Enchanted Forest*. Oil on canvas. C. 1895. Collection
Maurice Rheims, Paris.

Gustave Moreau's work eludes classification. One can say only that he worked
in isolation, resisting Impressionism, the end-result of Realism, and asserting his
will, as Huysmans described it, "to remain outside the centuries, to give no
indication of his origin, country, and period." Gustave Moreau pretends to fall
into historicism but only in order to lead the spectator more thoroughly astray
into "extraordinary palaces, in a confused and grandiose style." Thus he
invents "sumptuous chimerical robes." He was a prodigious colorist, envisaging
color in the same way as Runge, who said "that it should be the supreme art,
which is and must remain mystical."

Il ne faut pas offenser la pudeur des divinités du songe.

"The divinities of dreams are chaste and reticent;
do not seek to violate their reserve."

(Gérard de Nerval)

Of what species, we wonder, is the alarming animal
which is threatening the dreaming reader enclosed in
"the inlaid cabinet of sleep"? In the case of Heine it
would be beside the point to talk in terms of Romanticism, Realism, or Impressionism; he seems rather to
have dealt in deliberately calculated frenzy. Lines like
cephalopods curl round the graceful slender bodies of
his *demi-vierges* who are daughters of Rossetti's goddesses
and sisters to the treacherous mannequins of Beardsley.
K. O. Czeschka, Otto Eckmann, and Peter Behrens
showed enormous skill in conveying phantasms in
pictorial terms, but Thomas Theodor Heine surpassed
them all.

154 ▨ XAVIER MELLERY. *Fall of the Last Leaves of
Autumn.* Mixed media. 1902. Musée des Beaux-Arts,
Brussels.
The dream of flying is a theme which has been much
treated by the poets. A friend of Octave Maus',
Xavier Mellery exhibited several times at the Salon de
la Libre Esthétique in Brussels.

155 ▨ FERNAND KHNOPFF. *I Lock My Door upon Myself.*
Oil on canvas. 1891. Neue Pinakothek, Munich.

J'ai tant rêvé, j'ai tant rêvé, que je ne suis plus d'ici.

"I've dreamed so much, so much, that I don't
belong here any more."   (Léon Paul Fargue)

An Austrian by birth, Khnopff studied under Gustave
Moreau before settling in Belgium. This picture and
its title sufficiently demonstrate the complex personality
of the artist, who was fond of saying that he gave away
the symbolism as a bonus. Certain aspects imbued with
an ambiguous mysticism (Khnopff exhibited at the
Salon de la Rose Croix in Brussels) relate him to the
Pre-Raphaelites; his relish for finely executed detail
puts him in the company of the Flemish medievalists.

156 ▨ CARL STRATHMANN. *Stylized Landscape.* Ink and
watercolor. 1896. Städtische Galerie, Munich.
Under the eyes of Strathmann, a strikingly unusual
landscape painter, leaves and branches and trees took
on a frozen, mosaic quality. Novalis had the same
vision of nature, "a petrified magic wand." Like
Franz von Stuck or Hugo von Habermann, Strathmann belongs to that minority of Jugendstil painters
who liked to combine bizarre detail (see, for instance,
the glove under the bird's foot) with an overblown
eroticism: an example is his *Salomé*, a fat-cheeked
dancing girl saucily facing a serpent, an enormous
sausage with a lubricous stare.

157 ▨ RICHARD RIEMERSCHMID. *Cloud-spectres.* Watercolor. 1892. Städtische Galerie, Munich.

*La matière tend à se volatiser, l'esprit s'emparant de la
sensation pour la projeter à mi-chemin entre le concret et
l'abstrait....*

"Subject and medium become vaporous, the mind
seizing upon sensation and projecting it into a region
halfway between the concrete and the abstract...."

(Marcel Raymond, *De Baudelaire au Surréalisme*)

Riemerschmid was a painter as well as a decorative
designer. In general character, his work is symbolic and
dematerialized, an exact parallel to the phenomenon
observed by Marcel Raymond in the work of Mallarmé
and Moréas.

158 ▨ GIOVANNI SEGANTINI. *Infanticide.* Mixed media.
1894. Kunsthistorisches Museum, Vienna.
Fascinated by nature while still in his 'teens, Segantini
ran away from home to live with shepherds in the high
Alps; after completing his education, he settled there
in the Engadine. This strange artist drew his inspiration
from the Alpine massifs, the last refuge of the divine
and the demoniacal. Despite his impatient, rebellious
temperament, he became an enthusiastic adherent of
Divisionism, insofar as that technique enabled him to
transcribe light as a shower of tiny colored particles.
His love of nature was his undoing; he died of pneu-
monia contracted while painting in the open air on the
Schafberg.

159 ▨ RALPH ALBERT BLAKELOCK. *The Vision of Life.*
Oil on canvas. C. 1895. Charles H. and Mary F. S.
Worcester Collection, The Art Institute of Chicago.
A native New Yorker who lived in Greenwich Village,
Blakelock refused to follow the example of other artists
of his generation and complete his studies in Europe.
A painter of the Far West and the Indians, Blakelock,
like Ryder, bore witness to the existence of an American
Symbolism.

160 ▨ EUGÈNE CARRIÈRE. *Decorative Panel for the Mairie
of the 10ᵉ Arrondissement.* Oil on canvas. C. 1904. Musée
du Petit Palais, Paris.
Not only did Carrière enjoy high regard among the
élite of his day, he also exercised a profound influence
on contemporary sculpture. Rodin, who owned seven
canvases by Carrière, the Italians Leonardo Bistolfi
and Medardo Rosso, and the Russian Prince Paul
Troubetzkoy, all expressed keen admiration for him.
Carrière was one of the few Symbolists to be free of the
fetters of historicism. Disdaining the artifices dear to
Gustave Moreau and Puvis de Chavannes, he was more
successful than Émile Meunier or Steinlen in idealizing
popular or bourgeois themes, from mother-love to the
family group.

161 ▨ ODILON REDON. *Pandora.* Oil on canvas. C. 1910.
Bequest of Alexander Max Bing, The Metropolitan
Museum of Art, New York.

*Une rayonnante figure...du milieu de ces planches
agitées, se levait sereine et calme, une figure de la
Mélancolie, assise, devant le disque d'un soleil, sur des
rochers, dans une pose accablée et morne.*

"A radiant figure... amid this confusion of planks
rose up in calm serenity, a figure of melancholy

seated on rocks before the disc of the sun, in a pose of sadness and defeat."

(J. K. Huysmans, *À Rebours*)

Apart from Moreau, Gauguin, Redon, and Louis Anquetin, there are not many Symbolists whose work exhibits the stigmata of Art Nouveau—hermeticism, depravity, fatalism, or the cult of the dream world. A pupil of Gérôme and Bresdin, a friend of Mallarmé and regarded by the Nabis as their spiritual leader, Redon, according to Huysmans, had the power of transposing "Edgar Poe's hallucinatory mirages and panic effects." He belongs to Art Nouveau partly by virtue of the careful finish and magical aspect of his detail, but primarily because of his individual use of charcoal and black chalk for portraying figures who are "possessed" and almost magical.

162 ⬜ FERDINAND HODLER. *The Chosen One*. Oil on canvas. C. 1903. Karl Ernst Osthaus Museum, Hagen.
"A day will come when man will be asleep and awake at the same time." (Novalis)

The Rosicrucian, Sàr Mérodack Péladan wrote in 1910: "At present M. Hodler is undoubtedly the most authentic of Switzerland's painters; he is better than any of his German colleagues. These two things are obvious, and I fancy they are enough to satisfy both this noble artist himself and the very legitimate desire of his race to achieve their own aesthetic autonomy, which in the person of M. Hodler they have already begun to do." The reproach has been leveled at Hodler, a Bernese Huguenot, sometimes handicapped by the tense, reserved manner in which he expressed his mysticism, of being a "monumentalist" in tendency but not by instinct. It is by means of repeated linear rhythms, "parallelism" as he himself called it, that he succeeds in symbolizing rectilinear objects. His art is certainly cerebral but founded on a remarkable stylization of reality.

163 ⬜ LUDWIG VON HOFMANN. *Nude*. Oil on canvas. n.d. Paffrath Gallery, Düsseldorf.
Quel est ton nom? – Constance. – Où vas-tu? – Je m'en souviens
De toi-même et retourne à toi-même. – Soulève
Ce linceul de ta face et que je sache au moins
Si tu ressembles à la sœur d'un de mes rêves.

(Jean Cassou, *Sonnets composés au Secret*)

The elegant bathers of Ludwig von Hofmann (who frequented the Académie Julian in Paris) make one think of Puvis de Chavannes and Albert Besnard, and also of Hodler, although his style displays a certain hesitancy. In the work shown here, we see something which is also to be found in a number of other painters of the time and which Marcel Raymond has detected in some of the poets: a "deliberate attempt to marry Symbolism and Classicism and to derive from them a supreme art in which thought and poetry are amalgamated in a pure language, radiant with the fire of a lofty lucidity." (*De Baudelaire au Surréalisme*, Paris, 1963.)

164 ⬜ AUBREY BEARDSLEY. *La Dame aux Camélias*. Pen and ink. 1894. The Tate Gallery, London.

Numerous adjectives—perverse, satanic, tyrannical, melancholy, precious, artificial—have been used to describe the motive power of this *monstre charmant* who influenced Klimt, Toorop, Will Bradley, De Feure, MacNair, and the Glasgow School, corrupting an entire generation who were thirsty for experience. In delineating his pallid Eurasians (creatures of yesteryear like those in Cosimo Tura, Mantegna, Crivelli, Burne-Jones, and—even—Utamaro), the febrile and, as it were, diaphanous Aubrey Beardsley (who died of tuberculosis at the age of twenty-six) employed India ink to create strange and carnal works.

165 ⬜ MARCUS BEHMER. *The Stolen Orchid*. Pen and ink. 1903. Collection Emilio Bertonati, Milan.

There was a Beardsley trend in both Berlin and Munich. Behmer, Thomas Theodor Heine, and Emil Preetorius were inspired by the English master, but their work leans too heavily toward the conspiratorial wink and, for want of the necessary spice of Satanism, is somewhat savorless.

166 ⬜ JAN TOOROP. *Souls around the Sphinx*. Black chalk and pencil. 1892–97. Gemeente Museum, The Hague.
Et dans le silence de la nuit, l'admirable dialogue de la Chimère et du Sphinx commença, récité par des voix gutturales, et profondes, puis aiguës, commes surhumaines:
"— Ici, Chimère, arrête-toi."
"— Non; jamais."

"And, in the silence of the night, began the admirable dialogue of the Chimera and the Sphinx, intoned in voices at first guttural, deep, and hoarse, then shrill and almost inhuman:
'Here, Chimera; halt!'
'No; never.'"

(J. K. Huysmans, *À Rebours*)

Toorop loads his compositions with dramatic detail: closed eyelids, hair which clings to bodies like a winding-sheet, emaciated arms and fingers. It is by means of these "elements of cultivated melancholy" (*éléments mélancolisants*), to borrow Huysmans' expression, that Toorop catches and holds the eye of the spectator.

167 ⬜ CHARLES RENNIE MACKINTOSH and MARGARET MACDONALD MACKINTOSH. *The Opera of the Sea*. Oil and collage. 1902. Private Collection, London.

The art of Mackintosh, apparently stemming from the Celtic movement, is largely instinctive, and shows a vigor often lacking in the work of the Dutchmen Toorop and Nieuwenhuis. In 1913, after breaking with his partner Keppie, Mackintosh, who had always shown a strong interest in painting, gave up architecture. In 1920, he settled in Languedoc, where he spent the rest of his life and painted noteworthy watercolors. The work reproduced here, done in collaboration with his wife, is based on a poem by Maeterlinck, and was painted for the Warndorfer Music Room in Vienna.

VI ▨ FRANZ VON STUCK. *Spring*. Oil on canvas. 1896. Eigentümer der Bundesrepublik, Bonn.
After studying at the Munich Academy in 1882, Von Stuck became a member of the Jugendstil movement. An entire generation of enthusiastic supporters of Neo-Romanticism passed through his studio. In this work, the blue, violet, and bistre tones, the enigmatic face with its deliberate echo of Leonardo da Vinci, and the pose illustrate the extreme refinement of the artist.

168 ▨ ADOLFO WILDT. *The King's Dead Child*. Mixed media. C. 1910. Collection Emilio Bertonati, Milan.

> "A union concluded even for death is a marriage, which gives us a companion for the night. Love is sweetest in death; for him who loves, death is a wedding night—the secrecy of gentle mysteries."
>
> (Novalis)

In Italy, Gaetano Previati, Alberto Martini, and Wildt, under the influence of August Endell, Hermann Obrist, Beardsley, and Edvard Munch, composed works which were already on the brink of Surrealism.

169 ▨ GEORGES DE FEURE. *Fairy Tale*. Ink and water-color. 1898. Private Collection, Munich.

> *Le printemps, le soleil, les bêtes en chaleur,*
> *Sont une chimérique et monstrueuse fleur;*
> *À travers son sommeil, ce monde effaré souffre;*
> *Avril n'est que le rêve érotique du gouffre,*
> *Une pollution nocturne de ruisseaux,*
> *De rameaux, de parfums, d'aube et de chants d'oiseaux.*

> "Spring, the sun, and beasts in heat,
> Are a chimerical and monstrous flower;
> In its sleep, this panic-stricken world is suffering;

April is only the erotic dream of the abyss,
A nocturnal emission of brooks,
Branches, scents, dawn, and birdsong."

(Victor Hugo)

Georges de Feure was one of the few French painters who succeeded in capturing the spirit of Beardsley. His world is an imaginary Île de France sown with extravagantly exotic plants, strange orchids among which are revealed disturbing faces.

170 ▨ CARLOS SCHWABE. *Death and the Gravedigger*. Oil on canvas. C. 1904. Collection Carlos Schwabe, Paris.

"I could not love except where Death
Was mingling his with Beauty's breath."

(Edgar Allan Poe)

Carlos Schwabe, who illustrated Haraucourt and Baudelaire, found his inspiration in pathos. The Neoplatonism which fascinated the Germans and Florentines in the sixteenth century reappears in the work of the Symbolists. This painting also contains those cobwebby shrouds so dear to Toorop and Segantini. In this work, the Angel of Death is summoning an aged gravedigger.

171 ▨ JEAN DELVILLE. *Souls in Love*. Mixed media. C. 1902. Collection Jean DeLuille, Brussels.

"...but presently a gigantic sea happened to take us right under the counter, and bore us with it as it rose—up—up—as if into the sky.... And then we came down with a sweep, a slide, and a plunge...."

(Edgar Allan Poe, *Descent into the Maelstrom*)

The works of this Belgian Symbolist, with their eddying spirals à la Behrens, express a *morbidezza* which also hovers round the works of Segantini and some of the Italian Symbolists.

172 ▨ LÉON FRÉDÉRIC. *Nature*. Oil on canvas. 1902. Collection Baron Frédéric, Bruges.

Du temps que la nature en sa verve puissante
Concevait chaque jour des enfants monstrueux.

"At the time when nature, in her powerful creative energy,
Was conceiving monstrous children every day."

(Charles Baudelaire, *Les Fleurs du Mal*)

Octave Maus said that Frédéric worked on the borderline between idealized expression and the human document. He belongs to the Populist movement. Beneath the proliferation of human figures—children and women with faces inspired by Mabuse or Franz Floris—we can perceive the Surrealist vision.

173 ▨ MAURICE DENIS. *Madame Ranson and her Cat*. Oil on canvas. 1892. Collection Dominique Denis, Saint-Germain-en-Laye.

An exponent of the doctrines of the Nabis, Maurice Denis states his thoughts on the epitome of what a picture ought to be: "A plane surface covered with colors assembled in a certain order." His art is related to that of Gauguin, Émile Bernard, Ranson, and

Sérusier, and in his early work gracefulness predominates at the expense of three-dimensionality. Subsequently, he combined religious feeling with a certain degree of Hellenism; the result was a slightly monotonous Symbolism with a Christian slant.

174 ▨ LEO PUTZ. *Woman in a Glass*. Oil on canvas. 1897. Städtische Galerie, Munich.

Concerning wine, Baudelaire wrote that he would not be astonished if, charmed by a pantheistic idea, a few reasonable minds endowed it with a kind of personality. Putz, a Tyrolean, is an anecdotal painter of the strange side of experience. His subjects are disturbing but tempered with humor, and seem to bear some mysterious kind of message.

175 ▨ GUSTAV KLIMT. *Portrait of Frau Adele Bloch-Bauer*. Oil on canvas. 1907. Österreichische Galerie des XIX und XX Jahrhunderts, Vienna.

Klimt, the better to expose and analyze the souls of his ladies of the bourgeoisie, surrounds their faces with a labyrinthine linear interplay. Here, arabesques are contrasted with richly polychromed rectangular areas. These jewel-studded trappings recall the cries of protest uttered by the Parisian *couturiers* when Sarah Bernhardt brought back some dresses from Vienna: "Curses on the head of this man Klimt, who adorns our female bicyclists in Byzantine, Merovingian, or Carolingian accoutrements!"

176 ▨ GUSTAV KLIMT. *Salomé*. Oil on canvas. 1909. Museo Internazionale d'Arte Moderna, Venice.

By what *Angst* is Salome tormented? Has this neurotic beauty suddenly been deprived of her usual drugs, or has she at last resolved to behead her "analyst"? By way of entertainment, imagine Freud's *Introduction to Psychoanalysis* with illustrations by Klimt (these two citizens of Vienna were born in the same year).

177 ▨ FELICE CASORATI. *Per se e per suo cielo concepe e figlia*. Gouache panel. 1907. Galleria Narciso, Turin.

Ferme les yeux
Tout est comblé.

"Close your eyes,
Everything is filled up."

(Paul Éluard)

The influence of Klimt was pervasive, as can be seen in this picture by Casorati. Even today, the Austrian painter Hundertwasser is a Klimt follower.

178 ▨ AUGUSTO GIACOMETTI. *Night*. Panel. 1903. Kunsthaus, Zurich.

Le moi, c'est la spirale vertigineuse,
Y pénétrer trop avant effare le songeur.

"The self is a giddy whirlpool,
To penetrate too far into it terrifies the dreamer."

(Victor Hugo)

In Switzerland, a country not greatly amenable to Symbolist influence, Giacometti remains a solitary

VII ⊠ GUSTAV KLIMT. *The Kiss*. Oil on canvas. 1911. Österreichische Galerie des XIX und XX Jahrhunderts, Vienna.

Klimt's wonderful combinations of violent color harmonies relate him to the Moghul miniaturists. Both he and Redon display a passion for "super-decoration"; the difference is that Klimt was the first artist who saw the world as if through a kaleidoscope, whereas Redon seems to have been afflicted by a beneficial myopia. Klimt's influence, as important at the time as that of Moreau or Beardsley, is seen in the works of Egon Schiele, Richard Gerstl, and Oskar Kokoschka in Austria; Melchior Lechter in Hungary; Khnopff in Belgium; L. Bonozza in Italy; and Augusto Giacometti, and possibly Hodler, in Switzerland.

pioneer. *Night*, highly finished and somewhat precious, may be regarded as providing a bridge between Klimt and Segantini.

179 ⊠ OLAF GULBRANSSON. *Portrait of Gemma Bierbaum*. Drawing. 1904. Städtische Galerie, Munich.
The Norwegian draftsman and painter Gulbransson, like Thomas Theodor Heine, worked on the Munich comic periodical *Simplizissimus*. A disciple of the Japanese style, and a caricaturist of genius, he eliminates secondary material and concentrates on the most telling features—eyes, mouth, and hands (as in his portrait of Duse); he tears apart the wrappings of his models to reveal the essentials.

180 ⊠ EDVARD MUNCH. *Madonna*. Lithograph. 1895. Munch-Museet, Oslo.
The Norwegian, Munch, was the first to depict the incommunicable: man's perpetual isolation amidst an equally impenetrable nature. There is no need to be a psychoanalyst to understand this painter. The mother, intoxicated with her own anxiety, is already separated from her child (the foetus has its eyes closed). To convey her isolation more effectively, Munch surrounded the compositions with straggling spermatozoa-like forms. The painting of this Symbolist, who was also the greatest of the Expressionists, leaves no room for anecdote. Munch's life, a succession of catastrophes (he lost his mother and two of his sisters at an early

age), supplied ample nourishment for his bestiary of *Angst*.

181 ⌘ FÉLICIEN ROPS. *The Secret Side of a Game of Whist*. Drawing. C. 1898. Musée du Luxembourg, Paris.

"She was a young person, as near to nakedness as the indecency of current fashion permitted: her eyes were heavily lined with kohl and her mouth bled with lipstick. Her spectral make-up transformed her into a vampire by Rops."

(Jean Lorrain, *Maison pour Dames*)

182 ⌘ LUCIEN LEVY-DHURMER. *Portrait of Georges Rodenbach*. Oil on canvas. C. 1896. Musée d'Art Moderne, Paris.

Gaston Bachelard contends that by writing *Bruges la morte*, the poet Rodenbach attempted the "Ophelianization" of an entire city. Levy-Dhurmer, who was obsessed by the work of Leonardo da Vinci, would seem to have interpreted Rodenbach's words admirably: "In this twilit autumnal solitude, with the wind whirling the last leaves away, he felt more strongly than ever the desire to finish his life; he was impatient for the tomb. It was as if a dead woman were stretching out over his soul from the towers; as if the old walls were offering him their counsel; as if a whispering voice were rising from the water (and the water came up to meet him, as Shakespeare's gravediggers said it came to meet Ophelia)." Gustave Soulier wrote of Levy-Dhurmer in 1899: "The danger for this talent enamored of an expressive, psychic art is that without continual vigilance and self-restraint it may become over-refined and irritating."

183 ⌘ EDOARDO GIOJA. *Summer*. Oil on canvas. C. 1895. Private Collection, Italy.

Among the Italians, English, and French of the period there was a tendency to paint *à la* Leonardo; this tendency is noticeable today in the works of certain painters who are on the fringe of Surrealism.

184 ⌘ UMBERTO BOCCIONI. *The Lovers on the Lake*. Etching. 1908. Collection Emilio Bertonati, Milan.

"But when the Night had thrown her pall
Upon that spot, as upon all,
And the mystic wind went by
Murmuring in melody—
Then—ah then I would awake
To the terror of the lone lake."

(Edgar Allan Poe, *The Lake: To—*)

The influence of Bresdin can be seen in Boccioni. Before Marinetti's Futurist Manifesto claimed his allegiance, Boccioni, like several other Italian artists, hesitated between Neo-Impressionism and the newer European tendencies.

185 ⌘ VICTOR VASNETSOV. *Christ on the Cross*. Oil on canvas. C. 1890-95. (Whereabouts unknown.)

This canvas, a "symbolic icon" which is of particular interest for a Mannerism (the pose of the holy women) quite unusual in Russian art, was commissioned from the painter by the manager of a government factory in Vladimir for the workers' chapel.

186 ⌘ NICOLAS ROERICH. *The House of God* (possibly a sketch for a stage-set for Rimsky-Korsakov's opera *The Invisible City of Kitezh*). Gouache. C. 1909. (Whereabouts unknown.)

The painter Nicolas Roerich was a latecomer to what was to be known as the *Mir Iskustva* group. A passionate delver into archaeology and folklore, he took part with Malyutin in Princess Tenisheva's artistic undertakings at Talashkino, and in 1898 persuaded her to finance Diaghilev's periodical, *Mir Iskustva*. From then until 1904, this remarkable magazine was to open the mildewed doors of Slav folklore to the surprising world of Western Art Nouveau. Roerich managed to give his landscapes a Slavonic strangeness which is also found in Gallén-Kallela—tender green of cool pine forests; blue glints of streams edged with hoar-frost.

187 ⌘ WASSILY KANDINSKY. *Night*. Tempera on canvas. 1906. Städtische Galerie, Munich.

From 1896 to 1904, Kandinsky lived in Munich. Artistically speaking (as with Mucha, Mikhail Vrubel, Sergei Malyutin, Frank Kupka, and Pougny), his adolescence was torn between the pull of home and the attractions of the West. His "daughters of the night" are already Expressionistic, yet still carry the imprint of Old Russia.

188 ⌘ IVAN BILIBIN. *The Bogatyr Volga Vselavitch Metamorphosed into a Pike*. Ink and watercolor drawing. 1903. (Whereabouts unknown.)

Bilibin, like certain German artists such as Carl Strathmann, created a simple, powerful universe alive with oddity and humor. The spirit of Jugendstil and Art Nouveau was revealed to the *Mir Iskustva* group by a French diplomat, Charles Birlé, who, as early as 1892, exhibited in Russia works by Gauguin, Seurat, Van Gogh, Thomas Theodor Heine, and Steinlen.

189 ⌘ LÉON BAKST. *Nymph* (costume design for the ballet *Écho et Narcisse*). Watercolor. C. 1915. Musée des Beaux-Arts, Strasbourg.

The reaction against bourgeois realism was initiated in 1880 by the "Nevsky Pickwickians." This group, led by Alexandre Benois, included Dimitri Filosofov and the Symbolist writer Dmitri Merezhkovsky. In 1890 it was joined by Diaghilev, Valentin Serov, and Konstantin Korovine (who has been called the Russian Henri Rivière), who banded together and later issued the periodical *Mir Iskustva* ("The World of Art"). This splinter group, which also included Alexander Golovin and Bakst, aimed at regenerating the art of the theater. Until then, throughout the West, décor and costume were the work of designers after the manner of Paul Delaroche—imitation ferns, trellises—and elaborate, gaudy costumes were *à la* Ponson du Terrail. Diaghilev, working with Bakst, who was nicknamed the Delacroix of costume, revolutionized not only décor but also choreography throughout the world. The first performance by the Ballets Russes in Paris took place at the Théâtre du Châtelet on May 18, 1909.

190 ▨ MAURICE DE VLAMINCK. *Landscape*. Oil on canvas. 1900. Private Collection, Paris.
Even in the earliest canvases, Vlaminck's work is Expressionist. The composition shown here, with its rapidly retreating lines and general tumult and torment, charges the landscape with profound dramatic intensity. Yet the painter is still searching for his own style. The agitated brush strokes and a linear preoccupation recall the works of Segantini and the Italians.

191 ▨ CUNO AMIET. *Winter Landscape*. Oil on canvas. 1902. (Whereabouts unknown.)
This highly talented Swiss painter would have attained a personal style had he not assimilated all too well the paintings of his fellow pupils at the Munich Academy and the Académie Julian in Paris. His love of nature and a tendency to prefer color to contour make him akin also to Gallén-Kallela.

192 ▨ AKSELI GALLÉN-KALLELA. *Winter Landscape*. Oil on canvas. 1902. Ateneum Art Museum, Helsinki.
Nuit blanche de glaçons et de neige cruelle...
"White, sleepless night of icicles and cruel snow..."
(Mallarmé)
A pupil of Bouguereau, Gallén-Kallela is one of the most interesting, complex figures in Art Nouveau. His works first appeared in Paris at the Universal Exhibition of 1900: he was responsible for the frescoes in the Finnish pavilion. A naturalist and Symbolist, and influenced by Japanese art *via* the Nabis, Gallén-Kallela depicts a nature frozen and icy, apparently empty landscapes which seem to be waiting with a barely restrained tremor of impatience for the first moment of springtime and liberation.

193 ▨ CARL LARSSON. *Söndagsvila*. Oil on canvas. 1890. National Museum, Stockholm.
Carl Larsson was a member of a group of Swedish artists who called themselves the *Parisersvenskarna*, and who worked in various Parisian *ateliers* between 1875

and 1890. A painter and designer, Larsson takes enormous care in painting the obvious details—table, tools, and vases of flowers—as if to convince the viewer that he is a specialist in still life. But in reality the spectator is interested only in the two crossed hands, the enigmatic portrait of a young woman and, above all, the tiny key hanging to the left of the window, doubtless the key to the mysterious cupboard. We find here the same dominant silence and disquiet as in the pictures painted today by Balthus.

194 ▨ ALEXANDRE BENOIS. *Classical Landscape*. Watercolor. 1903. Collection Emilio Bertonati, Milan.
Benois, whose French ancestors settled in Russia during the reign of Peter the Great, was one of the founders of *Mir Iskustva*. Painter, art historian, critic, and stage designer, his ambition was to create a Russian art sensitized, rather than influenced, by Western painting and certain tendencies derived from Japanese art.

195 ▨ HANS SCHMITHALS. *Composition in Blue*. Oil on canvas. C. 1910. Städtische Galerie, Munich.
"Mythology," said Gaston Bachelard, "is the primitive view of meteorology." Anguish fills the spectator confronted by these abstract vortices, tragic spirals which have remained captured in glacial ice for the last few millennia.

196 ▨ FRANZ MATOUSEK. *Composition*. Oil on canvas. 1907. (Whereabouts unknown.)
As early as 1903, the Czech painter Matousek was producing strange configurations which may have been inspired by Klimt but are also prophetic of Klee.

197 ▨ FRANK KUPKA. *Linear Fantasy*. India ink. C. 1902. Collection Karl Flinker, Paris.
Prague at the beginning of the century was a remarkable center of artistic activity. At the beginning of his career the paintings of Kupka, like those of Kandinsky, were impregnated with Slav folklore. These were soon followed by arabesques intersecting with straight lines, rather similar to the early work of Kandinsky, Endell, and C. O. Czeschka. Kupka was the first to tread the path leading from Art Nouveau to abstraction.

THE STYLE NOUILLE
(Pseudo-Symbolism, Historicism, Bourgeois Realism)

198 ▨ WILLIAM LINDSAY WINDUS. *Too Late*. Oil on canvas. 1859. The Tate Gallery, London.
In this picture with social overtones, illustrating the

Des femmes folles de leurs corps, en faille bardoculées.
"Women with crazed bodies, with the rumps of jennets, dressed in faille."
(Jean Moréas, *Chronique du Symbolisme*)

theme that "a girl can't take risks," there is a residue of Pre-Raphaelite romanticism.

199 ☒ ERNST BIELER. *Apple Picking*. Oil on canvas. C. 1900. (Whereabouts unknown.)

Dix-sept ans! Tu seras heureuse.
Oh! les grands prés...

"Seventeen years old! You'll be happy.
Oh, the great meadows..."

(Rimbaud, *Ce qui retient Nina*)

In Switzerland about 1900, there were stirrings of a Pre-Raphaelite and Sezession tendency. Results were not always convincing, but the experiment did allow Bieler, Cuno Amiet, and Welto to express their sincere love of nature.

200 ☒ WALTER CRANE. *The Rolls of Fate*. Oil on canvas. 1882. Collection Emilio Bertonati, Milan.

This picture points to the comic-opera side of some historicist paintings at the end of the nineteenth century; the traditional myths have lost their intrinsic power. Another characteristic to be noted is that the masculine face registers emotional disorder less readily than the feminine.

201 ☒ ANSELME FEUERBACH. *Portrait of Bianca Capello*. Oil on canvas. 1868. Kunsthalle, Hamburg.

In Germany about 1820, a Raphaelite and Romantic trend emerged, led by Johann Friedrich Overbeck, the "Nazarene" group, and Maria Albertie, Novalis' friend. These artists were the Teutonic counterparts of the Pre-Raphaelites, but there are profound differences between their Romantic over-sensitivity and British emotional deviation. This particular vein of Romanticism runs through the nineteenth century, imbued with conventional paganism in the work of Hans von Marées, and with lyricism, of a very "Burgtheater" variety, in that of Feuerbach.

202 ☒ SIR LAWRENCE ALMA-TADEMA. *An Apodyterium*. Oil on canvas. C. 1890. Collection Charles Jerdein, London.

Worldly, fashionable historicism was the genre in which Alma-Tadema excelled. Only the setting has been retained from Pre-Raphaelitism, but its worldly beauties have been replaced by silly young ladies belonging to the "best" of society in the Roman Empire.

203 ☒ CLÉMENTINE HÉLÈNE DUFAU. *Composition in Antique Style*. Oil on canvas. C. 1900. French Embassy, Vienna.

Et l'Art vide aujourd'hui comme un sommeil sans rêve
Ressemble à ces dieux morts qui roulent sous nos pas.

"And art, which is as empty today as a dreamless sleep,
Resembles those gods over whose dead bodies our footsteps pass."

(Nicolas Beauduin, *Glas sur le siècle*)

In a few French academic painters (Mlle. Dufau and Besnard, for example), there can be perceived the intention of wedding Symbolism to Classicism in an attempt to achieve a supreme art. There was a similar episode in literature: opposition between the Symbolist poets and the "Méditerranéens."

204 ☒ FRED and PICKFORD MARIOTT. *Enchantment*. Gesso panel with metallic leaf and tempera. C. 1900. (Whereabouts unknown.)

Où tout n'est qu'or, acier, lumière et diamants,
Resplendit à jamais, comme un astre inutile,
La froide majesté de la femme stérile.

"Where there is nothing but gold, steel, light, and diamonds,
That shines forever, like a useless star:
The cold majesty of the barren woman."

(Charles Baudelaire, *Les Fleurs du Mal*)

The cult of the dream world has toppled into melodrama. Fred and Pickford Mariott, the better to render the pseudo-Wagnerian Byzantinism dear to Sarah Bernhardt, used gesso, a mixture of glue and plaster, which enabled them to model their work in relief. Some contemporary artists have adopted the same technique.

205 ☒ FRANCIS INNOCENT. *Fable*. Oil on canvas. C. 1903, (Whereabouts unknown.)

Je suis la Sphynge, je suis l'Isis,
l'hiératique, l'immarcescible.

"I am the Sphinx, I am Isis—
the hieratic and unfading."

(Willy)

206 ☒ JOSEPH EDWARD SOUTHALL. *Herod's Daughter*. Oil on canvas. C. 1895. (Whereabouts unknown.)

In Great Britain, Southall and Robert Anning Bell, by dressing figures with elegant, emotionless faces in heavy costumes, contributed to the emergence of the Pre-Raphaelite Mannerism which enjoyed much success in Europe between 1895 and 1914.

207 ☒ FREDERICK LEIGHTON. *Psyche's Bath*. Oil on canvas. C. 1890. The Tate Gallery, London.

Historicism was prone to a certain coy naughtiness; in this picture we reach the very verge of bourgeois Art Nouveau.

208 ☒ JOHN REINHARD WEGUILIN. *The Mermaid of Zennon*. Watercolor. 1904. (Whereabouts unknown.)

Dans la bête qui s'agenouille
J'ai surpris un regard humain:
Je puis être changé demain
En hibou, lézard ou grenouille.

"In the kneeling beast
I have perceived a human gaze:
Tomorrow I may be changed
Into an owl, a lizard, or a frog."

(André Mary, *Petit Berger de Calydon*)

The middle classes (like everybody) were avid for new, strange experiences. Many painters in France were ready to satisfy customers who wanted demonology, of a safe kind, suitable for any woman who attended Mass

regularly. Even so, supply barely kept pace with demand. One of the masterpieces of this genre was a
certain picture by Gaston Latouche entitled *L'Accident*.
A six-cylinder, one-hundred-horsepower De Dion
Bouton automobile, 1901 model, stands at the roadside;
its driver, an elegant, pretty young woman, is sitting
on the curb with her legs apart, applying first aid to the
arm of a bearded faun who has been knocked down by
her car, while a little monkey in the uniform of a
hospital orderly holds out a bandage. In the paintings
of Debat Ponsan, Annie-A. Beebe, Falero, Penot,
Wagrez, and Weizy, fatuity is tempered with satire and
bawdiness.

209 🖉 ANTON ROMAKO. *Admiral Tegetthoff during the
Battle of Lissa*. Oil on canvas. C. 1880. Österreichische
Galerie, Vienna.

> *Les jours de rage militaire*
> *Quand vibre et siffle et passe et se répand partout*
> *L'obus précis, ardent, volant et fou,*
> *Dites les gens, les pauvres gens entendez-vous?*

> "In the days when Mars is raging,
> When vibrating, whistling, all-pervading,
> The shell—accurate, ardent, flying, mad;
> Tell me, people, you the poor: do you hear?"
>   (Emile Verhaeren, *L'âme paysanne*)

The Austrian painter, Romako, seems to participate in
this crucial battle scene. The ship is ramming her
enemy: the event takes place directly in front of the
observer, and one can almost feel the impact of the
collision.

210 🖉 ARNOLD BÖCKLIN. *The Play of the Waves*. Oil on
canvas. 1885. Neue Pinakothek, Munich.
Böcklin, a Germanicized Swiss from Basel, was a
Romantic Expressionist, full of frightening humor but
lacking true dream-world inspiration. He is at his best
in the company of naïve monsters—centaurs locked in
bloody battle, or going off to be shod by the smith. The
imaginative tricks of this singular but very fine painter
succeeded in converting the German school to fantasy.
He had many pupils, among whom was the caricaturist
Hans Sandreuter.

211 🖉 NORMAN WILKINSON. *Richard II Holding the Red
Rose of Lancaster*. Oil on canvas. C. 1895. (Whereabouts
unknown.)
Symbolist painters were not generally interested in
depicting men, but exceptions were made for certain
"initiates"—drug addicts, homosexuals, and those possessed....

212 🖉 GUSTAV ADOLF MOSSA. *The Engulfed City*. Oil on
canvas. 1906. Musée Chéret, Nice.
As early as the beginning of this century, the first
stirrings of Surrealism can be detected in works of
Mossa, Maurice Feuillet, Reginald Francton, and
Wilfred Gabriel de Glehn (whose astonishing *Ulysses
and the Sirens* was first exhibited at the New Gallery,
Edinburgh, in 1900).

213 🖉 GEORGES ALFRED BOTTINI. *Oriental Scene*.
Gouache. 1898. Musée d'Art Moderne, Paris.

> "Harlots with padded bodices sip icy liqueurs
>   through straws."
>   (Jean Moréas and Paul Adam, *Demoiselles Goubert*)

No one could compete with Bottini in his use of
gouache, and in his hybrid style (Persian and Japanese)
in presenting scenes of intimate life, in which young
women of putative virtue seem to be drowning their
melancholia in alcohol or drugs.

214 🖉 ANTON VAN WELLIE. *Solo*. Oil on canvas. 1896–
99. Private Collection, Paris.
It must have been from the troubled waters of one of
those mirror-like ponds located on the grounds of private sanatoriums for rich drug addicts seeking with-
drawal, that Van Wellie fished out this strange soloist.
He would seem to be the twin brother of the Duc Jean
des Esseintes: "a slim, frail young man of thirty,
anemic, nervous and hollow-cheeked, with cold steely
blue eyes, a straight nose with flaring nostrils, and dry
slender hands." (J. K. Huysmans, *À Rebours*.) Touches
borrowed from Gustave Moreau will be noticed in the
landscape background and the sunset radiance of the
light.

215 🖉 ETTORE TITO. *The Lagoon*. Oil on canvas. 1892.
Museo Internazionale d'Arte Moderna, Venice.

> *Des femmes de Venise, au lever du soleil,*
> *Répandent dans Saint-Marc leur hésitante extase.*

> "At sunrise, women of Venice
> Let their hesitant ecstasy take wing in the
>   Cathedral."
>   (Anna de Noailles, *La Messe de l'Aurore à Venise*)

In this work we see how *morbidezza* has degenerated into
affectation and vacuity.

216 🖉 JOHN SINGER SARGENT. *Study for a portrait of
Madame X* (Mme. Pierre Gautreau). Oil on canvas.
1884. The Tate Gallery, London.
Sargent, as a society painter, seeks to show off to the
best advantage the profile of the lady who has commissioned the portrait.

217 🖉 JAMES MCNEILL WHISTLER. *Portrait of Théodore
Duret: Arrangement in Flesh Color and Black*. Oil on
canvas. 1883. The Metropolitan Museum of Art, New
York (The Wolfe Fund).

> "In the unit which is called a nation, professions
>   and castes introduce variety not only in gesture
>   and manners but also in the very form of the face."
>   (Charles Baudelaire, *L'Art romantique*)

An unusual portrait of a man. Théodore Duret, with
soft features and silky beard, holds a woman's fan in
his hand, and her cloak hangs over his arm. The portrait is signed with Whistler's quasi-Japanese decorative
butterfly.

218 🖉 CHILDE HASSAM. *Rainy Day, Boston*. Oil on
canvas. 1885. The Toledo Museum of Art, Toledo, Ohio.

Childe Hassam, a painter of daily life, fulfills in the United States the same function as Béraud in France. He excels in rendering atmosphere, light, and characteristic attitudes. Yet despite concentrating on "the transitory, the fugitive, the contingent," he gives his pictures the accent of unchanging truth. He has not recorded merely the outward appearance of a certain street in Boston with the contours of its buildings diluted in the teeming rain, and people with bent heads hurrying along over the shining pavements; he has succeeded in conveying the chill, penetrating monotony of rain anywhere.

219 ▨ FREDERICK KARL FRIESEKE. *Society Ladies on the Beach.* Oil on canvas. C. 1900. (Whereabouts unknown.) The United States, as a young country, felt the need to have its own "Society" with a capital S, like that in the Old World. As painters of high society, Europe could boast of Boldini, Helleu, and La Gandara; in the United States, Frieseke, who decorated the Shelbourne Hotel and other public buildings in New York, and Austin Abbey, who was one of the artists who provided the murals for the Boston Public Library, were among those who strove to emulate Vuillard, Maurice Denis, and Puvis de Chavannes.

VIII ▨ LOUIS ANQUETIN. *Gil Reading.* Pastel. 1890. The Tate Gallery, London.
At Pont-Aven, little scope was allowed to passion. Here, the face itself has become decoration, part of a cloisonné design.

220 ✎ CECILIA BEAUX. *After the Meeting*. Oil on canvas. 1914. The Toledo Museum of Art, Toledo, Ohio.
Some American painters, shackled not by the strength of tradition but by its absence, remained faithful to Art Nouveau when European painters had passed on to other things. An example is Cecilia Beaux, who in 1914 was still working in a "Japanese" style. The birth of avant-garde movements in the United States is a comparatively recent phenomenon.

221 ✎ JEAN BÉRAUD. *At the Café*. Oil on canvas. 1889. Musée Carnavalet, Paris.
Béraud's range of vision was purely objective. In this canvas he re-creates the very Parisian atmosphere of the Symbolist cafés, the dejected, elegant manners of familiar members of a *cercle*, and the exact pose of a relaxed errand-girl. More profound observation he left to Degas and Forain.

222 ✎ JULES CHÉRET. *Dancer with a Tambourine*. Oil on canvas. 1901. Musée Chéret, Nice.
> "Emerging from a nether world, proud to be appearing in the blazing artificial sunlight of a stage, girls of the little theaters—thin, frail, still adolescent—use their sickly virginal bodies to shake and waggle absurd travesties which belong to no period and which they simply adore."
> (Charles Baudelaire, "Les Femmes et les Filles,"
>   in *L'Art romantique*)

Chéret was a better poster artist than painter; he was quick-witted and abreast with the eye of the time, but he lacked personality. The "steam-driven Watteau" (*le Watteau à vapeur*), was Forain's description of him. He successfully assimilated the eighteenth-century masters and imposed a Chéret style which is commonly regarded as being "very 1900."

223 ✎ ALPHONSE MUCHA. *Sketch for a Poster*. Gouache. 1900. Collection Mucha, Prague.
> "I have said that every period had its own gait, glance, and gesture."
> (Charles Baudelaire, *L'Art romantique*)

On the day before the opening of his private exhibition in February, 1897, Mucha, the dancing dervish of the graphic line, received the following note from Sarah Bernhardt:
> "My very dear Mucha,
> You have asked me to present you to the Parisian public. Well, dear friend, be advised by me: exhibit your works, they will speak for you; I know my dear Parisian public. Your delicate draftsmanship, the originality of your compositions, the admirable coloring of your posters and pictures, will be found enchanting, and I predict that your exhibition will make you famous. Both my hands in yours, dear Mucha,
>   Sarah Bernhardt"

224 ✎ KEES VAN DONGEN. *Woman in her Corset*. Oil on canvas. 1904. Private Collection, Paris.

Before he emerged as a leader of Fauvism, Van Dongen was an enthusiastic advocate of a sensual type of Expressionism.

225 ✎ SVAR CEROSENIUS. *Varafton*. Oil on canvas. 1906. Private Collection, Sweden.
> *C'est l'heure où les maris, le travail achevé,*
> *Reviennent et la paix du soir emplit les âmes.*
>
> "This is the hour when work is over and husbands come home, and evening peace fills every soul."
> (André Dumas, *Le village*)

This is an example of that fierce humor, "the doglike appearance of these men reflected from eight angles," touches of which appear in France in the work of Albert Guillaume, but which flourished especially beyond the Rhine in Thomas Theodor Heine, who excelled in imitating the failings of "Mitteleuropa" society.

226 ✎ JOHN SLOAN. *Haymarket*. Oil on canvas. 1902. The Brooklyn Museum, New York.
> "At the entrance to a café, lounging against the door whose plate glass is lit from within and without, stands one of those brainless creatures whose elegance has been fashioned by his tailor and whose head by his barber."
> (Charles Baudelaire, "Les Femmes et les Filles,"
>   in *L'Art romantique*)

In the United States as in Europe, a style of "social" painting emerged on the borderline between Impressionism and Expressionism.

227 ✎ WILLIAM J. GLACKENS. *Chez Mauquin*. Oil on canvas. 1905. Friends of American Art Committee, The Art Institute of Chicago.
At the close of the nineteenth century the same duality can be found in the United States as in Europe: two tendencies, one Symbolistic (Albert Pinkham Ryder, Ralph Blakelock), the other bourgeois, representational and Post-Impressionistic (Childe Hassam, Cecilia Beaux, and Glackens).

228 ✎ PAUL HELLEU. *Au Salon*. Etching. C. 1900. Private Collection, Paris.
The figure is full of melancholy—the melancholy which springs from emptiness. This is one of the elegant "déhanchées" of Helleu making the rounds of the fashionable art exhibits.

229 ✎ GIOVANNI BOLDINI. *Portrait of Robert de Montesquiou*. Oil on canvas. 1892. Musée d'Art Moderne, Paris.
> "...even when he was motionless, that colouring, more marked in him than in any other of the Guermantes, like the sunshine of a golden day solidified, gave him, as it were, such a strange plumage, transformed him into such a unique and priceless specimen that one would have liked to own it for an ornithological collection; but when this flash of light transmuted into a bird also put itself in motion, in action, when, for example, I

saw Robert de Saint-Loup come into a gathering where I was, he had such a way of throwing back his head, gaily and proudly crested with its tuft of golden hair a bit thinned out, and such proud and coquettish suppleness in the movements of his neck—like no other human being—that, seeing the curiosity and admiration, partly social and partly zoological, which he aroused, you wondered whether you were in the Faubourg Saint-Germain or at the Zoological Garden, and whether you were watching some noble lord walk across the salon or some wonderful bird walk about in its cage.''

(Marcel Proust, *The Past Recaptured*— trans. Frederick. A. Blossom)

Boldini is one of that flock of artists generally regarded as the standard-bearers of a typically 1900 style. In reality, he was the painter belonging to the category of mediocre people who played a minor role in the movement, whose idol was their own insolence, whose bard was Robert de Montesquiou. A curious fact is that

the adult male (perhaps because he is usually more impassive than women) plays hardly any part in the visual symbolism of Art Nouveau.

230 ▨ RAOUL DU GARDIER. *On the Beach*. Oil on canvas. C. 1900. Private Collection, Paris.

"Memories, so frail, wan, and melancholy, gliding into the blue tinge of the distance."

(Gustave Kahn, *Palais Nomades*)

Jacques-Émile Blanche, Du Gardier, and James Tissot are the painters of elegant tea parties, pretty dresses, accessories and manners, conversation nicely adjusted to go with the hat, a delicate feeling for different materials and the whole *mise en scène* of what will be worn this season, from the style of parasol to the style of soul. This was the limit of their talent; it was for others to illustrate the depths of life, life painful and exalted, with its unsatisfied cynicism, its thwarted impulses toward better things, its vanities and its hatreds.

GAUGUIN, SEURAT
(Pointillists, Populists, Nabis, Art Nouveau)

231 ▨ PAUL GAUGUIN. *"Bonjour M. Gauguin."* Oil on canvas. 1889. National Museum, Prague.

About 1888, Gauguin and Émile Bernard, full of admiration for the technical methods of the Japanese— simplified forms, suggested rather than stated, and large flat areas of color—decided to abandon Impressionism. It was due to Gauguin and especially to what he learned from the technique of the woodcut, a lesson absorbed from him by Munch, that Symbolist art was able to unite its lot with that of Expressionism.

232 ▨ HENRY VAN DE VELDE. *In the Garden*. Oil on canvas. 1892. Neue Pinakothek, Munich.

Van de Velde's pictorial technique alternated between Neo-Impressionism and rationalism. Like Toorop and Van Gogh (who sent him sketches from time to time from Saint-Rémy), Van de Velde drew streaming lines which, in his own expression, are "like organ tones." But it was Gauguin who gave the final turn to the young painter's increasingly abstract tendencies. Van de Velde was barely twenty-seven when he decided to give up painting and devote himself to architecture and decoration.

233 ▨ GEORGES SEURAT. *Study for La Grande Jatte*. Oil on canvas. 1884. The Metropolitan Museum of Art, New York.

The date of this painting explains the importance of Seurat in relation to the art movements of the end of the century. He was the first to use "mechanical" techniques as a reaction against the reigning bourgeois devotion to sensory impressions. René Huyghe writes that Seurat "exploded space" and filled it with dust

motes which today would be called atomic. Does not his particular way of posing his models ("they seem to be expecting some mysterious event") and of enveloping them in a nocturnal universe, as seen in his drawings, make Seurat into something of a Symbolist?

234 ▨ JAMES ENSOR. *Masks*. Oil on canvas. 1896. Kunsthalle, Hamburg.

Plenty of "isms" can be invoked in connection with Ensor: Symbolism, Impressionism, Expressionism, and even Fauvism. The fantastic was his realm, and he was the first to anticipate Rouault in ensuring the renewal of the traditional imagery of medieval religion. But whereas Georges Rouault possessed total faith, Ensor's grotesque masks suggest that behind them lie sarcasm, fear, and doubt.

235 ▨ JOSEPH GRANIE. *Portrait of a Woman*. Oil on canvas. 1895. Musée d'Art Moderne, Paris.

The Art Nouveau movement cannot be separated from social and political movements. The spread of world Socialism, the literature of popular protest and reform, Anarchism, world's fairs—all these encouraged the ferment of ideas and the weakening of class barriers.

236 ▨ THÉOPHILE ALEXANDRE STEINLEN. *Poverty*. Drawing. 1899. Collection Maurice Rheims, Paris.

Steinlen occupies a remarkable place in revolutionary-minded populist art. He was tremendously adept at the pictorial transliteration of poverty, unemployment, and the atmosphere of the first big strikes, whereas artists like Forain specialized in minute observation of a squalid, recently enriched bourgeoisie.

237 ⬚ Richard Gerstl. *The Two Sisters*. Oil on canvas. 1905. Österreichische Galerie des XIX und XX Jahrhunderts, Vienna.
Gerstl, like Egon Schiele, was one of the minority who combined Expressionism and the Sezession style. *The Two Sisters* was exhibited in the entrance competition for the special painting class at the Academy of Fine Art, Vienna.

238 ⬚ Pablo Picasso. *The Letter*. Charcoal and watercolor. 1895. Collection Maurice Rheims, Paris.
In Barcelona at the end of the last century there was a school of Symbolist painters who concentrated on pictures of poverty: Isidro Nonell y Monturiol painted gypsies and tramps and Ramon Casas did sketchy portraits in a style rather like that of Lautrec. The scenes chosen by the young Picasso were love, maternity, popular uprisings, and death, all conceived in a Symbolist style close to that of Steinlen.

239 ⬚ Édouard Vuillard. *Reading*. Oil on canvas. 1896. Musée d'Art Moderne, Paris.
Although he remained much influenced by Synthetism, Vuillard, like Carrière, though with different methods, managed to give a deeply sensitive rendering of contemporary middle-class society in its familiar surroundings.

240 ⬚ Louis Valtat. *At the Café*. Oil on canvas. 1899. Collection Maurice Rheims, Paris.
The work of Valtat, like that of many other painters of the period, went through a brief Art Nouveau phase.

241 ⬚ Pierre Bonnard. *Goose Girl*. Charcoal drawing. 1901. Collection Boas, Paris.
Bonnard as a young man was employed as a clerk in a civil registry office. He had practically no leaning toward Symbolism; it was indirectly, through his genius for absorbing Japanese pictorial elements, and through the deep influence which he soon exercised on the fledgling school of Munich, that his early works (especially posters) occupy an important place in Art Nouveau.

242 ⬚ Joaquin Sunyer. *Variety Theater*. Oil on canvas. C. 1896. Private Collection, Germany.
In the work of Sunyer, Symbolism eventually disappeared through contact with Expressionism.

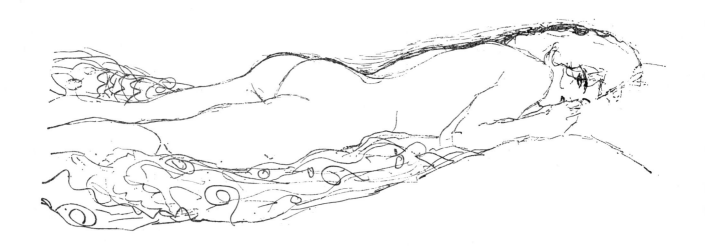

142

143

144

145

146

147

148

150

151

152

153

155

156

157

Musée du Petit Palais. 1527. Panneau pour la décoration de la Mairie du Xe - CARRIÈRE. V. phot.

160

161

162

163

164

165

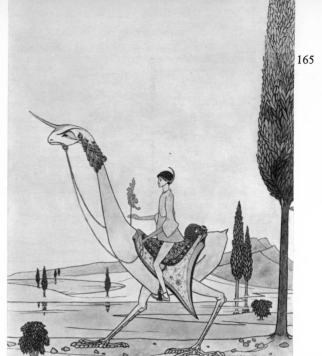

166

167

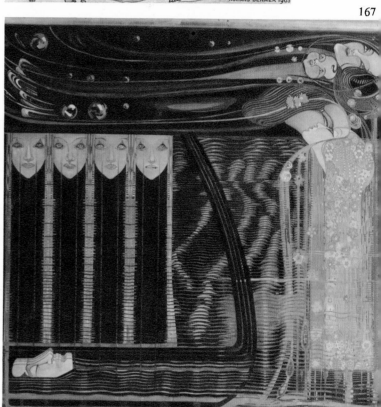

168

169

171

172

173

174

175

176

PER SE E PER SUO CIEL CONCEPE E FIGLIA

177

178

179

180

181

182

183

184

185

186

187

188

189

190

191

192

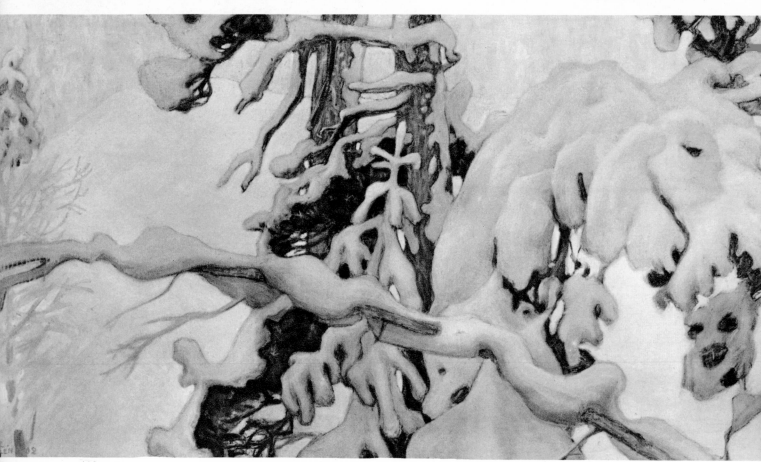

193

194

196

FR. MATUŠEK 13.I.1907

195

197

199

2

201

207

208

210

211

212

213

214

215

216

217

218

219

220

221

222

223

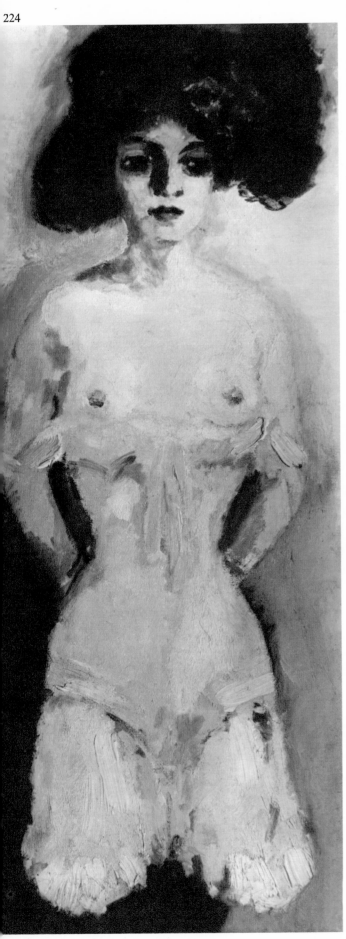

224

225

226

227

228

22

230

231

232

233

234

236

237

238

239

241

242

Sculpture

WHEN one sets about studying the sculpture of the turn-of-the-century, the question arises whether there is, in fact, an Art Nouveau sculpture.

Less independent, because more closely controlled by bourgeois taste, sculpture would appear not to have excited the same fever of innovation as painting. It was still the art of the Salon or the salons, conceived for the pleasure of the well-to-do middle-class customer and, ultimately, in the secret hope of being chosen to embellish a city square. Here and there, within this restricted frame, individual fantasy struggles for expression. One sculptor shows a bias for orientalism; another descends directly from the masters of the eighteenth century; and a third cuts his stone with such sensuality that his work borders on flagrant indecency—the kind which is enjoyed with special relish because, as a work of art, it can be contemplated with impunity. To sculptors, the essential thing was the body; the public demanded that they render flesh, portray it soft and round, firm yet tender, and overflowing with feeling. Feelings there were in plenty: conventional fine feelings; poignant, atrocious, or heroic feelings; sublime ones too on occasion, in which case it was compulsory that the eyes be raised to heaven. The figures in sculpture laughed or killed or suffered; their inspired eyes and tortured hands masked the immodesty of body and attitude.

It was the triumph of the *pompier* (which may be briefly defined as banality, stuffiness, and pomposity), a paroxysm of hypocrisy, the acceptance of perversion and even obscenity, provided they were suitably sad, veiled in noble intentions, and stamped with the recognized sign of approval—a prize at the Salon. Taste was degenerate, sadism unacknowledged. Desperation was lovely if grief divested her of her garments; she could be poverty-stricken on condition that poverty had not spoiled the shape of her breasts. Oriental or barbaric women were much appreciated. Of course their morals were not the same as ours, but then that was a question of authenticity, local color, was it not? The art of statuary was exhausted; in its senility it erred all the more for trying to follow in the footsteps of Clodion, Carpeaux, and Dalou. It copied attitudes but could not recapture the spirit. It appears to have remained wedded to these tendencies even at the height of the Art Nouveau period, and the few outstandingly gifted sculptors who did glimpse the social revolution going on around them made only occasional borrowings from it.

Against this, however, we ought in justice to remember that sculpture has always been intended to occupy a definite place, whether a public square or a private apartment; it can therefore disengage itself from official standards of taste only with difficulty. Unsold canvases can be stacked in a studio; sculptures, if only for reasons of space, cannot. Sculpture is still an art ruled by commissions and regulated by the law of supply and demand.

The buyers of sculpture were of two kinds: official organizations and private individuals. Miniature pieces, which the latter sought, were usually close to eighteenth-century traditions. Few sculptors were eager to commit themselves to large works, a field largely monopolized by

Rodin and Meunier—dangerous rivals for anyone to take on. Because of this there was a plentiful outpouring of statuettes, carefully worked trifles exactly in line with bourgeois taste. Some sculptors nevertheless made cautious forays into Symbolism. But while large-scale allegorical effusions might have been within their powers, small Symbolistic sculpture posed more difficult problems, and it wavered between the pretty-pretty and the grotesque. Direct, emotional themes were discarded in favor of mysterious ones, emblematically treated; one of the favorite themes was typified by Masseau's *The Secret*: a woman resembling an idol who, her robe half parted, holds a mysterious casket close to her enigmatic face (*see* plate 251).

It would be wrong to condemn all the sculpture which appeared around 1900 for having been totally untouched by the new artistic movements. Consciously or otherwise, some sculptors were affected by modern theories. Curiously, however, the new tendencies were expressed mainly in works whose importance goes beyond that of Art Nouveau, like those of Rodin and his school.

Rodin is one of those unusual beings whose genius is too vast to be contained in any movement: he is not merely a man of his own century. He is a Symbolist, but is classed among the Impressionists; he is Baroque, yet his works have the greatness and grandeur of Classic monuments. He is in himself an entire epoch, school, and tendency, which, however, cannot be conceived and understood without recourse to Art Nouveau. From the Impressionists he borrows the ceaseless movement of objects in light, but he enriches that movement with the characteristic dynamism of his time; every line vibrates, every volume throbs. From emotion he elicits a depth which sets him apart from both the realism of his predecessors and the emotionalism of his contemporaries. His texture is always alive, expressive, endlessly diverse, in tune with the massive varied nature of the stone itself (*see* plate 257). It never takes on that prettified, washed-out, soapy quality which others were at such pains to achieve. The curves are never flaccid; passion does not sink into rhetoric, nor love into affectation. He is all strength and power; his vital impulse never flags.

Although it was never possible to regard Rodin as belonging to any particular tradition or school, he influenced a large number of young sculptors who looked up to him as their master. One of them, Camille Claudel (*see* plate 258), sister of the poet, working in unusual materials (onyx and bronze together, for example), infused her sculpture with such fire and energy that it stands apart from other work of the period.

There is, broadly speaking, a certain unity in the sculptural themes of the end of the century. Sadness or joy, motherhood or mourning, confidence or despair, all these were seen as indwelling feelings rather than outbursts of emotion, and were meant to touch the heart without bewildering the eye. And not only the subject, but its physical treatment bear witness to the need for tenderness and affection which was manifested by sculpture at that time. Sharp ridges, brutal lines, and abrupt angles had given way to curves; volumes are supple, smooth, and refined, bathed in gentle light. Obsidian, marble, and bronze have become fluid and misty; the native directness and solidity of sculpture has been dissolved into evanescence.

This tendency was particularly strong in Italy. Justice has never been done to the way in which Italian sculpture, and especially Italian funerary art at the end of the nineteenth century, blossomed afresh, passing rapidly from popular realism to the most poignant Symbolism. Abandoning academic clichés, the Italians created new, powerful, strange works whose equivalent is to be found in no other style (*see* plates 259, 261, and 263). Never had anguish and distress been expressed with such intensity; never had such primitive imagery been so felicitously married to a dazzling technique. The same tendency was displayed by the Swede, Carl Milles (*see* plate 262), and by the Icelander, Einar Jónsson (*see* plate 260), both of whom could handle stone in such a way that it seems to flow like a liquid, a feat of virtuosity to which other sculptors were fairly quick to react.

While it must be admitted that 1900 sculpture is based on the cult of sentiment, it is important to note that this tendency consisted of two distinct streams. The first was love and its sorrows, and the usual collection of family emotions. The second, while remaining faithful to acceptable emotional patterns, glorifying manual labor and depicting the sufferings of the proletariat, made a deliberate attempt to be modern and to come to grips with historical reality. Attractive yet irritating, paternalist and populist at the same time, this art was the product of irreconcilable contradictions. For while the sculptors no longer consented to carve bourgeois scenes and portraits, and depicted nothing but work or poverty, they saw their new subject matter through the eyes (and felt it with the emotional reservations) of the property-owning classes. And so, despite being involved in the life of the people, and especially that of the urban laboring classes, they were in effect continuing to work for bourgeois society and, while producing work in a popular vein, to give that society the satisfactions and even the reassurance which it wanted. The emaciated, exhausted bodies they fashioned, and the faces ravaged by fatigue or hunger, expressed not a particle of revolt. Far from it: their art was accepted as expressing the perfect equilibrium of society and the unalterable justice of fate. The worker, ennobled by toil and purified by privation, could look out over the world with a calm, clear gaze, his eyes shining with pride; he had done his duty. Far from disturbing anyone, this art was a comfort to the public for whom it was made. It declared that in the very depths of poverty a certain happiness was still possible—a happiness, noble and discreet, sustained by the old, simple virtues. But however much the implications of this sculpture may jar us, they need not make us overlook its intrinsic qualities of truthful naturalism.

Thus, through populism, sculpture was stepping out of the trappings of costume—goddesses, allegory, all the old glamour—and putting on modern dress. The pictorial and above all the sculptural representation of people in ordinary clothes was an even more revolutionary event than the acceptance of a neologism by the Académie Française. It became possible to speak more directly. Figures clothed in Antique drapery were no longer the required means of expression. Reality was worthy of presentation just as it stood, and the modern, workaday world was no longer automatically equated with vulgarity and ugliness. This was a large step forward, a much more decisive one than sculptors had made by modeling their sitters in the fashions of the moment. An expensive dress is a myth in itself, but a blue overall, a miner's helmet, or a mason's shirt lends no wings to fantasy. The admission of these things into art was an acknowledgment that they possessed a certain beauty. It permitted a glimpse of the not-too-distant day when the black smoky horizons, the factory chimneys, and even the machines would have their own painters and poets. It was a proclamation that modernity and art had never been really opposed. It amounted to accusing art of never having looked at modern life.

Populist sculpture, reactionary though it was from a purely social point of view, had a place to fill in the modern world. It shook the traditional aesthetic to the foundations; the words "noble" and "beautiful" pertained now to things formerly despised as trivial, as well as to the aristocratic and exceptional.

Of the many sculptures whose subject matter was provided by labor, the most beautiful and also the most moving are probably those of the Belgian, Constantin Meunier (*see* plate 265). In mentioning this fine artist, we must not forget Guilliot and E. Rothansl; or Naoum Aronson, "the sculptor of social suffering," who faithfully adapted his procedure to the demands of his subjects, but kept his modeling firm at all times; or Alfred-Jean Halou, whose handling of the medium expressed the harshness of laboring life.

In the northern countries, especially Belgium, the populist sculptors endeavored, some with more felicitous results than others, to escape from sentimental convention. While they did not abandon entirely their predilection for "pathetic" and "moving" effects, they did avoid affectation, and achieved an Expressionist realism by no means devoid of amplitude and power.

Vérisme—faithful reflection of real life—is not the only merit of the works of Minne (*see* plate 264), Wouters (*see* plate 266), and Mendes da Costa. Their compositions are the more intense and expressive for being controlled by equilibrium in both volume and line. Their sculptures depicting grief, love, or work have a vigor and harmony recalling both the late-medieval stone carving of Flanders and the energy of certain drawings by Van Gogh.

Tradition, Symbolism, and Socialism, with their variants and derivatives, constitute the three major tendencies of sculpture at the beginning of the twentieth century. But there are certain artists who remained outside the main currents and who claim a special place here, in some cases because of their total fidelity to earlier traditions, in others because of their complete originality.

One of them, Prince Paul Troubetzkoy (*see* plate 268), first appeared on the French scene at the Paris Universal Exhibition of 1900. The elegance and feverish modeling of his portraits place him in the same line as Carpeaux. These portraits in the realistic vein are natural and lively, as if done in a hurry.

Another figure who stands apart from the rest is Edgar Degas (*see* plate 267), who in his small bronzes continued the systematic study of movements and attitudes which he pursued in other media. His dancers and women, modeled in the heyday of Art Nouveau, seem to have nothing to do with any of its trends. They are stamped solely with the master's genius and belong to him alone.

Finally, we must name Gaudí, whose sculpture moved forward very rapidly from fantasy and the dream world to arrive at abstract expression. The perennial question of whether Gaudí ever really belonged to Art Nouveau, even momentarily, is still unanswered. All the evidence seems to point to his having allied himself to the movement only insofar, and for as long, as it enabled him to enrich his own mode of expression. Thus he drew inspiration from nature only in order to create, as she does, a world of strange and living forms whose like exists in no other realm. In so doing he was the annunciator of a revolution which was to be greater than any the plastic arts had known for many centuries.

Gaudí was one of the first to discover a new role for the artist: he was no longer an interpreter, but a creator, with no laws except the limits of his own imagination. At a point in history when technical progress had made it possible to reproduce reality without the intervention of the human hand, he showed unprecedented boldness in exploring a new universe, a new way of expression which was natural only in being of human provenance. To him, 1900 art was at once a last, inspired, brief flowering of the styles of the past, and a premonition of the uncharted future; a development and dual current were summed up in his work, from its neo-medievalist beginnings to its final destination in the language of the nonfigurative.

Art Nouveau sculpture seems therefore to oscillate between two poles. On the one hand, it is traditional, sentimental, and not infrequently mediocre; on the other, there is the achievement of the isolated geniuses who prefigure the style of the future but do not really belong to Art Nouveau.

It follows that a true 1900 style would consist of a compromise between these two extremes, but there are no signs that this golden mean was ever attained. Sculpture merely borrowed a few tendencies from the new aesthetic—predominance of the curve, soft, gentle modeling, fluid volumes, expressive line—at the same time as it was swayed by other currents about which there was nothing specifically Art Nouveau. The growth and development which took place in the applied arts have no equivalents in sculpture. Between the traditional miniature sculpture and the first works of Brancusi there is a great gulf. Detractors of the 1900 Style are in a strong position here, since it is a fact that there is no great Art Nouveau sculpture. There are only "moments" of Art Nouveau, clearly perceptible in the pleasing trifles such as small bronzes and ceramic pieces.

243 ▨ UNKNOWN ARTIST. *Carved Organ Case* (detail). Wood. 1900. Castle De Haar, Vleuten, The Netherlands. Sculpture is the field in which Art Nouveau made its least successful showing. All too often, inspiration was confined within the limits of Symbolism, which lacked the necessary connections with dream and the unconscious, and which tended to confuse the power of legend with the prettiness of a Romantic album for young ladies. In the Low Countries the tradition of medievalism remained strong, as is shown by this gigantic and curious complex of sculptural decoration at the Castle De Haar.

244 ▨ ALFRED GILBERT. *Monument to Queen Alexandra*. Cast bronze. 1925. London.
The date of this monument confirms the strength of the English fondness for medievalism. Alfred Gilbert and Alexander Fisher belonged to that Mannerist, Wagnerian band who, under cover of spirituality, indulged in a *Walpurgisnacht* of sexuality.

245 ☒ WILLIAM REYNOLDS STEPHENS. *Genevieve and the Nestling*. Gilt-bronze. C. 1902. Private Collection, London.
The medievalism of the Englishman Reynolds Stephens is akin to that of the Frenchman, Jean-Auguste Dampt. The vigor of his style saves his work from being over-mannered.

246 ☒ ARTHUR STRASSER. *Triumph of Mark Antony*. Cast bronze. 1898. Vienna.
Austria—the Austria of the "bureaucratic style"—played it safe by commissioning Strasser to represent it at the Paris Universal Exhibition of 1900. Though the Sezession was revolutionizing architecture and the decorative arts, it seems not to have exercized its charms upon sculpture.

247 ☒ MAX KLINGER. *Beethoven*. Mixed media. 1899–1902. Museum der Bildenden Kunst, Leipzig.
Hans von Marées was a powerful influence on German sculpture at the end of the nineteenth century. His disciples, especially Adolf Hildebrand, illustrate the preference for the Antique world which Max Klinger was to carry to its highest and most irritating degree. A painter, engraver, and sculptor, this German artist hoped to arouse the spectator's excitement by employing rich and precious materials in combination. His repertoire was drawn from shimmering substances—gold, silver, bronze, onyx, porphyry, agate, and ivory. Falling victim to the weakness of his time, he failed to make an uncompromising choice between naturalism and Symbolism. Thus in his *Beethoven* he used the composer's life-mask taken by Klein, yet did not hesitate to dress up his model as an inhabitant of Olympus (note the footgear). Max Klinger had an almost unbridled passion for his materials: the body is executed in dazzling white marble; the eagle in veined black marble; the draperies are onyx; and the throne is composed of polished gold with insets of agate, jade, and opal. This predilection for precious substances and Byzantine imagery reveals the artist's ambition to be the Gustave Moreau of sculpture.

248 ☒ BOHUMIL KAFKA. *Decorative Group for the Façade of the Prague Opera House*. Plaster model. C. 1900.
In Prague at the end of the nineteenth century a desire for new things was in the air. The Symbolistic inspiration of Bohumil Kafka was fed by tragic dreams and reveries; he was rather like Segantini. His contemporary, R. Franges Mihanovic, was mostly influenced by Meunier and Rodin, and produced works with a sound sense of structure.

249 ☒ JEAN-AUGUSTE DAMPT. *Reflective Mood*. Ivory, metal, and wood. 1898. Collection the Marquis de Ganay, Paris.
Dampt attracted much attention in the last years of the nineteenth century; he was one of those craftsmen who wore an ample leather apron, a figure with special charms for cultivated people who knew their Wagner.

He was distinguished from his colleagues, like Froment-Meurice and Falize, by his Symbolist leanings.

250 ☒ THÉODORE RIVIÈRE. *Adam and Eve*. Ivory. C. 1900. Musée Galliéra, Paris.
Here the sculptor has contrived to give his material a shimmering, silky quality, like the seventeenth-century ivory carvers. The titles of some of his works are significant: *Messalina in the Suburra, Salammbô Visiting Mâtho*, and *Sword-Dance*. Rivière was a disciple of the virtuosi of Byzantium and the East. He belongs to the generation of decorative sculptors who incurred the mockery of Baudelaire. He excelled in carving gold, ivory, and precious stones, using archetypal literary subjects taken from Flaubert, Leconte de Lisle, and J. M. de Hérédia. Similarly, did not the half-veiled woman pacing before the wall of Alexandria give Freud the model for his Gravida?

251 ☒ FIX MASSEAU. *The Secret*. Gilt-bronze. C. 1900. Collection G. Lévy, Paris.
Fix Masseau, who underwent a long training in Florence, is related to the line of Italianized artists which includes Bouval, Caussé, and Obiols.

252 ☒ GEORGES TONNELIER. *Temptation of Saint Anthony*. Ivory. C. 1900. Musée Galliéra, Paris.
These "temptations," a favorite iconographic theme, reveal the attitudes of respectable people toward the attractions of Satanism. In the Middle Ages, temptation took the form of fantastic monsters seeking to entice the afflicted hermit. During the reign of Louis XVI, Satan's delegates have become barely nubile nymphs, disguised as shepherdesses. By the late nineteenth century, the Evil One has insinuated himself into the bodies of well-endowed, pneumatic young ladies who seem to be threatening the unfortunate old man and terrifying him with their overly voluptuous charms. In the Art Nouveau period many artists, in both France and Great Britain, gave expression to this taste for unintelligent sensuality on the part of respectable society.

253 ☒ UNKNOWN ARTIST. *Memorial Group* (in honor of the Marquis de Dion-Bouton). Silver, ivory, and stone. C. 1904. Musée des Arts et Métiers, Paris.
High craftsmanship was a dying phenomenon. Fabergé and his contemporaries were its last representatives, disappearing with the political order under which they had flourished.

254 ☒ FREDERICK MACMONNIES. *Pan*. Bronze. C. 1898. Private Collection, Paris.
Historical forces pushed the young United States in the direction of Realism. At the same time, Anglo-Saxon prudery was at its height: hence the misadventure suffered by Augustus Saint-Gaudens who, having decorated the cartouches of the Boston Public Library with naked children, had his work refused by the indignant city councilors. Signs of intentional,

considered sensuality in American art around 1900 are hard to find. MacMonnies' works, such as his equestrian group (which is somewhat similar to that executed by Recipion for the Grand Palais in Paris), his *Bacchante* (Brooklyn Museum, New York), and this bronze *Pan*, are inspired by the Italian Renaissance.

255 ◻ RAOUL LARCHE. *Loïe Fuller*. Gilt-bronze. C. 1900. Collection Joseph Setton, Paris.
The nucleus of Loïe Fuller's following was a small but deeply devoted band of admirers. Pierre Roche designed and executed an amazing entrance for the beautiful dancer's own theater (*see* plate 11). Larche's style is full of the Mediterranean Mannerism then so much in vogue in the Salons; the same can be said of Joseph Chéret, and of Léonard, who designed a series of *coryphées* for the Manufacture de Sèvres.

256 ◻ LLUIS DOMENÉCH Y MONTANER. Palau de la Música Catalana. *Detail*. 1906–08. Barcelona.
As early as the end of the seventeenth century, churches on the Iberian Peninsula and in Mexico, Peru, and Brazil had begun to display the same features seen here—the desire of the eye to be led a dance, led astray and intoxicated by unexpected thrusts and dynamisms captured in stone and plaster. In the hands of Domenéch this tendency became the expression of a lyricism which had been brought under the control of reason; the undulations of his sculptural motif go hand in hand with the flowing architectural forms which support them.

257 ◻ AUGUSTE RODIN. *Pygmalion and Galatea*. Marble. C. 1910. The Metropolitan Museum of Art, New York. Though claimed by both Impressionists and Symbolists, Rodin was unique; he cannot be grouped anywhere. The reason he occupies a pre-eminent place in this anthology of Art Nouveau is the deep, warm-blooded passion for the human body which runs through his work.

258 ◻ CAMILLE CLAUDEL. *The Wave*. Onyx and bronze. C. 1905. Collection the Claudel family, Paris.
Camille Claudel, a pupil of Rodin, was one of the most original of Art Nouveau sculptors. She had her own way of combining media (especially rare metals and semiprecious stones), and here used onyx to give her subject a wonderfully silky, tactile quality. "Just as a man sitting alone in the countryside makes use of some tree or rock on which his eye has fastened as an accompaniment to his meditation, so a work by Camille Claudel in the middle of a room functions in the same way as the curious rocks collected by the Chinese; its very form makes it a monument of the inner life. It is a budding theme, an invitation to the private muse." These were the admiring terms in which Paul Claudel summed up his sister's work.

259 ◻ LEONARDO BISTOLFI. *Memorial to Segantini*. Marble. C. 1900. St. Moritz, Switzerland.

Bistolfi created this superb monument to symbolize the mountain which played so great a part in Segantini's inspiration. A highly gifted sculptor, Bistolfi's first important work was *Sacrifice*, commemorating Victor Emmanuel, in Rome. A poet, writer, and musician, he revealed a deep attraction to the mystique of death—death as a seductive, disturbing figure with a virginal face of surpassing beauty.

260 ◻ EINAR JÓNSSON. *The Wave of the Centuries*. Stone. 1894–1905. Einar Jónsson Museum, Reykjavik, Iceland.
Icelandic Art Nouveau had Einar Jónsson as one of its best exponents. His protean talent ranged from a Bistolfi type of Symbolism to the kind of "constructivism" best typified by Bourdelle.

261 ◻ EDOARDO RUBINO. *Female Figure* (for the façade of the Pavilion of Decorative Arts at the 1902 Turin Exhibition). Plaster model.
Italy was rich in remarkable nineteenth-century Mannerist sculptors, among them Rubino, Romagnoli, Antonio Ruggeri, Arturo Dazzi, and Antonio Maraini. Their full importance will not be realized until a full survey has been made of the sculptural treasures which appeared in Italy toward the close of the century, both in cemeteries and on the façades of buildings. These works are executed in a flowing, D'Annunziesque style which some have related (mistakenly) to Impressionism.

262 ◻ CARL MILLES. *Elephants*. Marble. 1904. National Museum, Stockholm.
Swedish sculpture from the beginning of the nineteenth century was stamped by conservatism, with the mantle of Canova's prestige falling on his disciple, Thorwaldsen. Carl Milles, who was influenced by Rodin, was ambitious to reflect Sweden's new artistic aspirations (the playwright, August Strindberg, had already achieved resounding notoriety). Milles often attempted projects which exceeded his talent; one is tempted to call him a Mannerist Expressionist.

263 ◻ MEDARDO ROSSO. *The Bookmaker*. Cast bronze. 1894. Galleria Nazionale d'Arte Moderna, Milan.
René Huyghe, writing of the "process of dematerialization" which occurred in the nineteenth century, goes on to say: "The undulating graphic line of Gauguin, derived from the Japanese arabesque, has its counterpart in the fluid modeling of Rodin and Medardo Rosso." (*Larousse Encyclopedia of Modern Art*, New York, 1965.) The weakness of evanescence is that it tends to become abstract. Sixty years later, a certain species of abstract art was to collapse in just the same way, undermined by its own preciosity.

264 ◻ GEORGES MINNE. *Kneeling Boy at the Fountain*. Marble. 1898. Kunsthistorisches Museum, Moderne Galerie, Vienna.
Minne successfully kept apart from both populist

realism and the skillful deliquescence of the Italian sculptors at the end of the century. This figure is a perfect example of Art Nouveau sculpture as it ought to have been.

265 ▨ CONSTANTIN-ÉMILE MEUNIER. *The Soil*. Bronze. 1892. Musée des Beaux-Arts, Brussels.
The preoccupations of Constantin Meunier are made clear by such titles as *Glassblower*, *Man with a Hammer*, *Sower*, and *Firedamp*. He felt the despair of working-class life but avoided falling into paternalistic sentimentality.

266 ▨ RIK WOUTERS. *The Coquette*. Bronze. 1913. Musée des Beaux-Arts, Brussels.
Wouters' main objectives were solid construction and powerful rhythm. A weakness was his inability to throw off—even in this depiction of a coquette—a touch of populism: the elaborate flounced dress in this work creates a jarring note.

267 ▨ EDGAR DEGAS. *Dancer in a Tutu*. Bronze and cloth. 1901. The Metropolitan Museum of Art, New York.
The sculpture of Degas eludes formal classification. It nevertheless shows affinities to Art Nouveau: a populist tendency in the choice of subjects and a sense of effort in the pose.

268 ▨ PRINCE PAUL TROUBETZKOY. *Portrait of Robert de Montesquiou*. Bronze. C. 1902. Collection M. Mallett, London.
Troubetzkoy was perhaps the only Russian sculptor of his time who managed to throw off traditional Slav tendencies. Instead, he was a pupil of Rodin and displayed a leaning toward a certain type of Italian nineteenth-century Mannerism.

243

244

245

246

247

248

250

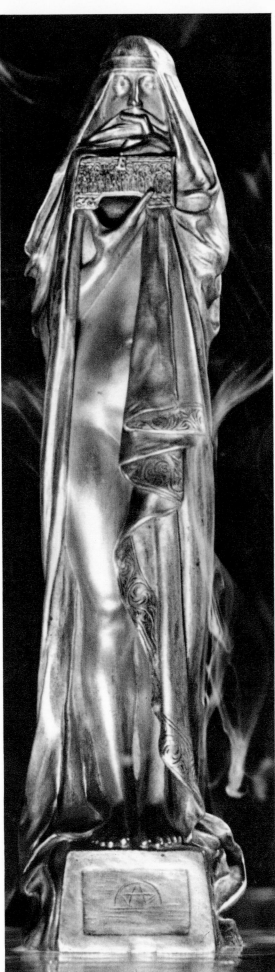

251

252

253

254

255

257

2

258

260

262

261

263

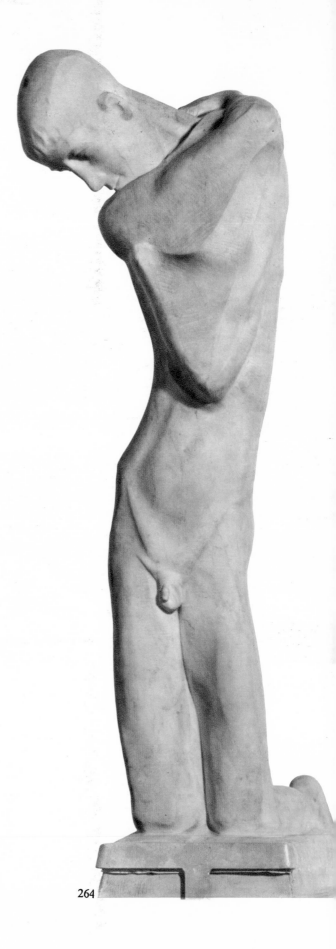

264

265

266

267

268

The Applied Arts

NOUILLE Style, Modern Style, 1900 Art, Stile Floreale—the names reflect differences not only of nationality but of attitude. However, in the end there was general agreement in favor of Art Nouveau, the name chosen by Samuel Bing for the shop he opened in Paris in 1896. Bing exhibited and sold furniture, textiles, ceramics, glass, and jewelry. *L'Art Nouveau Bing* was a furniture shop and an interior decorator's establishment where the minor arts were on display. It was precisely in this field that the most important innovations were taking place. Art Nouveau was providing an entirely new setting for daily life.

It is impossible to overlook the extraordinary revival of crafts—and of craftsmanship—which took place at the end of the nineteenth century. Not only did technical ability reach new heights, with a complete revision of the vocabulary of motifs, but there was an even more significant change: many artists turned aside temporarily or permanently from the so-called fine arts and devoted themselves to the applied arts.

Numerous causes—social, economic, and aesthetic—can be found for this. Nineteenth-century painting, sculpture, and architecture were commissioned and judged by the middle classes. There was a well-defined road which the artist was expected to follow. First came the art school, which in France meant the École des Beaux-Arts or one of the other official institutions, and after that the Salons, where artists exhibited their yearly output. Outside this *cursus honorum* there was no salvation and, moreover, no chance of making a living. Creative innovation was actually a handicap in attaining success, and was permissible only within strict limits. The prerequisite for prosperity and fame was a respect for tradition. For years artists struggled to escape these strictures, and in 1863, Napoleon III was obliged to authorize the opening of a *Salon des Refusés* in deference to the indignation of those who had been unsuccessful in satisfying the jury's tastes. There was an increasing determination on the part of artists to throw off the obligations which society imposed, and which they were no longer inclined to accept. Since this meant they could not subsist by painting, they diverted their talents to the poster and to a wide variety of craft avocations, and thus rapidly became aware of the bad taste dominating their surroundings.

The typical interior of a *fin-de-siècle* home was built around an astonishing collection of bric-à-brac. Little light and less air, heavy hangings, massive furniture cluttered with small objects—rooms full to the bursting point, solemn, tedious, appalling. The century was punctuated by successive waves of infatuation with Antiquity, the Middle Ages, and the Renaissance, with an undercurrent of conviction that the Louis XVI style was the best of all and could never be improved upon. Rooms were crowded with Henri II buffets, and the embroidered loves of troubadours or shepherdesses hung in perpetual suspension on net curtains, whose partings revealed glimpses of Romans perched on clocks and pugs immortalized in porcelain. The style of the nineteenth century, if it had one, was achieved by copying the styles of the past. Alfred de

Musset deplored this as early as 1836, in the *Confession d'un Enfant du Siècle*: "The apartments of the rich are cabinets of curiosities: a conglomeration of Classical Antiquity, Gothic, Renaissance, Louis XIII... something from every century except our own, a predicament which has arisen in no other period... so that we seem to be subsisting on the ruins of the past, as if the end of the world were near."

After another forty years, criticism had become still more violent:

"What do we see on every side? Wallpapers which wound the eye; against them, ornate furniture which wounds the eye; at intervals, a gaudily draped bay which wounds the eye; and every spare nook and cranny is hung with plates of spinach with decorative borders which wound the eye. Let the eye come to terms with all this as best it can." (*Art Décoratif*, 1899, No. 7.) Or again: "The subjects chosen to enliven the dining-room wallpaper are enough to put anyone off his food. The knives, forks, and glassware testify to a long and careful search to discover ugly and inconvenient shapes. The plates are either adorned with little punning devices calculated to induce neuropathological symptoms, or colored patterns of flowers and fruit created by school-girls who were taught porcelain painting as a genteel accomplishment to be sandwiched in between their sketching class and the piano lessons. Around the drawing room and bedroom mantels are clocks and wall sconces of indefinite shape, beds like gondolas, couches and sofas like instruments of torture, imitation gold frames and cardboard rose paneling are contemplated with serene satisfaction by the rent-paying occupant before settling down to sleep in this delightful setting." (Gustave Geffroy, 1900.)

New periodicals rained curses on the bastions of bad taste, and lavished illustrations and laudatory articles on designers of the younger generation who were striving to create a style.

But what had caused this sudden outburst of resistance? Why this abrupt disgust, these newly opened eyes, this desire to change the visual setting?

The discovery of Japanese art would seem to have been a principal factor. Enthusiasm for Japanese prints had been universal since about 1880, and their influence on painting was of capital importance. But they did more than inspire painters with a new outlook, new possibilities for humor, or new typographical composition or page layout. The greatest revelation they had to offer was simplicity, a capacity for delight in nature which the European eye had lost. A few boldly simplified outlines, filled in with broad patches of color and skillfully distributed on the page, were enough; there was a complete absence of anecdotal subjects and pompous clichés. This dazzling sobriety made everything Europe was producing at the time seem very artificial and heavy. A clean sweep was imperative; imitation styles, however adroitly confected, must be abandoned; ugliness must be banished; something new must be created.

Japanese influence also affected the *ensembliers*—interior decorators, as they came to be known. Exhibitions, galleries, and prints familiarized the Western eye with the supreme refinement of Far Eastern interiors which, unlike the European apartment, consisted of practically empty rooms, with walls which were in many cases quite bare.

Interior design and decoration, so important during the Art Nouveau period, were affected by two distinct and indeed opposing tendencies: on the one hand, architects and designers cast a nostalgic eye on the homogeneous styles which had governed past epochs; on the other, they were determined to make their interiors modern—that is, adapted to new needs and desires. They wanted to create a new style which would continue tradition but not copy it. The occasional echoes of the past which can be found in their work were unintentional; above all, what they were trying to recapture was the state of mind, the ideal (whether concrete or imaginary) which had presided over the creation of the models they admired. This ideal had in some cases not existed at all, but that is not the point. The creative artists concerned were convinced that at certain specially favored periods in history even the humblest craftsman had labored joyfully, making the most insignificant objects into works of art. Of all these inspired periods, the one chosen as exemplary was the Middle Ages—but not the Middle Ages as envisaged by the Romantics in the 1830's, a mysterious realm in which the shadowy, inseparable figures of love and death were forever moving, forever on the watch. On the contrary, the new model of the Middle Ages was compounded of simplicity, goodness, poverty, and hard work, and animated by disinterested faith, a world in which everyone had his own share to contribute in the making of beauty. The apostles of this new belief were many; the ones who left the deepest mark on their age were William Morris in England and Viollet-le-Duc in France.

William Morris was an ardent disciple of John Ruskin. Much earlier in the century Ruskin had condemned the spirit of the Renaissance, with its ideal of knowledge and perfection, and exalted the spirit of the Gothic age, whose leading aims were simplicity and freedom. To Ruskin's way of thinking, the violence of social unrest sprang from a sense of frustration on the part of the workers, who had been deprived of initiative and liberty, and therefore of joy and human dignity, rather than from any deep-seated resentment occasioned by the uneven distribution of wealth. The reason the laboring classes demanded a larger share of that wealth was that they did not know how to express their real need, which was for joy in work itself.

These arguments were taken up by Morris, who condemned not only the excessive division of labor, but any use whatsoever of machines. Human beings needed a human setting; their surroundings must be beautiful. Machines destroyed beauty and brought death to the spirit of man. In a lecture delivered in 1882, Morris analyzed the state of the various minor arts at that time. The only merit of the nineteenth century, he said in substance, was to have succeeded in making pottery and glass into ugly objects, a result attained by no earlier civilization, even the most primitive. Every time the machine was interposed between matter and the human mind the outcome was a debased article. To Morris, artistic truth and beauty lay in the imperfections which moved the soul, the trace of the human hand which alone was capable of giving life to matter. To the technical prowess of the Classical age, he preferred the clumsiness of the Middle Ages, which breathed sincerity and humility. In these he saw the expression of a simple, healthy joy which had been stifled by the Renaissance. He was no doubt manufacturing a legend when he depicted the medieval craftsmen as free and happy men; but, even if historically unjustified, Morris' vision was received by many artists as that of a "Paradise Lost," and the path to "Paradise Regained" had to be discovered before a new style could be created.

Morris must in any case be given credit for putting his theories into practice. When he came to set up house for the first time, he found nothing to his taste. He appealed to his friends, and with their help eventually composed an interior which satisfied his standards. When he studied the problems of book production, he did not confine himself to raising his hands in critical despair, or even to giving valuable advice; he founded the famous Kelmscott Press, which printed books from specially designed types on handmade paper. It was largely owing to his initiative that artists in various parts of Europe organized themselves into groups or guilds, under arrangements approximating the medieval condition of anonymity, to design and produce works of applied art. And he was perhaps not far wrong in attaching so much importance to the state of mind attributed by him to the craftsmen of the Gothic period, for by so doing he re-created the artist's humility toward his own handiwork. Thanks to Morris, it became more important, at least in theory, that a dish or a basket be practical and beautiful than that the maker's name be known. An even more laudable feature was that the object's beauty was regarded as springing solely from its perfect fitness for use, without thereby being relegated to second place. Both designer and craftsman submitted themselves to the laws of matter and function. They controlled and directed these elements, but were also in a sense directed and controlled by them.

This same subordination of decoration to form and function was insisted upon by Viollet-le-Duc, both in his architectural work and in his lectures. He discerned the most perfect realization of this principle in Gothic art and architecture but, whether from excessive admiration or a lack of confidence, he was more modern in his theories than in his buildings. It is not so much from the latter that his influence must be judged, but rather from his writings. It was the fashion to attack and ridicule him; nevertheless, he had the enormous merit of marvelously understanding the real, revolutionary essence of Gothic art and revealing it to his contemporaries. At the same time, he restored the applied arts to their rightful place and denounced the errors into which they had fallen. But, like Morris, he was still too close to the traditions and models of the past, especially the thirteenth and fifteenth centuries, and it fell to other men to create a truly new style. Because of the all-important initiative taken by Morris and Viollet-le-Duc, the next generation was able to fashion a truly modern style.

In tracing the origins of Art Nouveau, we are confronted by delicate and, as it seems, insoluble problems of historical precedence—all the more so in that any strict chronological account presents us with an interplay of influences so complicated as to be completely unreliable. In theory, Art Nouveau first appeared in England, then Scotland, and then suddenly expanded, extending to Belgium, France, Germany, and Italy. But the order in which these countries are named is simply a matter of individual preference on the part of historians, who frequently omit the importance of the movement in Scandinavia, Russia, and the United States. The truth is that there would not be much in common between most of these countries were it not that they were moved by a single underlying ideal: to settle accounts with the historicists. Irrespective of nationality, new ideas were, within a few years, to beget works which were original in relation to both the past and the present. This abrupt flowering between 1890 and 1895 was due to the influence of such groups as the Century Guild, founded in 1882 by Selwyn Image and Arthur Heygate Mackmurdo. In 1883, Mackmurdo designed the title page of *Wren's City Churches* (*see* plate 519), which was one of the first characteristic manifestations of Art Nouveau. At about the same time, the art of glassware was being revolutionized by Émile Gallé in France, and a new repertory of form and decoration was being created in Scandinavia in the Royal Copenhagen and Rörstranp workshops of Denmark and Sweden.

There was not one point of origin but several, and the flame was lit almost simultaneously, the spark coming in each case from the work or personality of some outstanding individual—such as Mackmurdo, Gallé, Carries, Chaplet, Van de Velde, or Tiffany—who brought about a complete renewal of one or more techniques of production. This amazing epidemic, which spread to so many countries at once, was propagated by international exhibitions and by periodicals dealing with the decorative arts; the latter, with their abundant illustrations and lyrically enthusiastic commentaries, fostered a laudable spirit of emulation. If we are to discuss dates at all, let us confine ourselves to demarcating the period when Art Nouveau was predominant. It was born, as we have noted, in the early 1880's, but that was only the first emergence of the seedling. By 1890, the style blossomed all over Europe, and its fanciful and fiery youth occupied the last five years of the century. The subsequent history of this art, which is erroneously labeled "1900," is one of mal-development and decline over the next ten or fifteen years. Some people give 1902 as the date of its decease, and adduce the Turin Exhibition as evidence of death. Doubtless the "art of the *fin de siècle*" had become a dead letter by then. But was not the simple style which followed it, stripped of nonessentials, the real Art Nouveau? First the Cubist revolution, and then the outbreak of the First World War, which forced the nations of the Old World to face the immediate reality of the twentieth century, marked its end. Nevertheless, substantial echoes of it can still be found as late as 1928, notably in architecture and funerary art. With the 1920's came Art Décoratif, whose debt to its predecessors was enormous.

Thus, the life span of Art Nouveau would seem to cover twenty years. This leads us to certain observations which may give a clearer focus on the character and consequences of the Art Nouveau style, which is inadequately understood even today.

There is no longer any excuse for confusing Art Nouveau with the "style of the langorous noodle," which is typical of the *fin-de-siècle* aesthetic. These fantastic excesses (which in any case were peculiar to France and Belgium) lasted only a few years. Art Nouveau is far more than just a tentacular art, peopled with cephalopods and drowned women. To reduce it to these terms would be to deny its very existence. In reality, impassioned curves, fainting flowers, and swarming tendrils were only one aspect of it, a trend which was resisted as early as 1900, and in some cases even earlier, in the name of the principles of Art Nouveau itself. This resistance is particularly noticeable in the applied arts. Whereas an aquarium-like sinuosity and mystery dominates the early works in bronze, pewter, and ceramics and the first redecorations of restaurants, these are followed almost at once by something simpler and more austere: definite and often angular shapes with pure, rigorous lines. Settings and objects conjured from the depths of haunted ponds passed quickly out of fashion, making way for a more rational, less tormented conception—less baroque, to use the word so often bandied about in connection with Art Nouveau. So it can be seen that after a temporary passion for the strange and morbid, there was a real regeneration of decoration and the crafts, a renascence which definitively pushed out effete formulas in favor of new, simple forms, conceived for a rational use.

For the last sixty years we have been—perhaps without realizing it—living in a setting which owes almost everything to Art Nouveau. Indeed, our whole attitude toward interior decoration, our demand for something harmonious and intimate, is inherited from the 1900 period. It is probably idle to speculate what our surroundings would have been like without Art Nouveau; its mark is everywhere, even in the smallest details. A good many of the shapes which we take for granted would never have developed without Art Nouveau; and when we study the lamps, vases, and other small objects of that period, it comes as a shock to realize how many ridiculous, ugly objects are still being produced today. Alas, we are the last people who should criticize an art which is called "decadent" or "*fin de siècle*," in view of our tardiness to avail ourselves of its benefits. Only the Scandinavian countries have succeeded in going forward on the path initiated more than fifty years ago. Looking at some of the examples in this book, whether they be flatware by Riemerschmid (*see* plate 478), a cup and saucer by Van de Velde (*see* plate 397), or Austrian or Scottish interiors (*see* plates 341 and 325), the reader will doubtless find himself exclaiming, "But that's modern!" No, not modern, but typically Art Nouveau, which is to say not *fin de siècle*, not late nineteenth century, but early twentieth. In a few short years the minor arts made a prodigious stride forward. We, sixty years later, are still living on the capital they accumulated.

Of course, Cubism, and the schematized Art Décoratif style, and abstract art have, in their turn, transformed the way we visualize objects. Surprisingly, however, while some of the forms realized during the last ten years in furniture and in smaller, more casual objects seem to have no connection with the aesthetic of the early part of the century, and while others are totally Manneristic (as seen in the exhibition *Objet Art Décor* held in Paris in 1962) and look as if they have sprung fully armed from the senile imagination of a few survivors from the *Belle Époque*, the fact remains that the great majority, however revolutionary they may seem, reflect the same solicitude for functionalism, comfort, and, in some cases, sober design which originally entered the world with Art Nouveau.

Consequently, it is no longer paradoxical to argue that Art Nouveau paved the way for a salutory return to simplicity. Objects have lost the false modesty, as it were, which made it compulsory to disguise them as something else, not only in form, but even in material. During the first three quarters of the nineteenth century the aim was not to make beautiful things, but things which looked expensive. The reaction of artists and craftsmen to this hypocrisy focused their attention on folk art and commonplace materials. They took to earthenware and pewter, used string for embroidery, and designed glorious brass settings to enhance the radiance of an artificial pearl.

Their insistence on complete sincerity led them to reject any decoration arbitrarily imposed upon a surface or volume. Their eyes had wearied of plain backgrounds on which hackneyed ornaments were applied at random, of medallions from which the profiles stood out rigidly, and of senseless flower patterns on plates. What their souls thirsted after was an intimate connection between background and motif. There must no longer be decorated surfaces, but only decorative surfaces. That was the reason planes were kept firmly restricted to their statutory two dimensions; to add a third would have been to tell a visual lie, and would, moreover, have amounted to dividing into two what was essentially one, by distinguishing between the value of the decoration and that of its ground. And for the same reason it was no longer possible for artist and craftsman, architect and carver, designer and executant, to work in isolation from each other.

Art Nouveau is sometimes written off as a reactionary, bourgeois phenomenon, an absurdity, an illusory attempt to return to craft conditions which had disappeared forever. Instead of indulging in condemnation or absolution, let us rather say that artists at the beginning of the century found themselves in an intolerably false situation, caught between the aesthetic bankruptcy of mechanization and the necessity for creating a style. In the absence of an environment in which such a style could have been developed, they turned toward an artisan-based society which was disappearing under the pressure of an economic and social evolution. But the problems at the beginning of the twentieth century reached beyond the bounds of art. They were double headed, at once sociological and humanistic, and perhaps we are still waiting for the solution.

Furniture and Decoration

C LASSICAL art has reassured conservative people for the better part of twenty-five centuries. It raises no awkward questions; it is always respected by the critics and venerated by those who take their opinions from the critics. It creates confidence. Rome in 1550, England and France in the eighteenth century, the United States about 1820, Munich in 1860—all these held Greco-Roman Antiquity in high esteem because it drew on the adventures of the past to stir people's imaginations decorously, comfortably—not too little, not too much.

This passion for Antiquity lives on today in motion pictures. People buy their tickets to sit in the dark and share the intimate life of Cleopatra.

Art Nouveau was not lacking the foible. There are chairs designed by Von Stuck which would not be out of place in Pharaoh's court as envisioned by Cecil B. DeMille.

As a compromise, the Middle Ages were a frequent source of inspiration for designers anxious to provide an interior both reassuring to the mind and pleasing to the eye.

MEDIEVALISM

The fashion for medievalism had its origin in emotional factors. In France the style of the mid-nineteenth century—the Restoration, Duchesse de Berry, "Keepsake"—with its sideboards and chairs reinforced with flying buttresses and acanthus decorations, delivered the country from the solemn Empire style and its reminders of the immediate past.

The upholsterers, who had not yet started calling themselves "decorators," surrounded their customers with a style imitated from the medieval court of Bourges. "Medievalism and polished walnut" could have been the slogan of the cabinetmakers of the Faubourg Saint-Germain or the Vallée de la Loire, who did well for themselves by turning out *dagoberts*, *huchiers*, and *caquetières* (medieval chairs with low seats, tall backs, and no arms). Havard's dictionary of furniture gives no fewer than one hundred names for the various imitations of this kind. We can imagine the exclamations any of them might have elicited from Mlle. Dolly, a character in a novel by Jean Lorrain (*Les Pelléastres*). Here is her own account of her visit to Monsieur Dormoy, a collector of Gothic weapons who is also a bit of a satyr:

"He prostrated himself before me: 'But you're Bradamante! Clorinda! la belle Heaulmière!'

"'Now just you mind your manners!'

"I showed him I wasn't standing for any of his sauce. But do you suppose that was the end of it? Oh dear me no, he had only just begun. What does he do but get down a lot of old ironmongery off the wall—a breastplate, and a lot of other old pieces to fit on your arms, your thighs and your stomach, in fact the whole body as you might say, and this crank wanted to lock me up inside that lot! Inside that hardware, I ask you, and me with my sensitive breasts, not to mention my tender thighs! So then I became really angry with him:

"'Now that's enough from you, you old poop! You go and take a bath—no, a cold shower, that's what you need. You must be a lunatic, escaped from Charenton... I've seen enough of you!'"

In Great Britain, Chippendale and Regency furniture, the latter of which was a combination, often a very happy one, of *rocaille* forms, was abandoned by the fashionable furniture dealers in favor of "French Renaissance" style. To push up their sales they guaranteed that their furniture was "in the purest François I taste" and that, as Sir Walter Scott wrote in 1838, it presented "the appearance of a curule chair, ancient distinction, Greek majesty, echoes of Italy."

Irritated beyond bearing by this mongrel eclecticism, which reached its nadir in the High Victorian period, Owen Jones (in *The Grammar of Ornament*) declared in 1856: "The world has become weary of the eternal repetition of the same conventional forms which have been borrowed from styles which have passed away."

In German and Austrian furniture and decoration mediocrity reigned supreme, and the revolt against the haphazard Empire revival of the dealers was particularly aggressive. Germany was flooded with horrors, of which the *brasserie* style was a relatively mild example. *The Studio*'s critic wrote in the issue of October 15, 1901:

"There has never been any genuine style in Germany, as far as the city-dweller is concerned... whenever something a little bit better was wanted, recourse was made to horribly complicated carving or to an imitation of the furnishing of the old French courts: there was nothing to be seen but gilt and stucco.

"In Imperial Germany things were even worse; there was only imitation. As the impression sought after was one of wealth, sumptuousness or (in a word) gold, rich moldings and very heavy furniture were predominant. But the middle-class person, who could afford only moderately priced articles, was forced to resort to imitation. There is varnish instead of gold, plaster or stucco instead of marble, papier-mâché instead of leather, and veneer instead of solid wood. Such was ordinary furnishing in Germany between 1880 and 1890."

FOLK ART

Folk art, medievalism's poor relation, flourished in the nineteenth century. Local interests and local legends were embodied in fabulous creatures, dragons, and geometrical repeated patterns.

These authentic themes became an all-too-ready prey to debasement when, under cover of "tradition," they were exploited by mass production. Venerable rustic relics such as Norman cupboards and Breton chests and settles were not only piously preserved; they were copied by the thousand. This fetishistic appetite for folk art was so strong at the end of the century that, in Russia, the idea of defying the "Old Russian" spirit by designing new furniture must have seemed as sacrilegious as an attempt on the life of the Tzar. At Talashkino, therefore, as in Scandinavia and Switzerland, designers working in the spirit of the Sezession had to disguise their furniture by giving it a traditional, old-fashioned air.

PERSISTENCE OF THE LOUIS XV STYLE

The eighteenth century was "invented" in the nineteenth by the Goncourt brothers and also by Huysmans—it is well to remember that the latter was fonder of the Louis XV taste than of Art Nouveau. But a preference for the eighteenth century had been in the air all along. Even as late as 1830, Louis XV articles were still being produced. Indeed, an apprentice who had signed his indentures in 1775, could have carried on quite happily under Louis Philippe, who reigned from

1830 to 1848. A certain class in society, which included many of the leaders of fashion and which made fun of the *petit bourgeois'* fondness for medievalism, remained tied to the eighteenth century, to which it looked back with longing and whose splendors it persistently hoped to revive. At court, the entourage of the Empress Eugénie professed touching sentiments for "our poor martyr, Marie Antoinette," and while the heavy, composite architecture of Napoleon III's reign eludes definition, the furniture which went with it remained faithful to the *rocaille* convention. The chairs, with their acanthi, their cambered feet, and their shimmering mother-of-pearl inlays lighting up the surrounding ebony, are by no means ungraceful or lacking in originality.

THE *CHIFFON* STYLE

The war of 1870 brought the decline not only of medievalism but also of the Napoleon III style. Instead of paneling modeled on that in the Château de Chenonceaux, the upholsterers now supplied heavy drapes hung in Turkish or Indian fashion, with openings like those of stage curtains. Rosewood chairs, varnished like patent-leather shoes, with tight, tufted upholstery, replaced the Gothic-type pieces covered with what was called, by courtesy, Cordova leather. Occasional tables were inlaid with brass and mother-of-pearl, and were usually cluttered with imitation Limoges enamel chalices or Palissy dishes, or their tops were adorned with coats of arms in niello work (pseudo-antiques of this kind were manufactured in the little workshops of the Marais quarter of Paris). It was, as it were, Franz Joseph "at home" to Marie de' Medici.

Today, this taste for such fripperies seems both surprising and amusing, but it was intrinsic to the Symbolist spirit. Huysmans gives this description of the bedroom of M. Des Esseintes in *À Rebours*:

"Having pondered the question from every angle, he concluded that what his objective really amounted to was this: he must use pretty, pleasant things to create a gloomy effect; or rather, while keeping the room as ugly as it really was, he must impart some kind of elegance and distinction to the whole. The *optique du théâtre* was to be reversed. On the stage, tawdry fabrics were made to appear luxurious and expensive. The effect he had to achieve was exactly the opposite; genuinely magnificent fabrics must be made to look like rags. In a word, he must devise a monk's cell which would seem genuine without, of course, being so."

Symbolist Mannerism, which was the final spasm of bourgeois taste before the coming of Art Nouveau, manifested itself throughout Europe. In Italy, the Stile Umbertino was no more than a distorting mirror for various glories of the past. Anyone exploring some of the immense palazzos in the vicinity of Milan, and examining the gilded chairs inspired by the ornamental carvings of the seventeenth century, may find it difficult to distinguish the ones made on the eve of the Risorgimento from those of a much earlier date. Add to this the Biedermeier style, which was raging all the way from Turin to Venice, and a clear impression of these fossil edifices will result.

The same spineless "style" was in evidence everywhere. Russia, Austria, and England were replete with it. The novels of the closing years of the century make the reader feel that the heroes of Maupassant, Tolstoi, and D'Annunzio must all have had their houses furnished and decorated by the same firm. The aesthetes, on the other hand, men like Huysmans, Robert de Montesquiou, and Jean Lorrain, were no longer content with the formula. Where there had been black they spread a rash of gold, and they substituted precious stones for the cloth buttons on upholstery, the better to lacerate their characters' skins.

The Americans followed a similar path. The rustic "Early American" style gave way to the Saracenic, which was considered very smart. Dark fabrics, contrasting with artificially tarnished braid, were draped on rosewood and ebony inlaid with mother-of-pearl and ivory. The transatlantic antique dealers, quick to exploit the new fashion, imported the "Thiers" monstrosities which were falling into contempt in Europe. Edgar Allan Poe's description (in the *Philosophy of Furnishing*) gives us a picture of one of these New York interiors:

"Two large low sofas of rosewood and crimson silk, gold-flowered, form the only seats, with the exception of two light conversation chairs, also of rosewood. There is a pianoforte (rosewood also), without cover, and thrown open. An octagonal table, formed altogether of the richest, gold-threaded marble, is placed near one of the sofas. This is also without cover; the drapery of the curtains has been thought sufficient. Four large and gorgeous Sèvres vases, in which bloom a profusion of sweet and vivid flowers, occupy the slightly rounded angles of the room. A tall candelabrum, bearing a small antique lamp with highly perfumed oil, is standing near the head of my sleeping friend. Some light and graceful shelves, with gold edges and crimson silk cords with gold tassels, sustain two or three hundred magnificently bound books. Beyond these things, there is no furniture, if we except an Argand lamp, with a plain, crimson-tinted ground-glass shade, which depends from the lofty vaulted ceiling by a single gold chain, and throws a tranquil but magical radiance over all."

The wretched pseudo-Renaissance sideboards, which now languish unsold in auction rooms and junk shops, indicate how strong was this mania for "antiques," affecting both the middle-income group and the rich. From about 1895, the catalogues of the big stores offered Louis XV or Louis XVI suites at "highly competitive" prices, payable in monthly installments. Some of the well-to-do were irritated by this "poor man's luxury," and there was no lack of mercenary scribblers, such as Arthur Millet, who described in 1899 the "delights" of working-class life and the dangers threatening it:

"I once lived for years in a working-class district and I observed the people at first hand. At every street corner in that district there is a bar, of vast dimensions and swimming in artificial light, like the cafés on the boulevards. When the workshops empty the bars fill up. Like the more prosperous districts, poor ones have their *heure de la verte* [absinthe-drinking time]. From six to eight in the evening an intolerable stench of absinthe fills the streets. How has all this come to pass? Wily industrialists, anxious at once to make their contribution to the people's happiness and to line their own pockets, have produced a cheap absinthe which sells at ten centimes a glass. Others have concentrated on increasing the luxury of working-class interiors. The furniture in these homes is now infinitely more luxurious than it used to be; there are Renaissance sideboards and Louis XV beds which, however, fall to pieces if the family moves a few times. The lower classes have other new enjoyments; they like horse races and are acquiring a taste for going to the seashore. In short, they are intent on proving that class is nonexistent and that they have the right to enjoy themselves as much as the rich. What they are doing, unfortunately, is squandering both their savings and their health. Aristocracy was undermined, and finally destroyed, by the abuse of pleasure. I am very much afraid that democracy may suffer the same fate. To me, this rapid growth of cafés, concerts, and every other kind of entertainment and enjoyment looks decidedly ominous."

The Art Nouveau artists were in revolt against an entire century of mediocrity and pastiche. As in architecture and the applied arts, two trends were at work: one was Symbolist and ornate, a welter of historicism in most cases; the other was modern-minded and sought simplicity. The sideboard (*see* plate 296) designed by Gallé in 1892, which has a Symbolist-inspired back and heavy Louis XIII feet, contrasts sharply with the simple, functional furniture designed a few years later by Eliel Saarinen and Frank Lloyd Wright (*see* plates 360 and 361).

THE SYMBOLISTS

The Symbolists were very diverse in their stylistic leanings; they might be naturalists (Gallé, Majorelle, Basile), rococo (Selmersheim, De Feure), exponents of the dream world (Gaudí, Rupert Carabin), Wagnerian (Gotthold Riegelmann), Orientalists (Toorop, D'Aronco, Tiffany), Medievalists (Berlage), Celtic (Mackmurdo), quasi-Japanese (Whistler, Ferdinand Boberg), or folk-art oriented (Princess Tenisheva's group). But they had one thing in common: they were all

Mannerists, perhaps the most complete Mannerists the history of art has ever known. Though often at variance in matters of aesthetic theory, they were united by a single ideal: they aspired to improve the setting of daily life, within the financial and social limits imposed by their clients.

From 1890 on, this missionary state of mind was manifested by the creation of innumerable groups in Paris, Vienna, London, Helsinki, and Glasgow. Craftsmanship was restored to its former eminence, and painters such as Van de Velde, De Feure, and Brangwyn, not content with having thrown the drawing-room doors wide open to decorative designers, finally joined their ranks to become craftsmen themselves.

ORIENTALISM

Samuel Bing was instrumental in opening new vistas as he imported various objects from Japan and ordered his designers to capture and translate their essence. Exasperated by the *turqueries* which Fromentin and Decamps were so fond of and which enraptured Sarah Bernhardt, Whistler and Bing sought to adapt exoticism to the Western eye. This formula created a refined aesthetic of decoration which can be seen in Whistler's Peacock Room, Bagery's chairs, the printed materials by De Feure, and Baillie Scott's salmon and rose-pink hangings (*see* plates 280 and 297).

But however influential the Orientalists were, the Nancy School was even more so; it created a truly Symbolist furnishing style which is of capital importance in the history of Art Nouveau.

THE SCHOOL OF NANCY

The plans and aims set forth by the School of Nancy stated a unified ideal: the revival of an artistic center which would draw its originality from the spirit of the ancient province of Lorraine, a regional aspiration not unlike that of the Medical School under Charcot.

We can gain information on the various ideals entertained by the youthful School of Nancy by reading its manifestos. They are rather reminiscent of those issued by supposedly left-wing parties animated by sincere, generous convictions but which, being partly sponsored by the well-to-do, become the most ardent defenders of capitalism.

Gallé wanted his works to be available to the masses, but they were so refined and so expensive to produce that only the rich could afford them. The same dilemma separated Ruskin and his disciple Morris, who wanted everyone to have beautiful things to enjoy, but fell into the clutches of mediocre manufacturers.

The School of Nancy succeeded not only in joining animal and flower motifs in its decorative schemes but also, by enlarging a field poppy, for example, or a gnat, achieved a kind of supernatural effect; this is its most remarkable characteristic.

The designers at Nancy were so enamored of unusual effects that they wandered into abysses inhabited by formless monsters. Similarly, some furniture by Gallé and Majorelle makes the hallucinated imagination of the artists of earlier centuries look like tamely realistic modeling.

Working on lines parallel to those of the School of Nancy, a few creative spirits such as Rupert Carabin, Jean-Auguste Dampt, and Gaudí went beyond the frontiers of Symbolism and successfully transliterated delirium into stone or wood. They penetrated deeper than anyone had before into the realm of dream and fantasy—deeper than Andrea Brustolon or the late-fifteenth-century Florentine cabinetmakers. The Gaudíesque mirror (*see* plate 306), Endell's staircase (*see* plate 318), the cabinet by Carabin (*see* plate 300), and the astonishing table by an unknown designer (*see* plate 301) are spirited, amusing, disquieting masterpieces, which would be quite at home in surroundings dreamed up by Hieronymus Bosch or Edgar Allan Poe.

Paris was more amenable to the styles advocated by the fashionable upholsterers and the Goncourt brothers, and was somewhat intractable at first when presented with the ideals of the

School of Nancy. France's first new, revolutionary interior must be credited to the adventurous spirit displayed by the owners of the Café de Paris and Maxim's. The work of Sauvage and Sara-zin at the Café de Paris, and the rooms in the private house designed by Schoellkopf for Yvette Guilbert, yield an impression of license, preciosity, and originality; standing in front of mahogany partitions, inlaid with volutes and arabesques of different kinds of rare wood, the unusual furniture seems to be dancing a strange lascivious ballet in the light falling from perverse can-delabra which coil and twist like angry cobras. The ordinary run of customers inevitably resisted this type of decoration, and in order to keep the commissions coming in, Schoellkopf and his colleagues had to draw in their horns.

The undeniably important position held by France in Art Nouveau was largely won by Émile Gallé, the movement's leader, and by countless cabinetmakers and decorators—such men as Majorelle, Émile André, Gautier, and Jacques Gruber—who made the most of the arboral sinuosities of the style without transgressing the example set by nature, the supple energy and formal construction of fibrous growth.

IMPASSE

A glance at the furniture and examples of decorative art included here will show the reader that this Mannerist art lacked roots, both spiritually and socially. When we contemplate this excess of affectation (and indeed of vulgarity, to which it often descended), we feel that the failure of Symbolism involved that of decoration also, or rather of super-decoration.

This was why the Nouille Style, which was the bridge between the world of yesterday and the world of tomorrow, was slaughtered by the public's lack of understanding. One can indeed sympathize with the irritation of some of the critics, one of whom wrote in *Le Gaulois* in 1899:

> "The Art of Decoration has been reborn. Are you thirsty? Try buying yourself a drink in a brasserie. Don't be nervous, go on in…. But alas! at once you will feel the chill of the ceramics descending on your soul, and the menace of the tormentedly rising candelabra suspended over your head…."

Like Dali, the writer goes on to complain of "the flaccid twists and turns of these appurte-nances created for a democratic clientèle" and is "nauseated by their ordinary, workaday appearance."

In many cases, especially where the applied arts are concerned—the very term "applied," as Jean Cassou rightly points out, "reveals the absurdity, sophistry, and unnecessary complication of the curves, their reckless eclecticism"—we are confronted by "a jumble which simply does not, and cannot, constitute a unity." (*Les Sources du XXᵉ Siècle*, Exhibition Catalogue, Paris, 1960–61.)

BELGIUM

Belgium made such progress on every artistic front, especially that of the decorative arts, that the end of the century found her in an exemplary position.

Two tendencies, often in conflict, held the field. One was the vein of Symbolism and fantasy associated with Horta, Hankar, and Gustave Serrurier-Bovy, and fairly closely related to the School of Nancy and the British. The other was created by Van de Velde and was resolutely functional; it "set up an experimental formula in opposition to the religious exaltation of Ruskin and the generous socialism of Morris." The idea of experiment underlay everything attempted by the young architect, who had adopted Michelangelo's statement that "beauty lies in the elimination of superfluities."

Van de Velde first turned his attention to simplifying the décor of everyday life. His gorge rose at:

"...the insane follies which the furniture makers of past centuries had piled up in bedrooms and drawing rooms.... Processions of fauns, menacing apocalyptic beasts, benevolently hilarious Cupids (bawdy in some cases and complaisantly anxious to please in others), and swollen-cheeked satyrs in charge of the winds."
His reaction to this décor was unequivocal:

"Reason is revolted by this perennial cowardice, this persistent refusal to seek out the right form, the form which is simple, truthful, and absolute."
And he rejects a certain deeply ingrained misconception:

"Style and beauty are two sharply differentiated things; neither of them depends on the other; indeed, either may exclude the other. To strive for style does not necessarily mean striving for beauty. Style results from the general connection arising between all the manifestations of creative thought in a given period. Style includes all the characteristics which constitute the family; some families are beautiful and others are ugly. So the same is of course true of styles.

"In architecture and the industrial arts it is dangerous to pursue beauty for beauty's sake. Such a quest can end only in baroque confusion."

(Henry van de Velde, *Formule d'une Esthétique Moderne*)

Henry van de Velde was just turned twenty-six when he was admitted to membership in the *Cercle des XX*, the group of painters in Brussels who were fighting for a new aesthetic.

An idealistic Socialist in the manner of his time, Van de Velde was anxious to connect the lot of art with that of society, to unify the civilization of thought with that of the machine. It was in this spirit that in 1895 he built his own house, Bloemenwerf, at Uccle (*see* plate 59), designing not only the building itself but also the furniture, lighting fixtures, and hardware, and creating an ensemble which was revolutionary for its time because it was completely, consistently modern.

The finished ensemble drew the attention of artists from all over Europe, and the French dealer, Samuel Bing, was so enthusiastic that he began exhibiting works by Van de Velde as early as 1897; Germans of various sorts and conditions—Count Harry Kessler and the art critic Julius Meier-Graefe, Walter Rathenau, and the Grand Duke of Saxony—became ardent supporters of his work and ideas.

Between 1897 and 1900, there was still a certain unity in Art Nouveau, regardless of whether its country of origin was Belgium, Britain, France, Germany, or Austria. The distinctions which were soon to arise between Art Nouveau and modern art had not yet appeared in any significant way; the same sense of line (though of course with individual variations) was displayed by the School of Nancy, Horta, and Van de Velde.

But, as one year followed another, Van de Velde eliminated "superfluous ornament" from his furniture, ceramics, and fabrics; at the same time, however, unlike Josef Hoffmann and more especially Adolf Loos, he retained from his Brussels period and the bewitching influence of Horta a certain fondness for the style which he made so much his own, and into which he appears somehow to have translated the slow, irresistible surges of the sea.

Van de Velde was therefore the one artist who achieved a balanced position between the excesses of the School of Nancy and the arid simplicity of the pioneers of the Bauhaus. His standpoint was that line was fundamental, that its shining excellence came from its having "derived its strength from the energy of the man who drew it," and that it should never be disguised or concealed. Despite being so hostile to superfluity and to the pursuit of beauty for its own sake, Van de Velde was well able to perceive the good side of Symbolist Art Nouveau. Years later, he wrote:

"The same critics who have nothing but enthusiastic exclamations for Gothic and Renaissance ornament are ever ready with severity when evaluating the execution and artistic value of contemporary works. But they have no right to depreciate the quality and inspiration of the men who guided the industrial arts in the flourishing days of the Jugendstil in Germany, Art Nouveau in France, and the style which borrowed briars and lilies—lilies and chlorotic girls with opulent tresses—from the English Pre-Raphaelites.

"If [Art Nouveau and Nouille Style] fell so rapidly into discredit, the reason lay in the strikingly poor execution of the objects it was trying to get the public to accept. With the furniture and other utilitarian objects of the Middle Ages and Renaissance it was just the reverse: the workmanship was so superlative that the inspiration of the artists of those periods has never since been safeguarded against criticism; only today has the suspicion percolated that the quality of the inspiration was inferior and possibly even corrupt! Once again we come up against the important truth that workmanship alone does not constitute beauty."

(Henry van de Velde, *Formule d'une Esthétique Moderne*)

An axiom of Leonardo da Vinci's which was taken up by Van de Velde, that "beauty and utility can exist together, like castles and men," became the battle cry not only of Art Nouveau, but also of the new age which followed it. Thus, when the directors of the Magasins du Louvre in Paris announced, in 1896, a competition for the design of a motorcar which was to look like a genuine automobile, not just a carriage minus the horses, they were contributing to the birth of what is now known in France as *le stylisme*.

GERMANY

In France, with Bracquemond, Gallé, and Guimard, and in Britain, with Mackmurdo and Morris, decorative Art Nouveau arose from the work of specialists. In Germany its origins were different; its proponents appear to have been three intellectuals, Justus Brinckmann, who founded the Museum für Kunst und Gewerbe in Hamburg in 1877, the painter and collector Otto Eckmann, and Jacobsen, a pastor who set up a village weaving center.

Acting on motives similar to those of the founders of the Arts and Crafts movement in Britain, Brinckmann wrote in his introduction to an exhibition of contemporary posters in 1896:

"Art must be accessible to all… not only to those who can afford to buy pictures, but also to those who have the leisure to enjoy them in art galleries. To attain this goal, art must go down into the street and station itself in the view of the workers hurrying by, to whom you can offer neither time nor money."

The prominence and success which the movement attained in Hamburg were due partly to another pioneer, Alfred Lichtwark, who communicated his passion for the art and horticulture of Japan to intellectual and industrial circles in that ancient Hanseatic city.

Between 1892 and 1900, the flame of the new movement was lit simultaneously in Munich, Darmstadt, Berlin, and Pforzheim. Whereas in France Art Nouveau remained a local phenomenon, largely confined to Nancy, in Germany every city contributed through its own originality to the creation of a general national style.

Munich, where the success of Art Nouveau was total, became the mecca of all these aspirations. The periodicals *Jugend* and *Pan* opened their pages not only to German artists but to anyone, no matter where he came from, who was eager to battle for the same cause. The spearhead was provided by *Simplizissimus*, whose liveliness and malice were reinforced by drawings, many of which were contributed by Thomas Theodor Heine.

The Germans, with admirable intuition, were much quicker than the Belgians to appreciate the genius of Van de Velde. Berlin, Munich, Darmstadt, and Hagen vied with one another to secure his services as teacher and designer. And although court and aristocratic circles sneered at his revolutionary efforts, big business, in the form of shipping companies, gave him commissions, as did craftsmen—the former for the interior decoration of ships, and the latter for shops.

Munich also attracted Mackintosh and the Hoffmann section of the Sezession from Austria. Olbrich, Obrist, Riemerschmid, and, above all, Endell found there exactly the climate in which imagination could expand and bloom.

The French had developed an inferiority complex about Germany after their defeat in 1870, and their reactions to this seething cauldron of artistic activity make an interesting study. They were both astounded and humiliated. For two centuries, Germany had been devoted to the charms of French art; now, with the indisputable success of this strange new movement, she had achieved her aesthetic independence, and in France not only the painters, but the dealers as well, were alarmed. A French critic wrote in 1897:

"Germany, as we are beginning to realize, has entered a period of magnificent development. No sooner had she attained military supremacy than she set about winning supremacy in the industrial and commercial fields; and this is now almost in her grasp. Today, her eyes are on artistic supremacy. Some of our own people believe this is an unattainable dream. They are wrong. A few years ago, if anyone mentioned the jewelers trained at Pforzheim and Hanau, they used to laugh disdainfully. But they have stopped laughing. German jewelers' shops can be seen in the boulevards. The center from which the whole world draws its supply is no longer Paris, but Pforzheim. If anyone thinks I am exaggerating, let me inform him that one of the leading French firms has just set up a branch in that city. I could cite several other no less convincing facts.

"What the Germans have done for their army, their industry, their trade—and for many other branches of their activities—they are now determined to do for their decorative art. Let us make no mistake about this. It is all part of the same struggle, and it will be waged with even greater tenacity and patience, if that be possible, because their previous successes have given the Germans boundless self-confidence. Will our own blindness be equally boundless? Alas, I am much afraid it will. In any case, I hereby sound the alarm; I would be failing in my duty if I did not. This time the struggle is at least taking place in the full light of day. German periodicals, its most active instruments, far from concealing the aim in view, publicly proclaim it; and they are displayed for sale in the windows of our bookshops."

AUSTRIA

Art Nouveau and "Modern Style," and even Jugendstil, eventually allowed themselves to be tinged with a certain pervasive dandyism. Vienna was different; it resisted. The adherents of the Sezession, who were the spiritual brothers of Mackintosh and his pupils, were up in arms not only against the old traditions, but also, and just as strongly, against the decorative ideas of Otto Wagner; their ambition was to move directly from the "bureaucratic" style, so lovingly cherished at the court of Franz Joseph, to a truly contemporary style. To the new "wreathing, writhing, and fainting in coils," they preferred straight lines, and, to the resounding contraptions of Max Klinger, surfaces in light or pale colors sprinkled with abstract geometrical ornament. But while it preserved an unbroken respect for the forms created by Mackintosh, Voysey, and Baillie Scott, the Sezession underlined the rigor of those forms with startling inlays of pearl, silver, and jewels, as if to remind the world that Vienna was nearer to Constantinople than to Glasgow.

The balanced masses and elegant geometrical patterns of Olbrich, treated in severe harmonies of black and white, are an early prefiguration of Cubism and Art Décoratif.

GREAT BRITAIN

In 1861, three of the best Pre-Raphaelite painters, Ford Madox Brown, Dante Gabriel Rossetti, and Edward Burne-Jones, joined William Morris in launching the firm of Morris, Marshall,

Faulkner & Co. The venture was inaugurated with a flourish, and copies of their prospectus urging radical reform in both furniture and decoration were widely distributed.

Morris' group came just at the right moment to satisfy the ambition of the English to have a national art of their own. Some of them, influenced by Ruskin, had already had their houses torn down and rebuilt; these modern buildings now required appropriate decoration and furniture. The transformation of English art was the work, directly and indirectly, of William Morris, a painter, weaver, printer, typographer, glazier, decorator, and dealer who also found time to write poetry, edit a Socialist journal, and give lectures.

The character of his preferences recalls Gallé rather than Van de Velde or Loos. He looked for examples among such relics of Celtic and Saxon handicraft as he could find in farmhouses and in the provinces generally. Jean Lahore wrote of Morris in 1898:

"In his magnificent endowment of natural gifts he resembles the 'universal men' of the Renaissance. He is by turns an outstanding poet and an admirable wood carver; he designs wallpapers; he prints and weaves chintzes and damasks and velvets. And these latter are masterpieces of line and color and inspire a whole youthful school. They compel emulation from such particularly talented men as Voysey and Walter Crane. They make a new and charming art come bursting, branching, and flowering into life on wallpaper and fabrics."

There has been some argument about the validity of Morris' work, because of the varied nature of his output; it was a mixture of cheap items turned out by ordinary manufacturing processes, and expensive ones produced by craftsmen. But it has been rightly observed by Kurt Dingelstedt that Morris' success was of prime importance insofar as he reformed and re-invigorated the craftsman's life, both technically and aesthetically:

"It was he who made it subsequently possible for the relationship between the raw material and the machine to be clarified, as Van de Velde also did. Morris' works were too rich and rare to be within the means of any but a small circle of amateurs, and were therefore completely inconsistent with the social convictions and aspirations of Morris himself. But it was unavoidably necessary to make a start in this non-social way in order to restore the status and savor of the craftsman's position and liberate him from the industrialization which he had undergone in the nineteenth century."

As can be seen from this chapter's illustrations, the English and Scottish schools resembled those on the Continent in that they frequently represented the conflicting currents of historicism and modernism. Ashbee and Baillie Scott succeeded in both respecting British tradition and striking (though not as boldly as Mackmurdo) an original note. Mackintosh and the Glasgow School, with their severe lines, both daring and graceful, shaped the future growth of the decorative arts not only in Scotland and the rest of Great Britain, but throughout Europe. The Blue Bedroom and the White Bedroom at Hill House are among the most remarkable examples of late-nineteenth-century decoration, and Mackintosh's stepped chairs have an unsurpassable beauty.

George Walton, regarded by Hermann von Muthesius as one of the best decorators of the period, was Great Britain's most interesting all-round interior designer after Mackmurdo. A feature of his elegant creations is the floral frieze with which he not infrequently covered the whole wall. George Walton, J. S. Henry, and a number of other English and Scottish artists gave a new impetus to the design of fireplaces, a speciality in which the British have always excelled.

FURNITURE DESIGNED BY ARCHITECTS

It is almost true to say that in earlier centuries money was no object; the architect could make the furniture match the building. Indeed, the master mason or his later counterpart often designed the woodwork and furniture himself.

During the greater part of the nineteenth century, architects left these matters to others, but toward the end of the century, their interest in interior decoration revived. D'Aronco in Italy,

Guimard, Plumet, and Selmersheim in France, Horta and Van de Velde in Belgium, Berlage in Holland, Gaudí in Spain, Eliel Saarinen in Finland, and many others attempted to realize a total unity. Guimard's designs for apartments included wallpapers, the settee on a stairway landing, the fireplace for the concierge, and all the necessary moldings, but this tendency, which grew stronger with the interest to which it ministered, was thought to be too expensive by real-estate promoters and builders from about 1905 on. The corruption of taste which they enforced was encouraged by the increasing trade in art objects, both privately and in auction rooms, and newspapers devoted a considerable amount of space to the art object market. The decorator's profession, moreover, was pursued by furniture dealers and upholsterers who had no imagination and were stubbornly resistant to reform. In 1905, a Parisian decorator boasted of having given Louis XV interiors to hundreds of New York apartments.

TOWARD MODERN ART

A glance at the pianos by Majorelle (*see* plate 362) and Hoffmann (*see* plate 367), or the desk by Saarinen (*see* plate 360), enables us to see what these designers were aiming toward, and the directions in which they were moving.

Majorelle, Gallé, Horta, Basile, and the Russians working in a folk-art style were leading decorative art toward an impasse. Their work sounded the knell of the old historicist and Mannerist styles.

Hoffmann's piano looks twenty years in advance of its time; it would have been at home in the 1925 Exhibition of Decorative Arts in Paris. This is because it represents a certain modernistic style tinged with a kind of Japanese aestheticism, which disappeared not long after that exhibition. Only Saarinen's desk, which would not be out of place today in a New York office building by Philip Johnson, affords direct proof that there was a successful variety of Art Nouveau, the ancestor of contemporary art.

CONCLUSION

It may still be too early to estimate the success of Art Nouveau in relation to the styles preceding it. The day before yesterday it was ridiculous; yesterday, irritating; today, it is what antique dealers call "amusing"; tomorrow, couches by Gallé and Gaudí and lacquered furniture by Mackintosh will assume their natural places among the masterpieces of all ages. Meanwhile, decorators are beginning to "do" their clients' homes in the 1900 Style, and are finding it no easy matter to reproduce the best of that style's achievements. One reason is that its life span was short: a bare ten years; another is that many of the things produced in its name were of poor quality—lack of unified design in some cases, poor materials in others. Moreover, duplicating the décor and especially its colors, which were all-important, is a delicate and perhaps impossible task because the fabrics to be copied—curtains, draperies, upholstering materials—have practically disappeared. (However, Liberty and Morris fabrics are now being reproduced in London, using the original plates and blocks.)

HISTORICISM, SYMBOLISM

STYLE JULES VERNE

269 ✎ Various Designers. The House of M. Jérôme Doucet, "Man of Letters" (sic). *Study.* 1902. Private Collection, Clamart.
The exterior of this simple, unpretentious house at Clamart is decorated with ceramics by Bigot, who also collaborated with Gaillard in executing the fireplace (which cost 2,500 francs—about $1,000). The murals, representing old tales and legends, are by J. M. Avy; the stained glass by Félix Gaudin; door and window hardware by Alexandre Charpentier; doors, wainscoting, cupboards, and *objets d'art* were supplied by Bing; the desk is by Eugène Colonna (cost: 750 francs), wooden chairs by Gaillard (each chair cost 350 francs). Not to be overlooked is the inevitable potted palm.

270 ✎ P. J. H. and Joseph Cuypers. *The Hall of Honor.* Castle De Haar. 1899–1900. Vleuten, The Netherlands.
In 1898, Baron van Zuylen replaced an ancient ruin with an immense fortress in stone and brick in an undiluted historicist style. Using medievalism as his basic style, the architect carried out an interior which is a Romantic-age "Folly," but one in which Art Nouveau details can be detected here and there. The total effect is as charmingly absurd as the architectural fantasies of Ludwig II of Bavaria.

271 ✎ Gotthold Riegelmann. *Staircase.* The German Pavilion at the Universal Exhibition of 1900, Paris.
At the end of the nineteenth century, Germany was still divided technically as well as aesthetically. Jugendstil was in opposition to both Wagnerism and Munich-style Hellenism. This decorative creation, in which Symbolism is still heavily impregnated with medievalism, recalls the doorway of the Pohjola building in Finland (*see* plate 68).

272 ✎ Michael Munkacsy. *Visiting the New Mother.* Oil on canvas. C. 1878. Neue Pinakothek, Munich.
As late as 1895, the *style Fallière*, Victorian style, and Rundbogenstil were dominant in well-to-do circles in Western Europe. Munkacsy, a fashionable Hungarian painter, takes us into the sitting room of a pretty young mother, decorated with potted palms (placed in the usual false brass *cache-pot* to hide the clay pot), Renaissance armchair, and "Japanese" hangings.

273 ✎ Unknown Designer. *Dressing Room.* The Rockefeller house at 4 West 54th Street. C. 1880. The Museum of the City of New York.
Toward the end of the nineteenth century the Rockefellers, who were already wealthy, modernized the inside of their house. To the existing "Duchesse de Berry" style (satinwood and other rare woods), the American decorator added a touch of "Saracenism." Only a few, "the best people," had dressing rooms,

which, however, were probably not as rare as bathrooms were in France. When in 1895 the Tzar Nicolas II resided officially in Paris at the Quai d'Orsay (the French Foreign Office), he had to go to the Ritz whenever he wanted a bath.

274 ✎ Henry Eyles. Rosewood armchair with ceramic plaque. 1851. The Victoria and Albert Museum, London.
Designed for Albert, the Prince Consort, this imposing armchair—a pleasant monstrosity, so to speak; the grandson of a Louis XV *bergère*—prefigures later excesses under Victoria and Napoleon III, and also Art Nouveau. It already calls to mind certain chairs by Basile.

275 ✎ Franz von Stuck. Ebony bench with ivory inlays. C. 1902. (Whereabouts unknown.)
The insatiable appetite for Classical Antiquity which dominates German architecture is also to be found in decoration and furniture.

276 ✎ Arthur Heygate Mackmurdo and Members of the Century Guild. Cabinet. 1886. The Victoria and Albert Museum, London.
Mackmurdo, architect and decorator, and a disciple of Ruskin and William Morris, set up the Century Guild in 1882; two years later he started a magazine, *The Hobby Horse.* He was an influential figure in the applied arts, and contributed to modifying British interiors. He was interested in all facets of decoration—wallpapers, fabrics. When the new century began, he decided to abandon the decorative arts.

277 ✎ George Gagey (attr.). Sideboard. C. 1902–04. Property of the Association des Mutilés de la face, Paris.
The School of Nancy and a number of architect-designers attempted to combine medievalism and Art Nouveau. This sideboard, which graced a fine 1900 house, is typical of the resulting hybrid style.

278 ✎ Unknown Designer. *Door.* Castle De Haar. 1898–1900. Vleuten, The Netherlands.
In this door, the Dutch decorator achieved a successful synthesis of the medievalist and Art Nouveau styles by orientalizing the decorative panel in the manner of Whistler or Toorop.

279 ✎ Jan Toorop. Interior. C. 1900. Gemeente Museum, The Hague.
In the early part of this century, Holland's decorative style was divided between her traditional tendencies and the influence of the Far East. (The same situation had occurred earlier, during the period of her East-

Indian conquests.) Five artists who were in love with Javanese art set about adapting it for Dutch use: Jan Toorop, Johan Thorn-Prikker, Gerrit Willem Dijsselhof, the ceramist Theodorus A. C. Colenbrander, and the sculptor Mendes da Costa. Toorop, who was born in Java, did not in any way tone down or tame Javanese symbolism; on the contrary, he made it more disturbing, pushing it to the brink of Surrealism. The room can be seen reflected in the mirror, and the very impassivity of the glass brings out the poetry of the wall decoration. Note the curved, angular pose of the hands on the figures decorating the frame. The pose is borrowed from the dancers of Bali and is noticeable in a number of Art Nouveau paintings.

280 ⬚ JAMES MCNEILL WHISTLER. The Peacock Room of the Leyland residence, London. 1876–77. Freer Gallery of Art, Smithsonian Institution, Washington, D.C.
The ravishing Peacock Room, replete with Japanese influence, is one of the greatest of Whistler's achievements. (Robert de Montesquiou said of Whistler that "he was like a rare bird; its crest was his forelock, its cries the painter's words.") This room announces the future American style (the "Saracenic") and the verticals dear to Koloman Moser, Loos, and the Art Décoratif style.

281 ⬚ WILLIAM DE MORGAN. *The Hall.* 8 Addison Road, London. C. 1899.
Orientalism had a considerable influence in Great Britain. The tiles and decorations in a Byzantine and Persian vein are a good example of the tendency. An excellent ceramist, De Morgan, like the Frenchman Metthey, played with harmonies of mauve, violet, and green. In contrast to the Byzantine decoration, the architect has introduced Art Nouveau details in the lighting fixtures, door handles, and switches.

282 ⬚ UNKNOWN DESIGNER. *Detail of Drawing Room.* Japanese Embassy. 1900. Avenue Hoche, Paris.
A curious exchange of influences can be seen here. Since 1870, Japanese art had been influencing the West; thirty years later, Art Nouveau was charming the artists of Japan. In 1900, the Japanese ambassador in Paris decided to give a 1900 appearance to his embassy. Since Japanese houses contain only the indispensable minimum of furniture, a certain amount of improvization was necessary. The Ambassador sent sketches of French furniture to the firm of Mitsui in Tokyo, requesting that they be transposed into an Oriental key. The result was successful, at least if one judges by the documentary evidence, which mentions salmon-pink hangings with a woven pattern of maple leaves near the bottom, chairs upholstered in gray and brown leather, woodwork with decorations in old gold, and white lacquered furniture.

283 ⬚ FERDINAND BOBERG. Side chair. 1900. Nordiska Museet, Stockholm.

The Swedish designer Boberg was particularly gifted with details: note the perforations of the cross bars on the chair legs, and the sun-ray design on its back. Like A. Wallenberg, he sought unusual effects: tables whose legs resembled those of women and whose tops were griffins' wings. This chair is yet another example of Japanese influence.

284 ⬚ TONY and PIERRE SELMERSHEIM. Rosewood settee. C. 1902. (Whereabouts unknown.)
The best French interior designers and decorators were Plumet, Barberis, and Tony and Pierre Selmersheim. The latter were opposed to Symbolism and aimed at creating an Art Nouveau based on historicism—Gothic, Louis XV, and even Directoire. They preferred decoration in a light key (with white walls), and achieved counterpoint in color by means of colonnades of semiprecious stone. Like the Anglo-Saxons, this French group was concerned with "functionalism"; this settee incorporates drawers and a glass-fronted niche for books.

285 ⬚ EUGÈNE VALLIN. Chair. C. 1900. Musée de l'École de Nancy, Nancy.
Eugène Vallin served an apprenticeship at Nancy under his uncle, who made ecclesiastical furnishings. He was a Symbolist who as a rule was less successful than Majorelle or Guimard in giving his work individuality.

286 ⬚ LÉON JALLOT. Chair. 1900. Bethnal Green Museum, London.
Between 1895 and 1910, a certain number of French designers who were irritated by the Symbolist historicism of Latin Art Nouveau began breaking the trail which eventually led to Art Décoratif. As early as 1903, Maurice Dufrêne was designing furniture in which three horizontal planes were connected by a richly inlaid stylized frieze—maple inlaid with marquetry in kingwood, ebony, mother-of-pearl, and ivory, in the manner of Hoffmann and Koloman Moser. Contemporaneously, Paul Follot executed enormous wainscots which he harmonized with the wall above in the manner of Van de Velde. Jallot, who designed the chair shown here, was one of the finest furniture makers in this group; it was to him, together with Gaillard, De Feure, and Colonna, that Bing entrusted control of the workshops of his Art Nouveau establishments.

287 ⬚ EUGÈNE COLONNA. Glass-fronted cabinet. C. 1902. Museum für Kunst und Gewerbe, Hamburg.
Colonna was one of the most accomplished exponents of Latin Art Nouveau. The spidery architecture of his furniture, with its dreamy, graceful, organic forms, makes him very different from Van de Velde, whose plastic sense is quite unemotional. In the Universal Exhibition of 1900 in Paris, on the Esplanade des Invalides, Colonna collaborated on Bing's Art Nouveau House, whose ceramic façade by De Feure made a striking contrast to the blatant folklore of the Breton

pavilion, which stood next to it. Watercolor sketches made at the time convey some idea of the special charm of which 1900 art was capable. They show walls whose satinwood paneling has insets of green plush; dressing rooms hung with Japanese silk printed in two colors; bedroom walls covered with embroidered silk—gray, blue, mauve, green—paneled with Hungarian ash, and bordered with upholsterer's piping; at the windows, hand-painted silk curtains, dusted with powdered gold, through which the light filtered gently.

288 ⬚ CHARLES PLUMET. Dressing table. C. 1900. Museum für Kunst und Gewerbe, Hamburg.
Functional, graceful, strong yet slender—this piece by Plumet is the perfect example of the Whiplash Style as interpreted by a Frenchman.

289 ⬚ VICTOR HORTA. *Entrance Hall.* The Solvay Residence (now the Wittamer de Camps Residence). 1895–1900. Brussels.
The stone sculpture is by P. Braecke. Horta, a contemporary of Maeterlinck and Théo van Rysselberghe was the first architect to break up the traditional interior anatomy of buildings by abolishing the usual passages and substituting an octagonal vestibule; a wide staircase services the rooms, which become independent entities. A passionate devotee of functionalism, Horta raised the status of utilitarian objects: steel, bolts, rivets, and naked stone became decorative elements in their own right.

290 ⬚ VICTOR HORTA. *Main Stairs.* The Solvay Residence (now the Wittamer de Camps Residence). 1895–1900. Brussels.
The stairs of the Solvay residence afford a glimpse of the startling genius of Horta. On the landing, framed by the volutes of the banisters, the magnificent panel by Van Rysselberghe assumes its full importance. Everything, even such details as the stair rods holding the carpeting, was designed by Horta himself.

291 ⬚ GUSTAV KLIMT (design), F. SIEGEL (marquetry), and ERWIN PUCHINGER (frame). Panel for a music room. 1900. Österreichisches Museum für Angewandte Kunst, Vienna.
"Symbolism *versus* functionalism" was the motto of the two fraternal yet contradictory tendencies which disputed the field in 1900. This panel (shown at the Universal Exhibition of 1900 in Paris), with strange motifs framed in copper, is an example of the subliminal fantasies favored by such Austrian artists as Klimt, Otto Wagner, and Moser. Adolf Loos, the apostle of simplification, rebelled against this tendency.

292 ⬚ J. J. GRAF. Marquetry paneling illustrating *Légendes Alsaciennes*. 1900. The Victoria and Albert Museum, London.
The spirit of this inlaid panel is pure Symbolism. Might this not be a stage-set as imagined by Gallé or Majorelle for *Tristan und Isolde?*

293 LOUIS MAJORELLE. Writing desk. 1899–1902. Musée de l'École de Nancy, Nancy.
The style of Majorelle is epitomized by this desk, whose bold yet graceful lines—note, for example, the splayed feet—recall the finest achievements of the eighteenth-century masters. Majorelle is the Charles Cressent (one of the greatest eighteenth-century cabinetmakers) of the Art Nouveau era. Despite its remoteness from the simplicity and functionalism advocated by Loos and Van de Velde, this piece, with its organic structure, is very much of its time.

294 ⬚ LOUIS MAJORELLE. Standing cabinet. 1899–1902. Collection Édouard Roditi, Paris.
It is difficult to separate reality from fantasy in the work of Majorelle. He was not content to derive his forms from nature; he developed them, carried them further. The muscular, trapezoidal feet of his pieces of furniture have a load to carry—the bony structure, as it were, represented by the woodwork above them.

295 ⬚ EUGÈNE GAILLARD. Chairs. C. 1900. Private Collection, Clamart.
These chairs have a tree-like touch disguising their essentially functional design. Gaillard was very talented, as can be seen, and (like Guimard) he was particularly adept at camouflaging the lines of force in his creations. This controlled lyricism is the hallmark of the Nancy School.

296 ⬚ ÉMILE GALLÉ. Sideboard, *Autumn Pathways*. 1892. Private Collection, Paris.
When delivering this piece to his customer, Émile Gallé accompanied it with a lengthy written message. In fulsome prose, which was a naïve imitation of the style of Mallarmé, he poured out his love of nature and his delight in work well done, and also gave detailed instructions for the cleaning, polishing, and preservation of the woodwork.
"*Autumn Pathways*:
"In the act of bidding farewell to a work which I brought forth not without pains and labor, I harbor within myself certain particulars concerning it, which I must now deliver to its purchaser. Allow me to dedicate them to you. They are but a slender tribute; these lines are not meant for the public eye....
"...On this occasion, my work was generated by its own joy in being magnificent, dense, and luxuriant, and in singing a song of praise to the warmth and abundance of harvest. My intention was to build a *crédence*, a Credo expressed in the accents of Autumn, a representation of might, growth, and majesty, whose festal gleam and orchestral shimmer would reflect not only the fanfares of life but also its muted voices and theological grace.
"All of us who love good work feel that it springs straight from the soul, and fancy that we hear the harmonies which presided over its birth. May this

present piece be to you as a forest growth rising from the floor to the beams of the ceiling.

"You are to imagine, then, that this handiwork of mine sprang integrally out of the burgeoning of two gnarled and ancient vine-stocks whose wood is brother to the clustered grapes and the year's new shoots and the supporting elm with its wrinkled bark, and the lizards and other little creatures round about....

"...The sense of decoration in this sideboard is exclusively based on the deliberate contrast between the representation of tangible things and the vision of certain lofty realities, those mysteries which we desire and must divine if we can.

"Look below. There the ornament makes contact with our ancient land and the life of the fields. Above, on the contrary, the depths are full of shadow; the decoration abandons naturalism to become misty and symbolic.

"Under your hands, therefore, are the animal and vegetable kingdoms of the vineyard 'in the heat of the day.' Here are its own peculiar plants, portrayed from the life in mosaics of wood and tints of August and September, from the woodspurge which opens at dawn to the golden buttercup. Here too are the winged guests of the site, the figpecker, and the tipsy thrush which feasts on the grapes; and the lines of the design are notations of bird-cries, the strident *tsic! tsic!* of the great scattered morning flights, and the autumnal refrain of the crested lark, *luli! luli!* .... [The description continues for two more pages.]

"*Patina!* I have emphasized the antithesis between realistic representation and symbolic adornment by applying a waxy patina only in certain places, where the relief has also been heightened by the use of encaustic. Elsewhere, on the other hand, I have taken a daring course which is without precedent in the cabinetmaker's art: the surface of the wood has been left in its natural virgin state, without varnish or patina. Nor has it been planed or sanded. Only the magical marks of an intelligently guided chisel have been allowed to remain. My colleagues may think little of the result—no matter. They have passively accepted the polish beloved by our forerunners, but that is only a passing fashion. The wood is sufficient unto itself. Waxes and pastes are by no means a guarantee of its indefinite preservation; it can lose its color in spite of them. In the grooves which hold the wings of the sideboard I have carved instructions to warn anyone undertaking repairs or restoration in the future against spoiling the matte surfaces.

"These have the powdery bloom of the heartwood, the veil of illusion which overspreads reality. And surely that is what we all so greatly need! So before the ravages of time and 'the moon which makes fabrics fade' (Montesquiou) shall have replaced the charm of youth by some other advantage which the maker will no longer be here to appre-

ciate, he wishes to say in what manner he has married the various hues of the wood with his mosaic designs....

"But now the craftsman is finishing his work and the master resigns himself to bidding it farewell.

"Sadly he inscribes his name upon it.

(Signed) Émile Gallé"

297 ☒ GEORGES DE FEURE. Settee. C. 1900. Private Collection, Paris.
The work of De Feure is characterized above all by refinement and elegance. One of the most versatile exponents of Art Nouveau, deeply interested in every kind of decoration, he loved to allow his creative spirit to wander into large expanses which he filled with strange flowers of the field. A predilection for luxurious materials caused him to upholster the fine Hungarian ashwood of his furniture with embroidered silk and to give a waxen glaze to the stucco with which he surrounded his fireplaces.

298 ☒ GEORGES HOENTSCHELL. Cabinet. C. 1900. Museum für Kunst und Gewerbe, Hamburg.
The style of Hoentschell has a more yielding, evanescent quality than that of Majorelle and Gaillard. It recalls the seventeenth-century Italian craftsman Andrea Brustolon and the designers of the fountains at the Villa d'Este. Algerian plane was one of Hoentschell's favorite woods.

299 ☒ EUGÈNE GRASSET. Cabinet with pier glass inset. 1898. Collection Brockstedt, Hamburg.
Only the 1900 Style could have produced this deliberate mixture of medievalism and Japanese influence.

300 ☒ RUPERT CARABIN. Cabinet. C. 1898. Private Collection, Paris.
To reveal the contents of this cabinet, it was necessary to lower the strangely sculptured panel (depicting bathers with their backs turned toward a carriage which is disappearing into the distance). A pair of entwined slugs, in bronze with a heavy patina, form the handle. The pedestal is formed by a bound woman whose grave expression is decidedly populist in style; she recalls the models of Gauguin, Sérusier, and Émile Bernard. Carabin, Dampt, Sarazin, Sauvage, and Schoellkopf manifested this tendency to out-symbolize Symbolism, somewhat in the manner of Gaudí, by integrating the sculptural theme into the main structure.

301 ☒ UNKNOWN DESIGNER. Inlaid olivewood table. C. 1898. Private Collection, Paris.
We have been unable to discover the origin of this curious piece. The kissing heads, which grow out of the raggedly contorted lines of the wood itself, are reminiscent of Carrière and of the carvers who decorated Milanese façades in the early part of the century. The marquetry of the table top, executed in pewter, mother-of-pearl, and semiprecious stones, and

the two reptilian women (who seem to be swaying to the rhythm of music which Debussy might have written) make one think of Klimt. The table bears two Gallé vases.

302 ▨ HANS BORGENSEN. Armchair. C. 1902. Private Collection, Sweden.
This chair (whose carving is applied rather than integral) bears a resemblance to some of the work of Ferdinand Boberg. The rings carved around the bases of the legs create an impression of strength and solidity; the forms at the ends of the arms are mysterious and hermetic.

303 ▨ ERNESTO BASILE and DUCROCQ. Gilded mahogany armchair. C. 1902. Private Collection, Italy.
Near the end of the century, the designer Ducrocq, who lived in Palermo, secured the collaboration of the architect Basile, the painter Maria Bergler, and the sculptor Augo. His furniture is among the most original ever made in Italy.

304 ▨ JEAN-AUGUSTE DAMPT. Armchair. C. 1902. Private Collection, Paris.
A sculptor, engraver, and decorator (he decorated the house of Mme. de Behague in Paris, which is now the Romanian Embassy), Dampt was also a cabinetmaker. He was part of the North European Symbolistic trend, closer to Huysmans than to Mallarmé.

305 ▨ UNKNOWN ITALIAN DESIGNER. Armchair. C. 1902. Collection Hélène Bouché, New York.
The shape and decoration of this chair (as in many other Italian designs of the time) are a compromise between Gaudí and the School of Nancy.

306 ▨ Attributed to FRANCISCO BERENGUER or ALEJO CLAPÉS. Pier glass. Collection Amigos de Gaudí, Casa Museo Gaudí, Parque Güell, Barcelona.
This mirror has a beautifully balanced quality, and recalls the bunches of seaweed left by the tides on the rock walls of tidal caves.

307 and **308** ▨ ANTONIO GAUDÍ. Carved armchair and chair. 1898–1904. Collection Amigos de Gaudí, Casa Museo Gaudí, Parque Güell, Barcelona.
The elegant carving and slender spiral forms of the chair (plate 308) give it the air of being ready to take wing. The architect Gaudí, who combined and sublimated all the styles of historicism and folk art, designed furniture, as did Guimard and many other architects. In this, as in other things, he was a genius, and turned out an incredible number of astonishing decorative creations.

309 ▨ ARTHUR BIBERFELD. Drawing room. C. 1900. (No longer extant.)
In this drawing room or boudoir by the Berlin designer Arthur Biberfeld, the accent is on the corner. The entire room is completely original. Note, for instance, the broad gesture of the hanging light, with its elegant

ellipses—a 1900 mobile—and the way in which the ceiling appears to have opened to conceal the fixture to which the light is attached.

310 ▨ JOSEPH MARIA OLBRICH. Drawing room. C. 1900. (No longer extant).
In 1880, the setting of daily life in Germany was still commonplace, vulgar, and depressingly aggressive. Fifteen years later, Olbrich, Endell, Riemerschmid, Pankok, and their disciples successfully united beauty with functionalism to enrich their country with a striking though ephemeral style. In this interior one feels that the decorator had breathed his spirit into the room, inflating it like a membrane of silk. The panels have a flowing quality, and the ceiling looks as if it had been wafted upward; wainscot, armchairs, couches, fireplace, and lighting fixtures are dovetailed and unified. A ravishing flowery manna descends on the wall, scattering its petals onto the furniture and carpets. The dynamic ceiling here, submarine rather than terrestrial, recalls Captain Nemo's cabin on the *Nautilus*. Jugendstil? No—*Style Jules Verne!*

311 ▨ RICHARD RIEMERSCHMID. Room for an Art Lover. 1900. (No longer extant.)
A room for an art lover had of necessity to surprise the eye with its daring and grace. The multiple-lustered hanging lamp resembles the interweaving flight of swallows, and the decorative frieze above the window and door is as delicate as eyelashes.

312 ▨ BRUNO PAUL. Armchair. C. 1900. Private Collection, Munich.
Bruno Paul, who took an active part in the founding of the *Vereinigte Werkstätte für Kunst und Handwerk*, was one of the leaders of the Munich School. His style is not easy to define: it is a combination of good taste, simplicity heightened by the ravishing oddity of a detail here or there, and comfort—the shapes of his chairs are open invitations to anyone who likes good living. Much of Bruno Paul's furniture is made of dark stained ash, with mahogany veneer insets.

313 ▨ HERMANN OBRIST. Tray table. C. 1900. Stadtmuseum, Munich.
Obrist studied pottery-making in Karlsruhe, sculpture in Paris, and embroidery in Florence. He later became director of the *Vereinigte Werkstätte für Kunst und Handwerk* in Munich. Much of his furniture appears to be conceived in a Gaudíesque spirit.

314 ▨ RICHARD RIEMERSCHMID. Cabinet. C. 1900. Stadtmuseum, Munich.
This partially glass-fronted cabinet and bookcase, with its bifurcated feet (also seen in works by Pankok, Bruno Paul, and Endell), is typical of German *fin-de-siècle* Symbolism.

315 ▨ BERNHARD PANKOK. Cabinet. C. 1900. Stadtmuseum, Munich.

A strange cabinet: perhaps the offspring of an illegitimate union between a steam shovel and a crab. Here again we have an example of the *Style Jules Verne.*

316 ⊠ AUGUST ENDELL. Table. C. 1900. Private Collection, Germany.
Endell's furniture, like Schilling's and Grebner's, has a strong affinity to that of Gaudí. This table can be compared with a sofa by the great master of Barcelona.

317 ⊠ BERNHARD PANKOK. Drawing room. C. 1900. Stadtmuseum, Munich.
Pankok was one of the masters of the Munich School. In this drawing room, the walls are broken up into panels showing Japanese influence. The panels themselves are cunningly related to the beams of irregular length which support the ceiling, a true vault, unusual in Art Nouveau. The light seems to flow from eleven brass hanging lamps, formed like the corollas of daisies. Emerald tones alternate with the pearly grisaille walls, a combination which accentuates the red upholstery of the furniture.

318 ⊠ AUGUST ENDELL. Vestibule of the Elvira Photographic Studio. 1897–98 (now destroyed). Munich.
From photographic records we can gauge the intensity of Endell's lyricism. Lines surge up everywhere: in stairs, walls, and ceilings. The Elvira Photographic Studio was a Gaudíesque construction (*see* plate 39) with dissonant contours, a submarine palace whose components feel the pull of conflicting currents. This is a long way from Van de Velde, Loos, and the Sezession and Glasgow styles.

319 ⊠ HENRI SAUVAGE and C. SARAZIN. Café de Paris. C. 1900 (now destroyed). Paris.
Stylistically, the Parisian architects Sauvage and Sarazin, who designed the Café de Paris, are related to Obrist and F. Siegel by their use of curved lines enriched with floral arabesques and abstract motifs outlined with mahogany. Some of Sauvage's furniture, imitating insect forms, is among the most surprising which the period produced.

320 ⊠ F. SIEGEL. Interior. C. 1904. (No longer extant.) Vienna (?).
The elliptical forms affected by the Austrian designer Siegel, like those of the French architects Sauvage and Sarazin, relate him to what we have called the *Style Jules Verne.* Siegel composed bentwood wall decorations whose elegant arabesques stand out against an unadorned, light background, relieved here and there by an open flower in the manner of the other Austrians and of Obrist.

ART NOUVEAU
(Functionalism, Slavism, Toward Art Décoratif)

321 ⊠ CHARLES RENNIE MACKINTOSH. Chair. 1900. The Museum of Modern Art, New York.
Mackintosh's genius contributed to a thorough reform of the decorative arts in Europe. His elegant, functional furniture was made of the commoner sorts of wood. Cheap and strong, painted white or waxed, it was easy to care for.

322 ⊠ CHARLES RENNIE MACKINTOSH and MARGARET MACDONALD MACKINTOSH. Writing desk. 1902. Österreichisches Museum für Angewandte Kunst, Vienna.
Mackintosh conceived his furniture in the same spirit as his buildings. It has a military strength enlivened partly with a few decorative motifs, like the armor of a jousting knight.

323 ⊠ EDWARD WILLIAM GODWIN. Sideboard. 1867. The Victoria and Albert Museum, London.
This sideboard clearly indicates that while European styles (Napoleon III, Victorian, Rundbogenstil) were still a dubious conglomeration of warmed-over scraps from the past, Godwin was already enthralled by Japanese art and was working toward the simplicity which inspired Ruskin, William Morris, and Mackmurdo.

324 ⊠ CHARLES RENNIE MACKINTOSH and MARGARET MACDONALD MACKINTOSH. Interior panel of the desk shown in plate 322.

This ravishing design executed in gesso is by Mackintosh's wife Margaret (they were married in 1900). Her sister Frances had married Herbert MacNair in 1899 (*see* plate 326).

325 ⊠ CHARLES RENNIE MACKINTOSH. Library Wing, Glasgow School of Art. 1907–09. Glasgow.
Mackintosh gradually abandoned architecture for decoration. The severe, functional interior he created for the library of the Glasgow School of Art is especially remarkable. Rigor and boldness are everywhere, from the library itself, which has been called "a masterpiece in the utilization of architectural space," to the upper loggia, from which the surrounding city and countryside can be seen like a vast panorama. It is almost unbelievable that the same man showed a completely different spirit in his elegant, almost frivolous tea rooms.

326 ⊠ HERBERT MACNAIR and FRANCES MACDONALD MACNAIR. Interior. 1902. (No longer extant.)
The interior decoration of Herbert and Frances MacNair is charming—perhaps even a little too charming. On walls of eggshell white, gossamer linear bouquets stand out in subtle harmonies of color: gray, light green, and lilac. Three-legged chairs, the front leg having a bracketed foot, add the final extravagant touch.

327 ⬚ OSCAR LEUWE. Dairy Restaurant. C. 1900. Nijmegen, The Netherlands.
In early twentieth-century Dutch offices, shops, and window displays, the English style was often espoused; but for its domestic interiors, the sternly dignified Dutch bourgeoisie preferred the austere decoration of K. P. C. de Bazel, with historicist furniture by Berlage, P. Joling (Amsterdam), or Willem Penaat (Haarlem).

328 ⬚ SIR FRANK BRANGWYN. Project for a drawing room. Watercolor. 1904. (Whereabouts unknown.)
Brangwyn was one of the *monstres sacrés* of the first part of the century. He was world-famous as a painter. As an interior designer and decorator he recalls Loos and Hoffmann. With his enormous, luxurious panels of wood separated by broad moldings, he anticipates Art Décoratif. The murals in this illustration are also by Brangwyn.

329 ⬚ E. A. TAYLOR. Sketch for a sitting room. Watercolor. 1902. (Whereabouts unknown.)
This sketch enables us to recapture the charm of this interior designed for the Turin Exposition of 1902. The white walls contrast with the pink and pale-green pastel shades of the doors and wainscoting; the part above the paneling is strewn with stylized floral motifs on a pearl-gray background, which is picked up again in a livelier key by the carpet and rugs. The lines of the piano are prophetic—very "1925." This simplicity and economy of means are characteristic of the English style of the period. Nauseated by overblown Victorianism and George Scott's Italian Gothic, English artists followed Morris' example and foreswore the pursuit of effect and sensation. Their influence was felt throughout Europe, especially in Germany; Hermann Muthesius, who was attached to the German Embassy as an architectural researcher, and Justus Brinckmann were both great admirers of English *Sachlichkeit* (objectivity) and constituted themselves apostles of the new tendencies.

330 ⬚ ARMAS LINDGREN. Sideboard. 1901. National Museum, Helsinki.

331 ⬚ LOUIS SPARRE and the IRIS GROUP. Table. C. 1902. Private Collection, Finland.
Underlying the renaissance of the decorative arts in Finland and the development of her architecture were two forces: reaction against German historicism and the attraction of Slavic folklorism. Louis Sparre was instrumental in the emergence of this "Kalevala style," as Édouard Roditi has so aptly called it.

332 and **333** ⬚ IRIS GROUP. Chair and interior for the Finnish Pavilion at the Universal Exhibition of 1900, Paris. (No longer extant.)
The decoration in general, the furniture—note the arched form of the table—and the simple iron hinges on the door are typical of the new Finnish style. The chair with embroidered upholstery is by Gallén-Kallela.

334 ⬚ CARL SPINDLER. Decorated cupboard. C. 1902. (Whereabouts unknown.)
The German designer Spindler has attempted to combine folk themes with the decorative ideas favored by the Englishman Baillie Scott.

335 ⬚ VARIOUS CRAFTSMEN. Princess Tenisheva's drawing room at Talashkino. C. 1902. Smolensk, Russia. (No longer extant?)
Whereas the Scandinavians, particularly the Finns, were resolutely modern and showed a marked preference for the Glasgow style, Russian progressives turned toward the Sezession and Symbolism, combining carving and painting in a stylized floral decoration.

336 ⬚ NICOLAS ROERICH. Couch with appliqué upholstery. C. 1902. Talashkino Workshops. (Whereabouts unknown.)
This couch, designed by Roerich for the Talashkino colony, is very different from the naïve works of the *Koustarys*, just as it is from the retrogressive spirit of the "Ambulants." Its delightful curves and stylized forms are very much in the *Mir Iskustva* vein. We are reminded of Diaghilev's Ballets Russes and of Alexandre Benois and Bakst.

337 ⬚ EDMOND FARAGÒ. Armchair, exhibited at the Hungarian Pavilion, Universal Exhibition of 1900, Paris. Bethnal Green Museum, London.
The spirit of the Sezession spread quickly from Vienna to the Balkans, and from Prague to Kiev. Budapest, weary of Vienna's neo-Byzantinism and Bureaucratic Style, invited Walter Crane to teach at the Museum of Decorative Arts. Edmund Wiegand adopted the Van de Velde line and designed furniture in a simple, unified style—fireplaces and bookcases in the manner of Ellwood. In Romania, Sterian injected new blood into the teaching of the decorative arts, and Petresco designed furniture in the Talashkino vein (eighty per cent Slav folk art, twenty per cent Sezession influence).

338 ⬚ VARIOUS DESIGNERS AND CRAFTSMEN. Furniture from Talashkino. C. 1902. (Whereabouts unknown.)
The Talashkino designers created their "New Russian" style by borrowing from both the Sezession style and folk art. Their work is built of massive volumes vividly picked out with geometrical or stylized decoration imitative of folk art. The result is something neither quite rustic nor quite modern. It represents an attractively original stage in the transition from one style to another.

339 ⬚ GUSTAVE SERRURIER-BOVY. Drawing room. C. 1902. (Whereabouts unknown.)
Like Van de Velde and Horta, Serrurier-Bovy was one of the great architectural decorators of Belgian Art Nouveau. But he was less bold than his colleagues; his ties to orthodoxy were closer. This interior, with its abundance of wavy lines and floral details, was very novel in its own day, but it lacks the inspiring breath

of modernism which enchants us in the work of his two celebrated contemporaries.

340 ⊠ ZINOVIEV. Armchair. C. 1900. (Whereabouts unknown.)
A mixture of Old Russia, paternalism, and the Sezession is noticeable in this chair. In the early part of the century, various sporadic movements in Russia laid siege to the ramparts of historicism. Their inspiration was similar to that of the Arts and Crafts movement in Britain. "It was in 1884," wrote Miss Netta Peacock, one of the organizers of the Russian rural industries section of the Universal Exhibition of 1902 in Paris, "that Hélène Polenoff first turned her attention to the study of the ornamental motifs of the Russian folk. The idea of doing so was suggested partly by the initiative of a friend, Mme. E. Mamontov, who in her country house at Abramtsevo, outside Moscow, had recently set up a school intended to give her serfs regular occupation during the winter months." This act of feudal paternalism aroused the enthusiasm of Princess Marie Tenisheva. Assisted by the painters Malyutin and Roerich, she founded a complete institute of the decorative arts at Talashkino. Peasant youths were trained in carpentry, ironwork, basket-weaving, wood-carving, and other crafts, and the girls in dressmaking, embroidery, or drawing.

341 ⊠ JOSEF HOFFMANN. Dining room of the Palais Stoclet. 1905–11. Brussels.
This dining room was built and decorated by Hoffmann, while the walls were decorated with friezes: marble, metal, and precious-stone mosaics by Gustav Klimt. The room illustrates the Continental differences between the Sezession and the various tendencies of Art Nouveau. Baron Stoclet of Brussels, a wealthy industrialist, was a collector and patron of the arts. He gave the young Viennese architect a completely free hand in designing his mansion, and Hoffmann proceeded to design everything, even the landscaping of the gardens. He sheathed walls and pilasters in yellow and ochre marble, and installed mosaic floors, with patterns of stylized flowers, to imitate carpets. Diffused lighting was achieved with spheres hung at different levels. The silver sconces, also designed by Hoffmann and placed at the angles of the walls, were made to look as opulent and precious as possible by being executed in "Cymric" style and inlaid with malachite.

342 ⊠ CARL WESTMAN. Interior of the Villa Saltsjö-baden. 1902. Sweden.
The architect, designer, and decorator Westman enlivened his cool, Glasgow Style interiors with a sprinkling of painted flowers on their snow-white panels. Carl Larsson's influence is noticeable in the painting of the furniture and the gay floral embroideries on white curtains. Another influence is George Walton, who made a deep impression on Northern Europe and was called by the critics "the

master builder of interiors" and "the artist of the home." Muthesius considered him one of the best decorators of the time. His own style, and his furniture after Chippendale, were both enormously successful.

343 ⊠ KOLOMAN MOSER. Ebony sideboard with marble inlays. 1900. Österreichisches Museum für Angewandte Kunst, Vienna.
This elegant piece, with its decoration of stylized fish, is a perfect example of the symbiosis that existed between the Japanese style and the Sezession. Koloman Moser was one of the founders of the *Wiener Werkstätte*.

344 ⊠ CLEMENT FROMMEL. Cabinet in boll hardwood. 1903. Österreichisches Museum für Angewandte Kunst, Vienna.
A happy amalgamation of Hoffmann's influence with that of Japan, and an anticipation of Art Décoratif, as seen in the fine wood, simple motifs, and rounded legs contrasting with the main cubic mass.

345 ⊠ ADOLF LOOS. Billiard room. 1898. (No longer extant.)
This billiard room has a beautifully balanced design. The vertical glass panels form a luminous counterpoint with the deeply set arched windows; the three strips decorating the ceiling suggest the crossbar of a scale, with the billiard table itself as its base. Loos was preoccupied with simplicity, and disapproved of Modern Style ornaments, which he regarded merely as a survival of Symbolism—that is to say, obsolete. Steiner's shop in Vienna, with its unadorned surfaces and its glass front two stories high, and the Kärtner Bar, built in the same year (1907), demonstrate what Loos felt to be the dominant characteristics of the Sezession movement.

346 ⊠ SIGMUND JARAY. Wardrobe. C. 1905. Österreichisches Museum für Angewandte Kunst, Vienna.
This wardrobe is part of a suite of bedroom furniture designed by Sigmund Jaray "for an unmarried workman." The line is simple, and the agreeable floral carving prefigures Art Décoratif. In Belgium, Serrurier-Bovy, with his passion for Socialistic amelioration, created "interiors for artisans," and in Paris, Maurice Lucet and Raymond Perraud founded the "American Combined," whose purpose was to allow credit terms to young couples for "wardrobe-beds" containing "a concealed washstand." These articles of furniture for customers with small incomes had their origin in the theoretical side of Art Nouveau, whose spokesmen proclaimed: "Nothing without art" (Roger-Marx); "Cheapness must be combined with usefulness and good taste" (William Morris); "To perpetrate ugliness is to sin against one's own conscience" (Van de Velde). Such men were in opposition to a certain section of the wealthier classes, whose mouthpiece was Arthur Maillet: "Is it true that the people, as Octave Mirbeau would have us believe, demand beauty? I

have no hesitation in answering, No!" The owners of the department stores, vigilantly watching for new consumer markets, soon began exerting themselves to supply "the useful and the pleasant" to the working and lower middle classes whose purchasing power had recently increased.

347 ◪ Rosa Drenn. Cabinet. C. 1905. Österreichisches Museum für Angewandte Kunst, Vienna.
It is evident that the designer of this cabinet, who was a pupil of Hoffmann, had already begun to leave Art Nouveau behind. Both its shape and its decoration

prefigure certain works by Jouve, an illustrator active around 1925, who owed much to Far Eastern influence.

348 ◪ Josef Hoffmann. Cigar cabinet. 1910–14. Österreichisches Museum für Angewandte Kunst, Vienna.
An ancient stepped ziggurat? No, a cigar cabinet! The rigidity of the form is softened by mother-of-pearl and ebony, semiprecious materials such as were later to be much used by Émile-Jacques Ruhlmann and the practitioners of Art Décoratif.

FURNITURE DESIGNED BY ARCHITECTS

349 ◪ Hendrik Petrus Berlage. Table and chairs. C. 1900. (Whereabouts unknown.)
Berlage's efforts to arrive at a truly modern style always appear hampered by Dutch historicism, from whose grip he could not quite break free. This inward conflict obliged him to disguise his innovations; he always returned, as if in spite of himself, to slightly rustic forms with a strong tincture of medievalism.

350 ◪ Ernesto Basile. Tea cart. C. 1900. (Whereabouts unknown.)
All curves and little flowers, this tea cart was designed by the Italian architect Basile for the decorator Ducrocq of Palermo. Looking like a cross between a tricycle and a Japanese fan, it would surely have upset an arch-functionalist such as Van de Velde.

351 ◪ Victor Horta. Rocking chair. Solvay Residence (now the Wittamer de Camps Residence). 1895. Brussels.
The design of this muscular yet graceful chair has the tensile strength of iron, the great Belgian architect's favorite material. Horta's works separate Van de Velde from Guimard.

352 ◪ Hector Guimard. Chair. C. 1900. The Cooper Union Museum for the Arts of Decoration, New York.
All the Guimard archives and the greater part of his furniture and bibelots were presented by Mme. Guimard to the Cooper Union Museum. With superb indifference, France allowed this historic collection to cross the Atlantic. In this chair one can appreciate the highly personal linear style of the artist whose genius found its happiest and most natural form of self-expression in certain aspects of Art Nouveau style. The steadiness and balance of this piece are in no way impaired by the grace of the slopes and curves.

353 ◪ Henry van de Velde. Desk. 1897–1900. Österreichisches Museum für Angewandte Kunst, Vienna.
One of Van de Velde's maxims was: "To conceive reasonably is new and ancient simultaneously: it leads to extremes, not to the tried and true." Elsewhere he wrote: "The temptations and unconscious insinuations

of Romanticism will induce us to twist and bend these skeletons, these schematic constructions, and to present them as ornamentation. This is the function of construction or, equally, construction imbued with the rhythm of linear ornament." "Skeleton," a word frequently used by Van de Velde, applies nicely to this desk, whose perfection nonetheless carries a disturbing quality, like the dry bones of some unknown monster.

354 ◪ Hector Guimard. Desk (designed for the architect's house at 122 Avenue Mozart, Paris). 1903. The Museum of Modern Art, New York.
In this desk Guimard surpassed himself; the inanimate wood has been given life. This asymmetrical "object" would hardly be out of place among the water lilies floating on the surface of a pond.

355 ◪ Charles Rennie Mackintosh. Table. 1900. The University of Glasgow.
No other cabinetmaker would have thought of describing this incisive, slender line, which curves toward its upper extremity to swell invitingly. This simple piece of kitchen furniture, painted white, is one of the most successful creations of Art Nouveau, and would have been worthy of gracing the cell of one of Zurbarán's nuns.

356 ◪ Otto Wagner. Chair. C. 1900. Österreichisches Postsparkassenamt, Vienna.
Otto Wagner was the missionary of the "absolute primacy of structure over decoration." This functional piece reflects no time, no epoch; it could have been designed in Egypt in the eighteenth dynasty or in twentieth-century Finland. Its rigorous metallic armature recalls a Samurai weapon.

357 ◪ Mackay Hugh Baillie Scott. Sideboard. 1901. (Whereabouts unknown.)
"To make war on ugliness and establish beauty in daily living" was the message of Van de Velde. The interest taken by architects in decoration is one of the most interesting characteristics of the movement. This sideboard, with its carefully wrought, highly charged inlaid arabesques, illustrates how Art Nouveau

brought architect and craftsman together for the first time, so that furniture and other objects of daily use were more closely in line with the house and the life going on inside it.

358 ⊠ CHARLES FRANCIS ANNESLEY VOYSEY. Writing desk. 1896. The Victoria and Albert Museum, London.
This desk has a quality of perfect equilibrium; the slim lateral uprights sound a note of elegance reminiscent of the great cabinetmakers of the late eighteenth century, Molitor for example. The only "effect" the artist has allowed himself is the decorative wrought metal of the door hinges.

359 ⊠ JOSEF HOFFMANN. Desk and chair. 1904. Palais Stoclet, Brussels.
Ebony and ivory decorate this desk and chair made of rare woods. Hoffmann has successfully combined functionalism and deep refinement. When not in use, the chair can be pushed away neatly under the desk so as to become part of it, creating a rectangular mass in complete harmony with the room.

360 ⊠ ELIEL SAARINEN. Desk. 1899–1900. Finnish Society of Crafts and Design, Helsinki.
This piece is fifty years ahead of its time. Where is the contemporary architect who will send some of our present-day interior decorators into forced retirement? For the last fifty years they have been emasculating creative taste by decorating apartments from the Avenue Foch, Paris, to Fifth Avenue, New York, in a spurious "Neo-Louis" style.

361 ⊠ FRANK LLOYD WRIGHT. Office chair. 1904. The Museum of Modern Art, New York.
This chair by the American architect was designed in 1904, the year in which Tony Garnier exhibited his projects for an Industrial City. As René Huyghe once wrote: "Dynamic forms are introduced everywhere, even where they are not needed. It is perfectly logical to think of a chair in terms of a problem posed by the weight of the seated body, and to set up the design by combining the flexibility of the upholstery and the elasticity of the supporting metal." (*Histoire Générale de l'Art*, Vol. II.) Here, Frank Lloyd Wright has not even bothered with upholstery.

MUSIC

362 ⊠ LOUIS MAJORELLE. Piano. 1898–1900. Musée de l'École de Nancy, Nancy.
Van de Velde accused Majorelle of designer's elephantiasis. In this case, this *monstre délicieux* designed by the illustrious master from Nancy, one feels that the Belgian architect was not far wrong.

363 ⊠ LÉOPOLD SAVINE. Piano. C. 1895. (Whereabouts unknown.)
Pleyel commissioned the decoration of this piano from Savine. Symbolism? No. Decaying Mannerism.

364 ⊠ ANDRÉ METTHEY. Models for a music stand, harp, and stool. C. 1900. (Whereabouts unknown.)
A delirious concert: the music stand has been transformed into a fluttering dancer, while the harp seems to be humming and vibrating to the touch of a possessed musician. These pieces were designed by the ceramist, Metthey, on a commission from the Pleyel firm in Paris.

365 ⊠ GUSTAVE SERRURIER-BOVY. Piano. C. 1902. (Whereabouts unknown.)
Serrurier-Bovy, a master in the art of floral and serpentine decoration, designed this piano, whose hefty legs are lightened by fretwork metal bouquets of campanulas.

366 ⊠ LEONARD WYBURD. "Valkyrie" upright piano, executed by the firm of Hopkinson. C. 1902. (Whereabouts unknown.)
Wyburd supported the keyboard not with the usual console, but with substantial vertical supports, and added shelves jutting out at either side for holding extra music.

367 ⊠ JOSEF HOFFMANN. Piano. 1905–06. Palais Stoclet, Brussels.
This piano by Hoffmann is one of the great Viennese architect's most interesting creations. There is a difference of only ten years between this and the piano by Majorelle (*see* plate 362); the difference in style is much greater, illustrating the fundamental differences between the School of Nancy and the Sezession.

368 ⊠ ALEXANDRE CHARPENTIER and ALBERT BESNARD. Piano. 1902. Musée Chéret, Nice.
The design and the carving of this ebony piano are by Alexandre Charpentier. His aim was to make the instrument superlatively light and graceful. The decorative paintings by Besnard are one of its most interesting features. On the inside of the lid the painter has attempted to embody the ecstasy of musical enjoyment in the nude figure depicted in gray monochrome on waves of gold. Along the side of the case he has extended an illuminated frieze; using flat colors with a dark outline, he has represented all the passions excited by music, from dream to crime. The general style is not typical of Besnard's work. Our attention is caught particularly by one figure in the frieze, the soldier beside the white horse; he is exactly like the *Cuirassier* by Roger de la Fresnaye, dated 1910 (Musée d'Art Moderne, Paris). Had La Fresnaye seen this piano?

269

270

271

274

275

276

277

278

279

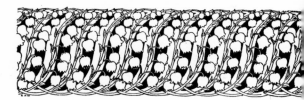

282

283

284

285

286

287

288

289

290

291

292

293

294

295

296

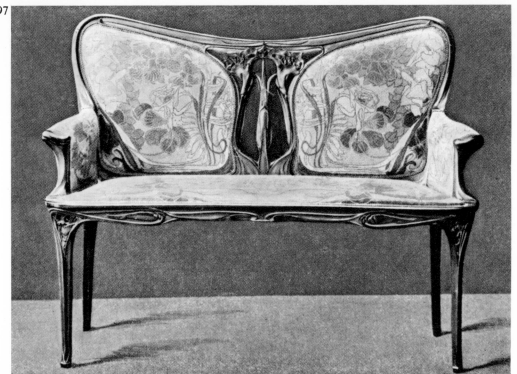

297

298

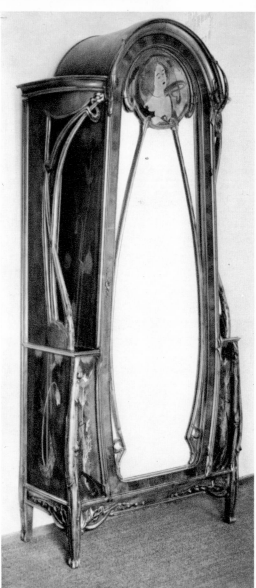

299

300

301

302

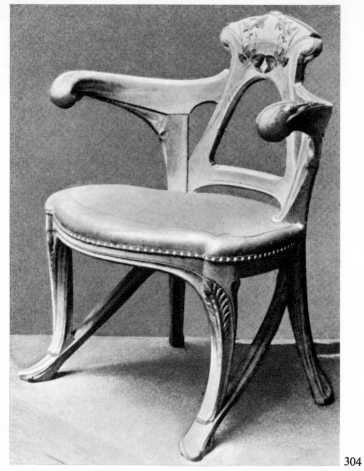

304

303

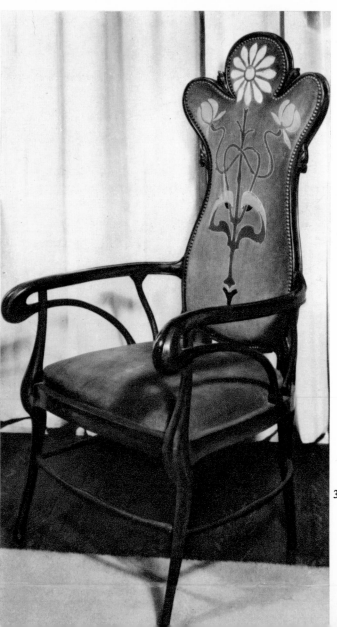

305

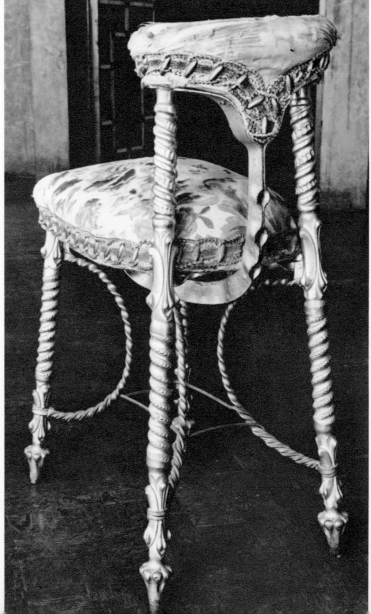

309

310

311

312

313

314

315

316

317

318

319

320

321

322

323

325

326

327

328

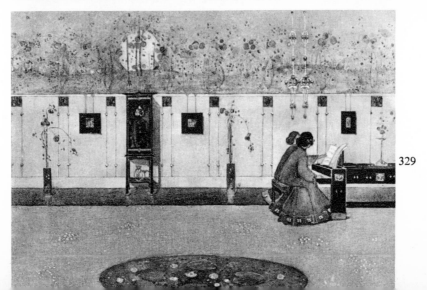

329

333

334

335

336

338

337

339

340

342

343

344

345

346

347

348

349

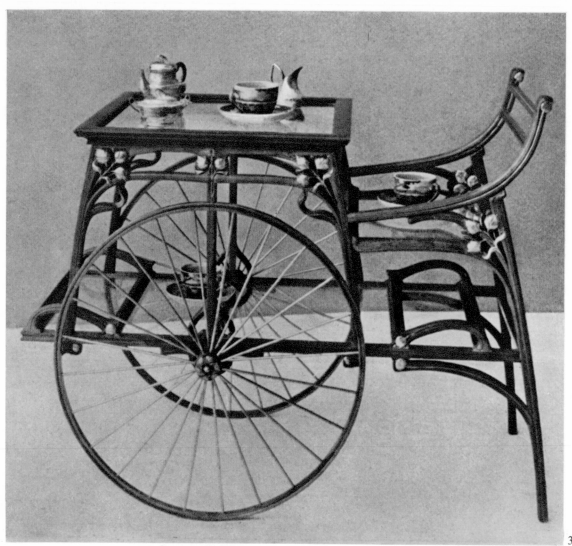

350

351

352

353

354

355

356

357

358

359

360

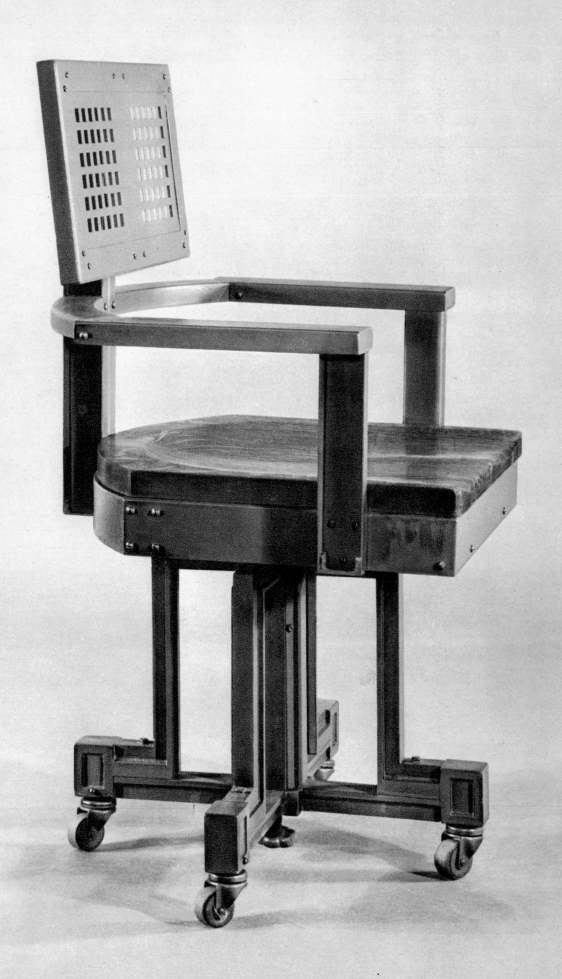

362

363

364

365

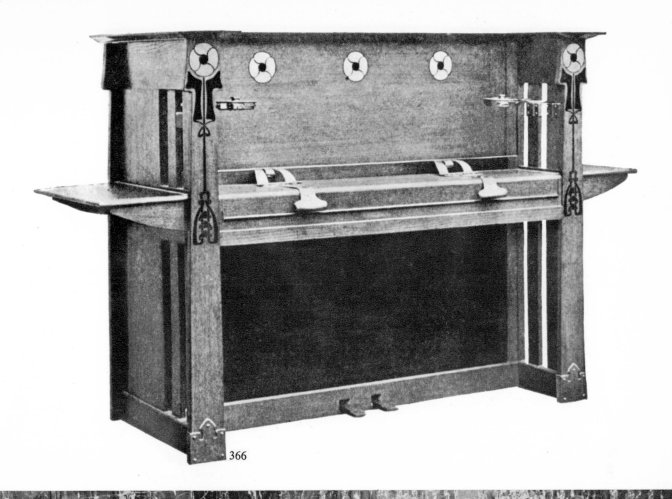

366

367

368

Ceramics

EVERY artist of any importance, in the period with which we are concerned, had many opportunities to display his decorative talents, in engravings, bookbinding, posters, wall-papers, carpets, or fabrics, in fact, in any medium where two-dimensional decoration was required. But ceramics, as a three-dimensional art, demands a more specialized approach; compared with the other applied arts, it is a special case. Although its laborious technique proved a deterrent to many designers, there were more potters at work than ever before. All over Europe and the United States ceramists of both sexes were building their own kilns and firing, decorating, and exhibiting their work with unprecedented enthusiasm.

This creative passion had begun around the latter part of the third quarter of the nineteenth century, and had sprung from several sources: Chinese and Japanese influences; a new interest in chemistry (in line with the scientific bent of the century); and the rediscovery by Ruskin and Morris of the craft virtues. The result was a complete renewal of the art of pottery which, like most of the other minor arts, had confined itself during the greater part of the century to the more or less successful reproduction of time-honored articles, with a traditional repertory of form and a limited range of glazes. The great national or royal porcelain works repeated the pieces for which they had become famous in the eighteenth century. Having attained near-perfection, they felt no urge to strike out in new directions. But in the light of recent importations from the Far East, their output suddenly acquired a monotonous, impoverished air. The shock of disillusion was hard to bear, but it had the beneficent result of forcing many craftsmen to discover the secrets of those rich Oriental colors, and a wave of activity ensued. There was a search for fade-proof colors and for glazes which would stand up to the high temperatures required in order to obtain great strength and impermeability. Hitherto it had always been believed that certain colors were incompatible with high-temperature firing; the Chinese and Japanese had now dazzlingly disproved this, and Western craftsmen were eager to emulate them. It is impossible to say just where the movement began. Production was enormous; every ceramist pursued his long, arduous experiments in the privacy of his workshop; all one can do is note the emergence in one place or another of highly original pieces with an astonishingly wide range of delightful colors and glazes.

In the latter part of the century, ceramics had its heroes and pioneers who soon discarded Italian and Oriental influences as they discovered their own styles. But they retained much from their early models: a fondness for neglected materials, especially earthenware, a passion for perfect craftsmanship, and the decorative sense which had been so painfully absent in the preceding decades.

There was a succession of pioneers who were looked up to as leaders by other European ceramists. A number of them were French: Théodore Deck, Ernest Chaplet, and Auguste Delaherche, for example. These three were fervent admirers of Japanese and Chinese earthenware. There were also fanatical seekers, such as Jean-Charles Cazin, Émile Lenoble, and Émile Decœur, who followed the example of Bigot and conducted bold experiments to find the proper glazes and temperatures which would yield warm, varied colors and new combinations of texture and luster. Mention should also be made of the curious and not very attractive faïence of Gallé, who obtained novel tints by mixing metallic oxides with the glaze. In England, the most representative figure during this period was William De Morgan, a perfectionist deeply enamored of fine glazes, who said of himself: "It is probable that I am a better chemist than many potters, and more of an artist than most chemists." This sally tells us much, not only about De Morgan himself, but about the motivation of the others.

They were at once virtuosi and men of science. They were as familiar with the qualities of the medium and the chemical properties of oxides as with the form and decoration of the particular piece they were creating. They were determined to make it beautiful; they also wanted it to be strong, useful, and practical. This resolve was intensified by the fact that most of them were not content merely with bowls, vases, and bibelots thrown on the wheel, but were interested in ceramics as architectural adjuncts. In France, Bigot and Muller played an important role in this field; in England a number of firms, as well as a great many individual artists, followed De Morgan's example and produced wall tiles. Pilkington and Royal Doulton were two firms much employed by architects. Alongside this industrial production, which was especially great in England, there were numerous individual craftsmen with their own kilns, and a few family concerns, such as that of the Martin brothers.

The movement was not confined to France and Great Britain. It was also widespread throughout Germany, Belgium, Italy, and the United States. Contemporary exhibitions were plentifully supplied with pottery from different workshops, all of which had their own individual styles, but were united in their pursuit of technical and artistic improvement. The public was dazzled by this display of ingenuity and aesthetic riches. Discovery and progress in ceramics were followed with acute interest. No other art seems to have attracted so much attention; there were so many ceramists, so many new works to look at, such surprises to be enjoyed! Ceramics appears to have been the field in which novelty was most obviously prominent and most widely appreciated. Critics writing about this regenerated art were eager to point out its beauties, and did not shrink from discussing its technical procedures and difficulties; both they and their readers, being aware of the obstacles, were all the more ready to admire the deep, warm reds, the delicate blues and greens, and the streaks, mottlings, and highlights adorning even the smallest of vases.

Artists were especially excited by the potentialities of earthenware. Porcelain was not neglected, but its development was different and slower, since its production was usually confined to the great royal or national establishments. Like the other branches of the arts, moreover, it had a great deal to learn from China. In 1884, Sèvres took pride in having devised a new hard earthenware which would stand comparison with Far Eastern work. But although there were improvements in the technical standard of French bulk production, there was little or no corresponding change in shape and decoration. The pioneer role seems to have been assumed by the Scandinavian countries, especially Denmark, where pottery imbued with the new spirit was being exhibited well before 1900. And while the Royal Copenhagen factory declined any abrupt break with the past and continued decorating its pieces with delicate landscapes in gentle colors, the workshop of the Bing and Groendahl firm used bright colors on a white ground, and floral decoration in relief. Both establishments, though, refreshed their vocabularies by a minute examination of natural forms: animals, plants, and landscapes became more real and more poetic, an example which the larger firms were soon trying to imitate. It must, however, be admitted that these various advances were of greater benefit to decorative than to utilitarian ceramics. Vases, drinking cups, and statuettes were more interesting to make than tableware, which consequently lagged behind. So did useful pottery in general; it was both plainer and less beautiful, rarely a work of art. Still, there were exceptions: in France, De Feure designed elaborate floral motifs in color harmonies of saffron, coral, and azure; in Belgium, Van de Velde drew abstract linear designs; and in Sweden, Wallander, who worked for the Rörstrand firm, decorated cups and plates with flowers in delicate relief. Other factories and craftsmen, notably in Germany, Austria, and Italy, produced interesting table pieces, but in general the renaissance of ceramics took place in other fields. Delight in the medium and a flair for unusual colors found readier expression in purely decorative work, and it was these which held the strongest attraction for both artists and purchasers.

369 ◿ ARTUS VAN BRIGGLE. *Lorelei* vase. C. 1900. The Brooklyn Museum, New York.
The American painter and ceramist Van Briggle was much influenced by the years he spent in France (1893–96). After working for Rookwood Pottery, he settled in Denver, producing works which quickly won for him an international reputation. In 1901, some of his vases, this *Lorelei* among them, were placed on sale in Paris. This side of Van Briggle's work illustrates the fondness of Art Nouveau for the dream world, the phantasmagoric side of human experience. No one has more successfully captured this spirit in the ceramic medium, and indeed, few people in any medium have so powerfully fulfilled the urge to create forms which were new and irrational yet obeyed an internal logic. This was one of the many aspects of Art Nouveau which captivated the Surrealists.

370 ◿ WILLIAM DE MORGAN. Earthenware plate. 1890. Private Collection, London.
Sixteenth-century Italian influence is dominant here, both in the geometric decoration and in the central medallion. Oriental influence is clearly evident in De Morgan's wall tiles. De Morgan, who began producing ceramics as early as 1859, was as much interested in Hispano-Moorish art as he was in Italian art. He allowed himself to be influenced by each in turn; his main interest was in rediscovering beautiful glazes, unusual colors, and the secrets of silvery or coppery highlights. It was in this area that he achieved his greatest influence. He was one of the originators of the revolution in English ceramics. A few French ceramists, such as Marius Fourmont, began exploring similar ideas, and achieved remarkable objects which, like De Morgan's, enriched the Art Nouveau style with metallic over-glazes of rare beauty.

371 ◿ MENDES DA COSTA. Earthenware plate. 1898. Gemeente Museum, The Hague.
The Dutch sculptor Mendes da Costa was one of the strangest figures of his time. What was said of him by contemporary critics, who admired him, can be summed up in four words: "A Goth from Java." In his small figures and ceramic pieces he liked to portray strange flora and fauna, whose forms and attitudes he stylized in a manner at once primitive and highly conscious. It is well known that Javanese art exercized a strong influence on Dutch decoration.

372 ◿ UNKNOWN CRAFTSMAN. Earthenware pot.

C. 1880. The National Gallery of Art, Washington, D.C.
This sober vessel, devoid of historicism or exoticism, has a timeless air and seems to stem directly from some ancient tradition. It looks like a highly successful piece of decorated folk art, but in fact it dates from after the middle of the nineteenth century and comes from a firm in Albany, New York. For several reasons, this simple pot is prophetic of Art Nouveau: it testifies to an interest in folk products which was almost unknown at the time, and its slender, lissome grace is accompanied by a somewhat formal handling of volume. It is a work of art.

373 ◿ UNKNOWN CRAFTSMAN. Porcelain vase. Limoges. 1898–1902. Museum für Kunst und Gewerbe, Hamburg.
This shows that even the Limoges porcelain works felt the touch of spring in the air, though its response was primarily on the luxury side of the trade. Where more ordinary objects, like this one, were concerned, the manufacturers were often accused of sacrificing beauty on the altar of utility. However, the material itself was always fine and the workmanship perfect. A dragonfly and a little foliage helped to bring out the transparency of the glaze.

374 ◿ UNKNOWN CRAFTSMAN. Stoppered porcelain decanter. Meissen. C. 1902–04. Museum für Kunst und Gewerbe, Hamburg.
Art Nouveau compelled all the royal or national porcelain manufacturers to revise and redesign their decoration, and to perfect their workmanship. Meissen was affected along with the others; it changed its style completely, enriched its palette, abandoned rococo and anecdotal styles, and took its themes from foliage and flowers. Here, each facet is adorned with an open carnation on the bulge of the body, and with a long stem ending in a bud on the neck, emphasizing the decanter's graceful form.

375 ◿ UNKNOWN CRAFTSMAN. Faïence vase. Gustafsberg. C. 1900. Museum für Kunst und Gewerbe, Hamburg.
Many faïence pieces made by the Gustafsberg firm have dark decoration on a light ground—deep blue on pale blue, as a rule—which was designed by such artists as Eriksson, Ekberg, and Wennenberg. Greenish matte glazes were also used, although brilliant colors were employed for more ordinary work. The freely

treated floral motif encloses the form in a network of felicitous decoration.

376 ⬚ UNKNOWN CRAFTSMAN. Vase. Rörstrand. C. 1900–04. Museum für Kunst und Gewerbe, Hamburg. Swedish ceramic factories were very active at the beginning of the century. The one at Rörstrand chose pink or pinkish-mauve, and soft greens, for the uncomplicated forms of its vases, on which a floral design in delicate relief rises to the rim, festooning it with a circlet of blooms. Simple forms and gentle colors make some of these pieces comparable to the Danish products—those of Bing and Groendahl (whose decoration, however, is brighter and stronger and covers the surface more emphatically), and those made by Royal Copenhagen.

377 ⬚ J. JURRIAAN KOK (design) and J. SCHELLING (decoration). Teapot. Rozenburg. C. 1900–04. Stedelijk Museum, Amsterdam.
Both the shape and the decoration of this teapot are very characteristic of Kok's Rozenburg porcelain. In all of this firm's wares sent to the Universal Exhibition of 1900 in Paris, we find these Oriental-type forms in which there are subtle transitions from rectangle to curve, extending without interruption into the handle and spout. The low-fired decoration also displays exotic touches; highly colored, streaky flowers, leaves, and birds make a strong contrast against the plain white ground.

378 ⬚ ÉMILE MULLER (execution and decoration) and VIBERT (design). Vase. C. 1900–04. Collection G. Lévy, Paris.
The ceramist Émile Muller is best known for his decorative architectural tiling. He executed a number of plaques in *"grès Muller"* (a type of earthenware named for him) for exterior and interior use. He also created a number of small ceramic pieces, such as the example shown here. The theme of this piece became very popular in Art Nouveau; the sculptor Vallgren, for instance, exploited it several times. The originality of this vase lies in its highly glazed surface, which catches the light and accentuates the contours and masses.

379 ⬚ AGNÈS DE FRUMERIE. *Ondine*. C. 1900. Private Collection, Paris.
Mme. Agnès de Frumerie was a Swedish artist living in Paris. Some of her works were cast in earthenware by Lachenal, others by Dalpayrat. Most of them are either small figures or vases with three-dimensional relief decorations. Her favorite subjects were women or children, seemingly wrapped in a mysterious atmosphere of Scandinavian legend. She was fond of clinging drapery, floating hair, and dreamy eyes, as in this *Ondine* who leans her pale head against a green rock. Her tenderly modeled shoulder barely emerges from the surface of the base, and her long neck sweeps up in a graceful curve. The structural trend of the piece is a

strong oblique movement arrested by the vertical force of the rock. No doubt there is an overdose of sweetness in this work; at the same time, no one will deny it a certain grace and excellent qualities of design.

380 ⬚ ALOYS. Ceramic figurine. C. 1900–04. Collection G. Lévy, Paris.
Ceramists could not remain content making only vases, however beautiful. They could not resist making figurines as well, especially ones of willful, coquettish women—the type one might have seen any day on the avenue, swathed in furs and wearing enormous hats. Through his modeling, color contrasts, and the play of light, Aloys has simultaneously transmitted the supple sweep of the figure and the opulence of her clothes.

381 ⬚ GÉBLEUX. Earthenware vase. Sèvres. C. 1900–1904. Museum für Kunst und Gewerbe, Hamburg.
In 1900, a stylistic revolution took place at the Sèvres works: old habits were sloughed off, nature was allowed to inspire a new type of decoration, the range of colors became richer, and technical procedures were reoriented. The result was a triumph at the Universal Exhibition of 1902 in Paris. Unkind voices whispered that these excellent results were merely the outcome of growing foreign competition. As if that mattered! At any rate, the results were there. An example is this vase decorated with ferns.

382 ⬚ ALBERT-LOUIS DAMMOUSE. Earthenware vase. C. 1900–04. Musée Galliéra, Paris.
Art Nouveau artists enjoyed using all varieties of earthenware. There were two trends: some artists simply cultivated the beauty of the material itself, unusual or infinitely delicate color, surprising forms, and the random effect of streaks and runs in the glaze; others, like Dammouse, enriched the surface with a simple, colored floral decoration to enhance the rotundities of the form.

383 ⬚ PAUL GAUGUIN. Double-mouthed earthenware vase. 1886–87. Private Collection, Paris.
Gauguin was the first great painter to become interested in the decorative arts and their technique. By 1886, he was already creating deliberately primitive pottery. These pieces sometimes verged on abstraction, like this example, which is decorated with cats and incised foliage. In Gauguin's work, the aesthetic formulas of the Nabis become a transparent veil; we can see through it and watch his passionate, uncompromising quest for the primary sources of art. There is nothing fortuitous in the asymmetrical form he chose here and the graffiti he scrawled upon it. On December 9, 1964, this piece, formerly in the collections of Gustave and Antoine Fayet, was sold at auction, at the Hôtel des Ventes in Paris, for 6,500 francs.

384 ⬚ UNKNOWN CRAFTSMAN. Earthenware bowl. C. 1900–02. Private Collection, Paris.

In addition to peasant-style pottery with deeply en-graved decoration and bright colors, Hungary produced a more select and expensive type of ceramic-ware which was very close to Art Nouveau and De Morgan's color schemes. A good example is this bowl, which has a handle consisting of two intertwining monsters. It exhibits the intimate harmony of deco-ration and form, the fondness for reptilian fantasy, and the sinuously interwoven lines characteristic of the entire period.

385 ⬚ VILMOS ZSOLNAY. Earthenware vase. C. 1900–02. Private Collection, Paris.
In 1892, Zsolnay founded a ceramics works in Pécs, an important Hungarian industrial city. In collaboration with a professor of chemistry, he invented a new type of reddish glaze, *vernis eosin*, which served to make the Pécs ceramics world famous.

386 ⬚ EDWIN MARTIN. Earthenware vase. 1897. William Morris Gallery, Walthamstow, England.
The four Martin brothers were among the first English craftsmen to pioneer the ceramics revival in Great Britain. Robert Wallace Martin attended the lectures of the great French ceramist and painter, Jean-Charles Cazin (who was teaching and working at the South Kensington Museum in 1871), which inspired him to pursue a career in the design and manufacture of pottery. His enthusiasm communicated itself to his brothers, and the four of them worked together in this field for over forty years. Each had his own speciality: Walter was the family's chemist and technician; Charles was the business manager and salesman (or the closest approximation to one that they had); and Robert and Edwin were responsible for the decoration. The latter, probably influenced by the Japanese, took his inspiration directly from nature. He ornamented his pieces with dragonflies and other insects, and aquatic scenes, delineated with exquisite delicacy. The free, supple, flowing lines of the fish and waterweeds on this vase admirably set off its roundness.

387 ⬚ UNKNOWN CRAFTSMAN. Pitcher. Rookwood Pottery. 1880–1900. The Brooklyn Museum, New York.

388 ⬚ UNKNOWN CRAFTSMAN. Vase. Rookwood Pottery. 1901. The Museum of Modern Art, New York.
Rookwood Pottery owed its existence to the initiative of one woman. In 1875, painting on china had become the fashionable pastime for ladies of leisure in Cincin-nati. In 1880, one of these ladies, Mrs. Maria L. Storer, set up a little pottery workshop which rapidly became one of the most important in the United States, its products winning special appreciation at the Chicago World's Fair of 1893. Rookwood Pottery has Rem-brandtesque colors: rich browns, reds, and yellows. It is also like certain Royal Copenhagen pieces. The best-known variety is *Tiger's Eye*, which has a glaze whose translucent masses seem to be flecked with gold.

389 ⬚ UNKNOWN CRAFTSMAN. Vase. Atelier de Glatigny. 1900. Museum für Kunst und Gewerbe, Hamburg.
The Atelier de Glatigny was run by a group of anonymous artists who devoted themselves almost entirely to porcelain. Added to this deliberate modesty, reminiscent of medieval guild workshops, was a resolve to produce comparatively inexpensive pieces, and to use only natural clay, as the Chinese did. Evidently, the spirit animating the Atelier de Glatigny was that of Art Nouveau. The same spirit comes through in the ceramics themselves, which are always intended for use. The decoration was derived from nature, explored either microscopically or by submarine observation. The beauty of this vase and its vertical segmentation is enhanced by a silver mounting, designed by Lucien Gaillard.

390 ⬚ VARIOUS CRAFTSMEN. Selected ceramic objects. C. 1900–05. Private Collection, Paris.
This shelf displays a selection of small ceramics from different countries. They show that while every country had its own style, there was nevertheless a common source of inspiration, a single Art Nouveau spirit: all of these pieces are decorated with, or repre-sent, animals or women's faces. The stylized pelican, elongated to fit the enclosing rectangle, is a Delft piece. The vase decorated with a severe profile, a contem-plative, very Klimtian face, smiling enigmatically and wreathed in floating tresses, comes from Austria, as does the head of a young girl to its left. The vase formed like a coiled snake is by the Hungarian, Zsolnay (*see* plate 385). The remaining piece is Italian and combines the two favorite themes of Art Nouveau, the woman and the flower. Its style owes much to both the fifteenth century and the Pre-Raphaelites. The thread which unites these very different works is a determination to achieve a truly decorative art, abandoning stock models inherited from past centuries and seeking themes from nature. Every human face or animal body is stylized and sometimes distorted in the interests of ornament. But this stylization is never conventional; all the plants, animals, and human beings retain life and truth; form is governed by the form of the object, but never becomes mere arbitrary decoration, gratuitously added.

391 ⬚ MAX LAEUGER. Vase and pitcher. 1903. Stadt-museum, Munich.
Max Laeuger, of Karlsruhe, was not a ceramist in the proper sense of the word, since he merely provided designs for execution by the Black Forest firm of C. F. O. Müller. But his copious output exhibits a style that is both original and simple; in his wall tiles, pottery, porcelain stoves, and mantelpieces the forms are clear cut, sometimes deliberately rustic, and tastefully decorated with brightly colored floral or abstract motifs.

392 ⬚ UNKNOWN CRAFTSMAN. *Dandelion* vase. Royal Copenhagen. C. 1900. Museum für Kunst und Gewerbe, Hamburg.

This Danish vase includes some of the familiar Copenhagen characteristics. The double row of petals in relief around the base is rather like the products of Bing and Groendahl, but the heavily ribbed sides and squat neck are out of line with the tenets of Art Nouveau. Though the form and decoration are still floral, a certain deliberate stiffness and the extremely schematic designs make this vase point to the style of the future. Sharp edges and almost straight lines show that the somewhat nonchalant grace of the end of the century is being abandoned for a new aesthetic, compounded of rigor and clarity.

393 ⬚ VARIOUS CRAFTSMEN. Talashkino Pottery. C. 1900. (Whereabouts unknown.)
About 1884, under the leadership of Elena Polenova, there arose in Russia a movement concentrated on encouraging folk art. Workshops were started for the peasants, one of the most important being that of Princess Tenisheva, at Talashkino, the source of these rustic and in some ways slightly naïve pieces. Much of the incised decoration is geometric and the shapes are very simple or, as in the case of the rather entertaining rabbit, stemming from ancient traditions. The intention was not to copy the past, but to restore life and authenticity to traditional motifs. On the face of it this is a long way from European Art Nouveau. But it should be remembered that the art of 1900 was not just a riot of whimsical curves, but a genuine quest for new decoration adapted to the object. All roads were legitimate, including that which led through the ancient folk art.

394 ⬚ UNKNOWN CRAFTSMAN. Vase. Rookwood Pottery. C. 1900. The Museum of Modern Art, New York.
The decoration of this vase is stylized almost to the point of abstraction, and retains only a distant link with its floral origin; the branches arranged in regular curves, and the simplified fruits or buds, are beyond the frontiers of Art Nouveau. The geometricized forms on this piece have a more modern look, verging on the Art Décoratif style.

395 ⬚ PHILIPPE ROSENTHAL. Soup tureen. 1904. Hessisches Landesmuseum, Darmstadt.
Here, English floral decoration seems to have been applied almost without modification. The long, thread-like stalks end in heart-shaped leaves ornamenting the cover and bowl of the tureen. Note how this utilitarian object unites elegance and simplicity. The designer has given it an elongated form which sits well down on its haunches without becoming squat or heavy. The handles do not interrupt the flowing line: the handle of the lid follows the gently rising curve of its profile, while those of the bowl reinforce its elongated slimness. Subtle harmony unites the elements of the design; the painted decorations extend both above and below, and the handles are complementary to one another, weaving an arrangement of pierced forms around the boundaries of the composition to create an impression of lightness.

396 ⬚ ALFRED WILLIAM FINCH. Tea service. C. 1900. Private Collection, London.
Finch was a Belgian artist who was forced to give up painting for financial reasons. He became a decorator and ceramist; his new profession took him to Finland, where Count Louis Sparre put him in charge of his ceramic workshops. Some of his pieces are brightly colored and brilliantly glazed; others are matte, slightly rough-surfaced earthenware. The forms he employed were fairly traditional, but the decoration he inscribed on them, with its graceful curves and dynamic lines, has an Art Nouveau character.

397 ⬚ HENRY VAN DE VELDE. Cup and saucer. C. 1900. Collection Dr. S. Wichmann, Starnberg, Germany.
A practical, very simple cup with a classic saucer; an everyday piece of porcelain, but stamped with the genius of Van de Velde. It is worth noting that the handle is not stuck on as a kind of afterthought: the space it encloses acquires significance and is dynamically included in the object. One of Van de Velde's great merits was his attempt to create useful objects which were works of art but were adapted to industrial production. He practiced what William Morris had only preached. Unlike so many European artists, he refused to confine himself to luxury ceramics; he was determined to beautify the humblest objects.

398 ⬚ LOUIS BENOUVILLE. Ceramic tiling. C. 1900. Rue Spontini, Paris.
In this house, Benouville left little room for ceramic decoration on the façade, but the interior contains large expanses of tile, ranging from blue to ocher, with a deeply incised floral motif. Facilities for firing large surfaces enabled him to make his decoration only two slabs high and to use a single large motif without dividing it several times.

399 ⬚ ÉMILE MULLER. Decoration. 1903. Rue Eugène Manuel, Paris.
The use of ceramic decoration in buildings made its reappearance in France in the middle of the nineteenth century. A few examples can be found in the polychromed friezes with which Gabriel-Jean-Antoine Davioud decorated caretakers' kiosks in public squares. But technical shortcomings made it apparent that a stronger material was needed, and earthenware took the place of glazed terra cotta. It was extremely durable and would take rich, brilliant glazes; a further advantage was that large surfaces could be fired. This house by Charles Klein is sheathed with soberly colored earthenware slabs on which a thistle motif emphasizes stories and bays. The material and its decoration were both by Émile Muller, who was called in by a number of architects.

401 ⬚ WILLIAM DE MORGAN. Plaque. 1888–98. William Morris Gallery, Walthamstow, England.
In 1869, De Morgan began to search for the secret of

blue and green Persian glazes. Such was his enthusiasm that by 1871 the products of his kiln could be seen throughout his house. In order to popularize the architectural use of ceramics in England, he created a large number of decorative panels. The decoration was painted on a transparent medium which was applied to the clay before glazing and firing; the medium was burned away, leaving only the decoration. His technical study of Persian and Hispano-Moorish art also influenced his choice of thematic material, as shown by this rampant lion surrounded by flowers.

400 and **402–405** ▨ Various decorative panels. C. 1900. These decorative wall tiles bring the *Belle Époque* to mind as assuredly as any floral design or curvilinear arrangement. The fashion for them was universal; innumerable cafés and shops were adorned with these brilliant panels. Various subjects were employed. At the Michelin garage in London (plate 400), the theme is the motorcar. At the Café Lipp in Paris (plate 403), a spray of flowers occupies the whole panel and is repeated in the adjacent mirrors; in another café in the Rue de Richelieu (plate 402), a street scene creates the illusion of an opening in the wall. The ubiquitous *petite femme* in the foreground casts a glance at every passer-by. At a bakery in the Avenue Jean-Jaurès (plate 404), we find a traditional character, the bread seller, a strongly built woman with shapely curves. On the front wall of a shop in Nevers (plate 405), a

woman's figure is enormously elongated to fit the tall, narrow panel. She stands on a softly and sensitively modeled pedestal, and the eye is caught by the decoration of her dress—floral, as might have been expected, and slightly Japanese. It is noticeable that these ceramic panels have taken the place of the old hanging shop signs. These wrought-iron emblems were too inconspicuous when placed against the extensive surfaces of modern buildings; they were no longer of any use in a street composed entirely of shops. Progress in ceramic techniques had produced weather-resistant panels in durable colors which made very effective signs.

406 ▨ ALFRED MESSEL. Ceramic tiles. Wertheim Department Store. 1900–04. Berlin.
This decoration announces the approach of the Art Décoratif style. On an irregular background (which has a decorative value in its own right) the artist has superimposed plaques of different shapes and sizes; their surfaces in relief set up a play of light on the wall. Like the building components with which they are closely integrated, these panels look as if they had been placed arbitrarily; the relief has the same value as the differently colored stone. Notice also the way in which the figures are subordinated to their background and treated in a somewhat medieval spirit. Surprisingly enough, this careful irregularity and deliberate archaism are probably responsible for the modern appearance of the ensemble.

Glass

NEVER has so much astonishingly beautiful glass been produced as at the beginning of the twentieth century. At the same time, never have artists created so many useless objects. Glass knick-knacks were turned out in much greater numbers than tumblers and decanters.

Unusual varieties of colored glass were eagerly sought after by artists. Transparency hardly interested them; they preferred a layer-cake of many colors, with deep, warm tones—cloudy grays, flecks of gold, rainbow shimmers, and brilliant reflections, all of which were admirable in themselves but quite contradictory to the normal function of table glass: the appreciation of the color of a wine, its density, or its transparency. Some people have dismissed all these objects as a symptom of decadence or Mannerism. This is, however, unfair, since this output of abstract objects (by virtue of their own decoration and their influence on the rooms containing them) had a positive value which should not be overlooked, if only for the role they played in forming the taste of our own time.

In Europe and the United States, as we have seen, numerous craftsmen (and even a few ladies of leisure) turned to ceramics. Glassworkers were rarer. A few great names dominate the period, headed by Émile Gallé and Louis Comfort Tiffany. These two had disciples and imitators all over the world: Brocard and the Daum brothers were profoundly influenced by Gallé, the master craftsman of Nancy; in Central Europe there was much copying of Tiffany, and Lötz-Witwe exhibited pieces which were simply duplicates of Tiffany vases. There were two major tendencies in the "art glass" of the period: the floral and the abstract—but it would be hopeless to attempt any classification by schools or countries.

Outside of the Gallé and Tiffany spheres of influence there are a few isolated special cases, such as Koepping. His work combined Bohemian and Venetian techniques, and has misty colors and delicate floral shapes. René Lalique, who began working in glass after 1900, reacted against Gallé's artistic aims and cherished the clarity or limpidity of the medium. Although he regarded glass as a precious substance and used it for works which were truly art objects, he was equally interested in industrially manufactured everyday glassware. Wineglasses and decanters with new designs and decorations were produced in cut glass by the Val-Saint-Lambert firm in Belgium. Of these nicely balanced creations, embellished with discreetly colored stylized flowers, Van de Velde wrote: "The finest of Val-Saint-Lambert glassware is a comfort to the eye; their strongly marked ribs underline the organic growth of the shape and strengthen the design."

In England, interest seems to have been centered mainly on manufactured pieces of moderate price. Industrial glassworks, such as Powell and Couper and Sons, secured the collaboration of well-known artists who, without deserting simplicity and time-honored tradition, turned out pleasantly imaginative work which was considerably indebted to the new spirit.

407 ⬚ Louis Comfort Tiffany. Vase. Favrile glass. C. 1900. Corning Glass Museum, New York.
The forms invented by Tiffany were always strange and sometimes fantastic. Here, a narrow stem opens out broadly into a flower—the kind of flower someone might see in a dream.

408 ⬚ Émile Michel. Vase. C. 1900. Musée Galliéra, Paris.
This opaque glass vase with flowers and foliage in relief is "very Japanese." The undulating stems decorate the blank spaces and make them more vivid; the flowers, like globules of darkness, emphasize the body of the vase.

409 ⬚ Antonin and Auguste Daum. Vases. C. 1900. Musée Galliéra, Paris.
The Daum brothers were deeply influenced by Gallé. They adopted a supple, asymmetrical, naturalistic decoration; broad leaves were stretched and elongated on the slender necks of their vases. But they were more sober than Gallé in their choice of shapes. The consistency of the material, also, is different, looking in many instances as if it had been hewn from a block and allowed to retain traces of roughness.

410 ⬚ Gabriel Argy-Rousseau. Bowl. C. 1900. Musée Galliéra, Paris.
Following the example of Decorchemont and Henri Cros, Dammouse and many other artists worked in opaque glass. The semi-translucent material was beautiful in itself and demanded little decoration. Argy-Rousseau was also interested in its possibilities; an example of his work is this restrained bowl decorated with lichens.

411 ⬚ Brocard. Bowl. C. 1899. Museum für Kunst und Gewerbe, Hamburg.
Brocard was a contemporary of Gallé who sought to revitalize the art by rediscovering the lost secrets of Islamic glass. He was later influenced by Gallé and, like him, found the source of his uninhibited, naturalistic decoration in plant life. On the surface of this piece branches, leaves, and berries unfurl as easily and naturally as they might in a garden.

412 ⬚ August J. F. Legras. Vase. Private Collection, Paris.
Gallé was universally admired: this vase by Legras is an example of the powerful influence he exerted, both decoratively and technically. The firm of Legras et Cie, of Saint-Denis, was awarded a *Grand Prix* at the Universal Exhibition of 1900 in Paris.

413 ⬚ Baccarat. Vases, decanters, and a "Fairy Light." C. 1900. Baccarat Collection, Paris.
The Manufacture Nationale de Baccarat brought about improvements in engraving, both with the burin and on the wheel. It also adopted the floral decoration of Art Nouveau and used it on tubular vases colored on the inside. Some of its pieces, usually those in monochrome, have a deeply incised geometric decoration which catches the light, while others exhibit a liberal display of carnations, dahlias, and irises.

414 ⬚ Thomas Fereday (?). Vase. C. 1910. The Cooper Union Museum for the Arts of Decoration, New York.
This cameo-engraved vase, executed for the English firm of Webb & Son, is thought to have been designed by Fereday. The decoration is naturalistic (Japanese) at a time when abstraction had captured the design field.

415 ⬚ Louis Comfort Tiffany. Vases. Favrile glass. C. 1900. The Museum of Modern Art, New York.
Tiffany devoted much effort to inventing a new, sensitive, opulent type of glass with a luster comparable to that found on pieces brought to light by excavation, which had been subjected to centuries of erosion and the action of mineral salts. During blowing, the glass was exposed to metallic vapors and other chemical reagents. The form of the vases was often rather ordinary: witness these two cylindrical vases, of which the one with a narrow neck is deliberately irregular and almost primitive, while the other has merely a slight inward fold of the lip at one point. What makes them rich and strange are the patches, streaks, and textures.

416 ⬚ Louis Comfort Tiffany. Vase. Favrile glass. C. 1900. The Museum of Modern Art, New York.
This vase is characteristically Tiffany. The glass looks like lava which was suddenly congealed while it was still flowing.

417 ⬚ Unknown Designer. Vase. Lötz-Witwe Glassworks. C. 1900. Museum für Kunst und Gewerbe, Vienna.
This might easily be mistaken for a Tiffany vase; it is, in fact, by a Bohemian glass firm which imitated the style and technique of the American master.

418 and **419** ⬚ Louis Comfort Tiffany. Vase and bowl. Favrile glass. C. 1900. The Metropolitan Museum of Art, New York.
Tiffany's forms, designs, and techniques, however original and personal they were, could be imitated; his variety and imagination could not. Marbled, veined, and mottled surfaces can always be integrated consciously into design, but in Tiffany's hands they retain a look of spontaneity.

420 ⬚ Karl Koepping. Wineglass. C. 1900. Museum für Kunst und Gewerbe, Hamburg.
This German designer is best known for his wineglasses in the form of flowers. In this example, a slender, capriciously twisting stem terminates in a lightly tinted calyx whose transparency is modified by a cloudiness in the material itself (which was not applied afterwards, as in many Tiffany pieces). Two leaf-like

ribbons of spun glass give the stem increased strength and underline the floral character of the piece.

421 ◪ Buchnau. Vase. C. 1900. Museum für Kunst und Gewerbe, Hamburg.
This vase is by the Bavarian designer whose work is closely akin to that of Lötz-Witwe. It is interesting to note that while the two greatest exponents of "art glass," Gallé and Tiffany, both had an immense following, their respective influences worked in different, and indeed contrary, directions. Gallé discovered a world of new possibilities which others could exploit without losing their own originality. Tiffany, on the other hand, could not be followed; he could only be imitated.

422 ◪ Émile Gallé. Vase. Glass, metal, and wood. C. 1900. Musée Galliéra, Paris.
"Yes, the different materials, forms, colorings, and natural decorations all spring from contemplating the reality of nature. Nature is wonderfully evocative of the certainties I present; things one can feel but not see. In my case, new ways of handling and treating the glass have always arisen from new expressive needs. These innovations, which come into play after en-graving, acid, and glazes have had their turn, are: glass inlay work, overlays of clear glass, and intaglio glass. These are calices in two senses: both flowers and cups, thirsting for light and air, form, in a word, a miniature floral anthology" (Émile Gallé).

423 ◪ Henri Cros. Plaque. Opaline glass. C. 1900. Collection Mme. B. Lorenceau, Paris.
Henri Cros, who died in 1907, was determined to find a durable material and absolutely permanent colors for polychromed sculpture. His experiments, which he began in 1884, caused a critic to dub him *"l'homme de la pâte de verre* ("the opaline-glass man"). This material (a kind of enamel) he employed in his bas-reliefs and memorial plaques. The secrets he was searching for had perished with Antiquity, and he himself was much influenced by ancient models. Most of his work has the curious charm which results when modernism is tempered with echoes from the distant past. The standing nude seems to have been borrowed directly from Greek works of the fourth century B.C., and the girl playing the double flute, as well as the standing figure holding two torches, are also eloquent of Greece. All these reminiscences and borrowings, however, are unobtrusively animated by the spirit of Art Nouveau.

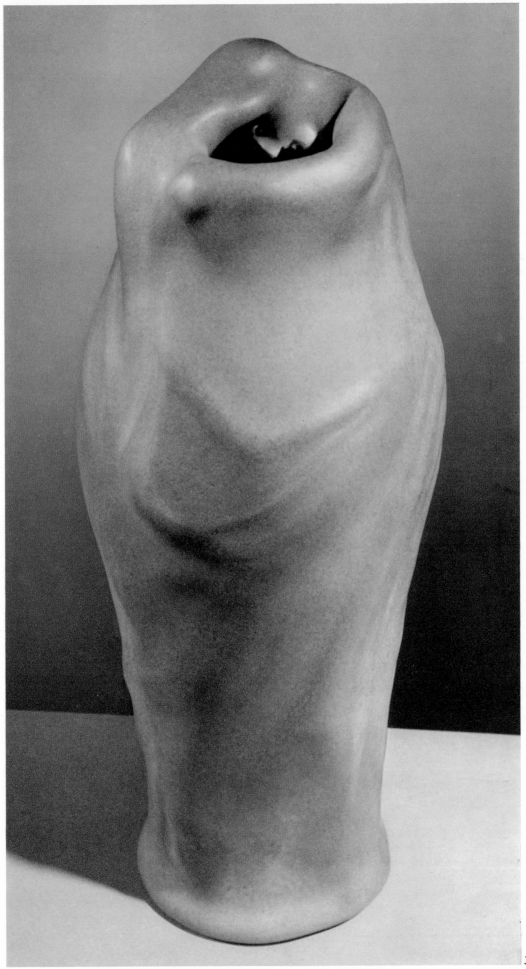

370

372

373

374

375

376

377

378

379

380

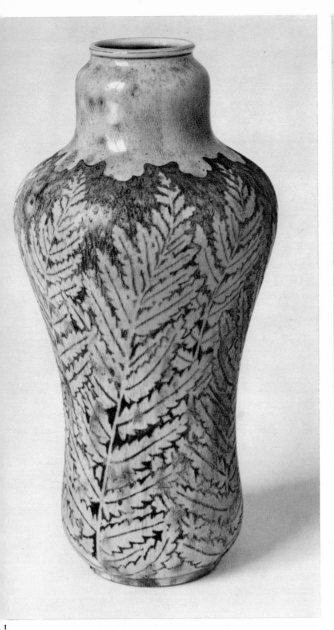

382

1

383

384

385

386

387

388

389

390

391

392

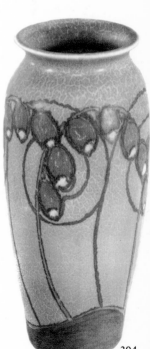

393

394

395

396

397

398

399

400

401

402

403

404

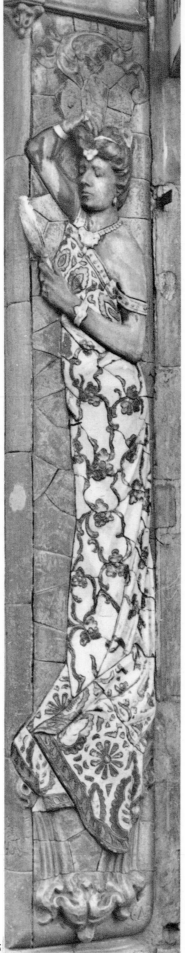

405

406

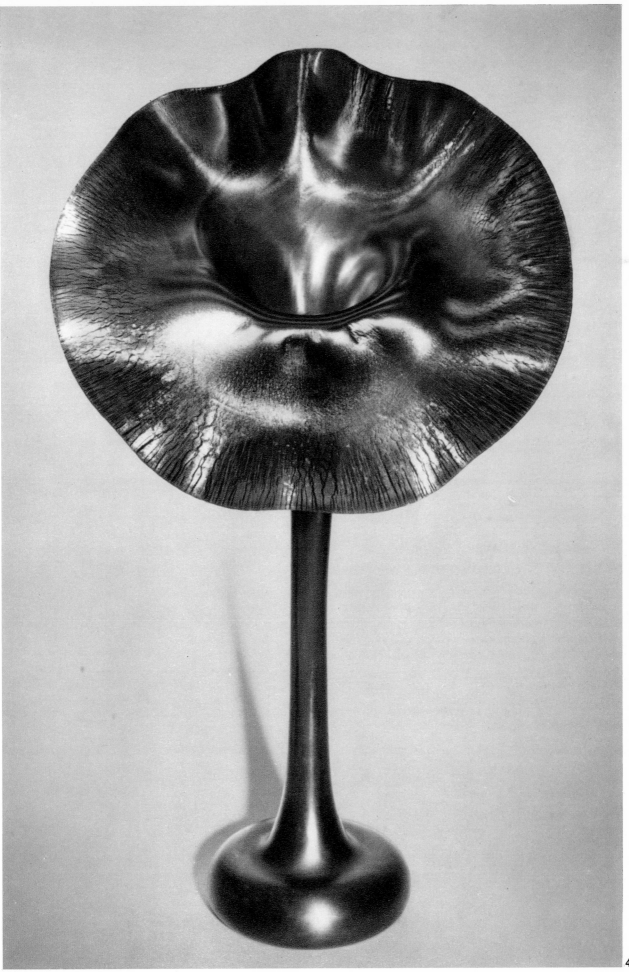

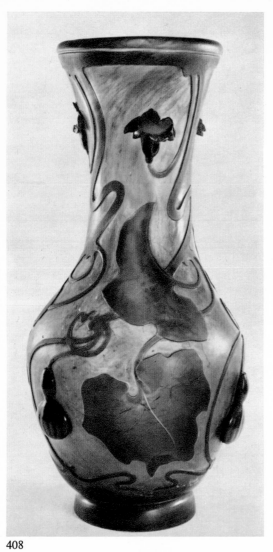

408

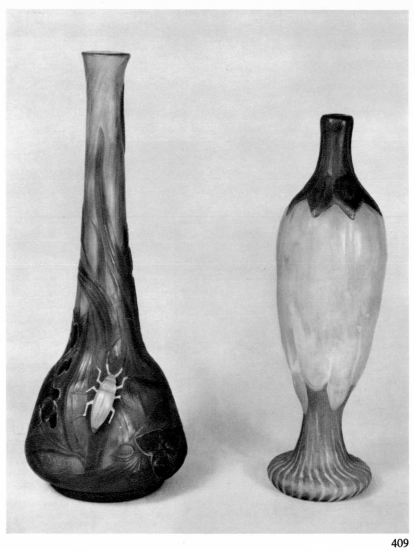

409

410

411

412

413

414

415

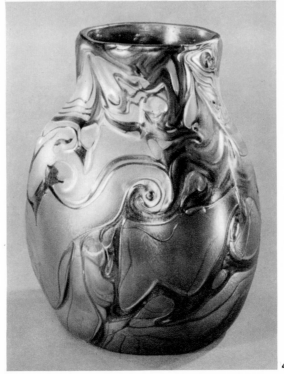

416

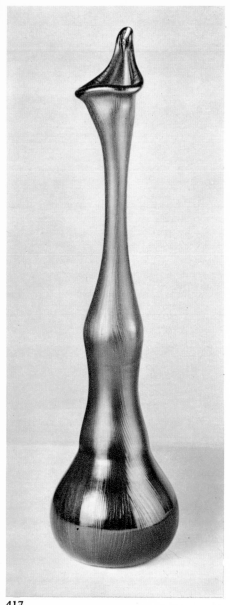

417

418

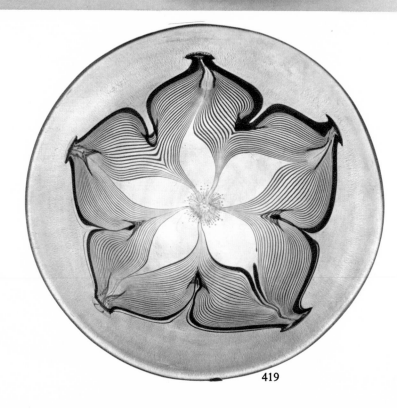

419

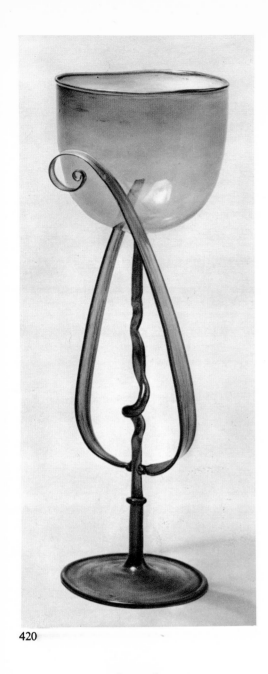

420

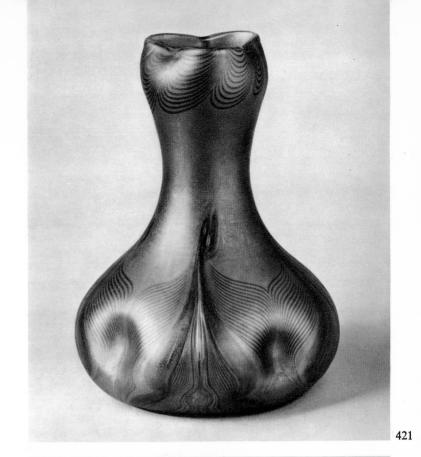

421

422

423

Lighting

ART Nouveau took full advantage of the possibilities offered by the electric light, which was still a relative novelty in 1890, but soon became widely used, and by the end of the century had been adopted by most towns and cities. Some people complained that the quality of the light was harsh, others that electric lamps were always tethered by their wire and could not be moved about freely. Electricity, nevertheless, was soon recognized as the lighting medium of the future. Even in its early days it generated its own special enchantment, a fairyland complete with inhabitants. One of these was Loïe Fuller, the celebrated American veil dancer; her art, which combined movement and rhythm with light, was an inspiration to many artists. Nor was the practical aspect of electric lighting disregarded. Despite certain essential requirements which had to be met, lamps could now assume a greater variety of forms; they could be blended into the decorative scheme, disguised as flowers, fitted with colored bulbs; they were something for imagination to play with. An electric lamp was both bouquet and bibelot, a floral element or an abstract interplay of line and globe; it became indispensable from both points of view: the practical and the decorative. The art of lighting was born with electricity. The placing and intensity of light could be controlled at will and used to break up the old obligatory grouping imposed by oil or gas lamps; the intimate character of a room could be creatively altered. The latest advances in the manipulation of metal and glass brought electric lamps into the field of decorative objects, including stained glass and even, on occasion, statuettes. Like other innovations, lamps gradually shed their wilder follies and assumed the forms used by decorators today.

424 ⊠ Léo Laporte-Blairsy. Electric lamp. Bronze. C. 1900. Collection Joseph Setton, Paris.
The bronze lamps designed by Léo Laporte-Blairsy are not flowers but women. About 1901, he brought out an unusually odd version, a girl leaning slightly forward and raising a panel of her dress, behind which the bulb is concealed. The operative part of a lamp was often disguised as a sleeve or an enormous chrysanthemum. The example shown here is a typical French object of the *Belle Époque*; the dreamy face, the ample, fluid modeling, as well as the mannered style and slightly overdone prettiness, were all highly appreciated around 1900. But the fashion was short-lived; public and critics alike had soon had enough of feminine silhouettes which had an equal chance of turning out to be, on closer inspection, inkpots, vases, lamps, or one of the statuettes which were the rage for a few years. In this

one, Léo Laporte-Blairsy has displayed the full range of his sculptural skill.

425 ⊠ Unknown Designer. Chandelier. Castle De Haar. 1899–1900. Vleuten, The Netherlands.
The size and style of this enormous chandelier were dictated by those of the room. The designer was obviously addicted to historicism (note the mounted knights in armor), but Art Nouveau influence is evident in the abundance of plant life. All the volutes, even those which form the horses' legs, are sprouting leaves.

426 ⊠ Louis Majorelle. Lamp. Gilt-bronze and glass. C. 1900. Musée de l'École de Nancy, Nancy.
Having won its freedom, the lamp could now become completely floral. Indeed, given a stem and a shade, this was the most natural form. Majorelle has here

divided the gilded bronze foot into three stalks crowned with glass blooms designed by the Daum brothers. One of the petals has been opened out in order to release more light. The floral motif is echoed in the base by a curling stalk which carries the switches. Almost all of Majorelle's lamps consist of more-or-less stylized flowers and have colored-glass shades.

427 ✎ FRANTZ JOURDAIN. Lamp. C. 1900. Magasins de la Samaritaine, Paris.
The graceful line of this tall iron support embodies fruit and flowers, but the lamp itself has been conceived as a separate entity. Endell and Horta gave this type of fixture a different treatment: the stalks carrying the bulbs sprang from the heart of the supporting foliage and the lamps became its flowers.

428 ✎ UNKNOWN DESIGNER. Lamp. Glass and bronze. C. 1900. Collection Peinture, Paris.
Art Nouveau designers were particularly attracted by the charm of water plants swaying in the current of a stream. This movement is communicated in the elegantly graceful example shown here, which is reminiscent of the Nancy School, but might with equal justice be attributed to a German designer.

429 ✎ HENRI BOUILLON. Candlestick. Bronze. 1899. Musée Galliéra, Paris.
By the end of the nineteenth century, electricity was already being installed, but gas, oil, and candles were still widely used. A study of the applied arts during the period reveals a number of candlesticks and gas, as well as electric, chandeliers. "The End of the Evening" was the title given by Henri Bouillon to this gilt-bronze candlestick. Around the base three women in cloaks are nodding off to sleep; chased on the central upright are the figure of a man and a girl kissing each other goodnight. The symbolism is simple and unobtrusive, and so is the object as a whole. The traditional form of the candlestick has been retained; what makes this a work of Art Nouveau is the decoration, and the soft, fluid modeling of the figures. Like many candlesticks of the period, this one is decorated with flowers. The base forms a broad leaf, with the stem curling back on itself to form the handle, and continuing toward the center to provide the candle-holder. Brass, copper, and pewter were the materials used for endowing candlesticks with a new charm before they disappeared from the scene as necessary household articles forever.

430 ✎ VICTOR HORTA. Chandelier. 1895–1900. Solvay Residence (now the Wittamer de Camps Residence). Brussels.
The chandeliers of the Solvay Residence are more emphatically floral than the rest of the decoration. In the dining-room chandelier, the accent is on line; the vertical metal stems are left bare throughout their length. The diminutive light bulbs are not hidden, but treated as an integral part of the decoration. Despite certain resemblances, this chandelier is at the opposite

pole from the French ideas of lighting design, which masked the source of light and changed its color in order to make it glamorous and mysterious. Here, the poetry is concentrated on the play of line rather than color. Horta has conceived his fixture from the point of view of a designer and architect rather than that of a painter.

431 ✎ JEAN-AUGUSTE DAMPT. Wall sconce. Copper. C. 1900. Museum für Kunst und Gewerbe, Hamburg.
Dampt is remembered primarily for his sculpture, but he also designed numerous chandeliers, standing lamps, and wall lamps, such as this one formed like a lily. He kept as much as he could of the natural appearance of the flower, and the distortion of the central petal, which houses the bulb, is hardly noticeable. The few lamps shown here give us an all-too-scanty idea of French lighting designs. In most cases, the lamp was formed like a flower or a bunch of flowers. This was the interpretation chosen by Dufrêne, Colonna, De Feure, Selmersheim, and many others. Not to be overlooked are the lamps of Gallé and Daum, which were so popular in their day that they were copied extensively (and badly) in the worst kind of mass-produced examples.

432 ✎ RICHARD RIEMERSCHMID. Music stand. Copper and wood. C. 1897–98. (Whereabouts unknown.)
Riemerschmid was a prominent member of the Munich *Vereinigte Werkstätte*. He was also a "Renaissance man": painter, architect, and designer of furniture, jewelry, glass, ceramics, fabrics, and wallpapers. This music stand is of stamped copper, mounted on wooden feet, and illuminated by a kerosene lamp. The combination of two purposes in one article is interesting, and is a good example of the search for simple, practical solutions characteristic of Art Nouveau. One of the great merits of the Munich designers was that they actually realized what others were content merely to formulate, namely the need for functional, beautiful furniture at a moderate price.

433 ✎ LOUIS COMFORT TIFFANY. Lamp. Cast bronze and Favrile glass. C. 1900. The Museum of Modern Art, New York.
Tiffany, like Gallé, created a vast number of lamps. We should remember that one of the earliest forms of decorative glass was the stained-glass window, an art form which combines glass, color, and light. The design of this desk lamp makes no effort to conceal its forms, which are based on plant life, but the treatment is quite different from French designs of the same type. The bronze base and stem of the lamp seem to be an upside-down mushroom, while the shade of Favrile glass is not part of the fungus at all. It is fair to surmise that a Frenchman working on the same theme would have left the mushroom in its natural position and used its cap as a shade. In Tiffany's design the shade conveys only a vague idea of the vegetable motif. It is a hemisphere which completes the general line in the

most harmonious way; the bronze and glass network provides a sumptuous, many-colored glow.

434 ⊠ JOSEPH MARIA OLBRICH. Candelabrum. Silver and amethyst. C. 1900. Hessisches Landesmuseum, Darmstadt.
Olbrich's artistic development moved toward a certain dry, geometrical style. He rapidly abandoned curves and flowers and concentrated on clear-cut form. In his many designs for typographic ornaments, jewelry, and fabrics, we can trace his progressive stylization of natural objects until they pass beyond recognition. In this candelabrum (one of a pair) he had already left his early work far behind and had entered his second period, in which he reacted against Art Nouveau fantasy. However, he never gave up his love of elegant form and fine materials. Here, shiny silver is set off by the mauve luminosity of amethysts.

435 ⊠ HENDRIK PETRUS BERLAGE. Candelabrum. Silver. C. 1900. Gemeente Museum, The Hague.
Berlage, undoubtedly one of the greatest Dutch architects of his time, is noted for the austere, truly modern line of his buildings. For the Amsterdam Stock Exchange he designed wrought-iron hanging chandeliers in the same bare style as this three-branched candelabrum. The decoration is very unobtrusive; what matters is the form, the alternation of solid members and empty spaces, and the balance of volumes.

436 ⊠ JOSEF HOFFMANN. Chandelier. Metal and glass. 1905–06. Palais Stoclet, Brussels.
Hoffmann eschewed both Symbolism and floral decoration in this chandelier which embodies a play of forms and volumes and has no decoration other than its own components: chains and light globes of white glass, among which hang small, solid crystal balls resembling electric bulbs. This chaste simplicity, which was characteristic of the Sezession, was to sweep all through Europe a few years later.

437 ⊠ KARL-OTTO CZESCHKA. Chandelier. Silver and glass. 1907. Museum für Kunst und Gewerbe, Hamburg.

In spite of its resemblance to a bouquet of flowers, this chandelier really represents a move away from Art Nouveau trends. The artist borrowed his theme from the immediate past, but treated it in a totally different spirit. The veins on the leaves and petals are quite arbitrary, and the elongated stems have hardened into formal volutes. The lamps designed by Gallé, Majorelle, and Dampt imparted the grace of growing plants to metal and glass; here, on the contrary, everything is ruled by functional laws which are alien to the vegetable kingdom.

438 ⊠ GERTRAUD VON SCHNELLENBÜHEL. Candelabrum. Silver-plated brass. C. 1911. Stadtmuseum, Munich.
This blazing torch with sconces for twenty-four candles may appear more dense and overgrown than the most contorted Art Nouveau examples, but its profusion of curves and volutes possesses a rigidity which relates it to the Art Décoratif style. The lines have lost their organic spontaneity, the design is colder, more calculating, and more logical than anything produced at the dawn of the century. It subscribes to a completely different aesthetic ideal.

439 ⊠ UNKNOWN CRAFTSMAN. Candlestick. Bronze. Talashkino Workshops. C. 1900. (Whereabouts unknown.)
This bronze candlestick, decorated with *champlevé* enamel (areas were first incised and the enamel then laid into them), was executed after a design by Princess Marie Tenisheva. Nothing like it was being produced in Western Europe at the time. It displays the deep originality of Russian art, which drew on national tradition to create novel form and decoration. Above the base, which is picked out with a simple geometric motif, two interlacing, knotted stalks of metal rise up, converge, fall away, and support two swans, one on each side. This piece can be regarded as one of the masterpieces produced at Talashkino; deft composition and perfect workmanship are at the service of delightfully fresh inspiration. It shows none of the symptoms of spurious naïveté or deliberate archaism; it is simple and elegant throughout.

424

425

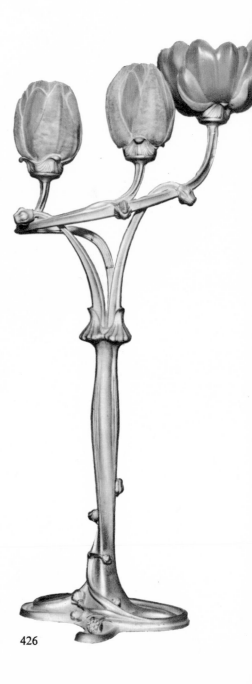

426

427

428

429

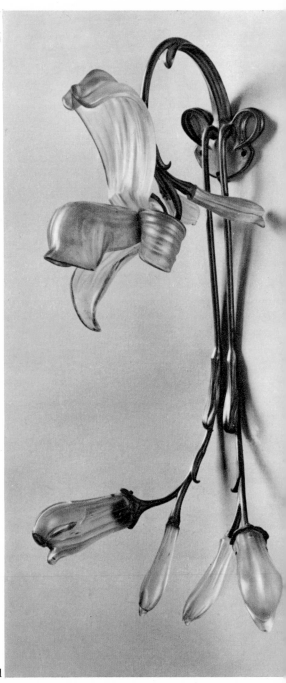

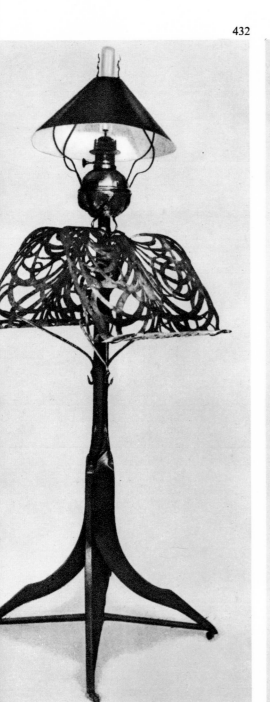

432

433

434

435

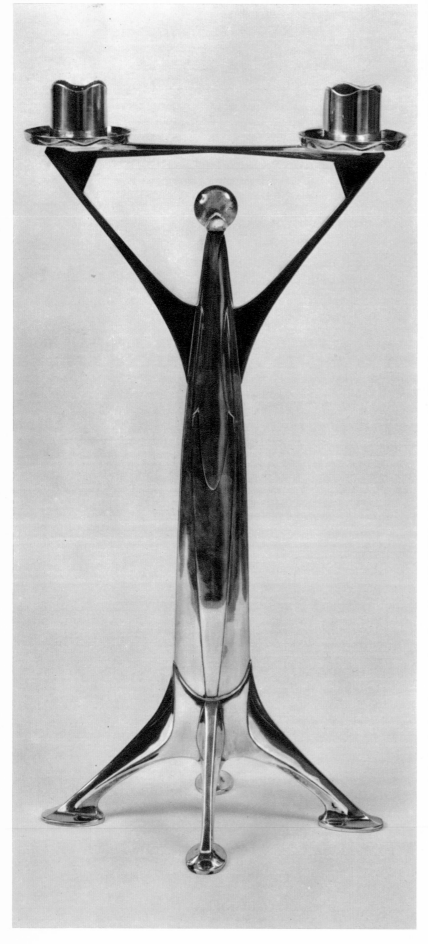

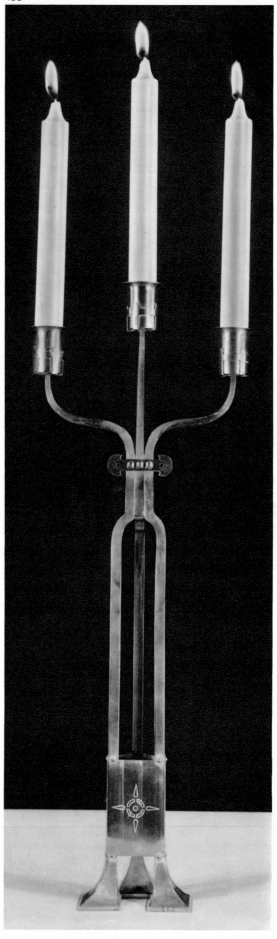

436

437

438

439

Wallpapers, Tapestries, Carpets

I N their desire to create a modern setting for daily life, the artists of the late nineteenth century were not content merely to give a new style to furniture and minor decorative objects. These were only two elements in a general harmony. Wall decoration also played an important role in the scheme of things.

It seems pertinent to point out that there are essentially two ways of decorating a wall. The first is the *trompe-l'œil*, which uses the illusion of the third dimension to make the room seem larger. This method reached its peak in the pseudo-Pompeian styles, whose practitioners covered the wall with perspective landscapes or theatrical vistas. These artifices were rejected by the Art Nouveau decorators; they used a "closed" conception which emphasized the flat, vertical quality of the walls and created a finite space. The old kind of escapism was deliberately barred. This second method sprang from a basic need, the need for creating an atmosphere of intimacy.

As a reaction against everything which had been done until 1880 or 1885, there was an attempt during the next few years to represent plants or trees in the most realistic and concrete manner. But the tendency overreached itself. Critics protested. "We saw irises with phenomenal blossoms thrusting up everywhere; delirious orchids, dropsical roses, pregnant azaleas, disheveled chrysanthemums like Papuan golliwogs, reeds as formidable as Priam's lance, little wild flowers mincing like pretentious aesthetes; a whole new genus of flora which seemed to have been glimpsed through distorting lenses or borrowed from antediluvian nature. In addition, hectically congested or pitifully anemic colors accentuated the morbidity of the outline" (Alphonse Germain).

Obviously, this jungle had to be cut back; it must be taught its place, allowed to decorate the wall and contribute its share to the general scheme, but no more. The wall was of necessity neutral, essentially discreet and unobtrusive. The first men to discover this secret were Morris and Voysey. The fame of English wallpapers soon spread throughout the world, and many Continental artists imitated them. Simplified or stylized flowers became decorative, yet sufficiently reticent; they provided a colored surface against which the furniture and pictures could assume their full value. William Morris covered his papers with a background of little flowers, superimposing larger ones at intervals, and connecting them by the wavy lines of their stems. Voysey's method was different; his flowers were larger, more stylized and closer together, giving a more abstract decoration to the wall surface. Mackmurdo was another leader who attracted a large following; in the closing years of the century he created an unmistakably English style which was universally admired and which led to the new spirit in wall decoration.

Every country adapted the British fashion in accordance with its own temperament. France and Italy remained faithful to flowers and trees. The Belgians covered their walls with a cunning play of lines. Germany wavered between a naturalistic style, strongly influenced by Japan, and pure abstraction. Scotland and Austria both tended to cover the wall with paper or fabric of a single color, or else dispense with these materials altogether and rely solely on paint.

It need hardly be pointed out that the principles of decoration still followed today were more powerfully anticipated by the Sezession than by any other section of the movement. But anyone interested in appreciating the contribution of Art Nouveau to our own lives should be careful not to overlook some of its most outmoded aspects.

440 ▨ ARTHUR HEYGATE MACKMURDO. Wallpaper. 1882. The Victoria and Albert Museum, London.
In his furniture and his typographic ornaments, in his designs for fabrics and wallpapers, Mackmurdo showed himself to be a precursor of Art Nouveau. In this example, we can recognize some of the significant elements of his own essential style, elements which were to become basic characteristics of "1900 Art." The naturalistic motif is treated in an exclusively two-dimensional fashion. As on the title page of *Wren's City Churches (see* plate 519), the flowers undulate and the foliage darts like flames. That is a characteristic Mackmurdo touch; another is the perpetual undulation which extends to the whole. It is set up here by the movement, the rhythm and counterrhythm of the plants and birds. A few years later, Voysey and the artists on the Continent were to take over Mackmurdo's decorative principles: rigorously flat surfaces, a predominance of curves, and the stylization of natural forms.

441 ▨ CHARLES HARRISON TOWNSEND. *The Arboreal Decoration* wallpaper. 1898. The Victoria and Albert Museum, London.
Wallpapers and wall fabrics were a battlefield, and the artists had a hard fight. After passing through a phase of imitation Middle Ages or Renaissance at the end of the century, conventional wallpapers tended to become imitation pictures or, in some cases, counterfeits of expensive, luxurious fabrics. England was the first country to produce a resistance movement to this trend, with the work of Morris, Voysey, Butterfield, and Townsend. The latter's stylized tree bears branches which are symmetrically knotted in a way that severs any connection with naturalism. The broad leaves overlap, yet produce no illusion of a third dimension. The artist makes no use of relief, modeling, or shadow; he has taken a natural motif as his point of departure in order to arrive at a purely ornamental design.

442 ▨ GUSTAVE SERRURIER-BOVY. Wallpaper. C. 1902. (Whereabouts unknown.)
Outside Great Britain, it was difficult to find an artistically presentable wallpaper—at any rate, before the end of the nineteenth century. People of taste, if unable to find something in England, often used a plain paper in one color and ran a decorative frieze across the top. Hence the vogue in France, for example, for stenciled friezes. Around 1902, Serrurier-Bovy made a number of such designs, sober and

refined, yet lively and intelligent. He employed trees and flowers; cyclamens, in the example shown here. All along the wall, supple stems climb upward, throwing out a few leaves here and there; only at the top is the motif allowed to open out. By this means the designer succeeds in connecting the frieze and the decoration of the wall; the delicate draftsmanship and vertical accent leave the sense of height undiminished, and the whole design is discreet and harmonious; it remains neutral without falling into insipidity. And, although the forms are stylized, Serrurier-Bovy has ingeniously taken advantage of the roots and flowers to adorn the base and topmost frieze. The drawback of this kind of design is that it has to be made to measure; Serrurier-Bovy solved this problem by printing his designs on lengths of paper suited to different ceiling heights. This solution, besides being almost unique, is interesting in its own right. Instead of covering the walls uniformly, the artist has taken into account their architectural character, exploited their verticality, and drawn attention to the top and the bottom. Repetition is not allowed to kill vitality; the pattern blossoms out just where it ought to, above the level of furniture and fixtures, where it can be seen to advantage. The conception is different from that of the English; we shall encounter it again in the work of one or two German designers.

443 ▨ LINDSAY P. BUTTERFIELD. Printed linen. Created for the firm of G. P. Baker. 1900. The Victoria and Albert Museum, London.
Butterfield, who also worked for the firm of Liberty, placed enormous stylized leaves and flowers on a background decorated lightly with a repeated linear pattern. Here (as in Townsend's wallpaper), the volumes have been reduced to flat surfaces; although the petals are curled back to show the inside of the flowers, everything is kept on one plane. A dark outline is used, but this, rather than making the forms stand out, binds them together and contributes to the decorative unity of the all-over design.

444 ▨ WILLIAM MORRIS. *Garden Tulip* wallpaper. 1885. The Victoria and Albert Museum, London.
William Morris designed some fifty wallpapers named after flowers or fruit. This design was also printed on fabric. Morris treated fabrics and papers in much the same way: he used a pattern of tiny flowers as background for stylized flowers on a much larger scale, spaced well apart and connected by curving stems which gave rhythm to the composition. The combi-

IX ▨ ALPHONSE MUCHA. Printed velvet. C. 1900. Collection Mucha, Prague.
Mucha not only designed posters (for which he became celebrated), but also produced a great deal of decorative work for interiors. In the three books he wrote between 1901 and 1905, *Combinaisons Ornementales*, *Documents Décoratifs*, and *Figures Décoratives*, he included numerous designs for wallpapers, jewelry, furniture, silver, and ceramics. Mucha's highly personal style was widely copied, and contributed greatly to the growth of a new visual repertoire. The figure of a woman combined with flowers was his favorite theme; whether he designed advertisements for cigarette papers or Sarah Bernhardt, when designing a poster or a decorative panel, he always presented—as in the fabric shown here—a long-haired beauty whose face is surrounded by a crescent or halo of flowers and foliage. He created a very special feminine type, with a meditative, dreamy expression, a great mass of intertwining tresses, and a sumptuous dress that is at once Oriental, barbaric, and refined. This type is so personal to Mucha and so completely Art Nouveau that we find ourselves wondering whether nature did not once more copy art, and whether women in 1900 were not trying to be women by Mucha. He used soft, gentle colors—tender greens, faded yellows, and diluted reds—and the effect of these reticent hues enhances his sumptuous forms and opulent drawing.

nation of the two motifs and the naturalistic drawing may seem to give this paper an Old-World charm; it was revolutionary for its time, however. It was an immediate precursor of the truly Art Nouveau papers designed by Voysey for Liberty, which also use large, simple flowers and rely heavily on line.

445 ▨ CHARLES FRANCIS ANNESLEY VOYSEY. *The "Tokio"* wallpaper. 1894. The Victoria and Albert Museum, London.
Voysey began designing wallpapers and wall fabrics in about 1884. Within five years he had made his name, and was working for leading firms. At first, he was influenced by Mackmurdo, but he soon found his own characteristic style: stylized birds, enormous flowers, and sometimes inexplicable shapes. He also had a tendency to make the wall as such seem to disappear, giving it a positive, purely decorative value, as in this example. The forms mix and overlap so much that it is sometimes hard to tell what they are. Thick outlines are used, and the details enclosed by them are either simplified or omitted. Voysey's crowded, natural forms, even more stylized in his fabrics than in his wallpapers, are made more abstract, more purely decorative, by being used in a repeating pattern. Voysey was more adept than any of his colleagues at taking some bit of the vegetable kingdom and transmuting it into a strictly two-dimensional decoration, which becomes a neutral background by virtue of its very abundance. William Morris used a background and a motif;

Voysey changed all that, constructing a surface out of forms and lines.

446 ⊠ GEORGES LEMMEN. Wallpaper. C. 1900. (Whereabouts unknown.)

With this designer we come to an example of purely abstract decoration which does not even remotely echo nature. This takes us away from French and English wallpapers and brings us very close to Van de Velde's conception of linear decoration. Georges Lemmen was a painter who early in his career developed an interest in the applied arts, especially the decoration of surfaces. He designed carpets, fabrics, wallpapers, and typographic ornaments. As a theorist he expressed ideas very similar to those of William Morris and the artists of Art Nouveau.

447 ⊠ WALTER LEISTIKOW. Wallpaper. C. 1900. (Whereabouts unknown.)

In this example, Leistikow paid great attention to the frieze at the top. In it he repeated the same motif used in the main part of the paper, but emphasized it by means of emphatic drawing and sharp color contrasts. His flight of wild swans with outstretched necks—a theme which might have been monotonous, but which he adroitly varies in three different arrangements—is given a schematic treatment reminiscent of Japanese art.

448 ⊠ OTTO ECKMANN. Wallpaper. C. 1900. (Whereabouts unknown.)

In this wallpaper, Eckmann employed the same principle as Serrurier-Bovy, but added an undercurrent of humor. The topmost frieze consists of a procession of swans; the rest of the wall contains only expanding circles, suggesting those seen on water. There is an amusing ambiguity in the draftsmanship: the artist has not sought to create the three-dimensional illusion; nevertheless, the rings on the water are seen in perspective. What he has done is to decorate a vertical wall as if it were a horizontal plane. At the same time, there is no *trompe-l'œil* effect; this paper is a true wall covering, most ingeniously treated. It is also a thoroughly competent piece of work, and not just a trick. The lower part, which is meant to provide a background for furniture and pictures, has been left almost bare; concentrated decoration is confined to the upper frieze. The two parts are not independent; although they have no actual motif in common, they are complementary as regards the theme (water), and the link between them is wittily established.

449 ⊠ OTTO ECKMANN. *Five Swans*. Tapestry. C. 1900. Museum für Kunst und Gewerbe, Hamburg.

This famous work, with its tall, slim dimensions, appears to contain a large number of peculiarly Art Nouveau elements. The Japanese influence is obvious —the horizon is at the top, and the ground surface, divided by a winding brook, occupies most of the picture space. Formally designed trees are reflected

wavily in the water. Between them float swans whose whiteness emphasizes the meandering stream. The peacock, for reasons both decorative and symbolic, was dear to Art Nouveau. The swan was almost equally treasured, for the same reasons. It was loved for its long, graceful neck and its impassive movement over the water. The composition of this design is also Japanese. The curve is the formal dominant; the verticals counterpointed against it—the trees, the swans' necks—are prolonged by their own sinuous reflections. The artist has rejected anecdote and illusion. Nature is represented for its own sake and has provided the artist not only with his subject, but with his decorative motifs as well.

450 ⊠ OTTO ECKMANN. Tapestry. C. 1900. Museum für Kunst und Gewerbe, Hamburg.

In this work the subject matter has been suggested by a fairy tale. The influence of German Romanticism is strong, but is counterbalanced by graphic and decorative talent of a high order. The graceful enchantment of the story is fully conveyed by a harmony of light, supple, predominantly curved lines.

451 and **453** ⊠ FRIDA HANSEN and GERHARD MUNTHE. Tapestries. C. 1900. Private Collections, Scandinavia.

A very different path was followed by Norwegian tapestry designers, as shown by these examples. For the most part, the artists sought their inspiration in ancient legends, folk tales, or national history. Human beings and animals are deliberately depicted in rigid, stylized attitudes. Munthe, in particular, was given to this somewhat barbaric primitivism, a cult of the archaic. Flowers are not exempt from the formula; they are distorted, coarsened, enlarged, and unnatural.

452 ⊠ VAINO BLOMSTEDT. Tapestry. 1902. National Museum, Finland.

The same characteristics are sometimes found in Finnish work, such as this tapestry by Vaino Blomstedt. The figures and landscape have been treated with the utmost simplicity. These Scandinavian works illustrate the least familiar side of Art Nouveau (to which, however, they do in fact belong; they are part of the same search for genuinely decorative expression). The sources of inspiration, the manner of stylization, and the treatment of motifs are different from those of the Belgian, French, German, and English artists, and sometimes, indeed, quite alien to them in spirit. The results, however, are parallel. These tapestries do not try to imitate paintings or to imitate the effect of *trompe-l'œil*. A tapestry is made for a particular purpose, with a particular technique, and these factors dominate the expression.

454 ⊠ SIR FRANK BRANGWYN. *Vine* carpet. 1896. Private Collection, Clamart.

This carpet was exhibited at the Paris Salon of 1899; it was thought most unusual and created a great stir. The vine has been stylized and geometricized into a colorful mosaic of a near-abstract character. The individual grapes are tiny squares, and almost none of the leaves are rounded. But although straight lines are the main feature of the design, and are accentuated by the branches weaving in and out among them, there is nothing rigid or sterile about the ensemble. On the contrary, what strikes one is the slightly Oriental opulence which was frequently so evident in the works of Brangwyn.

455 ▨ AKSELI GALLÉN-KALLELA. Carpet. 1905. Finnish Society of Crafts and Design, Helsinki.
Gallén-Kallela played a very important role in Finland's artistic life. He was one of the first painters to delve into the ancient poetic and artistic traditions of the country, and he exerted a powerful influence on his younger colleagues. Like many painters of the period, he was interested in the applied arts. Architecture and decoration had already familiarized the world with the sober Finnish style; we are confronted with it again in this carpet. It is very noticeable that, unlike what was being done in France, Belgium, and England, the plant motif has been simplified, geometricized, and reduced to a pattern of straight lines and circles.

456 ▨ VICTOR HORTA. Carpet. Solvay Residence (now the Wittamer de Camps Residence). 1895–1900. Brussels.
Although designs for wall fabrics and tapestries were very numerous, projects for carpets were decidedly uncommon. They presented the designer with a number of problems. The motif had to be such that it could be looked at from any direction, and if it was a floral one, it had at all costs to avoid *trompe-l'œil*. In France, Colonna and De Feure designed some very beautiful carpets, but England provided the chief influence for Continental artists. Voysey supplied designs for Liberty, and Brangwyn's carpets deployed stylized vegetation in a colored mosaic with a slightly Oriental flavor. In Belgium, Horta designed the carpets for the Solvay Residence in his very personal botanical and linear style. Indeed, it was by subjecting the plant to stylization that he gave it its decorative value. He turned it into a collection of volutes, denaturing it almost to the point of ornamental abstraction. This enabled him to avoid any illusion of depth; the treatment he achieved was genuinely two-dimensional. His carpets are discreet; the motif is not insistent, it is repeated indefinitely, and it does not importune the eye nor encroach on the importance of the hangings and furniture. These carpets supplied just the right finishing touch to the interior decoration of the house. Horta's inspiration never became stale, never repeated itself, and the powerful unifying force of his style ensured harmony throughout. Both in detail and in the over-all concept, he satisfied the urge for a pleasing, consistent interior—one of the major demands of the period.

WYNKEN·BLYNKEN
AND·NOD·ONE·NIGHT
SAILED·OFF·IN·A
WOODEN·SHOE·
SAILED·ON·A·RIVER·OF·
MISTY·LIGHT
INTO·A·SEA·OF·DEW!
WHERE·ARE·YOU·GOING
AND·WHAT·DO·YOU·WISH?
THE·OLD·MOON
ASKED·THE·THREE·
WE·HAVE·COME·TO·FISH
FOR·THE·HERRING·FISH
THAT·LIVE·IN·THIS·
BEAUTIFUL·SEA·
NETS·OF·SILVER·AND
GOLD·HAVE·WE·SAID.

WYNKEN
BLYNKEN
AND·NOD.

440

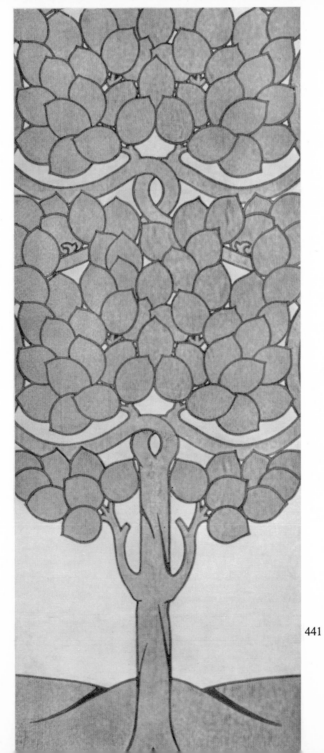

441

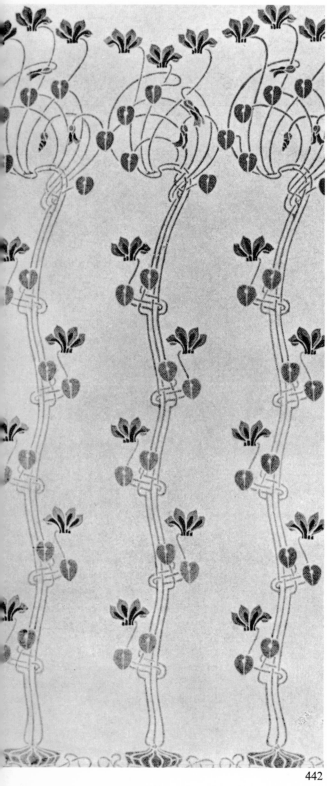

442

443

444

445

447

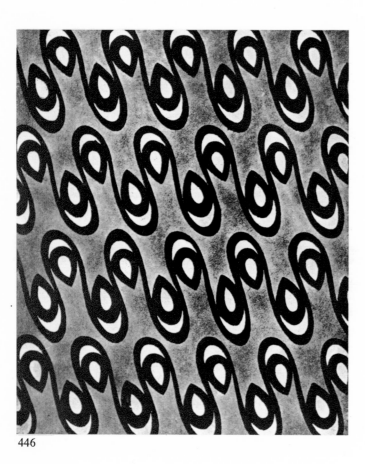

446

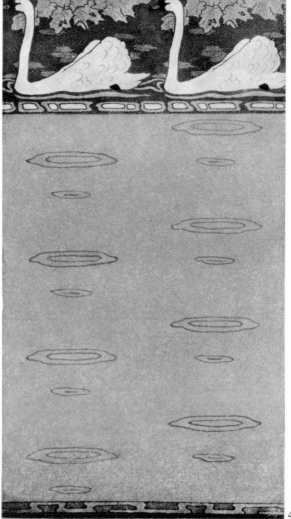

448

449

450

451

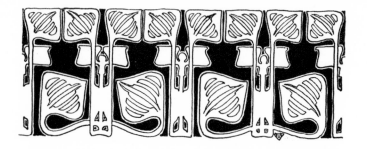

452

454

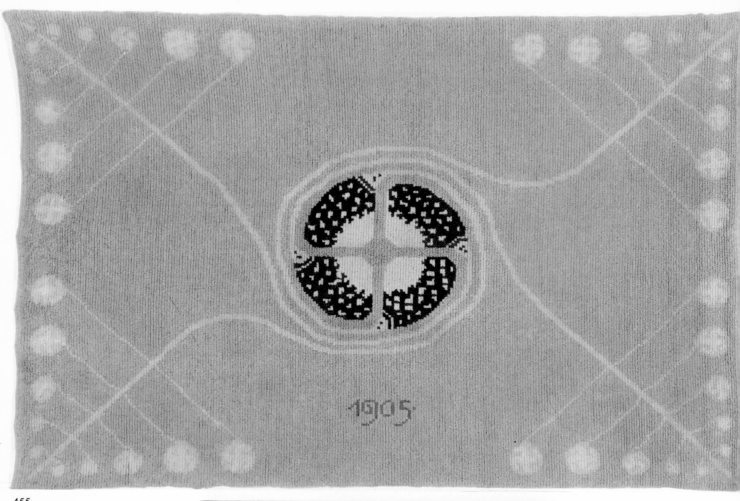

455

456

Bibelots

THERE came a time when vases by Gallé and Tiffany, and Koepping's airy flowers, lost their ability to please—not because they were fragile or useless, but because people had begun to prefer other objects which were equally fragile and useless, and which had the merit of being in a different style. One result of the growing popularity of these objects was the awakening of the public's interest in barbaric and primitive art, the first manifestation of our present-day taste for colors and volumes unencumbered by representational allusions.

Much bric-à-brac was cast out of interiors after 1890, but bibelots were not included in the holocaust. Actually, the reverse was the case. The crisis in painting and sculpture, compelling numbers of artists to invent new techniques, was reflected in interior decoration by a new wave of demand for *objets d'art*.

In this context it is instructive to look at the styles of interior decoration shown at exhibitions. Small objects in metal, pottery, or glass were far more popular than canvases, which were less favored than tapestry and stenciled wall decoration. Large sculptures were rarely seen, and statuettes took their place. The influence of Art Nouveau on sculpture was undoubtedly strongest in this subsidiary domain. Initially, there was a fashion for *petites femmes* adorning even the smallest objects (until the general trend toward simplification took over, affecting minor sculpture along with everything else). Flowers on long, flexible stems had also had their day, but were fairly rapidly subjected to stylization. The design of vases, objects on desks, picture frames, ashtrays, and clocks all became progressively simpler; the exuberant flora which had threatened to stifle them disappeared and the innate beauty of the material was allowed to emerge. In his jewelry Lalique brought certain unpopular gemstones back into fashion, and the same tendency can be observed in bibelots; all sorts of materials were examined and tried out. New thought in decoration was not the only factor in the rescue of the minor arts from the doldrums; there was also a passion for craftsmanship and pleasant, harmonious forms. Trends in fashions come and go, but the real value of Art Nouveau is permanent and cannot be denied. The leading characteristic of the movement was scrupulous attention to matter and form, and the perfect adaptation of each to the other. And is this not the very foundation of all aesthetic judgment?

457 ◩ UNKNOWN CRAFTSMAN. Inkwell. Pewter. C. 1900. Collection André Breton, Paris.
An octopus and a mermaid; evidently this unknown craftsman was fascinated by the poetry hidden in the depths of the sea, and attempted to capture its magic in pewter. The theme is characteristic of early Art Nouveau, representing the spell of submarine life—that strange world in whose rhythms plants and animals undulate with a grace unknown on land.

458 ◩ HENRI HUSSON. Salver. Silver. C. 1900. Musée du Petit Palais, Paris.
Henri Husson, the goldsmith, enriched the world with many examples of jewelry and silverware. This salver in hammered silver is a typical example of his style, which combines the new decorative repertoire of stylized motifs with frequent echoes of the Renaissance.

459 🗵 Eugène Feuillâtre. Compote. Silver and enamel. C. 1900. Musée Galliéra, Paris.
From 1898 onward, Feuillâtre was celebrated for his work in enamel. He gave up imitating the past and took his decorative inspiration from nature. He achieved milky and nacreous effects by applying his enamel to silver instead of confining himself to gold and copper. The mauve interior of his cup is decorated with translucent enamel. The silver stand is surrounded by a ring of bats.

460 🗵 Lucien Gaillard. Bud vase. Silver. 1902. Musée Galliéra, Paris.
This bud vase borrows the nervous coils and dynamic energy of the snake and the metallic reflections of its scales. The creature has not been stylized, merely tamed—its gaping mouth is greedy only for flowers.

461 🗵 Eugène Tourrette. Enamel plaque. 1895. Musée Galliéra, Paris.
Tourrette composed medallions entirely in enamel. In this example, around the white and pink of the face, the greens of the background and the dress provide harmonic contrast to the orange hair.

462 🗵 Ernest Moritz Geyger. Hand mirror. Silver. 1897. Museum für Kunst und Gewerbe, Hamburg.
Mirrors seemed to exercise a magnetic attraction on Art Nouveau designers. No matter in what material they were executed, their mounts invited the most extravagant decoration, with the range of themes selected from Antiquity to Symbolism. The examples shown here and in plate 463, display two different approaches and conceptions. The one shown here has a handle formed by a quasi-Hellenistic statuette of a standing man, whose upraised arms hold the mirror itself. The treatment of the relief decorating the back of the mirror is unusual and curious: the theme (a woman and three *amoretti*) comes from Antiquity, but the woman's disquieting expression and her nervous pose remind one of Beardsley.

463 🗵 Louis Comfort Tiffany. Hand mirror. Silver, enamel, and sapphires. 1900. The Museum of Modern Art, New York.
The handle of this mirror is formed by the long neck of a peacock turned back upon itself. The panel on the back of the mirror is decorated with another peacock, shown in full plumage and executed in brilliant enamels. The silver mounting of the frame and handle is decorated by cabochon sapphires which lend the ensemble a sparkling brilliance.

464 🗵 Carl Fabergé. Bowl. Silver. C. 1900. À la Vieille Russie, New York.
Is Carl Fabergé to be counted among the adherents of Art Nouveau? He was attracted briefly to the use of unusual materials, and he was influenced by Far Eastern art, but he is memorable chiefly as a re-markably independent, original figure who defies

classification. He designed this piece in the form of a firedrake, whose body is hollowed out to form a dish or basket. The stylized manner, the attitude toward decoration, and, indeed, the choice of theme reflect the combined influences of Byzantium and Japan. Possibly these are the only elements connecting Fabergé with Art Nouveau.

465 🗵 Eric Ehrström. Cache-pot. Copper. C. 1900. Finnish Society of Crafts and Design, Helsinki.
The return to the primordial sources of its national art which took place in Finland near the end of the nine-teenth century was not limited only to architecture; it extended to the applied arts as well. This large, hammered copper pot harks back to ancient folk traditions, but its underwater decoration—the water being suggested by three wavy parallel lines—relates it just as closely to Art Nouveau. Primitivism, naturalism, and an occasional touch of preciosity are perhaps the general characteristics of Finnish art in 1900.

466 🗵 Jules Brateau. Double-handled cup. Pewter. C. 1900. Musée Galliéra, Paris.
At the beginning of his working career, Jules Brateau's ambition was to align himself with the tradition of the Renaissance pewter work. This piece, decorated with a frieze of dancing children, shows the mark of his early aspirations, and also the influence of the Treasury of Boscoreale, now in The Louvre. The material is ad-mirably suited to the fluent modeling and the subtle relief of the little people encircling the upper body.

467 🗵 Alexander Fisher. Jewel box. Silver (?) and enamel. C. 1900. (Whereabouts unknown.)
Fisher was undoubtedly the greatest English goldsmith of his time. He was the man responsible for restoring true artistic value to the goldsmith's art in England, and reviving the taste for enamel, both opaque and translucent. Almost all his pieces are enriched with symbolic overtones; the miniature on this casket celebrates love.

468 🗵 J. H. Werner. Vases. Silver. C. 1900. (Where-abouts unknown.)
J. H. Werner of Berlin executed these vases after designs by O. M. Werner and Bruno Möhring. The clean, sometimes slightly rigid forms, varying between modernism and medievalism, were popular in late-nineteenth-century Germany. Here, we see three kinds of decoration: linear, naturalistic, and stylized. It unfolds on the most prominent part of the vase, accentuates elongations, expands wherever the form is protuberant, and vanishes wherever its presence would interfere with the unity and thrust of the work as a whole.

469 🗵 Ernst Riegel. Covered chalice. Silver-gilt. 1906. Landesgewerbemuseum, Stuttgart.
German craftsmen also looked back to earlier styles. Some, like Riegel, were attracted by the early Baroque

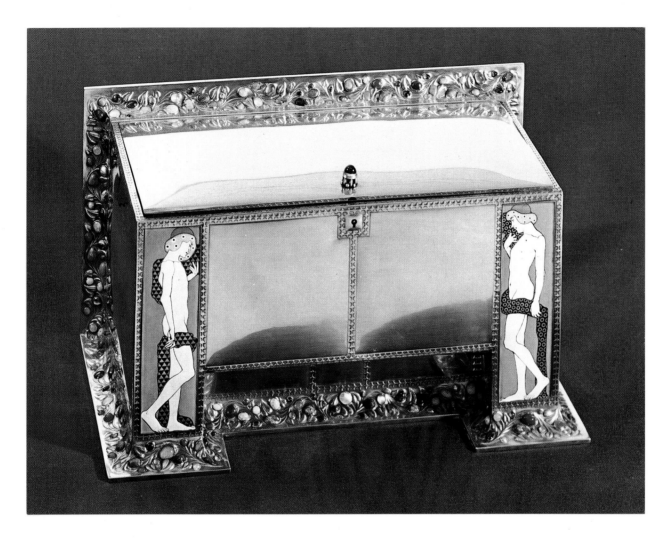

X ▨ Koloman Moser. Jewel box. Silver, enamel, and semiprecious stones. 1908. Österreichisches Museum für Angewandte Kunst, Vienna.

This jewel box was made when the aesthetic of the Sezession was dominant throughout most of Europe. The body of the casket is smooth and shiny, but a relief band decorated with different colored gems decorates the base and frames the back. A vertical panel at either side displays a delicately drawn youth, treated in a strictly two-dimensional style. Moser was one of the few members of the Sezession who was not an architect, yet the rigorous handling of planes and volumes in the treatment of this casket is in the spirit of a true builder. Decoration plays a subsidiary role to form, and is allowed to appear only where it emphasizes and strengthens the main lines of the structure.

and Late Renaissance, and sought to attain perfection in these styles. This curious chalice, in repoussé and incised silver-gilt, rises on its thin stem to expand into a pentagonal shape. Its finial is formed by a little figure of Fortune with a downward-pointed flowing cornucopia. Riegel made this piece the year he joined the Darmstadt artists' colony.

470 ▨ Unknown Craftsman. *Spring*. Silver. Made for Christofle et Cie, Paris. C. 1900. Museum für Kunst und Gewerbe, Hamburg.

After 1890, the work produced by this firm was influenced by Japanese art and the direct study of nature. Their dishes and goblets were decorated with flowers and fruit; tureens and sugar bowls took their shapes from pumpkins, cucumbers, and cauliflowers. This silver dish is a typical example of the new style;

the flower is used as a decoration, but is not allowed to control the form.

471 ▨ Jules Brateau. Saltcellar. Pewter. 1896. Museum für Kunst und Gewerbe, Hamburg.

The combined influences of the Renaissance and the eighteenth century are still very noticeable in this example, but they are a vehicle for strong Art Nouveau feeling. The mermaid's face owes nothing to the past, and the delicate floral decoration of the cellars and spoons belongs firmly to the maker's own time.

472 ▨ L. Kann. Teapot. Pewter and copper. C. 1900. Musée Galliéra, Paris.

Was Art Nouveau eager to popularize ugly creatures of ill repute: the octopus, bat, jellyfish, spider, and snake? Or, rather, did it make use of their repulsiveness to render them more fascinating—in the present instance, to force a shrinking hand to grasp the snake forming the handle and spout of this pewter and copper teapot? The body of the pot is formed like a gourd, cracked open by the creature's mobile head, which emerges from the belly of the pot to form its spout.

473 ⊠ LOUIS SPARRE. Trophy cup. Silver. C. 1900. National Museum, Finland.
An English critic, writing in *The Studio*, complained sadly that sports enthusiasts never looked at periodicals devoted to the arts, and were satisfied with trophies totally devoid of aesthetic value. The article was illustrated with drawings in which the leading English silversmiths had attempted to turn these prizes into works of art. This endeavor was not confined to Great Britain. In Finland, Count Louis Sparre designed this cup for presentation to a champion oarsman. The nature of the contest inspired the decoration (which is in contrast to the conventional shape) and the inscription in Gothic characters around the lip.

474 ⊠ UNKNOWN CRAFTSMAN. Teapot. Silver and enamel. Made for Tiffany & Co. C. 1900. The Metropolitan Museum of Art, New York.
The name of Tiffany is chiefly associated with Louis Comfort's Favrile glass, but it should not be forgotten that he came from a family of goldsmiths and jewelers. After his father's death, it was Louis Comfort who became head of the firm. Far Eastern influence is very obvious in the treatment of this teapot, whose exterior is entirely covered with colored enamels. The decoration is lavish and the shape a little heavy, but these blemishes are offset by the evident relish for fine materials (which also characterizes everything that came from the hand of Louis Comfort Tiffany).

475 ⊠ DAGOBERT PECHE. Coffee service. Silver and ivory. C. 1905–07. Historisches Museum der Stadt Wien, Vienna.
Dagobert Peche was still a student during the peak period of Art Nouveau. He belonged to the second generation of the movement's Viennese protagonists, and it was primarily around 1919–20 that he exercized a powerful influence on the applied arts in Germany and Austria. The handsome rotundities of this coffee service are typical of his work. He has made everything contribute to enhancing the beauty of the metal. The slantwise grooves disperse the light and accentuate the airy delicacy of the material. The large ivory handles lend balance to the form and contrast with its sparkling surfaces.

476 ⊠ HUGO LEVEN. Tea and coffee service. Silver. Made for Kayser Sohn, Krefeld. 1902–05. Hessisches Landesmuseum, Darmstadt.
The renaissance of pewter began in Germany. Numerous pieces were shown at the Paris Universal Exhibition of 1900. This service is subtly decorated with small, stylized roses, the stems and leaves in low relief. Its originality resides entirely in the forms and in the play of light over the highs and lows.

477 ⊠ UNKNOWN CRAFTSMAN. Spoons. Silver and semiprecious stones. Made for Liberty & Co. 1905–06. Collection Mrs. S. J. Bury, London.
The Liberty firm was so famous at the end of the nineteenth century that the Italians borrowed its name to label the new style: "Stile Liberty." The firm produced both simple, ordinary silver, and more expensive pieces set with enamels and precious stones. The great purity of line which is so striking in this set of spoons is thoroughly English, and the slight but unexpected curves of the handle, its slender stem, and the stylized flower with which it terminates are typical of the floral side of British Art Nouveau.

478 ⊠ RICHARD RIEMERSCHMID. Flatware. Silver. 1902–05. Deutsches Klingenmuseum, Solingen.
The painter, architect, and decorator, Richard Riemerschmid, worked in different metals; here is an example of his designs for flatware. He was particularly fond of gently curving handles which accommodated the shape of the hand. He kept the line simple and the decoration quiet, reducing the latter to a few engraved strokes echoing the main contour. These pieces are both decorative and functional; their elegant simplicity and formal boldness put them well ahead of their time.

479 ⊠ CHARLES ROBERT ASHBEE. Porringer and spoon. Silver. 1903. Collection Mrs. S. J. Bury, London.
The formal purity and linear elegance of these unusually shaped articles are very characteristic of Ashbee's work. Architect, designer, writer, and a prolific goldsmith, Ashbee played a prominent part in founding (in 1888) and running the Guild and School of Handicraft.

480 ⊠ CHARLES RENNIE MACKINTOSH. Fish servers. Silver. 1903. The Museum of Modern Art, New York.
The art of Mackintosh was original, even unique, in every field he entered. So true is this that some critics have actually regarded him as representing a reaction against Art Nouveau. Certainly this knife and fork have a very modern line. But we must emphasize once again that the "modern style" was not restricted to a short period of unbridled fantasy. It had also its functional, austere side—represented mainly by Scotland and Vienna—in which lay the germs of the art of today.

481 ⊠ GEORG JENSEN. Teapot. Silver and ivory. 1902–05. Jensen Studio, Copenhagen.
Georg Jensen was a sculptor and ceramist, as well as a silversmith. He was one of the most important Danish representatives of Art Nouveau. This plump teapot is in the traditional shape: simple, practical, and perfectly suited to its function. There is something familiar and comfortable about its stocky lines. The big flower forming the finial on the domed lid puts it unequivocally into Art Nouveau.

482 ▨ UNKNOWN CRAFTSMAN. Cigar lighter. Silver. C. 1900. Private Collection, Paris.
The 1900's were indeed a happy period, one in which the form of every object was thought out afresh and made more beautiful. This curious and elegant cigar lighter, with its slender stem and lengthy spout, is by an unknown designer.

483 ▨ HENRY VAN DE VELDE. Coffee and tea service. Silver and ivory. 1905–06. Stadtmuseum, Munich.
With this service, Van de Velde returned to less turbulent forms. The lines have lost nothing of their former grace, but they are calmer, more restful. Of course, Van de Velde was moving toward greater simplicity, like most of the artists of his time. However, in this example, as in all his work, he was not concerned merely with the decorative aspect. The two pots, the kettle, the milk jug, and the silver tray with ivory handles were all meant to be used, and their form and decoration are subordinate to their function. His earlier sinuosity has survived only in the legs of the little spirit lamp. Also to be noted are the boldness of the flat lids and the very elegant broken line of the ivory handles.

484 ▨ MAX KLINGER. Epergne. Oxidized silver. 1895. Museum der Bildenden Künste, Leipzig.
Max Klinger had reached maturity by the time Art Nouveau was born, and he was never less than faithful to a certain romantic mixture of Symbolism and mysticism. This epergne seems to conform to tradition rather than announcing a new age. With its two-stage support—a seated woman, borne up by a circle of dolphins—it has a monumental air; the arrangement of the baskets and vases is likewise very sculptural. The exploring spirit of Art Nouveau is undoubtedly evident in the balanced volumes and in the effect deliberately created by the empty space between the woman's extended arms. But the whole thing is overdone. A very few years after it was made, it would have been out of place in any modern interior.

Jewelry

COVERED in rich fabrics from head to toe, crowned with feathers or flowers, toying with parasol or fan, the 1900 Parisian woman enjoying an afternoon at the Longchamps track wore, and reveled in, twenty-five pieces of jewelry: six hatpins by Lalique; nine rings (two Classical, three Byzantine, and the remainder by Fouquet); three rows of Oriental pearls with a clasp by Henri Vever; a chain studded with opals, brilliants, and rubies, ending in a lorgnette by Fabergé; not to mention some half-dozen bracelets set with opaline glass and more-or-less precious stones. What must the horses have thought!

From the 1840's to the 1890's (that is, from King Louis Philippe to President Sadi Carnot), precious stones were worn primarily as a badge of wealth. From the time of the Second Empire, the discovery of new diamond mines diminished the creative role of the goldsmith. All that mattered was the purity of the stones—and, of course, their size. At the Tuileries, carats were the currency by which people reckoned their own and each other's fortunes. This was the state of mind against which Art Nouveau reacted.

The new start was made possible by the creative genius of René Lalique. He showed a few works at the 1889 Exhibition in Paris, but was not very successful. His first big triumph came at the Salon du Champ-de-Mars, in 1895. It was not long before he had an enthusiastic following both in France and abroad. People initially were astonished and shocked, and declared firmly that however admirable his bits and pieces might be, they could not be worn—they were fit only for window displays and the stage. But gradually the novel colors and shapes he introduced won over the public, and for a period of ten years most French jewelry reflected his influence.

At the close of the century, there was much talk of a return to nature, but for Lalique, this tendency took the form of a passion for metals and gems. If he fashioned narcissi, violets, thistles, and ears of corn, the reason was that they gave him the opportunity to juxtapose opals with carnelians, baroque pearls with ivory. The creatures he represented are not so much stylized as transposed. The life and grace of prototypes, real or imaginary, have survived intact in his enormous dragonflies with enameled wings, his gleaming lizards which grip an ivory bas-relief in their jaws, his thistles, his bunches of mistletoe, his pairs of swans with intertwining necks. Transformation into gold, enamel, and gems has not succeeded in making them lifeless.

After a few years, Lalique deserted bright, ringing colors for more discreet harmonies, subtler shades—the shimmering whites of opaline glass and engraved crystal. While retaining his originality to the full, he tempered the fantasy of his forms and evolved a more quiet but always fluent style which is evident throughout the wide range of his work: jewelry, glass, and decorative designs for rooms or houses. But for all his indisputable genius, Lalique remained faithful to tradition, whereas in the first years of the century Germany and Austria were beginning to produce geometrical and abstract jewelry which prefigured the twentieth-century aesthetic. The stones which Lalique arranged in bouquets of flowers were used by these innovators solely for their brilliance or strangeness, without any reference to nature. In this we can already detect an interest in the primitive civilizations which had been disdained for centuries, but were to acquire importance and significance only a few years later. This preference for the barbaric can be seen still more clearly in some Scottish and Scandinavian jewelry, inspired by the Celtic tradition.

But while different artists were inspired by different objectives, some striving for an apotheosis of the past and others seeking to anticipate the future, they had in common a passion for the intrinsic beauty of their materials: color, glitter, sheen, and iridescence. Their interest was in the artistic potentialities of the materials rather than, as in an earlier generation, their monetary value.

What counted now was not carats but the charm and beauty with which the craftsman-designer could succeed in endowing his work. This revolution in values was a boon to costume jewelry, which could win high esteem provided it was at once original and simple. Bronze rings no longer imitated silver, and colored glass abandoned the attempt to compete with emeralds and sapphires. Far from trying to conceal its humble origins, this jewelry exposed them for all to see, as if to proclaim that money was no longer a substitute for beauty. Every epoch has its own proper style in jewels. We may incline toward Cellini, or Fouquet, or Vever, but if so, the cause is a passion for the decorative object. Women today can no longer wear the elaborate ornaments conceived for long-haired Ophelias, who were dressed by Doucet and undressed by Toulet (a French novelist of the turn-of-the-century). From head to hip, the female torso in 1900 was a feast of possibilities for the jeweler's craft: a graceful armor of gems, a light buckler caught at the shoulder by a chain matching the belt buckle, and a comb of horn, tortoise shell, or ivory, surmounted by a jeweled spray *à la japonaise*. On the other hand, the necklace had shrunk in width and did not come lower than the neck itself. Sleeves were long, so bracelets were rarely worn.

Fans, rings, cufflinks, and the knobs of canes, executed in precious materials and with perfect workmanship, were the prerogative of a certain type of gentleman—"*ces messieurs*," and more especially the "*pelléastres*" (the name was partly a reference to Debussy's opera, *Pelléas et Mélisande*):

> "...handsome young men (almost all the Debussy-ists are young, very young), tender youths with long hair carefully pulled forward into a fringe, with smooth complexions, full, round faces, and big, deep eyes; jackets with velvet lapels and slightly puffed sleeves, overcoats a trifle too pinched in at the waist, copious satin cravats engulfing the neck or left floating free, or, if the Debussy-ist is in evening dress, a floppy bow tie negligently sprouting from a soft, turned-down collar; on the little finger (invariably, for they all have beautiful hands) a few precious rings from ancient Egypt or Byzantium, a turquoise scarab or a green gold caduceus —and they always go about in pairs."

> (Jean Lorrain, *Les Pelléastres*)

These *pelléastres* described by Jean Lorrain were the first representatives of that oligarchy of inverts who, as in the ancient world, were to dominate a certain segment of society. Beginning in 1900, homosexuality became the privilege of a closed circle, a social and intellectual élite which launched fashions, carved out reputations, and eventually exerted a real tyranny over literature and the arts. Homosexuality had come out into the open; it was no longer a vice, but a way of life.

At the beginning of the new century, homosexuals frequented well-known drawing rooms, and were dazzling figures both in conversation and in dress. What concerns us here is their influence in the aesthetic field, rather than considerations of their moral probity or sociological classification. Decadence was a thing of the past, and alert refinement had taken its place. The tastes of the homosexual were all guided by the beautiful. He surrounded himself with jewelry and bibelots to create that pleasing, well-ordered environment to which he of all men was exceptionally sensitive.

485 ⊠ UNKNOWN CRAFTSMAN. Pendant. Silver, malachite, turquoise, and pearl. C. 1885. Private Collection, Paris.
Nineteenth-century jewelry was marked by every taste in turn—Egyptian, Greek, Etruscan, Gothic, Renaissance, and Louis XVI. The sixteenth century provided the inspiration for this German or Russian pendant, an oval of flowers and seaweeds framing Saint George on horseback slaying the dragon. Certain stylized touches, and the plants appearing in the decoration, point forward to the jewelry of Art Nouveau.

486 ⊠ CHARLES FOUQUET (?). Comb. Gold, tortoise shell, and amethysts. 1899–1902. Museum für Kunst und Gewerbe, Hamburg.
Unlike Lalique, Fouquet and Vever reached out toward formal synthesis and the geometric. The "architrave" of this comb consists of a woman's face and hair, but here there are none of the clinging, streaming tresses of a drowned lady—that lady who appears so often in the designs of the period. On the contrary: stylization has been carried to the limit, transforming every lock into a neat little volute which provides the setting for an amethyst, and the whole resembles more some weird caterpillar than a head of hair. Under this strange crown of barbaric ornamentation, the comb acquires a faintly Oriental air, a mixture of memories from Japan and Byzantium.

487 ⊠ RENÉ LALIQUE. Brooch. Gold, enamels, chrysoprase, and brilliants. 1898. Gulbenkian Foundation, Lisbon.
Dragonflies appear frequently in the jewelry of Lalique. At this time, Lalique had not yet attempted to curb his imagination, and the insect's transparent wings are joined to the green torso of a woman. This piece was the property of Callouste Gulbenkian, who was the solitary pioneer collector of Art Nouveau jewelry early in the century. He lent this brooch to Sarah Bernhardt, and it was shown at two exhibitions, that in Paris in 1900, and the Turin Exhibition of 1902.

488 ⊠ PAUL ALBERT BEAUDOIN. Brooch. Gold, enamel, pearls, and brilliants. 1899–1902. Schmuckmuseum, Pforzheim.
In this brooch, the Paris jeweler Beaudoin surrounded a woman's face with a few violets and their leaves. These dreamy countenances framed by a halo of flowers were popular around 1900. They died out quickly, the result of innumerable repetitions on worthless pieces. The salt had lost its savor.

489 ⊠ CARL FABERGÉ. Cigarette case. Gold and sapphires. 1899–1902. Private Collection, New York.
Cigarette cases by Fabergé are still much in demand today, for their simple beauty and perfect craftsmanship.

490 ⊠ UNKNOWN CRAFTSMAN. Purse. Leather, silver, pearls, and sapphires. C. 1900. The Museum of Modern Art, New York.

Here, the mounting consists of writhing silver snakes framing a face. The mounting is set with baroque pearls and a few small sapphires, which add their brilliance to the decorative composition. The choice of subject matter makes it a typical creation of the period. The ominous sinuosity of the snake, one of the favorite motifs of Art Nouveau, is combined with a woman's face. The use of irregularly shaped baroque pearls is also typical.

491 ⊠ UNKNOWN CRAFTSMAN. Evening purse. Silver. 1903. Collection Ludwig Werner, Berlin.
The artistic jewelers of the period took wood, ivory, gold, and leather and fashioned them into lorgnettes, handbags, and other graceful, sophisticated objects. One of the most common decorative themes was the snake, as seen in this mesh bag. Mention should be made here of Lalique's embroidered handbags, the leather purses of L. Germain, and the numerous embroidered fans of lace, mother-of-pearl, or tortoise shell, as well as the parasol handles. Even men's walking sticks were subjected to decoration, proving that such frivolities were by no means confined to the fair sex.

492 ⊠ PERCY STAMP. Hat pin. Silver. Executed by the firm of Charles Horner, Halifax, England. 1900. Private Collection, New York.
This hat pin is very Art Nouveau; the line is full of movement and compels the eye to follow its restless twists and turns. English jewelry, with its linear and often abstract design, was practically unaffected by French influence.

493 ⊠ CHARLES RICKETTS. Ring and pendants. Gold, chalcedony, pearls, sapphires, etc. 1899–1902. Fitzwilliam Museum, Cambridge, England.
The English artist Ricketts was influenced by Japan, the Antique world, and Byzantium. The stones of this ring almost constitute a little Byzantine church with a dome of bluish-gray chalcedony. A gray stone in the interior of this miniature building lights up its "windows" in accordance with the movement of the hand. In the pendant on the right, the naturalistic portrayal of the bird contrasts with the deliberately archaic style of the whole.

494 ⊠ W. AUGUSTUS STEWART. Pendant. Gold, sapphires, and pearls. 1905. Collection The Worshipful Company of Goldsmiths, London.
Here, a woman's face is again the theme. This time the face is closely enshrined in her hair. But this aristocratic lady, fashioned by the London goldsmith W. Augustus Stewart, wears her enchantment with a difference: the face is mysterious, but in no way dreamy; the features are regular, but not tender. Perhaps we may read into it an inhuman, slightly malevolent coldness which makes the lady more akin to the fairies of the North than to the graceful *petite femme* of French Art Nouveau.

495 ◪ UNKNOWN CRAFTSMAN. Belt buckle. Gold. C. 1901. The Museum of Modern Art, New York.
Art Nouveau bracelets are rare, but Art Nouveau belt buckles are innumerable. They were so prettily and artfully devised that fashion decreed they should be worn behind. The one shown here is the work of an unidentified American craftsman. It consists of two feminine faces—the treatment of which is a little heavy-handed—encircled by their floating hair, which is adorned with flowers: an ever-familiar and recurrent theme.

496 ◪ HECTOR GUIMARD. Ring and hat pin. Gilt-bronze and paste. 1899–1902. The Museum of Modern Art, New York.
The octopus, which supplied the motif for this hat pin, also gave Guimard a pretext for indulging in the curves he so delighted in. As for the costume-jewelry ring, it must have been an act of almost sacrilegious provocation to suggest an engagement ring with a fake stone. Guimard was a lonely figure in his native France. Not only was he deeply influenced by the foreign origins of Art Nouveau, but he was ahead of his time in his taste for abstraction and things rich and strange.

497 ◪ KARL-OTTO CZESCHKA. Necklace with pendants. Gold, enamel, and opals. 1902–05. Österreichisches Museum für Angewandte Kunst, Vienna.
The very delicate linear design of this necklace can hardly fail to remind us of the decorations and jewelry which the Macdonald sisters were producing in Scotland. One of the curious things about Art Nouveau is this community of taste between Scotland and Austria, which was characteristic of the movement at a certain stage in its development. In this necklace by the Austrian, Czeschka, a system of tenuous chains connects oval plaques in which odd, convex, golden leaves are combined with opals and further decorated with birds and delicate little spirals. The botanical element is so powerfully and strangely stylized that at first glance one might mistake it for an abstract design.

498 ◪ FERDINAND HAUSER. Brooch. Gold, enamel, and moonstones. 1902–05. Landesgewerbemuseum, Stuttgart.
The wavy stems of little golden flowers, which have been simplified as far as possible, stream upward on a round, blue enameled plaque which features a large moonstone. The flowers above are balanced below by thirteen moonstones dangling from little chains, which follow the lines of the stems. This brooch is typical of the Sezession. The flowers are pure geometry, and stylization has left their vegetable origins far behind.

499 ◪ PHILIPPE WOLFERS. Choker. Gold, garnets, tourmalines, and enamel. 1902. Collection Wolfers Frères, Brussels.
Wisteria provides the motif for this necklace. The translucent enameled foliage unfolds onto sinuous

XI ◪ RENÉ LALIQUE. Brooch. Gold and enamel. C. 1898. Gulbenkian Foundation, Lisbon.
In drawing his inspiration from nature, Lalique looked toward her strange, disturbing side. This brooch was shown at the Universal Exhibition of 1900 in Paris. The writhing coils of nine snakes terminate in nine heads with gaping, threatening mouths. The lively, varicolored enamel lends diversity to the symmetrical arrangement of the heads.

branches picked out with garnets, and the solid clusters of tourmaline blossoms. The relatively naturalistic treatment of the motifs, in soft mauve-pinks and greens, shows an affinity with some of the work of Lalique; what differentiates it from his work is a deliberate air of extreme opulence.

500 ◪ C. W. MULLER. Pendant. Gold, amethyst, ruby, agate, and diamonds. 1905. Schmuckmuseum, Pforzheim.
In a sense, Pforzheim was the birthplace of the twentieth century, since it was the birthplace of the geometric forms which were to be on the crest of the wave around 1920. An example is this pendant, where, in a framework of gold with emphatic right angles, the agate plaque makes the amethyst and the red and white stones fairly sing.

501 ◪ KOLOMAN MOSER. Pendant. Silver, coral, lapis lazuli, agate, mother-of-pearl, moonstone, sapphire,

emerald, opal, turquoise, amethyst, and amber. 1900–03. Österreichisches Museum für Angewandte Kunst, Vienna.
Koloman Moser did not take long to abandon

naturalism for abstraction. He sought the combined beauty of form and matter—as in this pendant in which the jewels make a colored crown around a very stylized flower.

CLOCKS AND DESK ACCESSORIES

502 ⊠ GEORGES DE FEURE. Clock. Gilt-bronze. 1900–03. (Whereabouts unknown.)
Heroic figures of Julius Caesar and those personifying the bourgeois virtues have been replaced by more enigmatic symbols. Below the face, one of those typical Art Nouveau women with tall, slender, delicate figures, so much in fashion at the time, waves a final farewell to a vessel departing under full sail. Expectant hours and the flight of time are suggested in the design. The clock's rectangular face is surrounded by big, fleshy leaves. The marine landscape is continued onto the sides, and the back is decorated with a floral motif.

503 ⊠ HECTOR GUIMARD. Picture frame. Silver. 1907. The Cooper Union Museum for the Arts of Decoration, New York.
A prophet has no honor in his own country—least of all Guimard in 1900. He was accused of being too "Belgian," and of imitating Horta. And as soon as he described himself as an *"architecte d'art,"* some of his critics became indignant and others sarcastic. They damned his decorative abstraction and the undulating line to which, it must be admitted, he remained faithful for too long a time. This frame, designed in 1907, has an old-fashioned look; the clarity and simplicity which were to hold the field fifteen years later had already begun to struggle into existence.

504 ⊠ THEO NIEUWENHUIS. Clock. C. 1900. Silver and semiprecious stones. Gemeente Museum, The Hague.
Modernism and English influence are discernible in both the stylized leaves and the outline of this clock by this Dutch designer.

505 ⊠ UNKNOWN CRAFTSMAN. Clock. Inlaid wood. 1900–03. Private Collection, Munich.

The slender, functional shape of this clock is typical of the direction taken by Art Nouveau in Great Britain. The hands and face are the main design elements; everything else is subordinate. The case, adorned with a simple floral design, merely provides a support and a frame.

506 ⊠ LOUIS COMFORT TIFFANY. Inkwell. Bronze. C. 1900. The Brooklyn Museum, New York.
A catalogue of Art Nouveau inkwells would need a book to itself. In shape, style, and material, they are legion. There is Spicer-Simpson's symbolic silver inkwell on a marble base, entitled *The Mystery of Life*; a china octopus inkwell, like that by Henri Nocq; and Becker's *The Bramble*, in iron, boxwood, and ebony. The list would be incomplete without this "Egyptian" inkwell by Tiffany, a composition whose effect is deliberately monumental, decorated with large, simplified winged scarabs in relief.

507 ⊠ UNKNOWN CRAFTSMAN. Inkstand. Ceramic and bronze-gilt. C. 1904. Private Collection, Paris.
The period also produced simple inkwells, like this example. The containers stand at either end of the pen trough, and the metal base is lightly emphasized with a touch of floral decoration.

508 ⊠ UNKNOWN CRAFTSMAN. Clock. Bronze. C. 1900. Private Collection, Paris.
This clock was made in Chicago. The decoration features a rather androgynous winged figure (representing fleeting time?) with a disquieting expression. The clock face itself has no relation whatsoever to the Art Nouveau case containing it.

458

459 460

461

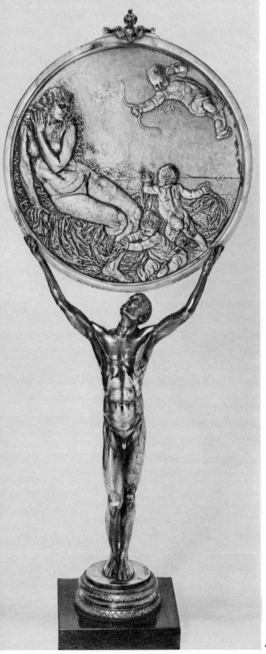

462

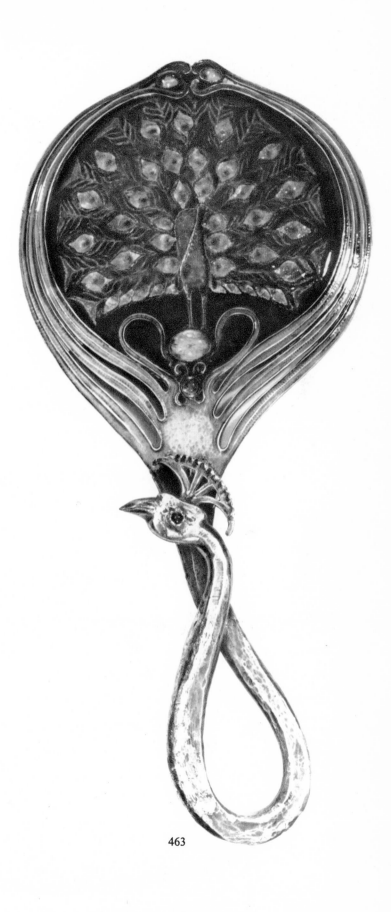

463

464

465

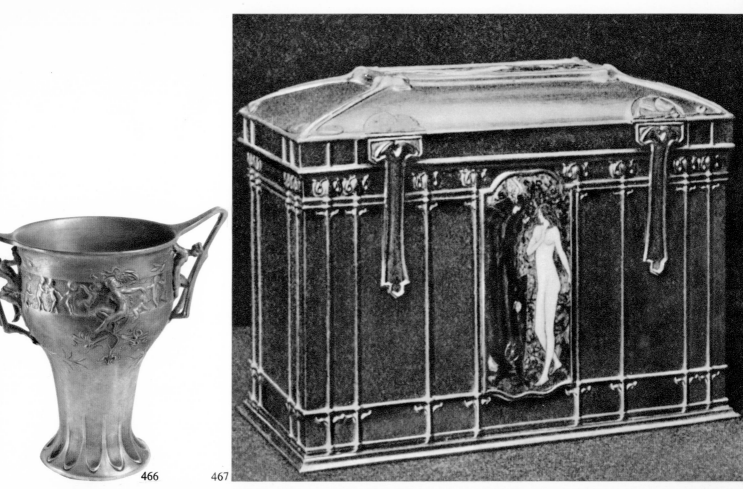

466 467

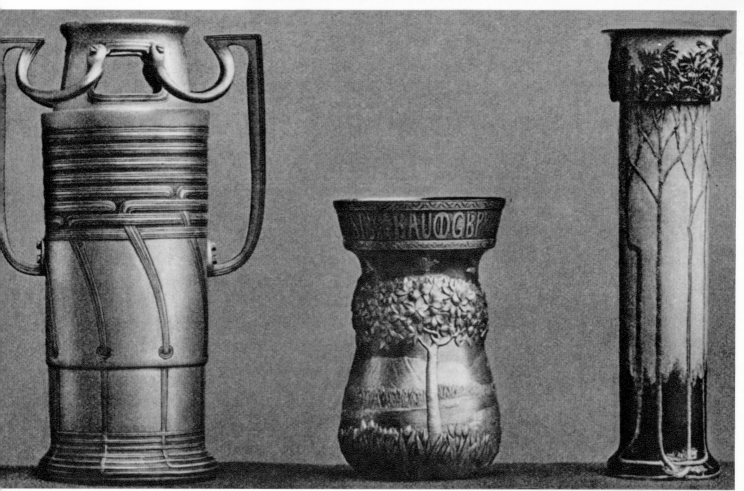

468

469

470

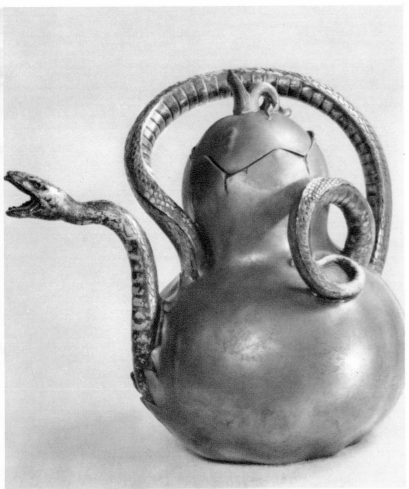

472

473

474

475

476

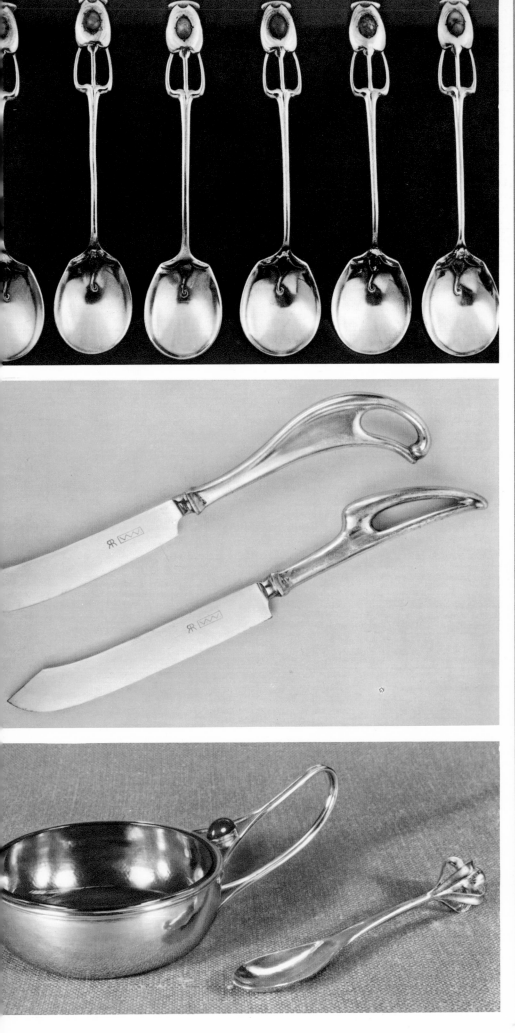

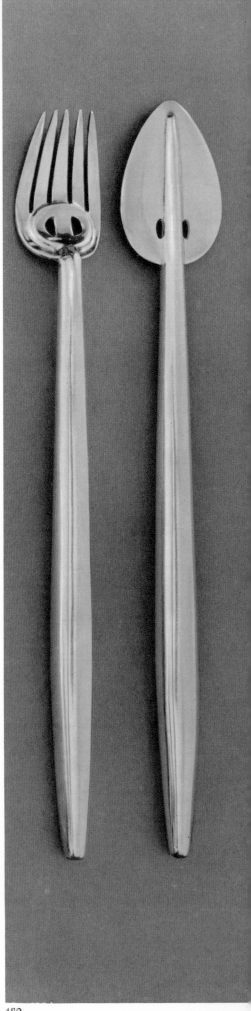

480

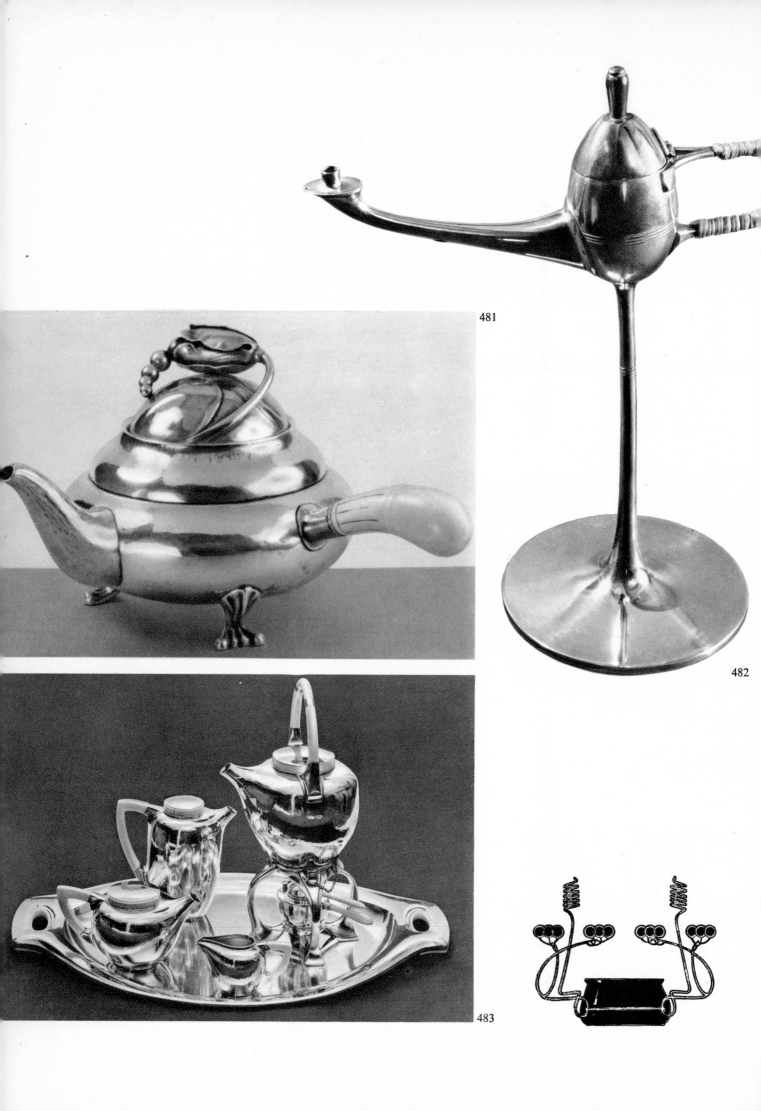

481

482

483

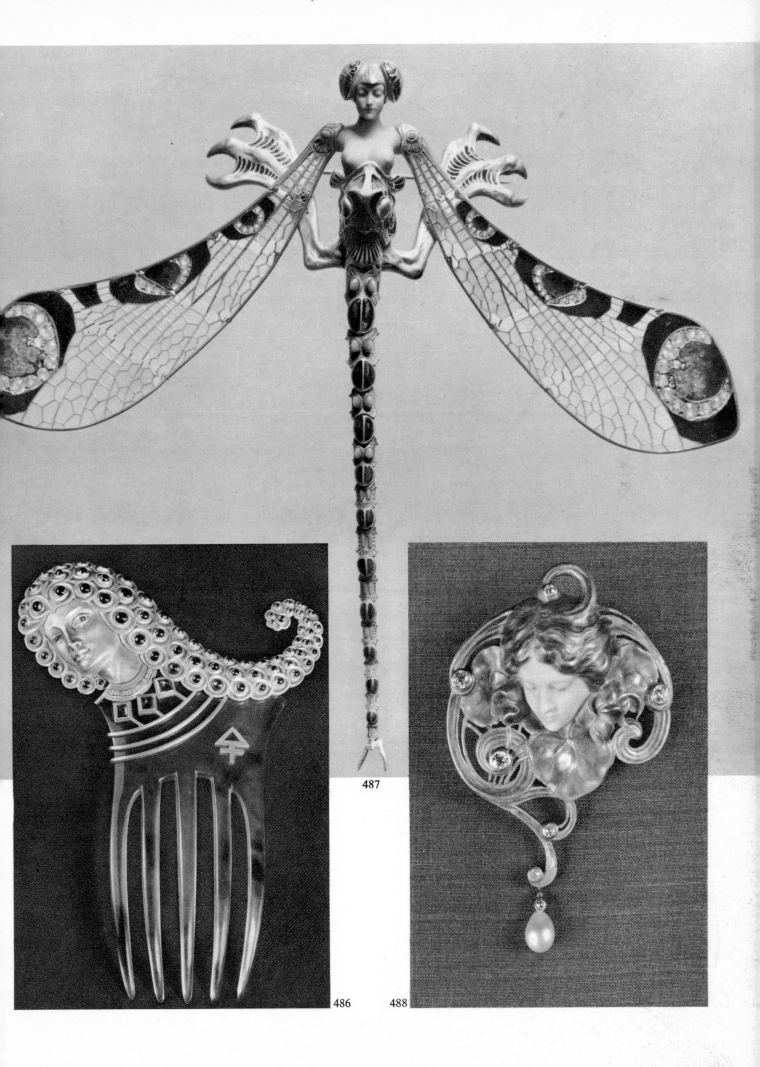

487

486 488

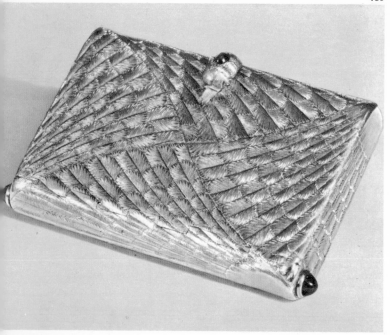

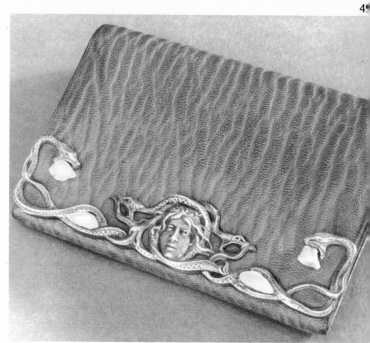

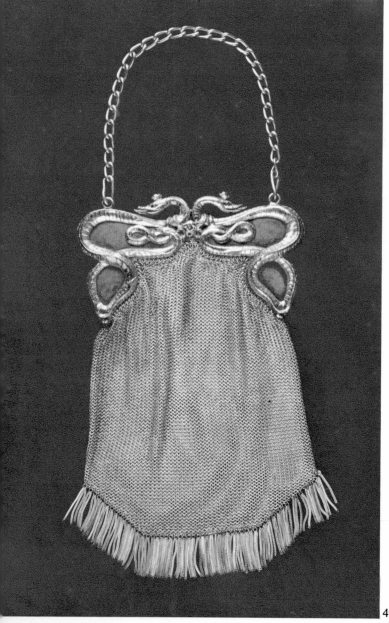

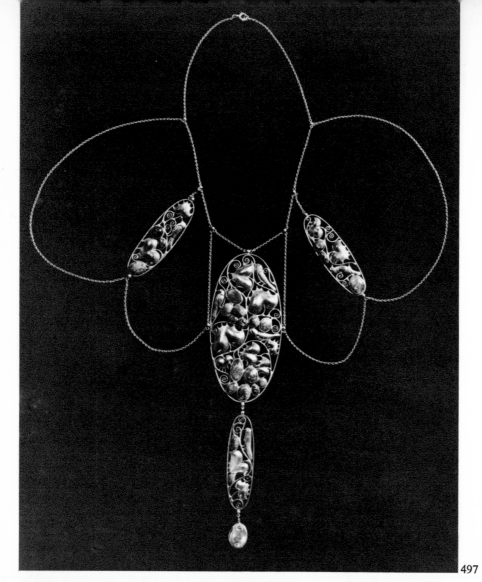

497

498

499

500

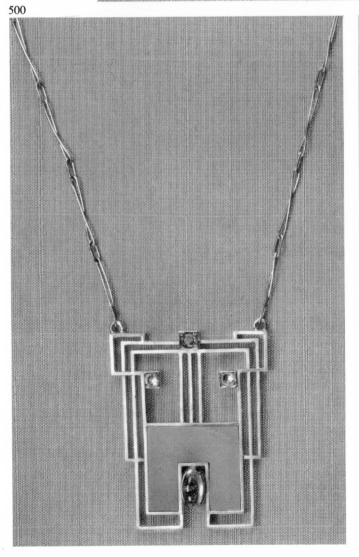

501

502

503

504

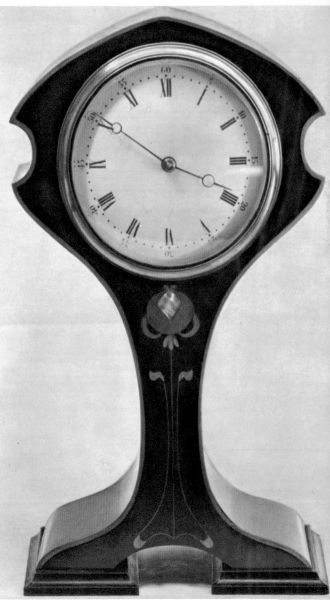

505

506

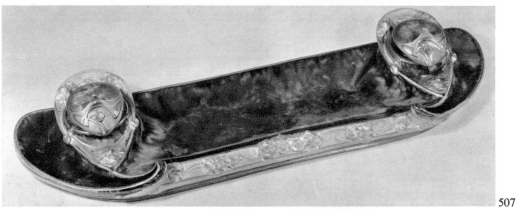

507

508

Fashion and Frivolity

THE expression "*La Belle Époque*" implicitly suggests an era of frivolous pleasure, a world which did in fact exist. To fashion, embroidery, and the luxurious little extras of life, artists and designers brought a serious approach and a standard of technical excellence which conferred high value on even the most superficial objects. The most ordinary fan or commonplace umbrella handle became a gem in its own right. Indeed, matters went so far that a woman tended to become a mere mannequin or dress dummy for creative ideals, an impersonal "area to be decorated." William Morris was one of the first pioneers of design to interest himself in fashion. He attacked it on the score of hypocrisy, the ridiculous attitude which insisted that the body be squeezed and pinched to fit the garment, rather than shaping the garment to fit the body.

By 1900, the "Eugénie crinoline" had been abandoned, but the feminine silhouette was still abused. Fashion plates, which exaggerate the lines considered essential, are most revealing in this respect. A slender waist and exaggerated curves are accentuated by a skirt which molds the hips and flares out at the hem. The belt is supported at the back by the buttocks, but in front comes down well below the waist, to lengthen the bodice. Nothing could be more unnatural than these two curves which, when seen in profile, make an S, with its mid-point at the waistline—the hour-glass silhouette.

Locked in a suffocating corset, with her buttocks sticking out and her bosom thrust forward, a woman was prevented from standing up straight. Though in the year of grace 1900 there were some women who refused to go on wearing "air balloon" bloomers, there was none who would let herself be seen without that indispensable item of the female uniform—her stays. A dress and its accompanying petticoats, which had been designed for a woman in a corset, would have lost all charm and style on a woman without one. Under the most clinging bathing costume, under the lightest or most mannish attire, even actresses or dancers had their waists constricted and their hips forcibly rounded by this cruel armor, which was a fertile source of stomach aches and fainting fits. Advertisements in fashion journals insisted on the virtues of this or that corset, recommended by doctors because it did not interfere with the digestive functions. It should be noted, in this connection, that plumpness, fostered by copious meals, was greatly appreciated.

"...as for her figure, and she was admirably built, it was impossible to make out its continuity (on account of the fashion then prevailing, and in spite of her being one of the best-dressed women in Paris) for the corset, jutting forwards in an arch, as though over an imaginary stomach, and ending in a sharp point, beneath which bulged out the balloon of her double skirts, gave a woman, that year, the appearance of being composed of different sections badly fitted together...."

(Marcel Proust, *Swann's Way*, trans. C. K. Scott Moncrieff)

This tyrannical cincture, in which a woman had to imprison herself every morning (with the indispensable aid of a maid's strong hand), far from being considered a mere piece of orthopedic apparatus, was actually an essential condiment in the graphics of eroticism: postcards of the kind called "artistic" frequently displayed a woman in nothing but her corset. And the evil which the corset did lived after it; when a woman took it off, her body remained misshapen. From the nudes of Courbet to the pornographic pictures of the late 1890's and early 1900's, the female anatomy shows the same deformation—atrophy of the waist, hypertrophy of the pelvis.

In dressing, the first item to go on was the chemise; over this came the corset, then the corset-cover; over that, the camisole, a little bolero of fine, heavily embroidered lawn. Next came the petticoats, molding the hips and garnished at the hem with a band of flounces or lace. Finally, the dress, often of lightweight material even in the most bitter weather, since the underclothes provided warmth. Boned collars were high and sleeves long, often prolonged to a point on the back of the hand. Long, many-buttoned gloves modestly concealed the lower arms, and women had nothing left bare except their faces. The legs, preferably plump, were clad in black stockings. Feet went into laced boots or shoes with high vamps. (Colette's Claudine, whose friends criticized the fine-drawn slenderness of her legs, showed exceptional boldness when she did not wear her stockings during a heat-wave.) An enormous hat, kept in place by lethal pins, completed the outfit, and there were the usual indispensable accessories: handbag, muff, and parasol.

At home, a woman would frequently put on a tea-gown, the work of a great couturier and as sumptuous as a court gown. In this attire she received her intimate friends. But on her "day" to receive, she was adorned from head to foot to meet the succession of envious or hostile glances as her guests entered the drawing room. At no time has dress been so much talked about, and never has it been changed so often in the course of the day.

A prosperous middle-class woman besieged her dressmaker with orders. This person, a sort of tyrannical employee, came to the house, advised, draped, and fitted the customer's dress for her next dinner or ball. The woman of fashion was dressed by one of the artist-tyrants with illustrious names like Worth, Redfern, or Rouff. These couturiers commissioned the most prominent painters to design new "creations," seek out materials, sketch embroideries, and create jewels. Georges de Feure was one of those who excited the critics' admiration:

"In the dresses designed for them by De Feure, women keep the graceful outline of their figures, which are lengthened a little but remain very supple. The dress, simply decorated at neck and shoulders, molds the waist and the hips; the skirt falls in straight folds, flares out with the grace of a reversed lily, and the hem is heavy with original embroidery whose design is never a repetition of what has gone before. Gold mingles with sombre gray. Startling reds enliven delicate beiges. Pearly pink stands out on dull green. And the transition from white to black passes through a hint of blue created by juxtaposing mauve and green."

DRESSES

509 ☒ Henry van de Velde. Dress. C. 1896. Kunstgewerbemuseum, Zurich.
The architect and decorator Van de Velde was above all a creator of harmony; everything, from the general lines to the smallest detail, contributed to the perfection of the whole. The artist in him ensured that when he designed a dress it would suit not only the wearer but also the surroundings in which she was going to wear it. We can well imagine this dark velvet gown in the setting of a Van de Velde drawing room. The linear motif accentuating them, and the set-in panel (a perfect use of appliqué), put the finishing touches to the decoration of the room. They sound the subtle, refined note which completes the harmony.

Though many artists concerned themselves with fashion and its light-hearted bits and pieces, none of them possessed Van de Velde's ability to create a universe apart, with its own laws and its own significant features.

510 ☒ Unknown Designer. Afternoon dress. 1902–05. Any pretty woman, heartbroken because she was a little too plump, could always turn for help to Mme. Blanche Leigh, 4 Rue de la Paix. Her advertisement promised results which were nothing short of magical: "The treatment is largely based on the inclusion of iodine in the various preparations used. Everybody knows how efficacious iodine is in dissolving adipose tissue and giving you a really slim figure, and what is especially delightful is that the cream, lotion, and bandage leave no marks on the skin."

511 ⊠ UNKNOWN DESIGNER. Ball gown. 1902–05.
February, 1899: "A charming evening dance was given by the Marquise de Moustiers; never has the light fantastic been more zestfully in evidence. Among the guests were: the Duchesse de Gramont, the Count and Countess Jean de Montebello, the Prince and Princess R. de Faucigny Lucinge, the Count and Countess de Cossé Brissac, Mme. Vagliano, Princess J. Murat, Mme. de Beistegui, the Count and Viscountess of Contades, M. and Mme. de Yturbe, the Marquise de Saint-Sauveur, Mme. Bemberg, the Countess de la Béraudière, the Countess Paul de Pourtalès, the Count and Countess Chandon de Briailles, the Count of Paris, M. Haas, the Countess Meunier de Haussoy, Boldini, Mme. de Kermaingan, M. Lazare Weiller, the Countess de Gontaut, the Marquise de Mun, the Marquise de Jaucourt."

512 ⊠ UNKNOWN DESIGNER. Afternoon dress. 1902–05.
To attract clients, the manager of the restaurant at the Ritz included the names of leading guests in his publicity material. You could be certain of meeting Lord and Lady Chelsea, Count de Gabriat, M.

Froment Meurice, M. Groult, the Duke of Devonshire, Mr. Beit, M. Jean Dupuis (the senator), Mme. Porges, M. Lebaudy, Baron Lejeune, and M. Hubert Faure.

513 ⊠ UNKNOWN DESIGNER. Ball gown. 1902–05.
Fashion journals were lyrical: "Here is a miraculous creation in coral-pink velvet with silvery highlights. The skirt is long, flowing and langorous, and is embroidered with an enormous spray of pale flesh-pink and sulfur-yellow roses. The skirt is slit to reveal an embroidered panel, the bodice, of a most strange and unusual design, has a shoulder-strap on the right and a cross-piece of Venetian lace; while on the left it is draped from a gold clasp connecting it with the back. The upper arms are bare, and extremely long, supple suede gloves rise high but not so far as to hide that superb shoulder, the belt is chiseled gold, a gorgeously rarified piece of work." Further selections from the fashion descriptions of the day must include: "chrysanthemum-colored, the flower of a dream, all the poetry of charm.... made of fine gold.... splashed with autumn rust.... wan and white as the sky in winter.... flushed like the roses of spring.... the myriad tints of summer.... wisteria velvet.... skirts of flesh-pink satin.... ultramarine blue velvet.... pearl-gray material.... meteoric crêpe...."

EMBROIDERY

514 ⊠ PATRIZ HUBER. Embroidery. 1895–1900. Hessisches Landesmuseum, Darmstadt.

515 ⊠ PRINCESS MARIE TENISHEVA. Embroidery. 1895–1900. Talashkino Workshops. (Whereabouts unknown.)
New themes and methods were adopted for embroidery, that essential ingredient of adornment. Embroidery for upholstery and interior decoration was made (by Mme. de Rudder in Belgium and Ann Macbeth in Scotland) by decorating the fabric with motifs in appliqué, outlined with braid. In France, Mme. Ory Robin made panels and screens by sewing pipingcord on coarse linen and heightening the effect with silver and old-gold thread. Embroidery was no longer an exclusively feminine art: Van de Velde, Hermann Obrist, Mackmurdo, Mackintosh, Bruno Paul, and Paul Ranson found new outlets for their imaginations in lace and guimping. Much was produced in this line; we have selected two examples. The first (plate 514) is an embroidered hanging with a red and yellow color scheme, made in Darmstadt after a design by Patriz Huber. The repeating pattern is a small group of feathers rising out of a circle, each unit being connected to its neighbor by lines reminiscent of a peacock's feather. The strongly stylized forms are designed for machine production. This readiness to make designs for industrial manufacture was one of the great merits of the artists of the early twentieth century. The

second example (plate 515) is Russian. The decorative pattern of this embroidery on canvas is a fusion of stylized vegetation and abstract shapes. The reader will have noted other instances of the special style emanating from these workshops, which were responsible for the most significant productions of Russian Art Nouveau. This skillful composition, both simple and modern in effect, is carried out in very soft mauves, pinks, and yellows, with staccato touches of dark violet and intense blue.

516 ⊠ HRDLICKA. Lace collar. 1902. Private Collection, Paris.
The *Wiener Werkstätte* played a leading role in creating new designs for lace and seeing that it was used in new ways. In 1902, Professor Hrdlicka published a collection of pieces designed by herself or under her direction. It included collars, fans, and handkerchiefs, which comprise some of the finest examples extant of plant and flower forms adapted to the technique of lacemaking. The stems and leaves are natural and in perfect conformity with the shapes they decorate, filling the curves and rhythms of those shapes with a sensitive arrangement of filled and empty spaces.

517 ⊠ FÉLIX AUBERT. Lace collar. C. 1900. Private Collection, Paris.
In this collar of multicolored lace, Félix Aubert chose the poppy as the basis of his design. A broad festoon

of the blossoms is blocked out around the outer edge, while the stalks, leaves, and buds stand out on an airier background. The designer displayed a sure understanding of composition, going beyond the simple ability to represent flowers cleverly. The decoration takes into account the shape of the collar, underlines it, and makes it stronger; motifs, material, and technique are in complete harmony with function.

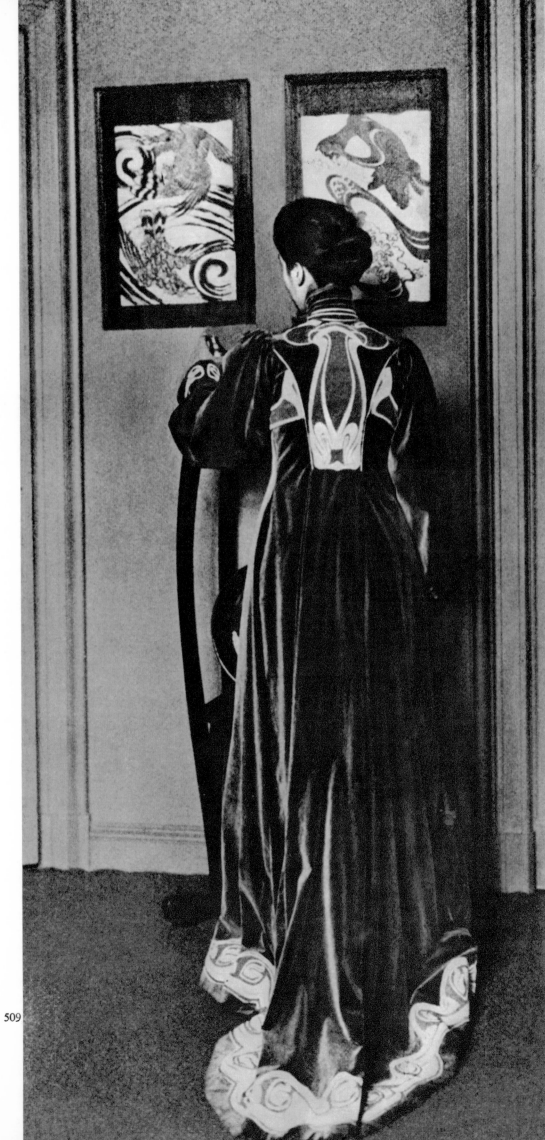

509

510

511

512

513

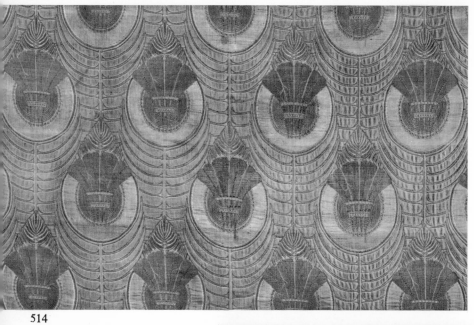

514

51...

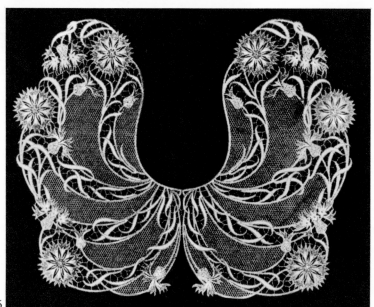

516

517

Typography and Bookbinding

IN the Symbolist period, writers and artists showed a new interest in typography, an interest which gradually extended to other aspects of the book as well. From its primary purpose as a vehicle for thought, the book as a physical entity became the object of a cult. For Des Esseintes and Dorian Gray, the container was as precious as the contents.

But others besides these unusual, and in any case imaginary, characters had become weary of the uninspired lettering and rules (in the typographical sense) gilding the spines of books. In the attempt to rediscover the true art of the book, a return was made to the sources: German and Italian incunabula. These prototypes were rare, sumptuous, and the work of craftsmen; they possessed just the qualities to charm the most exacting eye and mind.

The first books that William Morris printed are decidedly striking. The heavy, handmade paper is modeled on one produced about 1470; the text is compact, the margins wide, and the type, although devoid of complicated verticals and elaborate ligatures, is obviously inspired by Gothic models. This archaic touch is noticeable in a number of works produced between 1880 and 1890. Thereafter, the typographers began cutting new type faces.

The reworking of book design affected much more than letter forms and other detailed aspects of typography; the very conception of what a book should be had changed completely. Artists were tired of simply providing illustrations for the text; they longed for a closer connection between thought and picture. This quest for a deep underlying unity was extended to the binding.

After yielding for a time to the temptations of medievalism, bookbinding in the Art Nouveau period was permeated by Symbolism and the new taste for floral or linear embellishment. A special place of honor should be kept for the artists of the School of Nancy, whose work was original in every way and raised a storm of both protest and enthusiasm. It was between 1893 and 1899, that Martin, Wiener, and Prouvé designed and executed their pictorial bindings, in which a mosaic of leather and pyrography on the boards and spine create a single, continuous decoration, and bright colors abut directly, one upon the other, instead of being separated by gilt rules. These works, undertaken partly as feats of technical daring, were revolutionary in that they anticipated modern tendencies. As late as 1905, some designers were still adorning their bindings with Symbolist landscapes, the style used by Clément Mère and Waldraff in *Le Miroir du ciel natal*, by Rodenbach, and *Ramuntcho*, by Pierre Loti.

In addition to these highly specialized productions, there were other, more traditional designs which kept to the old form but sought a certain limited renewal by using floral themes, sometimes stylized, sometimes not. The bindings of Marius Michel are the most famous of these. Other names to note are those of Kieffer, Georges Canape, Petrus Ruban, H. E. Berlepsch-Valendas, and Eugène Belville.

It was in England, with the work of Beardsley, T. J. Cobden-Sanderson, and Douglas Cockerell, that the linear style took root and flourished. If the English, with their fine-drawn gilt tooling, appear to have made less radical innovations than some of the French, they were nonetheless the originators of the abstract tendency later adopted on the Continent by Behrens, Van de Velde, Bindesboell, Kersten, and Countess Sparre. Like their predecessors in the fifteenth and sixteenth centuries, these binders intended to startle and attract. To accomplish this they employed a wide range of materials: silver, copper, wood, or straightforward cloth, as in the bindings of Talwyn Morris, Theo Nieuwenhuis, Berlage, and Toorop.

This wave of novelty created a sensation. Books and periodicals, reaching a larger public than other art forms, broadcast the new aesthetic ideas. Posters, menus, greeting cards, and, in fact, even the most trivial pieces of printing benefited from recent advances in presentation and decoration. Finally, binding brought about a revival of interest in the art of leatherwork: panels, screens, and office furniture became again works of art.

TYPOGRAPHY

518 ☒ WILLIAM MORRIS. Title page of *The Golden Legend*. 1892. William Morris Gallery, Walthamstow, England.
It was in 1891 that William Morris, bent on reviving the art of typography, founded the Kelmscott Press in partnership with Emery Walker and Edward Burne-Jones. He designed new type, derived fairly closely from Gothic examples, and also endpapers and other ornaments. This title page is richly medieval in atmosphere. Significantly, Morris and his friends brought out new editions of various other medieval works, notably Chaucer's *The Canterbury Tales*.

519 ☒ ARTHUR HEYGATE MACKMURDO. Title page of *Wren's City Churches*. 1883. William Morris Gallery, Walthamstow, England.
This title page is generally regarded as the first manifestation of Art Nouveau. It contains all the elements which were to emerge triumphant ten years later: broadly stylized flowers, undulating stems, leaves rising like flames, integration of the type design with the decoration, and an arresting distribution of black and white, giving the background a positive decorative value.

520 ☒ GERRIT WILLEM DIJSSELHOF. Title page of *Kunst en Samenleving*. C. 1900. Private Collection, Amsterdam.
The originality of Dutch ornament—one might say of all Dutch art—at the end of the nineteenth century was due to the influence of Java. It was from that colony that artists borrowed the techniques of batik, a method of dyeing in which portions of the design are protected under a wax coating between various applications of color. What attracted the Dutch designers was not so much the technique itself or even the subject matter for which it had been used, but the peculiar effects obtained, which they thought to reproduce in other decorative media. An example is this title page by Dijsselhof, which also shows medieval influence.

521 ☒ MSTISLAV DOBUJINSKY. Title page of *Mir Iskustva*. C. 1902. Private Collection, Paris.

In the title page for this periodical, Dobujinsky achieved an amalgamation of new and old. The stippling and the nervous, whirling line recall the drawing of the "elliptical" portraitists of the late eighteenth century, while the lettering and layout show a creative desire for modernity.

522 ☒ GEORGES AURIOL. Monograms and type samples. 1898–1902.
Like Grasset and Giraldon, Georges Auriol designed a new type face. His alphabet, which uses some of the upper case forms in lower case, is plump and supple, as if drawn with a brush. Auriol worked for a number of publishing houses, including Flammarion, Hachette, and Larousse; he also worked for Enoch, who published the most successful songs of the time with covers designed by Lucien Métivet, Steinlen, De Feure, Chéret, and Henri Rivière.

523 ☒ WILL BRADLEY. Poster. 1895. Koch Collection, Chicago.
Will Bradley, one of the most interesting personalities in American Art Nouveau, is best known for his posters and book illustrations, but he also made numerous designs for interior decoration, wallpapers, and architectural projects. His reputation extended beyond his own country, and he was known and admired in Europe as early as 1894. His career continued long after the decline of Art Nouveau; until 1930, he was the best-paid designer in the United States. The example shown here is dated 1895, and is characteristic of his style, which owes much to Beardsley and Ricketts; nevertheless, his draftsmanship, and more especially his composition, are personal and original. He adopted the Japanese perspective and spatial synthesis, and like the other draftsmen of the period, he was fond of a profusion of curves. The treatment, however, is entirely his own. Bradley omits the third dimension and frequently disregards the normal articulation of the human body, altering its proportions and rejecting all allusion to natural models in order to accentuate the purely ornamental character of his design. He suggests forms by a mosaic of whites, grays, and blacks, the

arrangement of which obeys the laws of equilibrium rather than those of reality. A noteworthy feature is the prominence accorded the verbal content of the poster; Bradley gives it a decorative value almost equal to that of the figures.

524 ☒ THEO NIEUWENHUIS. Calendar. 1896. Private Collection, Germany.
In the work of the Dutch designer Nieuwenhuis, the revival of ornament was not confined only to books. It can be seen here on a page from an ordinary calendar, designed for a German client, in which flowering, snow-laden branches symbolize the departure of winter and the arrival of spring. Two years later, the French General Post Office brought out the first calendars adorned with the dreadful chromolithographs which were destined to be pinned up in so many cottages.

525 ☒ CHARLES RICKETTS. Title page of *Rubaiyat of Omar Khayyam*. 1902. The Victoria and Albert Museum, London.
Charles Ricketts, who founded *The Dial* in 1888, played an important part in the development of decorative art in England. Gifted with responsive curiosity, he was a great admirer of William Morris, Greek and Japanese art, and the paintings of Gustave Moreau. He was also particularly interested in German fifteenth-century woodcuts, whose influence is obvious in this title page. The title itself has been treated separately; the designer has tried to derive as much decorative value as possible from the letter forms, joining and superimposing them in a most unusual way.

BOOKBINDING

526 ☒ LÉON GRUEL. Binding for *Collected Tales of Edgar Allan Poe*. 1900–01. Museum für Kunst und Gewerbe, Hamburg.
This nocturnal scene depicts a black cat, back arched and tail bristling, silhouetted against the subtle tonal gradation of a fantastic moonlit landscape. It is reminiscent of the shadow-plays which were in vogue during the same period. Gruel, whose work was consistently admired, here displays high technical perfection together with real understanding of the book he bound. Many of his bindings are decorated with foliage or stylized flowers of startling effectiveness.

527 ☒ VICTOR PROUVÉ. Binding for *Salammbô*, by Gustave Flaubert. 1893. Musée de l'École de Nancy, Nancy.
This binding was executed by René Wiener. It makes full use of the different ways of treating leather: inlay, engraving, gilding, and glazing. Wiener adroitly uses the design of the veil of Tânit to connect the boards with the spine. This *Salammbô* is one of the earliest examples of a binding treated as a picture. Instead of merely illustrating a theme from the story, the binding tries to present the essential spirit of Flaubert's novel. Orthodox craftsmen were critical of these pictorial bindings, which they considered to be a betrayal of the art of the book.

528 ☒ M. LILLIAN SIMPSON. Book cover. Metal electrotype. 1896. The Victoria and Albert Museum, London.
The artist created this work while she was a student at the National Training School. This metal binding, with a cherub on its clasp, reminds one of an antiphonal; it typifies the dual source of the bookbinding revival in Great Britain: the Middle Ages and the Renaissance. Its opulent heaviness is somewhat lightened by the graceful nudity of the winged creatures adorning it.

529 ☒ SARAH T. PRIDEAUX. Binding. 1902. The Victoria and Albert Museum, London.
This binding is fairly close to traditional precedent, but the flowers and leaves are natural rather than conventional and reveal the awakening of a new decorative sense in England.

530 ☒ JOSEF HOFFMANN. Bindings for Adolfe Stoclet. 1911. Palais Stoclet, Brussels.
These bindings (and the inkwell) are typical of the style of the great Viennese architect. Like the Palais Stoclet itself, they are some twenty years ahead of their time.

531 ☒ AUBREY BEARDSLEY. Binding for Vincent O' Sullivan's *The Houses of Sin*. 1897. The Victoria and Albert Museum, London.
The essence of Beardsley's genius is in his pure, almost weightless line. Though extremely tenuous, it stands on its own, and serves to decorate the entire outside of a book. In his illustrations, it divides the white page in such a way that every part becomes extraordinarily intense through mere force of suggestion.

532 ☒ HENRY VAN DE VELDE. Binding. C. 1902. Museum für Kunst und Gewerbe, Hamburg.
The bindings designed by Van de Velde were executed and tooled by P. Claessens. They display the curves familiar from the other works of Van de Velde who, while maintaining the integrity of his own style, may also have learned something from the experiments of Cobden-Sanderson in England. In this example, the interlacing lines play up the value of the expanses of flat color between. According to Van de Velde, every line "owes its power to the genius of the man who drew it." From the lips of a lesser artist, such a statement might tempt us to smile, but from Van de Velde we can accept it.

Posters

OUR interest in late-nineteenth-century posters is not only in their inherent values, but also in the development and change of this art form. In a mere twenty years the advertising placard became a new art, embodying its own principles and techniques. It was no longer merely a printed notice, nor was it a picture; it became a decorative composition designed for a utilitarian, commercial purpose, combining image and letter, line and color. It had to catch the eye and charm it, the attractiveness of the design causing the mind to take in the text. It had to astonish, yet be easily understood. It was intended to be seen rather than looked at, grasped immediately and almost unconsciously. This type of poster art was born in France toward the end of the nineteenth century. Its progenitors were Toulouse-Lautrec, Jules Chéret, and Eugène Grasset.

There were several causes for the metamorphosis of the poster. Painters (other than prize-winners at the Salon) lived precariously and were often not far from starving. There were also financial and technical factors: business competition, the new techniques of lithography and zinc engraving, and the success of Japanese prints and drawings had provided the conditions for this entirely new combination of publicity and art. The poster became an essential part of the street as a visual entity—many people pointed out the likeness of walls and fences to a decorative frieze. Finally, a new species of business was created: the renting of suitable locations where these outsized creations could be posted.

There were further consequences and benefits. Posters not only trumpeted the virtues of Menier chocolate and Ripolin enamels; they also presented a new aesthetic. They augmented the color and gaiety of the street and familiarized everyone with a strange new concept of ornament; they accustomed the eye to a new repertory of line, color, and form, to modes of representation and decoration which may have been bewildering at first sight, but which through constant repetition rapidly created new visual perceptions and sensibilities. To its contemporaries at the time of its birth, the poster was a manifesto; and to historians it became a source of evidence, for it both launched fashions and reflected public taste. There was a tacit dialogue between designer and spectator, each imposing his preferences on the other. The poster thus deserves equal rank with its coeval, the motion picture, as the popular art form *par excellence* of the twentieth century. It also reflects the style of Art Nouveau peculiar to each country—the particular line, flowers, stylization, abstraction—and shows us how the specific national elements in each of these styles became more marked as time went on. At the end of the nineteenth century, the poster was international in style; the masters of the *genre* were almost all French, and it was from them that the other European countries took their cue. But by 1900, or even a little earlier, each country was discovering an easily discernible style of its own.

Grasset, Chéret, Capiello, and Steinlen created typically French posters, full of flourish and *brio*. The English designers, such as John Hassall and the Beggarstaff brothers, combined humor and a touch of caricature in a way which was entirely alien to France. The Glasgow group, here as elsewhere, showed affinities with the Sezession, but on neither side was there any loss of individuality. The Macdonald sisters and Herbert MacNair brought out posters exhibiting a typically Scottish preference for elongated, slender, slightly rigid forms, while Koloman Moser and the other Viennese designers settled for a more geometric stylization, a more emphatic rigor of construction.

A very special case is the work of the Dutchmen Toorop, Thorn-Prikker, and Nieuwenhuis, who availed themselves of Javanese influence to effect a renovation of their country's decorative stock-in-trade. Finally, the posters of Mucha lie outside all the main classifications: indeed, and in spite of their Byzantine flavor, they cannot be classified with any tradition whatsoever. They are the work of a genius whose uniquely personal style attracted imitators but did not found a school. It had little in common with the trends which made true poster art possible.

533 ◰ Julius Klinger. *Künstlerplakate.* 1912. Museum für Kunst und Gewerbe, Hamburg.
This poster by Klinger shows the ultimate outcome of the Viennese geometric tendency. In it we can recognize, on the one hand, some of the typical elements of Art Nouveau—schematic silhouettes, rejection of modeling, and an over-all treatment in expressive lines and decorative surfaces—and on the other, a premonition of Art Décoratif—extreme elimination of detail, and a stylization devoid of sentiment but not of beauty.

534 ◰ Jules Chéret. *Théâtrophone.* C. 1900. Collection Document, Paris.
For once, a *petite femme* by Chéret is found in a moment of relative repose. For a few short seconds she is captivated by the sound of the "*Théâtrophone,*" but at any moment she will be off again—she is already exploring the distance with her eyes. In spite of having settled down for a moment, she has lost nothing of her feathery lightness or her perpetual vibration, which her creator suggests by his nervous zigzag line and its sudden interruptions, by angular contours and transparent shadows. A few summarily drawn figures in the background indicate depth.

535 ◰ Jean Atché. Poster for a cigarette. C. 1900. Collection Document, Paris.
In this poster the influence of Mucha is manifestly present; the pose, composition, and treatment are reminiscent of his more celebrated posters devoted to Sarah Bernhardt, to Ruinart's champagne, and to Schaal's chocolate. The present example, whose intention is more interesting than its execution, aims to advertise the quality, and indeed the magical virtues, of a commercial product. To buy the brand of cigarette, whose smoke makes so graceful a halo around the lady's face, would not be to enjoy the tobacco for its mildness, its delicacy, and flavor; the purpose would rather be to approximate as closely as possible a certain ideal image. The poster's main subject is not the tiny cigarette but the woman—her elegance, the inclination of her head, and the curve of her uplifted hand.

536 ◰ Georges de Feure. *Chimères et Grimaces.* C. 1900. Collection Document, Paris.
Lithographed illustrated covers for sheet music were among the victims of photography. This type of illustration was still flourishing in 1900; people not only sang a good deal then, but they were also capable of reading music. Music both light and serious could be effectively and profitably diffused by publishing collections of songs or operatic arias. The most famous artists contributed to the illustration of music by designing covers for these collections and posters announcing publication of the latest pieces. This poster is a sample of the oddity and fantasy unfolded in the work of Georges de Feure. The confusion of hair and flowers is treated with much freedom and originality, and the exalted expression of the face framed by the lyre belongs to the enigmatic world of this artist, in which every promise is charged with menace, and every pleasure with fear.

537 ◰ Manuel Orazi. *Théâtre de Loïe Fuller.* C. 1900. Collection Document, Paris.
Certainly no dancer inspired so many artists as did Loïe Fuller. When we examine the works dedicated to her—statuettes, drawings, and posters—we find ourselves visualizing her in a perpetual whirlwind of transparent veils. To most of those who depicted her, Loïe Fuller was a gigantic billowing skirt under whose undulation the dancer's body is engulfed and drowned. Orazi rejected the idea of representing this volatile creature directly; he sought only to suggest her presence and movement, and therein lies his originality. Her face, torso, arms, and the muscular curve of her waist are all firmly drawn, but the rest of the body dissolves into a whirling mist; a few enlarged spangles explode colorfully in the foreground.

538 ◰ Joseph Maria Olbrich. Poster for the Darmstadt Exhibition. 1901. Hessisches Landesmuseum, Darmstadt.
This poster was designed for the exhibition of the Darmstadt artists' colony where Olbrich had been working since 1898. Its geometric character makes it

virtually a manifesto. The paving, which takes up more room than anything else, is seen in perspective; the trees are triangles; and the decorative border is schematic. The lettering is a characteristic example of Olbrich's typographical explorations; the angles are definite, yet the rhythm is fluid and undulating. The dovetailing and overlapping of the letters help to make each word a decorative entity in itself.

539 ✎ HENRY VAN DE VELDE. Three posters for Tropon. 1897–98. Private Collection, Paris.
For the Tropon firm, Van de Velde produced not only these famous posters, but a number of other designs which also show his taste for abstract ornament. The only naturalistic element is seen in the three little birds, and even they are strongly stylized into a triskelion. The simple design, a combination of lines of different thicknesses which render the rectangular frame of the page softer and more flexible, makes one forget the real surface on which it is inscribed, leaving one aware only of the surface the design encloses. Straight lines and right angles are excluded. Once again, Van de Velde is playing with our visual sense, yet not for a moment deceiving or tricking it. He imposes a special kind of space, with its own logic, rhythm, and perfection, and rejects all reference to a natural model.

540 ✎ KOLOMAN MOSER. Poster. 1899. Graphische Sammlung Albertina, Vienna.

For the fifth exhibition of the Sezession, Moser designed this poster, lithographed in blue, violet, and gold by A. Berger of Vienna. It is representative of both Moser's style at the end of the century and the general tendencies in posters at the time. It is full of broad curves, and also displays the growing trend toward abstract design, especially near the top of the composition. The seated genie, which forms the main subject and sets the structural scheme, is treated in a manner both naturalistic and decorative; the hair and wings are pretexts for a line play in which forms and curves extend and curl in defiance of natural appearances. The mosaic tendency, and the abstract forms and lines, prefigure Moser's later works.

541 ✎ RICHARD TESCHNER. Sketch for a poster. 1913. Graphische Sammlung Albertina, Vienna.
This design really comes under the heading of Art Décoratif. It contains the typical ornamentation of that style: stylized circular flowers. Discipline of form is evident everywhere; the curls of the letters, for example, are carefully calculated. We are already far from Art Nouveau—but without the extraordinary revolution and renewal it effected in all the arts, this poster could not have been created. Its debt to its pioneering predecessors is obvious—composition, repertory of ornament, and thoughtful creativeness in the design of the letters.

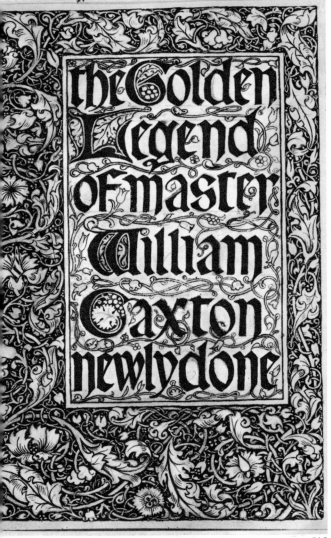

518

519

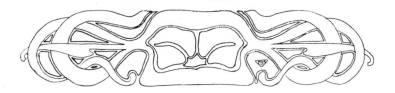

520

Kunst en Samenleving

naar: Walter Crane
door: Jan Veth

521

Историческая выставка предметовъ искусства

1904

52

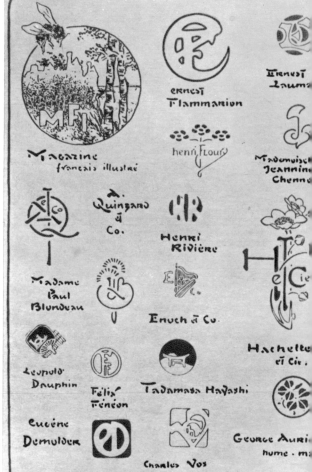

Magazine
français illustré

ernest
Flammarion

henri Floury

Шrnest
Laum

Madame
Paul
Blondeau

A.
Quinzard
& Co.

Henri
Rivière

Enoch & Co.

Madumoisel
Jeannin
Chenno

Leopold
Dauphin

Félix
Fénéon

Tadamasa Hayashi

Hachette
et Cie.

Eugène
Demolder

Charles Vos

George Auri
hume - ma

523

524

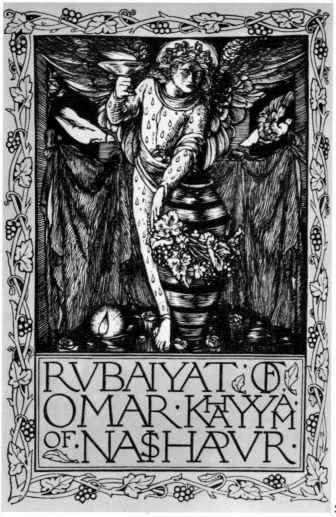

525

527

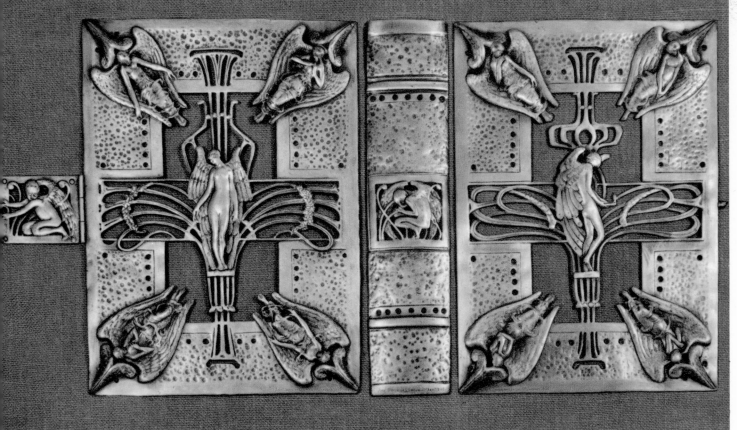

528

529

530

531

532

534

535

536

537

538

539

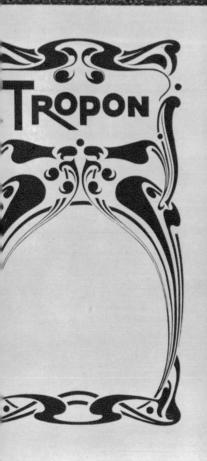

540

541

Graphics

ART Nouveau graphics demand a lengthy study, not just a brief enumeration. Such a study would range from colored woodcuts to *ex-libris* plates, and include landscapes, portraits, and typographic ornaments, each of these examined in detail. We shall simply point out general characteristics, fully aware that this summary treatment is all too superficial.

In lithographs and woodcuts, whether in black and white or in color, the decorative conception and treatment was of prime importance (especially in the case of the Nabis). This meant taking into account the flat surface and, consequently, being prepared to emphasize purely ornamental details at the expense of volume and the illusion of depth. Time and time again the designer felt that without a darker patch in one place or another, his composition would become unbalanced, and thus put in a shadow or thickened a line accordingly. Objects and people are frequently stylized, surrounded by a heavy outline and conveyed by a broad, flat treatment. Both in color and in monochrome the tendency was to make the print a mosaic of ornamental forms, a harmony of lines in which curves played the main expressive role. Decoration was not achieved through drawing alone; background itself had a definite form and was not merely an empty space lying alongside or behind the figures. Contiguous blacks and whites, each maintaining their own identity, were subtly matched and balanced. These characteristics are especially prominent in posters and typographic ornaments by Van de Velde, Toorop, Olbrich, Behrens, Will Bradley, Eckmann, Brangwyn, Grasset, and others—almost all the artists who were involved in the general decorative revival of the time concerned themselves at one time or another with typography and the design of printers' ornaments. Of special significance are certain English figures who were all more or less related to the Pre-Raphaelites: Walter Crane, Burne-Jones, and above all Aubrey Beardsley, that curious, disturbing genius who exerted a powerful influence on designers both in England and abroad.

542 ⬚ EUGÈNE GRASSET. *Drug Addict*. Lithograph. C. 1898. Collection Brockstedt, Hamburg.
This woman is an astonishing figure. Above her forehead rises the rebellious little lock of hair which is the speciality of Grasset's models. The rest of her hair streams down in heavy tresses over her violently tensed back and around her equally tense face. She is giving herself an injection. The keynote is expressiveness, brought out by the arrangement of whites, grays, and blacks—the top of the stocking provides a contrapuntal touch to the black mass of the hair—the concentration of the pose, the curved back, and the convulsive hands.

543 ⬚ HENRI RIVIÈRE. *Grazing Horse*. Lithograph. C. 1900. Private Collection, Paris.
Like many others in the period, Henri Rivière learned much from the masters of the Japanese woodcut. He did not learn the secret of their technique merely as a mechanical trick. In his *Twelve Aspects of Nature, Breton Landscapes*, and *Views of Paris* he shows a personal touch and conveys a poetic sensibility peculiar to himself. He does not isolate his forms by means of a heavy outline; he builds them up, using only an incidental accent here and there to bring out the relief or denote some irregularity of the ground. He aimed at

recording aspects and moments, not for their quality of transience but for their eternal content amid the ever-changing play of light. The moving melancholy of the landscape was his subject: the soul of the place, not the soul of Henri Rivière.

544 ✎ EUGÈNE GRASSET. *Autumn.* Woodcut. C. 1900. Collection Dr. Sachers, Munich.
Autumn was issued as a black-and-white woodcut and a six-color lithograph. The proof reproduced here is black and white. It is very characteristic of Grasset's style, with its wide areas surrounded by outlines, the rejection of depth and relief, and the absence of empty spaces. The design covers the whole page, and the background makes no attempt to suggest the third dimension. No evidences of light or shadow or gradations of color are present; line and surface alone are featured. The hair is a dark mass contrasting with the bright areas of the face and shoulder; the fruit, leaves, and branches are carried out in varying tones of gray. All the representatives of Art Nouveau we have encountered so far have this same resolutely decorative attitude. Here, it is particularly interesting because of its Janus-like quality, at once naturalistic and anti-realistic. The artist takes his subject matter from nature, and his people and plants are perfectly recognizable; but by depriving them of volume and light, he deliberately removes them from life. All that Grasset retains is the outline, which he transplants into two-dimensional space. As a result, every form becomes principally an ornament. The procedure is common to many artists, but is especially prominent in this poster. Objects are not stylized or distorted; on the contrary, they have been carefully studied and accurately drawn, subject only to a slight degree of formal schematization; but having lost their weight and their glitter, they have left reality. Grasset applies to the poster the formula laid down by Maurice Denis for painting: "a plane surface covered with colors arranged according to a certain order."

545 ✎ SAMUEL JESSURUN DE MESQUITA. Woodcut. C. 1899. Private Collection, Paris.
This woodcut by the Dutch artist Jessurun de Mesquita represents the tendency of Art Nouveau to use flat areas in which black and white are conceived as complementary opposites. The surfaces are kept intact, with only a sinuous line here and there to disturb them with a hint of modeling; every object is expressed by the shape of its silhouette. This work is modern, not only in style but in subject: a café scene, a snapshot of people in everyday clothes and casual attitudes.

546 ✎ PAUL RANSON. Program cover for Maeterlinck's *Les 7 Princesses.* 1892. Private Collection, Paris.
As a designer, Paul Ranson tried his hand at everything, but was best at designing carpets, fabrics, and wallpapers. The program reproduced here is an example of the flowing, essentially decorative lines which are characteristic of his work. Here, everything undulates,

and the nonchalantly drawn letters are deliberately out of proportion and fanciful. The background is completely covered with finely drawn lines in which the pen strokes stand out less than the white spaces between them. The figure of the woman, beautifully drawn with great restraint, balances the white expanse carrying the title.

547 ✎ THOMAS THEODOR HEINE. *Things We Have Stolen.* Lithograph. 1892. Private Collection, Munich.
The monthly review *Jugend* was started in Munich in 1896. Its title was the origin of the German term "Jugendstil" for Art Nouveau. This alone indicates how important a part it played and how wide was its influence. It was plentifully illustrated, and its contributors frequently included Steinlen, Otto Eckmann, Vallotton, and Thomas Theodor Heine. Heine also contributed to *Simplizissimus.* In both periodicals he was free to express his black humor. This example gives us a foretaste of a new style of illustration which did not fully emerge until a few years later. The simplified outlines, especially that of the woman's figure, show a Japanese influence, but the monster is typically Germanic.

548 ✎ EUGEN KIRCHNER. *November* (from the periodical *Pan*). Aquatint. 1896.
Here we have a Japanese-type perspective, leading up out of the top of the picture; Japanese humor is evident in the parallel silhouettes battling against the wind. It would be difficult to exaggerate the indebtedness of Art Nouveau to Japan.

549 ✎ WILHELM VOLZ. *Salome.* Lithograph. C. 1900. Collection Dr. S. Wichmann, Starnberg, Germany.
Salome was a figure of great interest for artists near the end of the last century. For Gustave Moreau and Aubrey Beardsley she conveyed a certain conception of woman. To them, as to Volz (a Munich artist), she was no longer the Salome of the Middle Ages, a charming little dancer. She was wanton, cruel, and sensual. It was from her that the delicate feminine creations of Art Nouveau acquired their streaming hair, both plant-like and serpentine, and also their air of mystery and perversion. In this example, the decorative composition (which is typically Jugendstil) is accompanied by a violent yet restrained realism; the tortured faces, depicted simply and economically, and the passionate twist of the body contrast with the calm lines of the background. This is not the light, carefree atmosphere captured so frequently in the works of the *Belle Époque,* but rather the most impassioned and bizarre aspect of Art Nouveau.

550 ✎ JAN TOOROP. Poster for *Het Hoogeland Beekbergen.* 1896. Collection S. Lankhout, The Hague.
Johan Thorn-Prikker and Toorop had a considerable influence on the applied arts in Holland. In this poster we notice the same style as in Toorop's paintings: vertical emphasis, elongated forms, and a mysterious,

mystical atmosphere. However, the decorative sense is different, being perfectly in accord with the different technique imposed by the medium. Toorop has rejected modeling; everything which would normally be expressed by the illusion of the third dimension has here been conveyed in terms of flat surfaces. The folds in the sleeves of the winged creature have become curves and volutes, and the bodies of the crouching figures have not been shown in the round, but flattened and purposely distorted. Everything possible has been done to give the impression of a flat surface covered with interwoven lines. The tendency, which had already become perceptible in some of Toorop's paintings, has here become deliberate and overt. On closer analysis, every detail would confirm this, from the lines surrounding the suppliants and infiltrating all the white spaces at the bottom of the composition, to the serrated fretwork of the lettering.

551 ⬚ HENRI DE TOULOUSE-LAUTREC. *La Grande Loge.* Lithograph. 1892. Museum für Kunst und Gewerbe, Hamburg.
As a draftsman, lithographer, and poster designer, Toulouse-Lautrec exerted a strong influence on the Art Nouveau graphics. Borrowing much from the Far East—its new way of depicting perspective, its flat patches of color, and its graphic synthesis—he found his "Salon" in the street. His humor and cruel realism helped him to delineate a silhouette in a few expressive lines. He renewed the artist's subject matter—no more eternal landscapes, grandiose scenes, or noble historic subjects; he was excited by reality and reality alone. Lautrec did for his own epoch what Callot, Goya, and Daumier did for theirs: he revealed the poetic aspect lurking in the weary, tragic round of banal habitual pleasure. It is impossible in a few lines to analyze the richness of his contribution. We shall therefore confine ourselves to this one lithograph and point out the elements which Art Nouveau was to borrow from him. It will be seen that he used perspective to transform and refine the architectural setting into a few unexpected curves. One notes in passing, that these lines both situate his characters in space and tell us that we are at the theater. The two figures in the foreground, a study in complementary opposites, are established by contrasting values which are created by only a few touches; in the woman's white coat, the shapes are underlined by a few strokes possessing an ornamental quality. As for the third character, a broadly laid on composition in black and white, the two strokes indicating eye and mouth convey his expression more effectively than any amount of detail.

552 ⬚ PAUL HERMANN. *The Cab.* Lithograph. C. 1900. Collection Dr. S. Wichmann, Starnberg, Germany.
This lithograph by the painter and lithographer Paul Hermann is a typical example of the Art Nouveau print. The treatment is in a very *japonisant* style, reminiscent of some of the work of Bonnard. Outlines have been almost omitted, and different values are juxtaposed without a frontier line between them: the identical bodices are rendered in a single color, as are the enormous bows on the hats. It was a common whim among lithographers to leave the drawing unfinished in this way, leaving it to the spectator to complete it in his mind. Félix Vallotton employs the trick with peculiar boldness; for a crowd, he uses an expanse of black, some white faces and hands, and nothing more. Hermann has conceived his composition as a patchwork of flat washes differentiated by their shapes, their colors, and a few decorative strokes within their boundaries. This may be regarded as a compendium of the leading tendencies in graphics around the turn of the century. The subject is contemporary life, but the main preoccupation is to create a decorative work.

Medallions

THE art of the medallion underwent a renaissance at the beginning of the present century. Perceptibly influenced by the style of the 1900's, it threw off the shackles of conventional pomposity and began to portray aspects of everyday life with a new freedom and fluency of modeling. At times it followed painting and sculpture into populism and sentimentality, but with restraint and without absurdity. We are indebted to the artists of the period for some extremely attractive works in the form of medallions and small plaques, which are not only admirable in execution, but aesthetically valuable through their purity of line.

553 ◪ DANIEL DUPUIS. Plaque commemorating numismatics. Bronze. C. 1900. Museum für Kunst und Gewerbe, Hamburg.

Daniel Dupuis was one of the artists who applied themselves to resuscitating the medallion, an art which had endured the last three centuries under the dead hand of official allegorical pomposity. In this instance, the artist has surrounded a nude figure with contemporaneous furniture. The pose is natural and the drapery supple and gracious. The improbable subject becomes acceptable.

554 ◪ CAREL JOSEPH BEGEER. Plaque commemorating an association of amateur photographers in Amsterdam. Bronze. 1895. Museum für Kunst und Gewerbe, Hamburg.

In this plaque by Begeer, Antiquity mingles with modernism. It appeared in connection with a photography exhibition in Amsterdam. It celebrates the triumph of modern technology in a deliberately traditional language reminiscent of the circumlocution employed by Pope Paul VI when he found himself obliged to translate "photographers" into Latin: "*Technici prepositi ad imagines ceremoniae luci experimendas.*" However, the allegorical figure has been rejuvenated by means of a modern hair style, and though she is holding out a laurel crown with one hand, the other rests on a camera in her lap. The artist has employed a smooth, unctuous relief, and the soft rotundities of the clouds are related to Art Nouveau.

555 ◪ ALEXANDRE CHARPENTIER. Medallion portrait of Émile Zola. Bronze. 1899. Museum für Kunst und Gewerbe, Hamburg.

In this admirable portrait of Zola, Charpentier has shown what he could do when he applied his talent to the medallion. Along with the delicate, fluid modeling there is an extraordinary ring of truth in the profile. Nothing is conventional, and idiosyncrasies of character are conveyed by telling details: deep folds in the neck, the slightly unkempt hair at the back of the head, the bushy moustache and beard, and the interrogative arch of the eyebrow rising behind the pince-nez.

556 ◪ LOUIS BOTTÉE. Medallion. Bronze. C. 1902. Museum für Kunst und Gewerbe, Hamburg.

In every field, Art Nouveau artists strove to create as close a relation as possible between background and decoration, so as to make them two aspects of a single entity. In the medallion, this is evident as a quest for a softer, more sensitive style of modeling. Bottée diminished the depth of the relief and surrounded both background and subject with the same "spatial envelope." Here, he uses a delicate modeling with progressive gradations of depth to depict his flying nudes, symbolizing the inspiration of the poet.

557 ◪ ERNST BARLACH. Plaque honoring Justus Brinckmann. Bronze. 1902. Kunsthalle, Hamburg.

This plaque displays the strong touch and intense expressiveness which in a few years led Barlach to the brutal but poignant Expressionism of the small figures he created about 1910. This broadly modeled profile, with its deliberate simplifications and omissions, fairly shouts with life and truth. The artist has led the light along the projections of the temple and over the hollows of the cheek and the eye socket. This portrait of the founder of the Museum für Kunst und Gewerbe in Hamburg gives us the likeness of the man created by a method totally different from that of Charpentier in his Zola medallion. Here, Barlach is not only the tormented sculptor with whom we are familiar, but a skillful designer as well: the inscription forms an integral part of the composition and plays an important ornamental role. This work is related to Art Nouveau by virtue of the undulating lines near the bottom of the plaque.

558 ◪ Rupert Carabin. *Girl with Cat*. Bronze plaque. C. 1898. Kunsthalle, Hamburg.
Carabin was above all a sculptor. This relief would appear to have been conceived in three dimensions, not two. The surface which the artist has left bare between the two figures is not a filled-up background, but rather a volume containing air and light. The naturalistic portrayal of the girl's body is characteristic of Carabin's style.

543

544

545

546

547

548

549

550

551

552

553

554

555

556

Iustus Brinck=mann

Ernst Barlach

dem Schöpfer
des Museums
für Kunst u. Ge
werbe in Ham
burg 1877-1902

557

R. Carabin

558

Machinery

I N the nineteenth century, the machine took over every area of technical production, causing a violent change in man's relationship to the world about him. The speed and precision of mechanical manufacture threatened to eclipse the artisan who was compelled to concede, inch by reluctant inch, the territory in which formerly his skill had made him master.

Physical devices have always been necessary to man to assist him in his undertakings and strengthen his control over nature. The attitude of Ruskin and Morris—with their refusal to recognize that mechanization fulfilled a need, was beneficial, and had a gigantic future—seems to us not only reactionary but futile.

It is not enough, however, to make the machine as useful a servant as possible; there is the further problem of making it fit to look at. Industrial aesthetics is a very modern science, the very possibility of which was unsuspected at the end of the nineteenth century. After a few half-hearted attempts, foredoomed to failure, the notion of encumbering machines with decoration was abandoned; it was clear that there was no point in trying to disguise them, and that they had better be left black and unadorned, sinister and functional. Since factories were manned, for the most part, by a kind of second-class humanity, the *lumpenproletariat*, it was unimportant whether the humming machines had any pretensions to artistic attractiveness. But the problem reappeared in the case of machines for the leisure classes: motorcars and airplanes, for instance. The first took some years before it shed its resemblance to a horse-drawn carriage, and during its infancy, the airplane had to look like a bird—although Clement Ader's, in name as well as appearance, looked like a bat (*see* plate 559).

Thus did modern man attempt to appease the past (and also reassure prospective customers) by veiling startling mechanical novelties in antique habiliments. In the early years, an engine was actually just what people thought it was, an auxiliary, an afterthought with a conventional covering. Its aesthetic power, its ability to engender new forms, was not admitted until much later.

559 CLEMENT ADER. *Chauve-Souris*. Musée des Arts et Métiers, Paris.
"...A further trial was held on 14 October [1897]. The *Avion* took off, skimmed the grass, was driven off the track by the wind and finally suffered severe damage on abruptly regaining contact with the ground. The distance thus traveled was about 300 yards. Although the Military Commission had expressed itself favorably and recommended that the experiments be continued, the Ministry of War considered this result inadequate and withdrew its subsidy...."
(Marcel Jeanjean, *Les étapes de l'aviation*, Paris, 1948)

560 Benz *Ideal* automobile. 1899. Deutsches Museum, Munich.
"They were curious machines, these early 'puff-puffs' with a tiny engine, big wheels, a horizontal tiller for steering, and no windshield. They began appearing timidly on public highways, raising clouds of dust, making a frightful noise, exhaling foul smells, and sowing terror among horses and the peasantry. The thoughtful shrugged their shoulders and predicted the early demise of so unsightly, noisome, and fragile a novelty. But the seekers persisted, and every year brought new improvements."

(Jacques Chastenet, *Histoire de la Troisième République.*
Vol. III: *La République Triomphante*, 1893–1906. Paris,
1955)

561 ▨ UNKNOWN DESIGNER. Bicycle. Photograph
Collection Coursaget.
In 1886, the bicycle was provided with a chain drive,
and the ugly duckling became a swan. While this prod-
igy was still in the fledgling stage, Jules Bois, a
journalist, foresaw a fabulous future for it: "The
motorcar will go out of fashion; the bicycle will remain
in favor but will become a flying machine allowing the
cyclist to stroll along through the air, avoiding the risk
of being run over...." (We are not sure, in this photograph, just how well this pneumatic nude lady will ride
the vehicle.)

562 ▨ Omnibus. C. 1875. The Museum of the City of
New York.
> *Les tramways se ruent, béhémots aux prunelles incandes-*
> *centes.*
> "Tramcars, behemoths with incandescent eyeballs,
> hurtle along."   (Jean Moréas)

This ancient American omnibus has been retired to a
museum. Although it is a touching relic from a past age,
it has not been put there merely to extract a pious tear.
Is it possible not to notice that it bears the wavy lines
and floral decoration of early Art Nouveau?

561

562

Religious and Funerary Art

So far we have seen renascence and rejuvenation on every side, but when we turn to religious art we find that the architecture and decoration of churches seem to have escaped the prevailing trends. Grandiose conventions held the field, and only superficial concessions were made to the new style. How are we to explain the stagnant condition of religious art during a period when all the other arts experienced a renewal whose vital sources were the Middle Ages, one of the most profoundly religious epochs in history? This curious paradox may perhaps be explained if we analyze the situation.

Essentially, the Catholic and Protestant churches in the late nineteenth century were official institutions. Belonging to either was like belonging to a social class or a political party. Their function and impact were political and social rather than mystical.

What, for the churches, were the great questions of the day? There was discussion concerning the temporal power of the pope and the separation of church and state. In France, there was a wave of hostility against Protestantism, caused primarily by rivalries between banking houses. Even the Dreyfus case eventually lost all but the remotest connection with Dreyfus himself and became a pretext (in the minds of some people, at least) for asserting that adherence to this or that religious belief determined a certain kind of political behavior. To all appearances, religion had become no more than a basis for external attitudes; it was no longer concerned with mysticism, metaphysical concepts, or the inner life.

Meanwhile, a powerful current of spiritualism and mysticism had been developing for many years, organizing itself outside the sphere of the churches. There was a multiplication of little sects and brotherhoods, of secret societies concerned with all the manifestations of supernatural powers. One end of the scale was occupied by black magic, the other by a hazy, scientific, humanistic spirituality which tried to be more broad-minded and more receptive than the traditional forms of belief. People wanted a more adaptable, living religion. They argued and interpreted, sought God by tempting the Devil, voted Christ a member of the Socialist Party. It may be that these spiritual and intellectual stirrings, and the little sects to which they gave birth, were really rather unimportant. But however insignificant some of them may have been, they did at least proclaim, even if they could not satisfy, the need for renewal in religious expression.

The official churches were ossified; they spoke in a dead language. No creative impulse could be expected from so cold and pompous a source. The artists left the churches to their own devices or, at best, designed their frigidly solemn buildings and used floral motifs in the decoration of religious objects, since the old symbols and themes had become empty of meaning. No artist or craftsman whose faith was real and vivid could nourish and express it inside the accepted framework of religion. It is not, therefore, in places of worship, large or small, that we must look for any artistic expression of spirituality. With few exceptions, it could find no place in them.

But the exceptions are important. In England, a new current appeared in the wake of church restoration activities, which were widespread. One of its champions was Sir William Reynolds-Stephens whose works include the interior decoration of the little Church of Saint Mary the Virgin at Great Warley, Essex. He lined the vaulting with aluminum and surrounded the choir with a screen of small metal pillars, like tree trunks, decorated with a horizontal floral band. Aluminum and bronze alternate with panels of green marble and carved wood. Natural objects—reeds and vine foliage—are treated with a graceful rigidity which has nothing to do with imitation Byzantine or Gothic.

The Sezession artists, notably Otto Wagner and Koloman Moser, were bolder still. In the Church of Sankt Leopold outside Vienna (*see* plates 569 and 571), their perfectly restrained approach and unadorned rigor of line and volume produce that deeply religious atmosphere which was so rare in the period.

Finally, the greatest exception of all was Gaudí, who expressed his mysticism in an original and indeed unique style combining medieval references with cubic contrasts of volume. The work of Gaudí, especially the Church of the Sagrada Familia in Barcelona (*see* plate 563), confronts us with the intense religious feeling which is to be sought in vain elsewhere. What the English and Austrians contrive to suggest by dint of linear strictness and discipline, the Catalan Gaudí utters spontaneously in an architectural and decorative language of inexhaustible variety.

Counterbalancing the stasis in church architecture, the cult of spiritualism invaded everything which concerned man's fundamental fear, his apprehension of death. In this area, notably in the decoration of tombs, emotional constraint and dogmatic control were absent. At the beginning of this century, funerary art enjoyed one of the most flourishing periods it has ever known; in the various tendencies of the Modern Style, it found exactly what it needed in order to blossom. Of all monuments, the tomb is ideally suited to grief-stricken symbolic figures. The setting and occasion sanction what would be considered excessive in other contexts.

It is significant that funerary art was not relegated to indifferent artists. On the contrary, much of it bears famous signatures: Sullivan, Mackintosh, Albert Bartholomé. Bartholomé is responsible for the great monument to the dead at the Père Lachaise Cemetery in Paris, regarded by the critics as one of the finest and most significant sculptures of its time. In it, the sculptor contrasts the serenity of a young couple on the threshold of the unknown with the grief and anguish of those who are still living. Through the discreet archaism and the realism comes an indefinable religious feeling which rejects the narrowness of the purely Christian concept and borrows from ancient Egypt and modern idealistic philosophy. By expressing the timeless anguish of man in the face of his own destiny, Bartholomé has given us one of his finest works. Like most sculptors of his time, he produced his best when giving utterance to this deepest and most disturbing of all human preoccupations.

It thus seems that cemeteries are the place in which to seek the most successful achievements of Art Nouveau sculpture. We shall also find there faithful testimony to the development of the bourgeoisie and their aesthetic in the nineteenth century.

The Père Lachaise Cemetery in Paris is a bourgeois burial ground, a Paris in miniature, complete with middle-class neighborhoods and aristocratic residential areas. During the first third of the nineteenth century it remained hidden away, humble and romantic; but after 1830 when the bourgeoisie disengaged itself from Romanticism and simultaneously consolidated its complex position in society, the gravestones became monuments and the paths between them assumed the proportions of streets lined by rich, lofty mausoleums, like the houses in a city of the dead. The *grande bourgeoisie* of the *XVIIᵉ arrondissement* (a fashionable section in Paris) established its quarters in "Monceau" style in one section of the Père Lachaise.

From that cemetery, however, we get only the bourgeois side of the picture. To realize what funerary art of that period has to offer, we must visit Italy, and particularly Genoa. There, in the huge cemetery above the city, the Staglieno, we can review, clearly and precisely, not only the evolution of the bourgeois aesthetic, but also the division between Symbolist and bourgeois art, which became more sharply marked as time went on. The evolution strikes us as the most natural expression of human grief, the grief of the common people as well as the rich. The division, on the other hand, passed from applied realism to haughty frigidity, loitered palely and perpetually on the fringes of mythology, and merely reflected the anxieties and preoccupations of a single class down the centuries.

In the period we are considering, the first preoccupation of this type of art, chronologically speaking, was to raise the bourgeois flag by displaying the bourgeoisie's wealth and power through an exact, minute portrayal of the worldly belongings which attest its position; the subsequent phase consists of rising above the common herd by disdainfully refusing to indulge in any concessions to symbolic expression. In the Staglieno, the monument of a rich Genoese family, consisting of a black cross on a white marble base, stands out from the other tombs, not because it is simple, but because it is insolent. Its spurious Jansenism is a mark of pride. The gulf deepens and widens in direct ratio to bourgeois prosperity. About 1880, the distinction was still not acute: Moreno (*see* plate 582), one of the oddest sculptors of that time (he must surely be the only one in the world whose statues included even the eyelashes!), touches our hearts with his realistic pathos. In his statues of men in their Sunday suits and women in moiré and lace, there is a quality truly of the people, a naïveté and good sense which are infinitely moving. Later, the bourgeoisie were to turn up their noses at allegory (which continued to flourish on the graves of the poor), expressing unashamedly the agony and bewilderment of the living in the presence of death.

If these baroque, over-ornamental mausoleums are allowed to remain intact, it will not be many decades before their merit is acknowledged. Homage will be rendered to the misunderstood, unjustly neglected talent, to the imagination and deep poetic sense, of such men as Besesti, Bringiotti, and Leonardo Bistolfi. Their monuments have an astonishing expressive power which makes them fit the definition put forward by a contemporary critic, H. Fierens Gevaert:

> "A tomb is the symbol of our afterlife, which we conceive as an endless existence untrammeled by vain complications. It is therefore the most concrete representation of the eternal and unchanging. As such, and through the purging of unnecessary detail, through the unity of emotion which it embodies and the immortal poetry of its purpose, it must be considered as one of the highest manifestations, perhaps indeed the highest, of which the decorative arts are capable."

The tombs designed by Sullivan, Sommaruga, and some of the Czechoslovakians are more sober, more architectural, already modern. They are steles, upright stones, almost undecorated. They anticipate a funerary art in which grief and fear are expressed with more restraint. And this is our own tendency today.

RELIGIOUS ART

563 Ⓩ ANTONI GAUDÍ. The Church of the Sagrada Familia. 1883–1926. Barcelona.

Gaudí devoted over forty years of his life to the Church of the Sagrada Familia. He died before it was completed; as he himself had said, "Saint Joseph will finish it." It was originally intended to be consecrated to the Holy Family, whose virtues it glorifies, and especially to Saint Joseph, who is much venerated in Catalonia. It also expressed a desire to expiate the sins of a materialistic age. Initially conceived as a neo-Gothic building throughout, it was transformed by Gaudí into something completely original. Its guiding intentions were reinforced by the mysticism and genius of its architect. From 1884 to 1893, he worked on the crypt and the apse; the façade and transepts were not built until 1903. Just as in an old church the successive periods of architecture can be distinguished, we can follow here the development of the architect's ideas. The bays of the porches are Gothic, but a new element is already apparent in the carving of the gables above the porches. Strange stalactites evoke the entrance of a cave hollowed out by the sea and the wind. Floating figures emerge on the surface of the stone, adding a note of fantasy. The towers soar like fountains and seem to be drawing the building up to heaven. They conform to the traditional verticalism of the Middle Ages, but their shape is entirely new. They are tower and spire in one. Their colored-tile finials, which belong strictly to Gaudí's cubic period, were added much later.

564–566 ⊠ J. B. Sedding (architect) and Henry Wilson (metalwork). Holy Trinity Church, Sloane Street, London.

After neo-Gothic, architects turned to neo-Romanesque and neo-Byzantine styles (for example, the churches in Montmartre and Fourvières). In England, Holy Trinity Church in London reveals Gaelic sources of inspiration, which are evident in the copper crucifix, the enamel and precious stones of the high altar, the copper sheathing on the arches, walls, and pillars, the carved capitals, and the embroidered altarcloth, in which medallion-framed figures alternate with similarly bordered symbols. The artists involved, overawed by the past, did not succeed in giving religious art a style of its own. Although often tasteful, their work leaves us with a certain embarrassment, the embarrassment which they, no doubt, felt in expressing themselves in an out-of-date idiom.

567 and **568** ⊠ Lucien Magne. Mosaics and high altar. Parish Church. 1900–02. Bougival.

The church at Bougival was restored by the architect Lucien Magne at the beginning of the present century. It was in a state of such dilapidation that this represented an enormous task. He first had to strengthen the structure itself. He then redecorated the church throughout in a neo-Gothic Art Nouveau style which he attempted to harmonize with the building. He did not seek to re-create the vanished furniture and ornament, but tried rather to produce a harmony of both spirit and form between his predecessors' work and his own. Thus, for example, he made the high altar completely traditional, but decorated it with Modern Style floral motifs. The same spirit appears in the treatment of the very fine door of the tabernacle, by Noiseux, and in the mosaic adornment of the arches we recognize the typically luxuriant, naturalistic, decorative flora of the period. Only Art Nouveau is capable of filling the space beneath an arch with such an embroidery of undulating branches. There is no trace of pastiche in the carvings. The sober treatment of the crucifix is very modern, and the sentimental note added by the two little angels prostrating themselves at its foot is thoroughly in the taste of the period.

569 and **571** ⊠ Otto Wagner. Church of Sankt Leopold. Steinhof. 1904–07. Vienna.

Otto Wagner's massive church at the top of the Steinhof in Vienna is striking because of its form. The cruciform plan, topped by a dome at the crossing, and the towers flanking the west door have been traditional elements in church architecture since the Middle Ages. But here, everything has been made over in a new spirit. Full scope has been given to the taste for simple geometric forms, clean-cut surfaces, and sober decoration. Religious art has been given an unusual, original path by the aesthetic tenets of the Sezession. The interior decoration, which is very *Wiener Werkstätte*, follows the same principles. In his mosaic over the high altar, Rudolf Jettmar has made the deliberately rigid figures of the saints lead upward in two symmetrical rows toward the central figure of Christ. Angles and straight lines have been accentuated by stylization, creating a contrast to the rolling ground of the site. The clearest indication of Oriental influence is in the arrangement of the high altar. However, the influence is interpreted with originality throughout, never becoming merely pastiche. Otto Wagner and his collaborators have succeeded in creating a modern idiom for religious art. This example is almost unique of its kind.

570 ⊠ Hector Guimard. Synagogue. 1913. Rue Pavée, Paris.

Guimard remained faithful to his style in this synagogue. The undulating façade, with a shallow concavity rising up the middle, marks the three main divisions of the interior: the central nave, and the aisles above which rise two galleries with seats for the women. The restricted breadth of the building is compensated for in its length and height. The motifs in relief which add an accent to the bays of the main door are repeated inside in the decoration of the ceiling and tall pillars. They are closely akin to those adorning Guimard's celebrated entrances to the Métro stations.

572 ⊠ René Lalique. Chalice. Silver and glass. C. 1898–1902. Collection Maurice Rheims, Paris.

There is nothing religious about this chalice except the name and the shape. The suave flow of the crystal glass can be seen between the openwork formed by silver pine-needles. It is comparable to a chalice in silver and enamel by Feuillâtre, who employed the same decorative theme. If exception is made for a few works by Bourgoin and Paussielgue-Durand, ecclesiastical appurtenances designed in France are distinguished more for their sumptuous appearance than for the aptness of their symbolism.

573 ⊠ Lucien Magne. Candlestick. Brass. C. 1898–1902. Parish Church, Bougival.

In the church at Bougival, Lucien Magne showed the same care for minute detail as he did for the total concept of his restoration of the church (*see* commentary to plates 567 and 568). This can be seen in the brass candlesticks he designed for the high altar. The shape is traditional, but the organic decoration and its gentle modeling put these pieces among the finest metalwork of the Art Nouveau era.

574 ⊠ René Lalique. Pectoral cross. Silver-gilt, enamel, and mother-of-pearl. 1898–1902. Collection Maurice Rheims, Paris.

This cross by Lalique, in its enameled silver-gilt mount, is a piece of jewelry rather than a religious emblem. It is indeed legitimate to wonder whether the form was not chosen more for its decorative value than for its religious significance. It certainly makes an admirable setting for the full-blown petals of these mother-of-pearl anemones.

STAINED GLASS

575 ⬚ KOLOMAN MOSER. Stained-glass window. C. 1898–1902. Church of Sankt Leopold, Steinhof, Vienna.

These windows echo the stress on verticals which is one of the dominant characteristics of the building. Saints, hieratic figures like those by Hodler, bearing their attributes, form a procession. Each figure fills a strict rectangular frame, which accentuates the deliberate rigidity of the composition. Except for the halos, the artist has used small pieces of glass, which underline the muscular anatomy of the figures, the folds of their robes, and the ornaments. The glass has not been heightened with paint or details in grisaille. These windows are simple, radiant, and richly ornamental.

576 ⬚ ALBERT BESNARD. Stained-glass window. C. 1898–1902. Hôtel des Gueules Cassées, Paris.

The Hôtel des Gueules Cassées (Home for Disfigured Veterans), at 20 Rue d'Aguesseau, is the perfect example of a style both Art Nouveau and bourgeois. Its proprietors have shown the good sense to protect it from regrettable alterations. The façade, the ironwork of the entrance, the balconies, the charming dining room, the ceiling of the large drawing room, and the ravishing stained-glass windows by Besnard speak for themselves. The window shown here is on the first-floor landing. It is entirely filled by a landscape whose predominant greens and blues are punctuated by a few small dashes of red. Besnard received numerous commissions for stained-glass windows, notably some in the Paris Hôtel de Ville. His designs were executed by Henri Carot. He used fine, lively colors and preferred to take his subjects from nature.

577 ⬚ ÉMILE GALLÉ. Stained-glass window (possibly for Sarah Bernhardt's dressing room). C. 1898–1902. Museum für Kunst und Gewerbe, Hamburg.

Is not every vase by Gallé a stained-glass window modeled in three dimensions? With his taste for color and light, and also for Symbolism, he could hardly have been otherwise than charmed by these transparent screens of colored glass, and the art of making them. He has covered this panel with airy foliage, the red of whose flowers seems to spill out over the entire surface without detracting from the transparency of the glass.

578 ⬚ JACQUES GRUBER. Stained-glass transom. C. 1898–1902. Musée de l'École de Nancy, Nancy.

One part of the house containing the Musée de l'École de Nancy was built about 1900. The transoms of the windows are panels by Gruber, who chose water lilies for the subject of their decoration. This was a typical Art Nouveau theme, especially in the early days when there was a strong bias in favor of the suppleness, movement, and magic of life, both on and under the water. Just as typical of the period is the use of colored glass. After three centuries of eclipse, the art of stained glass came to life again all over Europe at the end of the nine-teenth century. Such great artists as Grasset, Otto Eckmann, Van de Velde, Leistikow, and Patterson, to cite only a few, designed stained glass for churches and private homes. It was particularly in domestic interior decoration that the art struck out along new lines. The window had now become a surface inviting embellishment, and every artist who accepted the invitation brought along his own favorite style. (In France, architects frequently called in Socard to adorn windows with graceful floral designs.) This phenomenon was part of the general eagerness with which the new decoration was greeted, but it was also, perhaps, a result of that need for an intimate atmosphere, which became more and more urgent as cities became noisier and more populous. These windows masked the ugliness of the urban landscape, isolated the occupants of the house, and enveloped them in colored light.

579 ⬚ WALTER CRANE. Design for a stained-glass window. C. 1898–1902. William Morris Gallery, Walthamstow, England.

In this design, Walter Crane showed himself very much the Pre-Raphaelite. The figure and the setting are derived from the early Renaissance. The woman in Classical costume stands out from a background tapestried with leaves. Her figure and draperies freely overlap the frame with its decoration of grapes and vine leaves, and her pose has a grace which recalls Botticelli. This, and other such designs, shows Crane to be an important figure in the stained-glass revival. It is worth noting that he followed the sixteenth-century technique, using large pieces of glass on which he painted the subordinate details. He made the leading follow the outlines of the figure, instead of employing it as a decorative element in itself, as later practitioners were to do. The stained-glass window had not yet undergone the influence of the Nabis, who were to change its development and give it new direction.

580 ⬚ LOUIS COMFORT TIFFANY. Four stained-glass panels. C. 1900. The Museum of Modern Art, New York.

Tiffany's stained glass won him the admiration and astonishment of his contemporaries. His fame in Europe was great, and he received numerous commissions, notably one for windows in Bing's Maison Art Nouveau, which he executed in 1899 after designs by Brangwyn. Bonnard, Vuillard, and Toulouse-Lautrec also created designs for him, but most of the resulting windows have since disappeared. Occasionally Tiffany, who did work for both churches and apartments, made his own designs. He executed them in "American" glass, an opaline, multiveined substance which yielded richer colors than any previously used glass. On this glass he overlaid no glaze or pigment of any kind. As early as 1898, critics were enthusiastic over these "strange windows... through which the light filters

oddly, as though from a cloudy sky." Light was not
obstructed by his practice of combining several layers
of differently colored glass, and his almost habitual
exploitation of accidental streaks and iridescences
present in the glass. The glass acted as a sieve or filter,
transforming the light into colorful, opalescent gleams
whose charm cannot be reproduced in a black-and-
white illustration. We can only imagine the effect and
note the great originality of this man, who attached
little importance to drawing and was primarily interested in creating new harmonies of material and color.

581 ⊠ PETER BEHRENS. Stained-glass panel. C. 1898.
(Whereabouts unknown.)
Stained-glass design becomes almost abstract in the
hands of Behrens. Here and there it may be possible to
detect a botanical origin, but stylization renders it
difficult to recognize. It is with an example of this kind
that we may best conclude our account of the development of stained glass in the Art Nouveau period. If the
glass is strong enough it can be used in large pieces;
leading is then needed only to separate sheets of
different colors. Here, the leading traces the design and
does so all the more freely since it does not have to
serve also as a supporting armature.

XII ⊠ MARCEL MAGNE. *The Assumption.* Stained-glass
window. C. 1898–1902. Parish Church, Bougival.
The Magne family specialized in religious art. The
father of the family was the architect Lucien Magne,
who entrusted to his son Marcel the stained-glass
windows for the apse of the church at Bougival. The
narrow lancets made it necessary to use a vertical
composition which is crowned by the figure of Christ.
The characters and their faces are drawn in a modern
vein which remains faithful to the spirit of the building
and does not copy medieval styles. Where the artist has
sought to emulate his predecessors is in the glowing play
of color; his blues and purples and whites and ochers
color the incoming light as a Gothic window might
have done.

FUNERARY ART

582 🖉 ¼MORENO. Family tomb. 1891. Staglieno Cemetery, Genoa.

On the threshold of the unknown—which is suitably masked by a curtain so realistic that it might be real brocade—father and son bid one another farewell. This touching episode, staged in stone, is witnessed by two other deceased members of the family, whose faces can be seen on the wall, each encircled by a garland. These medallions are more than merely counterparts of the venerable family portraits hung in the home; they are a frighteningly vivid reminder of those who have gone before and have taken with them into eternity their starched collars and severe expressions, those visible guarantees of their bourgeois status. For that matter, the whole scene is designed to indicate the social position of the protagonists: their unobtrusively expensive clothes, the carefully displayed bowler hat, the quality of the curtain material, and the restrained expression of emotion—all are signs of wealth and a good upbringing. The real anguish of death seems not to exist, or at least it has not been allowed to show. This sculptured group simply displays a setting and an attitude, seeking to edify the spectators rather than to expose the feelings of the performers.

583 🖉 JOSÉ DE CHARMOY. Sainte-Beuve's grave. 1903. Cimetière Montparnasse, Paris.

A bust at the top of a column rises among these faceless crosses and commemorative gravestones. Thus a great critic, who was in love with truth, towers over his buried contemporaries; for this is Sainte-Beuve. The studious face, inclined in contemplation, has been rendered with the ridges and furrows of age and the forceful interrogative line of the eyebrows, the mouth pursed in doubt. A wide drapery winding its way down from the shoulders spirals around the column and spreads out over the base. Paganism is revived by this realistic portrait and the column which echoes the tomb sculpture of the ancient world: eternity is of the intelligence rather than of the soul, and virtue yields the first place to intellectual probity. The anonymous crowd lying under the surrounding stones is dominated by the thinker's face.

584 🖉 FROMENT MEURICE. Chopin Memorial. C. 1898–1902. Parc Monceau, Paris.

This is not a tomb, but, being a lament in stone for the death of the great composer, it can properly be included here, especially since both the conception and its treatment relate it to the style of funerary art in the 1880's. It is a mixture of the realistic and the symbolic, and the main impression it gives is that of an essentially bourgeois art, whose idea of expressing emotion was to depict a few fainting women. It would seem that, in spite of the piano (carefully protected by a cloth) and the importance conceded to the graceful motion of the player's hands, the monument has been raised not so much to the musician as to the regret caused by his

loss. On the artfully irregular stele, disingenuously simulating the ravages of time by its rough finish, there flutters a winged creature carved in that conventional, airy, slightly flaccid style which "sensitive" people found so affecting. Nothing has been left out, yet nothing has been said. Faced with such a display of hollow eloquence, it is easy to understand why Art Nouveau should have reacted with its symbolism or realism, both of which were often overdone, but were at least expressive.

585 🖉 E. PELLINI. Funerary sculpture. C. 1898–1902. Cimitero Monumentale, Milan.

586 🖉 LEONARDO BAZZARO. Funerary sculpture. C. 1898–1902. Cimitero Monumentale, Milan.

When Italian graveside sculptures abandoned portraits or family groups, they nevertheless retained a wide variety of symbolic expression, as can be seen from the few examples shown here. The tomb in plate 585 depicts a girl who hides her weeping face behind her hands. From side to side, over her slender arms, runs a strip or fillet which binds her forever to her new home, the grave. This figure, with its slightly morbid sentimentality, expresses the human urge to resist oblivion. The sculptor has laid stress on the unhealthy and tragic, and has suppressed every aspect of death except the moment of high pathos. The opposite attitude is represented by the heedless joy of the children playing around the tomb in plate 586. What are we meant to conclude? That life is only a game? Or should we regard these gay little children as symbolizing the indifference of time and of the living in the presence of death? One child holds a cross and raises her eyes to heaven, but the gesture is slightly theatrical and does not carry much conviction.

587 🖉 SAASSI. Gravestone. 1910. Cimitero Monumentale, Milan.

The decorative detail on this large monument is still abundantly floral, supple, and sinuous, and curved lines are dominant in the relief. The cross surmounting the urn has been put there to cancel the impression of paganism given by the angels, some of whom are dancing among flowers, while others are encouraging the dead to join them in their revels.

588 🖉 BOHUMIL KAFKA. Gravestone. C. 1898–1902. Prague.

This extremely simple memorial embodies a curious piece of decoration. On the face of his severe monument the artist has placed three funeral wreaths, which a critic described as follows: "The drooping flowers have almost faded, the palms have begun to wither, and the weather has spoilt the ribbons; the work of decomposition and death has begun." This symbolic representation of decomposition is discreetly done, yet is somewhat startling. It illustrates nicely the Mannerist tendency which is frequently found in the Art Nouveau of Eastern Europe.

589 ▨ Leonardo Bazzaro. Monument. C. 1898–1902. Cimitero Monumentale, Milan.
Some artists took their themes from the myths of the ancient world, crowning a monument with a funeral urn or giving their statues the cold indifference of souls in Hades. This Classically draped figure, standing on a construction built of cyclopean blocks, is a typical example of the work of Bazzaro.

590 ▨ Max Pfeiffer. Funeral urn. C. 1898–1902. Prague.
Funeral urns were still abundant in the early twentieth century. Made of marble, like this one, or bronze or silver, they mark a return to Antiquity (or rather, to an ancient world newly enriched by Romantic poetry) and an acceptance of Symbolism: "…Eternity, which has no end, no beginning, and presides over all the things of this world." The restrained decoration, allowing the form to play the leading role, is characteristic of this Munich sculptor.

591 ▨ Raimondo d'Aronco. Mausoleum. 1904. Cemetery, Udine.
D'Aronco devoted part of his architectural activities to the small town of Udine, which was near his birthplace. Some idea of his singular genius is given by this mausoleum, with its daringly modern cruciform superstructure which makes one think of Bourdelle. But the floral part from which it rises is still marked by Genoese symbolism.

592 ▨ José de Charmoy. Beaudelaire's grave. 1903. Cimetière Montparnasse, Paris.
This work was executed a few years before the monument to Sainte-Beuve (*see* plate 583), and was inspired by a similar idea: the body's mortality is contrasted with the immortality of genius. Looking down on the shrouded, recumbent figure is the torso of the man as he was in life: the stubborn, suffering rebel, now asserting his power from the beyond.

593 ▨ Louis Sullivan. Ryerson Tomb. 1889. Graceland Cemetery, Chicago.

594 ▨ Louis Sullivan. Getty Tomb. 1890. Graceland Cemetery, Chicago.
Very different from the European examples are those designed by the American architect Sullivan; this is Protestant territory. Whether it be a chapel or a simple rectangular monument, the work presents clean, severe lines. In most instances the decoration is abstract and in low relief. One of the tombs has the sloping walls of the Egyptian mastaba; funerary art is in fact the field in which the influence of ancient Egypt is most evident.

595 ▨ Giuseppe Sommaruga. Faccanoni Mausoleum. 1907. Cemetery, Sarnico.
In this mausoleum, Sommaruga gave Symbolism an almost exclusively architectural form. It is both a temple and a tomb, an uninhabitable monument in which nothing is on the human scale. With its raw masonry and its Mycenaean appearance, it expresses that quality of the inevitable and irremediable which is the stamp of human destiny.

564

565

566

567

568

569

570

571

572

573

574

YDEN NACKTEN KRANKEN
BERGEN BEKLEDEN BESVCHEN

580

581

583

584

585

586

591

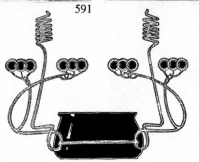

592

Index

Numbers in italics indicate plates; Roman numerals indicate colorplates. Numbers in parentheses indicate page
on which commentary to plate appears

Acknowledgments

(Numbers indicate plate numbers)

PHOTOGRAPHIC CREDITS

A. C. L., Brussels: 152, 265, 266; A la Vieille Russie, New York: 464, 489; Alexis, Brussels: 62; Annan, Glasgow: 32, 146; *Architectural Record*: 79; Archives Carnavalet, Paris: 72; Archives de la Samaritaine, Paris: 427; The Art Institute of Chicago: 159, 227; Ateneum Museum, Helsinki: 192; George Barrows: 480, 494, 580; Barsoti, Florence: 18; Bayerische Staatsgemäldesammlungen, Munich: 143, 144, 153, 155, 195, 210, 232, 272; Carla de Benedetti: 539, 595; Bevilacqua, Milan: 19, 100, 263, 585, 586, 587, 589; Bildstelle des Deutschen Museums, Munich: 560; Boissonas, Geneva: 8; Brisighelli, Udine: 591; The Brooklyn Museum, New York: 150, 226, 369, 387, 506; Bulloz, Paris: 2, 5, 15, 72, 86, 91, 95, 97, 121, 149, 221, 231, 239, 253, 255, 295, 458, 567, 568, 573; The Chicago Heritage Committee, Chicago: 55; *Connaissance des Arts*, Paris: 268, 485, 574; Conservatoire National des Arts et Métiers, Paris: 559; The Cooper Union Museum for the Arts of Decoration, New York: 352, 503; Dobos Lajos: 38; The Fitzwilliam Museum, Cambridge: 493; R. B. Fleming, London: 45, 46, 47, 49, 50, 51, 75, 118, 131, 133, 135, 244, 274, 276, 280, 286, 292, 323, 337, 358, 400, 428, 440, 441, 443, 444, 445, 477, 479, 525, 528, 529, 531, 564, 565, 566; Fotografen, Munich: 264; Fournier, Moulins, France: 73; The Freer Gallery of Art, Washington, D. C.: 281; Galerie Brockstedt, Hamburg: 397; Galleria del Levante, Milan: 168, 184, 194, 200; Gemeentemuseum, The Hague: 166, 279, 371, 435, 504; Giacometti, Venice: 176; Giraudon, Paris: 181; L. Gittleman, Institute of Design: 93; The Glasgow School of Art, Glasgow: 30, 31; S. R. Gnahm, Munich: 108, 312, 316, 355, 356, 391, 483, 484; André Gornet: 251, 380; Henriette Grindat, Lausanne: 26, 27, 28, 29, 115, 120, 256, 306, 307, 308, 563; Roger Guillemot: 485, 574; Jacqueline Guillot: 268; Hamburger Kunsthalle, Hamburg: 142, 201, 234, 557, 558; Peter Heilmann, Darmstadt: 41, 42, 43, 44; Peter Hess, Hamburg: 378, 542; Hessisches Landesmuseum, Darmstadt: 395, 434, 476, 538; H. J. Heyden: 139, 140, 299; Historisches Museum der Stadt Wien, Vienna: 475; Hulskamp en Hulskamp's Fotobedrijf, Utrecht: 243, 270, 278, 425; Ictimer: 455; Jonko-Lenanto: 465; Charles Jerdein, London: 167; Kleinhempel, Hamburg: 557, 558; A. Knecht: 313, 314, 315, 438; Kunb, Hagen, West Germany: 162; Kunstgewerbemuseum der Stadt Zürich, Zurich: 509; Kunsthaus, Zurich: 178; L. Lizon, Le Mont-Dore, France: 136; M. de Lorenzo, Nice: 222, 368; Lott, Nancy: 16, 17, 119, 362, 426, 527; G. Walton Mackintosh: 158; Mandel: 457; Manufacture de Baccarat, Baccarat, France: 413; Elfriede Mejchar, Vienna: 353; Melzian, Berlin: 40; The Metropolitan Museum of Art, New York: 53, 161, 217, 233, 257, 267, 418, 419, 474; K. G. Meyer, Vienna: 12, 33, 34, 35, 203, 246, 291, 322, 324, 343, 344, 346, 347, 348, 569, 571, 575; Milsom: 92; Morian, Brussels: 63, 84; William Morris Gallery, Walthamstow, England: 148, 386, 401, 518, 519, 579; Münchner Stadtmuseum, Munich: 438; Museo d'Arte Moderna, Venice: 215; Museum of the City of New York: 273, 562; The Museum of Finnish Architecture, Helsinki: 66, 67, 68, 82, 103; Museum für Kunst und Gewerbe, Hamburg: 139, 140, 287, 288, 298, 332, 374, 381, 389, 392, 411, 420, 421, 431, 437, 450, 451, 462, 470, 471, 526, 532, 551, 553, 554, 555, 556; The Museum of Modern Art, New York: 114, 132, 321, 354, 361, 388, 394, 415, 416, 433, 463, 480, 490, 492, 494, 495, 580; The National Galleries of Scotland, Edinburgh: 146; National Museum, Helsinki: 330, 331, 396, 452, 473; National Museum, Stockholm: 193, 225; Jacques Nestgen, Paris: 1, 3, 4, 6, 7, 9, 10, 13, 14, 81, 87, 88, 89, 92, 96, 99, 117, 249, 277, 293, 300, 301, 398, 399, 405, 454; Richard Nickel, New York: 56, 57, 58, 109, 129; Österreichische Galerie, Vienna: 175, 209, 237; Pierre d'Otreppe, Brussels: 101, 128, 130, 289, 351, 430; Pandolfi, Pesaro: 71; Mario Perotti: 21, 22, 107, 127; Pietinen, Helsinki: 110, 360; Paolo Piovattici, Pesaro: 25; Eric Pollitzer, New York: 90, 94, 102, 305; Ritter, Vienna: 373, 375, 376, 377, 417; Routhier: 510, 511, 513; Städtische Galerie, Munich: 156, 157, 179, 187; Albert Steiner, St. Moritz: 259; Studio Minders, Ghent: 36, 60, 61, 341, 359, 367, 436, 530; Studio Polma, Caen: 98; The Tate Gallery, London: 145, 147, 164, 165, 198, 207, 216; Taylor and Dull, New York: 489; The Toledo Museum of Art, Toledo, Ohio: 218, 220; Jacques Verroust: 85, 182, 213, 229, 235, 402, 404, 570, 584; Webster Brothers, New York: 54; Gerd Wipfler, Pforzheim: 469, 478, 481, 488, 491, 496, 497, 498, 499, 500, 501.

AUTHOR'S ACKNOWLEDGMENTS

Mr. Mario Amaya, London; Miss Elizabeth Aslin, the Victoria and Albert Museum, London; Mr. Andreas Badrutt, St. Moritz, Switzerland; Mme. Baran, Paris; Mr. Bertonati, Milan; M. Besset, Paris; Dr. Bott, Darmstadt; Mr. Brockstedt, Hamburg; Mr. Enric Casanelles, Barcelona; M. Jean Cassou, Paris; M. Paul

Cauchie, Brussels; Mr. R. Citroen, Amsterdam; Dr. Claude Couinaud, Paris; M. Jacques Damiot, Paris; M. Jacques Dars, Paris; Dr. Kurt Degen, Hessisches Landesmuseum, Darmstadt; M. H.-M. Delaage, Paris; M. Dominique Denis, Saint-Germain-en-Laye; The Editor of *Arts in America*; *Documents*, Paris; M. Bernard Dorival, Paris; M. Louis Duroueix, Secretary-General of the Association des Gueules-Cassées, Paris; Mr. K. L. Essayan, Lisbon; Mrs. Bernadette Fenwick, Paris; Mme. Jeanne Fillon, Paris; M. Karl Flinker, Paris; Marquis de Ganay, Paris; Mr. Aldis Graham, Chicago; M. Guillaume Gillet, Paris; M. Robert Giron, Brussels; Prince Windish-Graetz, Curator of the Museum für Kunst und Gewerbe, Hamburg; Dr. Haussmann, Museum of Decorative Arts, Berlin; Dr. Heiss, Munich; Dr. Herta Hesse, Director of the Städtisches Karl-Ernst Osthaus Museum, Hagen, West Germany; Mrs. Harta Hirn, Muinaistieleellinen Toimikunta, Historiallinen Ostaso-Kansallismuseo, Helsinki; M. Barlach Heuer, Paris; Mr. Charles Jerdein, London; Mme. Jean-Pierre Jouffroy, Paris; Mme. S. Kahn, the Petit Palais, Paris; Baron Lambert, Brussels; M. Langui, Director of the Beaux Arts de Belgique, Brussels; M. Vincent Lavirotte, Paris; M. Gérard Lévy, Paris; Mme. B. Lorenceau, Paris; Miss Sara Lubitz, New York; M. Jean Lullin, Geneva; Professor Mate Major, Budapest; Mr. Malett, London; M. Manoukian, Paris; Mrs. Joyce Mansour, Paris; Miss Pearl Moeller, The Museum of Modern Art, New York; Mme. Gilles de Monbrison, Paris; *Peinture*, Paris; M. Pierre Moisy, Bonn; Museum für Kunst und Gewerbe, Hamburg; Mr. Richard Nickel, Chicago; Count Christian de Nicolay, Paris; Dr. Fritz Novoty, Vienna; Mr. Paul N. Perrot, the Corning Museum of Glass, Corning, N.Y.; Maître Pescheteau, Paris; Mr. Paolo Piovattici, Pesaro; Mrs. Ragnar Kulin, Stockholm; M. G. Renan, Paris; M. Édouard Roditi, Paris; Baronne Alix de Rothschild, Paris; Mr. Theodore Rousseau, The Metropolitan Museum of Art, New York; Mr. Asko Salokorpi, Finland; Mr. Alexandre Schaeffer, New York; M. Joseph Setton, Paris; M. Jacques Stevens, Treasurer of the Association H. van de Velde, Brussels; Mme. Stoclet, Brussels; M. K.-H. Strauss, Paris; Mr. von Tischowitz, Cultural Attaché, the German Embassy, Paris; Mr. Petur Thorsteinsson, Icelandic Ambassador, Paris; Mr. E. J. Vehmas, Assistant Curator, Ateneum Museum, Helsinki; M. Robert Verdon, Clamart (Seine); Dr. Phil. Stephan Waetzoldt, Berlin; Dr. Siegfried Wichmann, Starnberg; Mr. Carl Winter, Fitzwilliam Museum, Cambridge; C. F. S. de Winton, Esq., the British Council, France; M. and Mme. Wittamer de Camps, Brussels; M. Marcel Wolfers, Brussels; Baron T. van Zuylen, Vleuten, Netherlands.

I wish also to thank my admirably helpful publisher, M. O'Meara (Arts et Métiers Graphiques, Paris), and Marie-Anne Pini, whose research and collaboration have been invaluable to me in the preparation of this book.